The

CULT

of the

PRESIDENCY

America's Dangerous Devotion
to Executive Power

The

CULT
of the
PRESIDENCY

GENE HEALY

CATO
INSTITUTE
WASHINGTON, D.C.

Paperback ISBN (2024): 978-1-952223-94-5
Ebook ISBN (2024): 978-1-952223-95-2

Library of Congress Cataloging-in-Publication Data available.
LCCN: 2024940205

Healy, Gene, 1970–
    The cult of the presidency : America's dangerous devotion
      to executive power / Gene Healy.
    p. cm.
    Includes bibliographical references and index.
    ISBN 978-1-933995-15-1 (cloth: alk. paper)
    ISBN 978-1-933995-19-9 (paper: alk. paper)
    1. Presidents—United States. 2. Executive power—United States.
    3. Executive-legislative relations—United States.
    4. United States—Politics and government—2001–
    I. Cato Institute. II. Title.
    JK585.H43   2008
    352.230973—dc22   2008005701

Cover design by Jon Meyers.

Printed in Canada.

CATO
INSTITUTE

1000 Massachusetts Ave. NW
Washington, D.C. 20001

www.cato.org

TABLE OF CONTENTS

Midway through President George W. Bush's second term, I started writing a book on "the most powerful office in the world," how it got that way, and why we should fear it. Somebody told me I needed an "elevator pitch": two sentences that sum up the book's thrust before the doors open and your captive audience escapes. I went with "It's about the presidency. I'm against it."[1]

A snarky synopsis but close enough to the mark: the book that emerged takes aim at the *modern* presidency, an office that, in its long march toward full-spectrum dominance of American life, has become both absurd and menacing.

In *The Cult of the Presidency*, I made the case that for far too long, Americans have looked to the presidency for far too much. No longer a limited constitutional officer charged with faithful execution of the laws, the federal chief executive has been transformed into a quasi-messianic figure, expected to create jobs, teach our children well, advance freedom worldwide, and serve as a living American talisman against hurricanes, terrorism, stock market turmoil, and spiritual malaise. Our political culture has invested the office with preposterously vast responsibilities and, as a result, the officeholder wields powers that no one human being ought to have.

Turns Out, It's Worse Than I Thought

At the time, I thought I'd offered a suitably dark and pessimistic diagnosis. So it's disorienting to look back, a decade and a half down the road, and realize the book wasn't nearly dark and pessimistic *enough*.

In *Cult*'s penultimate chapter, I scoffed at Alexander Hamilton's prediction in *Federalist* no. 68 that "there will be a constant probability of seeing the [office of the presidency] filled by characters preeminent for ability and virtue."[2] Slim chance, I argued; instead, the modern presidential selection system, "a Darwinian contest rewarding bottomless ambition and moral flexibility," drives "the worst [to] get on top . . . and get worse."[3] Now, peering into the hellmouth of the 2024 presidential contest, it seems I didn't know the half of it.

It's humbling to recall that early in the 2016 cycle, I thought the then-likely matchup between another Bush (Jeb) and another Clinton (Hillary) was the most depressing choice imaginable (oh, you sweet summer child). Both candidates were at least fully *compos mentis* and awful "within the normal parameters."[4]

As the 2024 campaign loomed, a voter survey found that the most prevalent sentiments were "dread" and "exhaustion."[5] Americans looked certain to endure a repeat race between a man who ginned up a riot hoping to overturn the last election and a sundowning octogenarian whom 69 percent of *Democrats* even then thought was "too old to effectively serve."[6] At this writing, 10 days after a stumbling, shambolic debate performance revealed the extent of President Biden's decline, that certainty has diminished, but dread persists. Toward the end of Cormac McCarthy's novel *Suttree*, the ne'er-do-well protagonist, having lately recovered from a barfight skull fracture followed by a bout of typhoid fever, muses to himself: "There are no absolutes in human misery and things can always get worse."[7]

Fifteen years and three presidencies since *Cult* was published, it's worth taking stock of what's changed and what hasn't in America's pathological relationship with the presidency—if only to gird ourselves for fresh horrors to come.

The political scientist Theodore Lowi once proffered a mordant "Law of [Presidential] Succession," which holds that each new president enhances the reputation of his predecessors. (Corollary: "This is the only certain contribution each president will make.")[8] The forced march through the Obama, Trump, and Biden presidencies has left Americans somewhat more jaded about the office's potential as a wellspring of national redemption. How could we not be? Even so, each of those men managed to seize new powers, leaving the office stronger than they found it. The presidency of 2024 is, if anything, even more formidable and menacing than the presidency of 2008.

These developments were predictable, and predicted, to some extent, in the first edition of *Cult of the Presidency*. What I didn't anticipate, however, was the rise of mass partisan hatred, or what's recently been dubbed "political sectarianism."[9] American politics has gone feral over the past 15 years, and that's made the president's unilateral power a direct threat to social peace. We've raised the stakes of our political differences dramatically. The presidency itself has become a central fault line of polarization because the president, increasingly, has the power to reshape vast swaths of American life.

American Idolatry

When I wrote *Cult*, I fancied myself ripping the veil off what we'd allowed the office to become, rubbing our noses in our creepy, idolatrous orientation toward the modern presidency. The president described in the *Federalist* was to have "no particle of spiritual jurisdiction."[10] Yet American political culture had endowed the role with quasi-mystical significance, charging the president with responsibility for all things great and small, from the price of a tank of gas to the state of the "national soul." This "vision of the president as national guardian and redeemer," I wrote in *Cult*'s opening pages, has become "so ubiquitous it goes unnoticed."[11]

Lately, though, it's all getting a bit too on the nose. "God Made Trump" is the refrain of a campaign ad the former president posted on Truth Social earlier this year: "And on June 14th, 1946, God looked down on his planned Paradise, and said, I need a caretaker. So *God gave us Trump*," the narrator intones.[12]

On the campaign trail, Trump's self-deification takes on a more apocalyptic tenor. "The seal is now broken," he raves: "either we surrender to the demonic forces" assembled by the Biden administration, "or we defeat them."[13] For the site of his 2024 kickoff rally in March, Trump picked Waco, Texas, where in 1993 an armed standoff between federal agents and cult leader David Koresh's Branch Davidians ended with over 80 dead. "For those who have been wronged and betrayed . . . I am your retribution," Trump thundered, "2024 is *our Final Battle*."[14]

Actually, it's a "*Battle for the Soul of the Nation*," President Biden insists. In a September 2022 prime-time address with that title, delivered from the steps of Philadelphia's Independence Hall, the president railed against the MAGA-hatted forces of "chaos" who "live not in the light of truth but in the shadow of lies." Then he drifted off into metaphysical theology: "I believe the soul is the breath, the life, and the essence of who we are. The soul is what makes us 'us'" and so on.[15]

Yet you have to wonder how much anyone, including the candidates, takes these pretensions seriously. Is Joe Biden capable of tending to anything as elusive and ephemeral as the "national soul"? Even before his disastrous debate performance in June, he rarely seemed capable of even finding the podium without a handler. Does Donald Trump have the requisite attention span to serve as an instrument of divine vengeance? Before taking office, the 45th president told his aides to "think of each presidential day as an episode in a television show in which he vanquishes rivals." In that light, Trump's apocalyptic ravings can be understood as another iteration of his long-running shtick: part of the grift that keeps on giving.[16]

The mystique of the presidency has taken a well-deserved hit in recent years. Whether on MSNBC or the *New York Times* op-ed page, dewy-eyed pundits still sometimes quote Franklin D. Roosevelt's dictum that "the presidency is pre-eminently a place of moral leadership."[17] But ordinary Americans are finding it increasingly difficult to look upon presidential politics with anything but revulsion. That's in no small part thanks to Trump himself, who did an "amazing job" puncturing the romance of the presidency and making it hard to take presidents seriously as moral leaders.

In an earlier era, the release of the Watergate tapes tarnished the office's aura of majesty by revealing that the president could be a petty, paranoid, foul-mouthed [expletive deleted] crook. The character flaws Nixon displayed in private—and fought to prevent revealing—Trump broadcast publicly and proudly to millions of followers on a Twitter feed that felt like the Watergate tapes unspooling in real time. With his insult-comic pep rallies, his "smash-and-grab attitudes toward governance," and his general inability to act like a grown-up in a grown-up's job, the 45th president "sanded the faux majesty off the office and freed the masses to direct their worship to other, more credible gods," *Politico*'s Jack Shafer wrote in 2017, predicting that "as long as he remains a prisoner of his impulses . . . we can look forward to seeing the prestige of the office decline."[18]

Decline it has, at least in terms of the trust Americans invest in the executive branch, which, according to recent numbers by Gallup, has fallen to within three points of its record post-Watergate low.[19] But, in contrast to the post-Watergate era, Americans' resurgent skepticism hasn't yet translated into reforms that re-limit presidential power. In fact, in the 15 years since *Cult* was published, the "most powerful office in the world" has grown even more powerful.

The Incredible Expanding Presidency

Of the three presidencies we've endured since the book came out in 2008, Barack Obama's looms largest, both in terms of the cultlike, tent-revival atmosphere surrounding him and his aggressive expansion of executive power.

As a candidate, Obama had pledged to "turn the page on the imperial presidency." But by the time he hit the podium at Oslo to accept his precipitously granted Nobel Peace Prize in December 2009, Obama had already launched more drone strikes than George W. Bush managed in eight years.[20] He'd leave office as the first two-term president in American history to have been at war every day of his presidency.[21]

Along the way, our 44th president did more than any predecessor to strip away the remaining legal limits on presidential war-making. Less than a year after his Peace Prize acceptance, Obama launched his first "war of choice," in Libya. When the Muammar el-Qaddafi regime failed to collapse on schedule, Obama defied the limits imposed by the 1973 War Powers Resolution, advancing the novel theory that you're not engaged in "hostilities" if the foreigners you're bombing can't hit you back.[22] And it was Obama who was largely responsible for warping the 2001 Authorization for the Use of Military Force—passed three days after the 9/11 attacks to target al Qaeda and the Taliban—into an enabling act for endless war, anywhere in the world.[23]

In September 2011, Obama added yet another innovation: the remote-control execution of a U.S. citizen without due process, far from any battlefield. With the targeted killing of Anwar al-Awlaki, a New Mexico–born radical cleric, via Predator drone strike in northeastern Yemen, the president claimed unreviewable authority to serve an "executive death warrant" on any American he deemed a terrorist threat.[24] Nor did citizenship offer any special protection from the executive branch's expansive surveillance powers. In the summer of 2013, thanks to National Security Agency whistleblower Edward Snowden, the public learned that the administration had been engaged in a massive, covert effort to collect domestic phone data, monitoring Americans in the name of protecting them from terrorism.[25]

Even where no national security claim was available, our 44th president managed to forge new frontiers in the abuse of executive power at home. As I wrote in *Cult*, "crisis is the health of the presidency," and the 2008 financial collapse proved no exception.[26] The months leading up to Obama's inauguration saw the collapse of the housing market, a paralyzing credit crunch, and two of the Big Three American automakers teetering on the edge of bankruptcy. In that panicked atmosphere, our 44th president played a role akin to commander in chief of the U.S. economy, flouting bankruptcy rules to shaft Chrysler's creditors and reward his union allies, forcing the company to merge with Italian automaker Fiat, and summarily firing the CEO of General Motors.[27]

As the crisis receded, Obama continued to govern by executive fiat. "I've got a pen, and I've got a phone," the president bragged, and he proceeded to use them to unilaterally grant lawful status and eligibility for federal benefits for nearly half of the 11 million unauthorized immigrants in the country; invent a presidential "power of the purse," spending billions of dollars Congress never appropriated on health care subsidies; and issue regulatory "guidance" documents strong-arming colleges and universities into growing their diversity, equity, and inclusion bureaucracies and tightening restrictions on campus speech.[28]

In private, Obama had been heard to worry that his executive-power innovations would lie around like a "loaded weapon" for future presidents to abuse.[29] And on January 20, 2017, he passed that fearsome arsenal on to Trump, who used it aggressively and added a few new inventions of his own.

The most dangerous of these came in January 2020, when Trump used the targeted-killing machinery set up by George W. Bush and perfected by Obama to kill Iranian general Qasem Soleimani. The Soleimani hit was something new under the sun: it marked the first time an American president publicly ordered the assassination of a top government official of a country we were not legally at war with. It was also a major usurpation of congressional power: killing a senior government figure with a drone-fired missile is something every country on Earth would consider a declaration of war, a decision our Constitution rightly reserves for Congress.[30]

Trump's other key innovation was in the use of presidential emergency powers. In February 2019, he declared a national emergency to "build the wall" on the U.S.-Mexico border, diverting over $5 billion to a pet project Congress had refused to fund. It seems not to have occurred to any president before Trump that he could use a bogus "emergency" claim to do an end run around Congress in a budget battle. Yet that's precisely what President Trump did, and Congress proved powerless to stop him.[31]

Then, in early 2020, a *genuine* national emergency arrived, in the form of the COVID-19 outbreak. In terms of lives lost and economic damage, the pandemic rapidly eclipsed the two prior crises of the 21st century: 9/11 and the financial panic of 2008.

That spring, with Trump regularly punching "send tweet" on unhinged theories of executive power, it seemed certain he'd follow the pattern established by past presidents. In March 2020, the president threatened to impose a federal "QUARANTINE" on New York, New Jersey, and Connecticut—something that would almost certainly require the U.S. military to enforce.[32] In April, he claimed "ultimate authority" to force governors to reopen their states, and in July, he floated the idea of "Delay[ing] the Election until people can properly, securely, and safely vote."[33] Yet COVID-19 ultimately proved to be one crisis Trump was willing to let go to waste. In each case, Trump quickly backed down, leaving the impression that the real "ultimate authority" he coveted was dominance over the news cycle.

Instead, his successor, Biden, seized on the pandemic to justify rule by decree, ordering Americans to mask up on public transport, forbidding landlords to collect the rent, and mandating that workers show their COVID-19 papers in order to keep their jobs.[34] By early 2022, it was becoming clear that, in the name of "public health," the Biden administration had been engaged in a massive, covert effort to suppress political speech. As the Twitter Files and related litigation would reveal, "very angry" Biden officials had pushed social media companies to blacklist and shadowban alleged "disinformation" (much of it actually accurate) about the COVID-19 lab-leak theory, pandemic lockdowns, and COVID-19 risk.[35] This "coordinated campaign" of "unrelenting pressure," the Fifth Circuit Court of Appeals noted in an opinion that fall, "had the intended result of suppressing millions of protected free speech postings by American citizens."[36]

In the summer of 2022, COVID-19 also served as the rationale for a sweeping plan to cancel up to $600 billion in student loan debt for some 43 million borrowers. Drawing inspiration from Trump's border-wall gambit, Biden invoked the COVID-19 crisis to trigger a 2003 emergency-power statute aimed at providing relief to U.S. soldiers then deployed in Iraq and Afghanistan.[37] The Supreme Court rebuffed the plan—as it had the vax-or-test mandate—ruling that it exceeded the authority granted in the law. Undeterred, the administration has been mining other sources of statutory authority in the hopes of delivering a new multi-billion-dollar jubilee prior to November's election. "The Supreme Court tried to block me from relieving student debt. But they didn't stop me," Biden boasted via X, formerly Twitter, in late May.[38]

The Cult in the Age of Political Sectarianism

Meanwhile, as the presidency accrued new powers to reshape American life and law, something else was happening that made centralized control more dangerous. Americans were growing so far apart that they could barely understand—or *stand*—each other anymore.

The first two decades of this century marked the dawn of "an acute era of polarization," the Stanford political scientists Shanto Iyengar and Masha Krupenkin report, one in which "partisans' mild dislike for their opponents has been transformed into a deeper form of animus."[39]

A key measure of partisan hostility is the so-called feelings thermometer, a long-running series of surveys in which respondents rate their own party and the other party on a temperature scale of 1 to 100. In the 1970s, Democrats and Republicans gave their own party a balmy 74 degrees and opposing partisans a slightly brisk 48 degrees. By 2020, however, the average temperature rating for the other side had plummeted to a bitter 20 degrees.

Americans aren't just cold to the other team: they hate and fear them. Majorities of highly politically engaged Republicans (62 percent) and highly politically engaged Democrats (70 percent) tell pollsters that the other party makes them feel "afraid."[40] Politics now divides Americans more than race, sex, or religion. In fact, in disturbing ways, politics has taken the place of religion.

In the fall of 2020—midway between lockdown/George Floyd summer and the Capitol riot on January 6, 2021—a group of leading polarization scholars published an article reframing the phenomenon in religious terms. What's come over us is best described as "political sectarianism," they argue, characterized by "strong faith in the moral correctness and superiority of one's sect." Like Sunni and Shia in the Middle East or Catholics and Protestants in Northern Ireland, large numbers of politically engaged Americans have come to see their political opponents as "alien," contemptible, and "iniquitous."[41]

As recently as 2016, the idea that the other team was morally debased was a minority view among partisans, but by 2022, the Pew Research Center reported that 72 percent of Republicans and 63 percent of Democrats had come to regard members of the other party as "more immoral," with similar majorities agreeing that the folks across the aisle are "more dishonest."[42] And in a 2019 study titled "Lethal Mass Partisanship," researchers found that over 42 percent of Republicans and Democrats agreed with the statement that members of the other party "are not just worse for politics—they are downright evil." When asked, "Do you ever think: we'd be better off as a country if large numbers of [the opposing party] in the public today just died?," 15 percent of Republicans and 20 percent of Democrats owned up to occasionally wishing mass death on fellow Americans who don't vote like they do.[43]

Partisans no longer worship their party's president quite as fervently as they did in George W. Bush's or Obama's first terms. But they're increasingly desperate to prevent the ascendancy of the rival sect. "Viewing opposing partisans as different . . . dislikable, or immoral, may not be problematic in isolation," the authors of "Political Sectarianism in America" write, but "when all three converge, political losses can feel like existential threats that must be averted—whatever the cost."[44]

A Divider, Not a Uniter

Here's a thought experiment: if you had to design institutions from scratch to govern such a deeply divided people, how would you proceed? The prudent answer, it seems to me, is *as gently as possible.*

To preserve social peace, you'd want contentious issues settled close to home, where there's more common ground. Where having one national policy is unavoidable—as in trade or war—you'd want elected representatives in multiple branches of government deliberating and forging consensus. The last thing you'd want to do is maximize the number of zero-sum, one-size-fits-all decisions made at the top, with a single political leader making the call.

Instead, over the past couple of decades, we've been running a dangerous experiment. As our politics took on a quasi-religious fervor, we've concentrated vast new powers in the executive branch. Fundamental questions of governance that used to be left to Congress, the states, or the people are now increasingly settled—winner takes all—by whichever party manages to seize the presidency.

In all the hand-wringing over polarization, law professors John O. McGinnis and Michael B. Rappaport warn in an important 2022 article, "Presidential Polarization," a key factor "has gone largely undiscussed: the deformation of our federal governing structure." The drift toward one-man rule both intensifies partisan fury and makes it more dangerous.[45]

Where the original constitutional design required broad consensus for sweeping policy changes, "now the president can adopt such changes unilaterally," McGinnis and Rappaport write, and whenever the presidency changes parties, rules affecting almost every aspect of American life shift with the party affiliation of the president.[46]

When one man decides what your health insurance covers, whether you're on the hook for your student loans, whether we have a trade war with China or a shooting war with Iran—when so much turns on who holds the White House, it's a safe bet we're going to fight about it bitterly. The modern presidency by its very nature is a divider, not a uniter. It's become far too powerful to be anything else.

Worse still, as national harmony has frayed, recent presidents have used their burgeoning powers to pick at the seams. In the years since *Cult* was published, the weapons of presidential power have increasingly been deployed to impose forced settlements on the issues that divide us most. In the age of identity politics, the modern president has become our culture warrior in chief.

Earlier battles in America's perennial "culture wars" were rarely fought with the "pen and phone." Presidents weighed in on flashpoint issues of the time, like school prayer, abortion, and "family values"— but their efforts were largely performative. In the 1980s and 1990s, presidential culture-warring was mainly waged from the bully pulpit.

If a president wanted to signal that he was *really* serious about a particular culture-war dispute, he'd throw his weight behind a constitutional amendment designed to settle the issue. In 1982, President Ronald Reagan proposed a school-prayer amendment; in 1989, President George H. W. Bush backed another prohibiting "flag desecration." Lip service and long-shot constitutional amendments remained the key tactics in presidential culture-warring at the time I began writing *Cult*. In the 2004 and 2006 election cycles, President George W. Bush proclaimed his support for a Federal Marriage Amendment defining marriage as "a union of man and woman."[47] Like the school-prayer and flag-burning amendments, it sputtered out well before reaching the goal line.

Throughout this whole period, no president seemed to imagine that he could wade into culture-war fights and settle them with the stroke of a pen. Perhaps the closest any came was with the executive order, first issued by Reagan in 1985, requiring U.S. foreign aid recipients to certify that they wouldn't perform or promote abortions. Starting with Bill Clinton, subsequent Democratic presidents turned the Mexico City Policy off—Republicans, on again—with the requirement blinking in and out of existence each time the office changed parties, without meaningfully affecting any American's rights.[48] But in the 15 years since *The Cult of the Presidency* was published, the consequences of a shift in party control of the office have grown far more sweeping.

Few issues divide Americans more than race; nevertheless, one of Biden's first acts as president was to issue an executive order guaranteed to divide us further. Biden's day-one Executive Order on Advancing Racial Equity makes rooting out "systemic racism" a central organizing principle for the federal government.[49] On that basis, the administration began mounting a frontal assault on equality before the law. In 2021, for example, the Biden administration began handing out emergency COVID-19 relief funds—debt relief for farmers, grants to restaurants—on explicitly racial grounds. That principle even extended to lifesaving drugs. Minority status alone could move you to the front of the line for COVID-19 antivirals in states following guidelines from Biden's Food and Drug Administration.[50]

On the contentious issue of transgender rights, once again, what the country's getting is forced settlement through unilateral edict and administrative order.[51] Title IX of the Education Amendments Act of 1972 prohibits discrimination "on the basis of sex" in any program receiving federal financial assistance. New regulations issued under that authority by the Biden Education Department in April make the president commander in chief of the girls' room, empowering him to decide which kids get to use which bathroom in nearly every K–12 public school and college in America.[52] At the same time, Biden's Department of Health and Human Services is moving to implement a rule that requires doctors and hospitals to provide "gender-affirming care"— puberty blockers, cross-sex hormones, and "top" and "bottom" sex-change surgeries—including for minors. Private insurers—and the taxpayer, via Medicaid—will be required to foot the bill.[53]

It seems there's no contentious social issue too parochial to escape the notice of the current culture warrior in chief. Lately, President Biden has been hell-bent on making a federal case out of how local school districts curate their grammar-school library shelves. At the White House Pride Celebration in June 2023, the president announced the appointment of a "book-ban coordinator" in the Education Department's Office for Civil Rights (OCR): "We're taking on these civil rights violations, because that's what they are," he told the crowd.[54] If local taxpayers decide Maia Kobabe's cartoon-porn memoir *Gender Queer* is too hot for the bookmobile, they may have to face a federal inquisition over creating a "hostile environment" for LGBTQ students.[55]

If he takes power again, Trump has no intention of declaring a federal ceasefire. Instead, the "Agenda 47" section of his campaign website promises to arm the other side of these culture-war battles. He'll take OCR off the "book ban" beat and sic them on any teacher who covers critical race theory or transgender issues or forces "other inappropriate racial, sexual, or political content on children." They'll face "severe consequences" under federal civil rights law.[56] His education platform includes a plan to take over teacher certification from the states and "create a new credentialing body to certify teachers who embrace patriotic values and the American way of life."[57] And what Biden deems "gender-affirming care," Trump calls "child sexual mutilation," and he's pledged to put the full weight of the federal government behind that view, tasking the Justice Department with investigating pharmaceutical companies that make puberty blockers and pushing for a law "prohibiting child sexual mutilation in all 50 states." No doubt he'll encourage some creative prosecutions when he discovers the federal female genital mutilation law that's already on the books.[58]

The Most Important Election in History?

One of the key benefits of "energy in the executive," Alexander Hamilton argued in the *Federalist*, is that it would provide "steady administration of the laws."[59] In the modern era, it's had the opposite effect, as laws change radically from administration to administration, depending on the policy preferences of the president. In the service of presidential culture-warring, puberty blockers and so-called gender-affirming care can go from compulsory to forbidden every four to eight years depending on which political party wins the presidency. And on a host of other controversial policies—from immigration to racial preferences to energy and the environment—"energy in the executive" now means whipsawing between extremes whenever power changes hands.

"In the last decade," the *New York Times* recently reported, "environmental rules in particular have been caught in a cycle of erase-and-replace whiplash" that makes it nearly impossible for industries to plan.[60] New tailpipe emissions restrictions issued by the Biden Environmental Protection Agency in March are designed to "ensure that the majority of new passenger cars and light trucks sold in the United States are all-electric or hybrids by 2032," and regulations finalized in April 2024 will force coal plants "to either deploy technology to capture virtually all their emissions, or shut down."[61] Here again, Trump promises a 180-degree turn, reversing these policies and setting oil and gas producers free to "drill, baby, drill, right away."[62]

Partisans have always told us that next November's is the "Most Important Election in History"; we used to take it with the requisite grain of salt. In 2000, only 45 percent of Americans told pollsters it really mattered who won that year's presidential contest. It's only gone up from there: 63 percent in 2012, 74 percent in 2016, and 83 percent in 2020.[63]

Maybe Americans think it matters because *it matters*. If everything from what car you can buy to what books go on grammar-school library shelves turns on which party controls the White House, good luck convincing people to take an electoral loss in stride. "The imperial administrative presidency," McGinnis and Rappaport note, "raises the stakes of any presidential election, making each side fear that the other will enjoy largely unchecked and substantial power in many areas of policy."[64] That fear encourages the dangerous conviction that *every* election is a "Flight 93 election"—charge the cockpit, do or die.[65] The relentless growth of executive power has made the federal government the central catalyst of social strife.

Americans have an inchoate sense that something's gone wrong: a majority of voters recognize that our "system of checks and balances dividing power among the president, Congress, and the courts is not working well these days," according to a recent survey from the Associated Press and the University of Chicago.[66] The same survey shows that "the abstract idea of a president with nearly unchecked power remains unpopular," for what little that's worth. The rub comes when we go from the abstract to the particular; the Associated Press summed up the survey results succinctly: "Americans think a president's power should be checked—unless their side wins."[67]

Yet anyone capable of thinking past a single presidential election cycle should recognize the dangers of giving presidents an even freer hand. In a country as fractious as ours has become, that's a prescription for turning our as-yet-metaphorical civil war into *real* "American carnage."

Instead, for the sake of domestic tranquility, we need a sustained effort aimed at limiting the damage that presidents can do and lowering the stakes of presidential elections—reining in emergency powers, war powers, authorities over trade, and the ability to make law with the stroke of a pen. Our most pressing need is for structural reforms that limit the harm we might do to each other amid the fog of partisan war.

I wrote *Cult* because I believed the American presidency had become an extraconstitutional monstrosity and a libertarian nightmare, "the source of much of our political woe and some of the gravest threats to our liberties."[68]

The past decade and a half has given me little reason to change that assessment. But as I look back at what I wrote then, I fear that I understated the dangers we'd face by failing to re-limit executive power. In certain passages, I seem to suggest that the wages of constitutional sin would be frustration: eternal recurrence of the "timeworn pattern: outsized expectations, dangerous centralization of power, and inevitable failure," a "perennial cycle of disappointment and centralization."

Fifteen years later, the risks strike me as far more dire than that. In our partisan myopia, we've unwittingly laid down the infrastructure for autocratic rule and sectarian warfare. The danger isn't that we'll wind up *disappointed*; it's the prospect that the presidency will tear the country apart.

It's said that God protects fools, drunks, and the United States of America. But it is also written: "Thou shalt not tempt the Lord thy God." Just how far do we want to keep pressing our national luck?

INTRODUCTION

On the morning of January 28, 2007, Mike Huckabee went on NBC's *Meet the Press* to announce that he was running for president of the United States. It was a bold move for an undistinguished former governor of Arkansas, best known for losing 110 pounds in office and writing about it in a book called *Quit Digging Your Grave with a Knife and Fork*. Bolder still was Huckabee's rationale for seeking the nation's highest office. He had decided to run, he told host Tim Russert, because "America needs positive, optimistic leadership to kind of turn this country around, to *see a revival of our national soul.*"[1]

Russert didn't make the most of his opportunity for follow-up questions, but the candidate's remark might have suggested several. First, was the "national soul" really in such a desperate state that its last, best hope was . . . Mike Huckabee? Second, and more importantly, what sort of office did Huckabee imagine he was running for? Is reviving the national soul in the job description? And if reviving the national soul is part of the president's job, what *isn't*?

The Bipartisan Romance with the Imperial Presidency

Huckabee wasn't the only candidate to wax messianic about the president's role. His fellow contestants in campaign 2008 also seemed to think they were applying for the job of national savior. Sen. John McCain (R-AZ) invoked Teddy Roosevelt as a role model, noting that TR "liberally interpreted the constitutional authority of the office," and "nourished the soul of a great nation."[2] Sen. Barack Obama (D-IL) ran on "the audacity of hope," a phrase connoting the eternal promise of redemption through presidential politics (is "audacity" the right word for that kind of hope?). For her part, Hillary Clinton seemed to see the president as the lone figure who could restore a sense of purpose to American life: as she put it in May 2007, "When I ask people, 'What do you think the goals of America are today?' people don't have any idea. We don't know what we're trying to achieve. And I think that in a life or in a country you've got to have some goals."[3]

The man they hoped to succeed, George W. Bush, has made clear on any number of occasions just how broadly he views the president's job. After a tornado ripped through central Kansas in May 2007, the president visited the hardest-hit town and told the assembled residents, "I bring the prayers and concerns of the people of this country to this town of Greensburg, Kansas." He had arrived, he said, on a mission to "lift people's spirits as best as I possibly can and to hopefully touch somebody's soul by representing our country, and to let people know that while there was a dark day in the past, there's brighter days ahead."[4]

The president as described by George W. Bush was no mere constitutional officer charged with faithful execution of the laws—he was a *soul-toucher*, a hope-bringer—a luminary who carried with him the prayers and concerns of the American people—not to mention plenty of federal aid.

Nearly six years earlier, September 11 had inspired similar rhetorical excess, but with far greater consequence. The week after the attacks, President Bush invoked America's "responsibility to history" and declared that we would "answer these attacks and *rid the world of evil*."[5] A mission that vast would seem to require equally vast powers. And the Bush administration has made some of the broadest assertions of executive power in American history: among them, the power to launch wars at will, to tap phones and read email without a warrant, and to seize American citizens on American soil and hold them for the duration of the Global War on Terror—in other words, perhaps forever—without ever having to answer to a judge.

Those assertions have justifiably given rise to fears of a new Imperial Presidency. Yet, many of the same people who condemn the growing concentration of power in the executive branch also embrace a virtually limitless notion of presidential responsibility. Today, politics is as bitterly partisan as it's been in three decades, and the Bush presidency is at the center of the fight. But amid all the bitterness, it's easy to miss the fact that, at bottom, both left and right agree on the boundless nature of presidential responsibility.

Neither left nor right sees the president as the Framers saw him: a constitutionally constrained chief executive with an important but limited job: to defend the country when attacked, check Congress when it violates the Constitution, enforce the law—and little else. Today, for conservatives as well as liberals, it is the president's job to protect us from harm, to "grow the economy," to spread democracy and American ideals abroad, and even to heal spiritual malaise—whether it takes the form of a "sleeping sickness of the soul," as Hillary Clinton would have it, or an "if it feels good, do it" ethic, as diagnosed by George W. Bush.[6]

Few Americans find anything amiss in the notion that it is the president's duty to solve all large national problems and to unite us all in the service of a higher calling. The vision of the president as national guardian and redeemer is so ubiquitous that it goes unnoticed.

Is that vision of the presidency appropriate for a self-governing republic? Is it compatible with limited, constitutional government? The book you're holding argues that it is not. Americans' unconfined conception of presidential responsibility is the source of much of our political woe and some of the gravest threats to our liberties. If the public expects the president to deal with all national problems, physical or spiritual, then the president will seek—or seize—the power necessary to handle that responsibility. We're right to fear the growth of presidential power. But the Imperial Presidency is the price of making the office the focus of our national hopes and dreams.

Cursing the King, Pining for Camelot

It may seem strange to charge that American political culture—so often derided for its cynicism—suffers from romanticization of the presidency. There's no doubt that we're less starry-eyed about our presidents than we were half a century ago, when three-quarters of Americans trusted the federal government to do what was right most of the time and over 60 percent told pollsters that the president should take the lead in deciding what the country needs.[7] Post-Watergate America is more likely to distrust any given president, and respect for the office has declined. But at the same time, the inflated expectations people have for the office—what they want from a president—remain as high as ever.

A year before September 11, National Public Radio, the Kaiser Family Foundation, and Harvard's Kennedy School of Government released an extensive survey of American attitudes toward government, summing up the results pithily: "Americans distrust government, but want it to do more." Though nearly half the respondents saw the federal government as a threat to their personal rights and freedoms, the survey also showed that Americans "would like to see the government do more in a wide range of areas."[8]

So too with the presidency. Today, we're far more open than our grandparents were to the idea that the president may be a crook or a clown; yet, we still expect the "commander in chief" to heal the sick, save us from hurricanes, and provide balm for our itchy souls. If F. Scott Fitzgerald was right that the mark of a first-rate mind is the ability to hold two contradictory ideas at the same time, then, intellectually, the American electorate is second to none. We don't trust the president. But we demand that he fulfill our every need.

That tension suffuses the American view of the presidency from low culture to high. And in their rhetoric, presidents stoke the public's inflated expectations, promising moral leadership and government action that can heal the country and the world. Americans don't quite believe it, but can't bring themselves to give up the dream. From popular culture to the academy to the voting booth, we curse the king, all the while pining for Camelot.

Is the president a tyrant or a saint? A crook or a Lincolnesque redeemer? All the above, if popular culture is any indication of American sentiment—and what better indicator could there be? Americans' conflicted views of the presidency play themselves out on small screens and large: the pop culture president is at turns malevolent, pathetic, and ridiculous . . . or righteous, heroic, and noble. He molests Girl Scouts and gins up a phony war to distract the public, as in 1997's *Wag the Dog.* Or he's a two-fisted action hero, ready to personally vanquish any foreign threat—as with Harrison Ford's President James Marshall, who duked it out with Russian terrorists that same year in *Air Force One.*

Martin Sheen's President Jed Bartlet never got quite as physical, but few movies or TV shows from the 1950s or 1960s ever embodied the heroic view of the presidency as completely as did NBC's hit series *The West Wing.* Bartlet was unbearably decent and admirable, a Catholic theologian-cum-Nobel laureate in economics—just a slight cut above the sort of person we usually get for the job. Even his scandals were noble: in Season 3, Bartlet suffers a congressional censure vote for concealing his valiant struggles with multiple sclerosis—a far cry from the thong-snapping hijinks of the Clinton years.

Meanwhile, much of the same audience that adored *The West Wing* laughs along nightly as Comedy Central's *The Daily Show* skewers President Bush's arrogance, incompetence, and difficulties with the English language. Martin Sheen is their president, but Jon Stewart is their comedian—and no one seems to notice any tension between the two views.

Like other Americans, historians prefer a cinematic presidency—not for them the stolid, boring competence of a Calvin Coolidge. Instead, presidential scholars insist that America's great presidents are the nation builders and the war leaders—men who overturned the settled constitutional order during periods of crisis. That's nowhere clearer than in the periodic polls of scholars ranking the presidents, a practice introduced by Arthur Schlesinger Sr. in 1948 and repeated by his son, the author of 1973's *The Imperial Presidency.* That book was a powerful critique of executive aggrandizement and the decline of Congress, which makes it all the more ironic that Schlesinger Jr.'s polls, like his father's, heavily favored imperial presidents.

Summing up the results of his 1962 survey, Schlesinger Sr. noted that "Mediocre Presidents believed in negative government, in self-subordination to the legislative power."[9] And scholars continue to see it that way. Thus, in Schlesinger Jr.'s 1996 survey, 5 of the top 10 presidents were war leaders: among them James K. Polk, Harry Truman, and Woodrow Wilson. Polk's major achievement was starting a war of conquest. Truman launched our first major undeclared war and had to be rebuked by the Supreme Court for claiming that his powers as commander in chief allowed him to seize American companies. After running for reelection as a peace candidate, Wilson took the country into the pointless carnage of World War I and carried out perhaps the harshest crackdown on civil liberties in American history. Wilson's successor Warren G. Harding pardoned the peaceful protestors Wilson had imprisoned and ushered in the boom times of the Roaring Twenties. Yet, Harding comes in dead last in the Schlesinger poll.[10]

Correcting for partisanship doesn't change the scholarly bias toward imperial presidents. In October 2000, the Federalist Society and the *Wall Street Journal* conducted a presidential scholar survey balanced among experts on the left and the right. Ronald Reagan shot up 17 places, but otherwise the results were virtually identical to the Schlesinger survey.[11] Whether they're conservative or liberal, America's professors prefer presidents who dream big and attempt great things—even when they leave wreckage in their wake. The worst fate for any president, it seems, is to become one of history's timeservers, men like Hayes, Arthur, Harding, or Coolidge, who offered no New Deals, proclaimed no New Frontiers—men whose ambition was so contemptibly flaccid that they could content themselves simply with presiding over peace and prosperity. To be truly great, the modern chief executive needs to aim higher. Today's president can no longer merely preside.

All the President's Jobs

And it's been that way for quite some time. In 1956 prominent political scientist Clinton Rossiter published *The American Presidency*; in the book, Rossiter announced his "feeling of veneration, if not exactly reverence, for the authority and dignity of the presidency." The president had, Rossiter noted approvingly, come to be viewed by the public as "a combination of scoutmaster, Delphic oracle, hero of the silver screen, and father of the multitudes."[12]

Rossiter outlined 10 roles that the public expected the modern president to fulfill. At least five of those roles are nowhere to be found in the Constitution, and they reflect a breathtaking amount of responsibility and power. Among the roles Rossiter describes are

- *"World Leader"*: The president is responsible not just for the "common Defense of the United States," as the Constitution phrases it, but for the survival and flourishing of freedom worldwide.
- *"Protector of the Peace"*: He is charged as well with responding to any highly visible crisis, from labor unrest to bad weather. Faced with "floods in New England or a tornado in Missouri or a railroad strike in Chicago or a panic in Wall Street," Rossiter noted, "the people turn almost instinctively to the White House and its occupant for aid and comfort."
- *"Chief Legislator"*: Where the Framers' chief executive had recognized that Congress takes the lead on domestic policy, by the 1950s, the president had become the motive force in American government, responsible for setting the nation's policy agenda and pushing his legislative program to completion.
- *"Manager of Prosperity"*: Well before President Bill Clinton took office promising to "focus like a laser beam on the economy," Professor Rossiter recognized that the modern president had become responsible for the economic well-being of the country, a figure expected to "watch like a mother hen over all the eggs in all of our baskets."
- *"Voice of the People"*: The modern president had also become, in Rossiter's words, "the moral spokesman of us all," responsible for divining and implementing the general will. He is nothing less than "the American people's one authentic trumpet," a leader with "no higher duty than to give a clear and certain sound."[13]

Taken all in all, Rossiter gives us a remarkable vision of the president. He's our guardian angel, our shield against harm. He's America's shrink and social worker and our national talk-show host. He's a guide for the perplexed, a friend to the downtrodden—and he's also the Supreme Warlord of the Earth.

Rossiter wrote on the cusp of the New Frontier, before two presidencies had been broken on the rack of Vietnam, before the revelations of Watergate reawakened Americans to the dangers of the executive unbound. Thus, his exuberance about the promise of presidential power may strike the modern reader as naive and anachronistic. But the presidency remains much as he described it. None of Rossiter's roles has been transferred to any other government actor or returned to the people themselves. The 21st-century president remains our World Leader, the Protector of the Peace, our Chief Legislator, our Manager of Prosperity, and the Voice of the People—even if we're more likely than ever before to worry about the powers we've ceded to him.

Our Plebiscitary Presidency

During his 1912 reelection campaign, our 27th president, William Howard Taft, looked on with numb dread as that grandiose vision of the presidency began to emerge in the form of his former friend and mentor Theodore Roosevelt. Seeking to secure a third term by denying Taft a second, TR's campaign struck an apocalyptic note: in his address to the delegates at the Progressive Party convention that year, Roosevelt barked, "You who strive in a spirit of brotherhood for the betterment of our Nation, to you who gird yourselves for this great new fight in the never-ending warfare for the good of humankind, I say in closing . . . *We stand at Armageddon, and we battle for the Lord!* "[14]

Recoiling from Roosevelt's fanaticism, Taft offered a more realistic account of the presidency's potential. On the campaign trail, and later, in his book *Our Chief Magistrate and His Powers*, Taft insisted that the president was not responsible for solving every major problem in American life and should not have the power to attempt it. In one speech during the 1912 campaign, Taft protested that the president "cannot create good times . . . cannot make the rain to fall, the sun to shine, or the crops to grow."[15] At the height of the Progressive Era, however, American voters weren't in the mood to reward executive humility; the election went to Woodrow Wilson, a pivotal figure in the growth of the Imperial Presidency.

Few presidents since Taft have tried to lower public expectations for the office. Far more typical is the tone struck by Bill Clinton in his first inaugural address, in which he intimated that the ritual of presidential anointment could bring hope and life to the world: "This ceremony is held in the depth of winter. But, by the words we speak and the faces we show the world, we force the spring."[16]

Political scientists who have tracked the content of the inaugural and State of the Union addresses over time have found that presidential rhetoric has become much less humble and much more activist in tone.[17] Rossiter's roles abound in modern presidential speeches, which increasingly describe an alternate reality in which the "man in charge" is capable of putting right virtually every problem in modern American life. In his State of the Union addresses, George W. Bush has promised, among other things, to rescue America's children from gangs, fight steroids in sports, "move [America] beyond a petroleum-based economy," and "lead freedom's advance" around the world.[18]

There's good reason modern presidents talk the way they do: their rhetoric reflects what the office has become. The constitutional presidency, as the Framers conceived it, was designed to stand against the popular will as often as not, with the president wielding the veto power to restrain Congress when it transgressed its constitutional bounds. In contrast, the modern president considers himself the tribune of the people, promising transformative action and demanding the power to carry it out. The result is what political scientist Theodore J. Lowi has termed "the plebiscitary presidency": "an office of tremendous personal power drawn from the people . . . and based on the new democratic theory that the presidency with all powers is the necessary condition for governing a large democratic nation."[19]

If we're unhappy with the presidency we've got, Lowi suggests, we have ourselves to blame. The office as we know it is largely the creature of public demands. And like the transformed presidential role it reflects, the exultant rhetoric of the modern presidency is as much curse as blessing. It raises expectations for the office—expectations that were extraordinarily high to begin with. A man who trumpets his ability to protect Americans from economic dislocation, to shield them from physical harm and moral decay, and to lead them to national glory—such a man is bound to disappoint. Yet, having promised much, he'll seek the power to deliver on his promises.

Congressional Abdication and Overextension Abroad

Of course, no one cause can fully account for the enormous expansion of presidential power throughout the 20th century. The interplay between outsized public expectations for the office and presidential attempts to meet those expectations is central to the story of the presidency's growth, but other factors are at work as well.

A key factor is congressional abdication, the near-total failure of Congress to defend its constitutional prerogatives against aggrandizing executives. James Madison thought we could count on the constitutional architecture to harness man's lust for power, channeling it in a manner that would make the separation of powers largely self-executing. Ambition would counteract ambition, with the members of each branch fighting any diminution of their authority.

Unfortunately, the experience of the 20th century suggests that the ambitions of individual legislators do not provide them with sufficient incentive to resist executive encroachments on congressional power. The Madisonian scheme has been frustrated by legislators' eagerness to delegate legislative authority to the executive and to leave to the president the final decision over war and peace.

Another cause of executive power's growth is American expansion abroad. By creating a vast empire of overseas bases and stationing American troops across the globe, Congress has virtually ensured that the president would acquire enormous unilateral powers over foreign policy. But it's hard to see how public demands are responsible for America's imperial posture and the resulting expansion of presidential power. Public opinion polls reveal very little support among Americans for Wilsonian foreign policy adventures or for the notion that America should play the role of global policeman.[20]

Public demands may not be directly responsible for the institutional failures of Congress or for America's dangerous overcommitment abroad, but Americans' conviction that on all matters of policy the buck stops with the president makes it far easier for Congress to delegate authority and dodge responsibility. And the modern president's role as the guarantor of international peace greatly increases the odds of war and the centralization of executive power that war brings.

War Is the Health of the Presidency

"It is of the nature of war to increase the executive at the expense of the legislative authority," the *Federalist* tells us.[21] And modern commanders in chief tend to reflexively invoke the war metaphor when the public demands that they take action to solve the emergency of the month, real or imagined.

"War is the health of the state," Randolph Bourne's famous aphorism has it, but Bourne could just as easily have written that "war is the health of the presidency." Throughout American history, virtually every major advance in executive power has come during a war or a warlike crisis. Convince the public that *we are at war*, and constitutional barriers to action fall, as power flows to the commander in chief.

Little wonder, then, that, confronted with impossible expectations, the modern president tends to recast social and economic problems in military terms: war on crime, war on drugs, war on poverty. Martial rhetoric often ushers in domestic militarism, as presidents push to employ standing armies at home, to fight drug trafficking, terrorism, or natural disasters. And when the president raises the battle cry, he can usually count on substantial numbers of American opinion leaders to cheer him on.

Like intellectuals the world over, many American pundits and scholars, right and left, view bourgeois contentment with disdain. *Normal* people appear to like "normalcy," Warren Harding's term for peace and prosperity, just fine. But all too many professional thinkers look out upon 300 million people living their lives by their own design and see something impermissibly hollow in the spectacle. From William James's search for a "Moral Equivalent of War" that could unite Americans behind a common cause to the modern nostalgia for the "Greatest Generation," large swaths of our intelligentsia believe that war is the force that can give American life meaning.[22]

Our chief executives capitalize on that belief, declaring metaphorical wars on all manner of social harms or real wars on foreign adversaries. Again and again throughout American history, presidents have used the power of the bully pulpit—and their power to command the army—to redefine their role, transforming themselves from humble chief magistrates to domineering commanders in chief.

In the chapters to come, we'll explore that transformation. To show that the problems of the Imperial Presidency began long before George W. Bush's inauguration, we'll have to cover a fair amount of history. We'll begin, in Chapter 1, by looking at the Framers' vision for the presidency. The Constitution's architects knew human nature too well to concentrate enormous power and responsibility in any one man's hands. Instead, they carefully limited executive power, especially the power to take the country into war. And despite the best efforts of several aggrandizing chief executives, at the end of the 19th century, the presidency still greatly resembled the office the Framers had envisioned 100 years before.

In Chapter 2, we'll look at the early-20th-century reformers who sought to overturn that vision. The Progressives saw constitutional limits as a brake on progress and wanted the president set free to perform great works. By the third decade of the century, the Progressives had succeeded in transforming the office, in large part due to their keen appreciation of how war and crisis could be exploited to centralize power.

Chapters 3 and 4 trace the rise and fall of the Heroic Presidency, from the height of its power and public esteem in the early Cold War to its decline after Vietnam and Watergate, when Americans reclaimed their heritage of skepticism toward power. Oddly, though, just as most Americans were concluding that the presidency needed to be constrained, conservatives decided that it needed to be unleashed. The post–World War II right, led by William F. Buckley's *National Review*, had previously appreciated the dangers of concentrated power better than any other political movement of its time. But by the mid-1970s, motivated in part by the "emerging Republican majority" in the Electoral College, the right had largely abandoned its distaste for presidential activism and had begun to look upon executive power as a key weapon in the battle against creeping liberalism. Sadly, that pattern is all too common in political battles over the scope of presidential power. The tendency to support enhanced executive power when one's friends hold the executive branch—a syndrome aptly dubbed "Situational Constitutionalism"—is a recurring theme of this book.[23]

Chapters 5 through 7 treat the post-9/11 period. The al Qaeda threat led to the Heroic Presidency's triumphant return and the ascendancy of a constitutional theory that places enormous unchecked power in the hero's hands. Even as trust in the federal government, and in President Bush, has plummeted, the Bush administration skillfully employed the war metaphor to accumulate new powers. But given the nature of the war on terror, these were potentially permanent powers in a permanent war—available to all future presidents, virtuous or otherwise. That ought to trouble all Americans, regardless of their political leanings.

Given the staggering powers and responsibilities that go with the 21st-century presidency, it's more important than ever before that the person who holds the office is worthy of trust. Chapter 8, "Why the Worst Get on Top . . . and Get Worse," will provide little comfort on that score. Our current system for selecting the president favors men and women with extraordinary stamina and a burning desire to rule. And the surreal environment of modern White House life can hardly help but magnify the character flaws of anyone who wins the office.

In the final chapter, we'll ask what, if anything, can be done to restore the presidency to its proper constitutional role. Though we'll examine various proposals to curb presidential prerogative, in the end, there is no simple legislative "fix" to the problems of the presidency. Unless and until we change what we ask of the office—no longer demanding what we should not want and cannot have—we'll get what, in a sense, we deserve.

* * *

George W. Bush returned to the ranch in January 2009, to the relief of an ever-increasing majority of Americans. But replacing him will not solve the problem of presidential power. The pressure for centralization will remain, enhanced by the atmosphere of permanent emergency accompanying the war on terror. And future presidents will respond to that pressure by enhancing their power, becoming loved and admired, then hated and feared, in the binge-and-purge cycle that characterizes the American public's dysfunctional relationship with the presidency.

In an October 2000 "exit interview" with the *New Yorker*, Bill Clinton allowed that his tenure may have served to "demystify the job" of the presidency, and that, as far as he was concerned, that wasn't "such a bad thing."[24] "Demystifying the job" was a wonderful euphemism for alternately amusing and dismaying Americans with the image of a president with his trousers around his ankles. But a genuine demystification of the presidency is sorely needed. A political culture often condemned for its cynicism isn't nearly cynical enough when it comes to the nation's highest office. That office cannot deliver what it promises; and in the promising it sets the stage for further concentration of power.

Can that cycle be broken, and the presidency cut down to size? Is a presidency consistent with a constitutional republic possible in 21st-century America? This book, which contains far more diagnosis than prescription, may not answer those questions to the reader's satisfaction.

What can be said with confidence, however, is that a presidency of limited powers and modest goals was what the Framers gave us in 1787. It was the presidency we enjoyed for most of the first century under the Constitution. And it is worth fighting to restore.

1

OUR CHIEF MAGISTRATE AND HIS POWERS

The best rulers are always those to whom great power is intrusted. . . . It is, therefore, manifestly a radical defect in our federal system that it parcels out power and confuses responsibility as it does. The main purpose of the Convention of 1787 seems to have been to accomplish this grievous mistake.

    —Woodrow Wilson, *Congressional Government* (1885)

O n Friday, June 1, 1787, the Philadelphia Convention turned to the seventh resolution of the Virginia Plan introduced three days earlier, "that a national Executive be instituted, to be chosen by the national Legislature." With George Washington, the delegates' unanimous choice for convention president, looking on, James Wilson of Pennsylvania made a bold suggestion. He moved "that the Executive consist of a single person." After South Carolina's Charles Pinckney seconded the motion, "a considerable pause" ensued.[1]

What sort of officer would this be? An elected monarch, as several of the delegates feared?[2] Or something far less imposing?

The title the delegates settled on for the chief executive was humble enough. As commonly used in the 18th century, the term indicated the presiding officer of a legislature, with an emphasis on the "presiding" function, "almost to the exclusion of any executive powers," a position "usually [held by] men whose talents and reputations matched their office."[3]

Republican in Form and Substance

In fact, some found the very modesty of the title irritating. Even "fire companies and a cricket club" could have a "president," Vice President John Adams complained shortly after taking his place as presiding officer of the new Senate.[4] On April 23, 1789, three days after arriving in New York—then the seat of the national government—Adams delivered an extensive speech to the Senate insisting that the president and vice president needed honorific titles to lend an air of dignity and majesty to government. At Adams's behest, the Senate appointed a committee to confer with the House of Representatives on what titles would be appropriate.

The House wanted nothing to do with the idea. James Madison, then serving as a representative from Virginia, scorned Adams's effort.[5] "The more simple, the more republican we are in our manners," Madison told his colleagues, "the more national dignity we shall acquire."[6] When the joint committee recommended against "annex[ing] any style or title to [those] expressed in the Constitution," the House unanimously adopted the committee's report.

Yet, Adams wouldn't take no for an answer. At his urging, the Senate appointed a new Title Committee, which on May 9 proposed that the president be addressed as "His Highness, the President of the United States, and Protector of their Liberties."[7] When the Senate moved to postpone consideration of the report, Adams launched into a "forty minute . . . harangue" on the "absolute necessity" of titles.

In this debate, Adams had a formidable opponent, Sen. William Maclay of Pennsylvania, a man possibly more Jeffersonian than Jefferson, a partisan republican before factions had properly formed. In Maclay's private journal, which remains one of our best records of the proceedings of the first Senate, he condemned the "base," "silly," and "idolatrous" attempt to append quasi-monarchical titles to the nation's new constitutional officers.[8]

A first-generation American of Scots extraction, Maclay lived on a farm in the rural Pennsylvania interior, near Harrisburg. He served only two years in the Senate, and the members of what Maclay saw as an emerging, aristocratic "court party" were no doubt glad to see him go.

Maclay rarely missed a chance to needle his ideological opponents, whom he saw as beggars after "the loaves and fishes of government"—men who favored the "translation of the diadem and scepter from London" to New York.[9] He was up from his chair to object at the merest hint of anti-republican language, such as a reference to the president's "most gracious speech" or a resolution that suggested the president had "rescued" the United States from "anarchy and confusion." When a proposed resolution referred in passing to the "dignity and splendor" of the government, Maclay found even this offensive, telling his fellow senators:

> As to the seeking of sounding names and pompous expressions, I thought them exceptionable on that very account, . . . that "splendor," when applied to government, brought into my mind, instead of the highest perfection, all the faulty finery, brilliant scenes, and expensive trappings of royal government, and impressed my mind with an idea quite the reverse of republican respectability, which I thought consisted in firm and prudent councils, frugality, and economy.[10]

The Maclay that emerges from the journal is a dyspeptic grouch, the sort of personality that too few people properly appreciate.[11] Yet, as doctrinaire and exacting as Maclay could be, he was also funny and irreverent. He didn't take himself overly seriously, and thus found it impossible not to laugh at his self-important colleagues. Adams caught the worst of it. After the vice president agonized over a point of protocol, asking the senators for advice, "a solemn silence ensued." Maclay struggled to keep from cracking up: "God forgive me, for it was involuntary, but the profane muscles of my face were in tune for laughter in spite of my indisposition."[12] Maclay had to beg divine forgiveness again two weeks later, while confessing that, looking at Adams, he could not help thinking "of a monkey just put into breeches."[13]

When it came to the debate on titles, though, Maclay was deadly serious. Not only were such titles anti-republican, they were *unconstitutional*: "Let us read the Constitution," he demanded, pointing to Article I, Section 9, Clause 8: "No Title of Nobility shall be granted by the United States." "Appellations and terms given to nobility in the Old World," Maclay declared, were "contraband language in the United States," and could not be applied "to our citizens consistent with the Constitution."[14] Even the phrase "Protector of their Liberties" was objectionable: "The power of war is the organ of protection," Maclay reminded the senators, "this is placed in Congress by the Constitution. Any attempt to divest them of it and place it elsewhere, even with George Washington, is treason against the United States, or, at least, a violation of the Constitution."[15]

In response to Adams's suggestion that citizens of other countries wouldn't respect our constitutional officers unless they arrived bearing fancy titles, Maclay responded with classic American indifference: "As to what the common people, soldiers, and sailors of foreign countries may think of us, I do not think it imports us much. Perhaps the less they think, or have occasion to think of us, the better."[16]

Maclay won the point, and we've ever since referred to the president simply as "the president." But Adams's central role in the debate earned him a title of his own: Proto-Jeffersonians in the House and Senate began referring to the portly vice president as "His Rotundity." The entire episode irritated Washington, who later wrote that Adams had acted without his knowledge and contrary to his wishes.[17] Throughout his presidency, when Washington referred to the office he held, most often he called it the mere "chief magistrate."[18]

The titles debate was significant because it reaffirmed the constitutional settlement: the new president would not be an elected king. The chief magistrate had an important job, but he was not responsible for saving the "national soul": the president would have "no particle of spiritual jurisdiction," the *Federalist* tells us.[19] Instead, as presidential scholar Jeffrey K. Tulis has put it, unlike "polities that attempt to shape the souls of their citizenry and foster certain excellences or moral qualities by penetrating deeply into the 'private' sphere, the founders wanted their government to be limited to establishing and securing such a sphere."[20]

A government thus limited had no need of a chief executive invested with the powers and responsibilities described by Professor Rossiter in 1956's *The American Presidency*. As our early constitutional history makes clear, the Founding Generation did not see the president as Rossiter's Protector of the Peace, except perhaps in the narrow, constitutional sense that they expected him to respond to sudden attacks by hostile powers. Neither was he the Voice of the People, the Manager of Prosperity, nor the Chief Legislator. His main duty, as Article II, Section 3, explains, was faithful execution of the laws.

It's difficult for 21st-century Americans even to imagine a president with such a modest role. For as long as any of us have been alive, the president has been the central figure in American political life. But the Framers never thought of the president as America's "national leader." Indeed, for them, the very notion of "national leadership" raised the possibility of authoritarian rule by a demagogue who would create an atmosphere of crisis in order to enhance his power.[21] To foreclose that possibility, the powers of the chief magistrate would be carefully limited.

This chapter will explore the constitutional presidency as envisioned by the Framers. We'll begin by examining the leading modern challenge to the constitutional presidency, unitary executive theory, which, at its most radical, envisions a president with the foreign affairs powers of an elected king. We'll see that, contrary to the arguments of many unitary executive theorists, the Framers explicitly rejected royal prerogative as a model for the republican executive. They left it to Congress to decide whether and when the country would go to war.

We'll then turn to the president's constitutional role on the home front, where republican mores prevented him from bypassing Congress through direct appeals to the American people. The legal and cultural restraints on presidential activism remained surprisingly strong for over a century after ratification. Despite several notable exceptions to the rule, in the 19th century, as Theodore Lowi put it, "chief executives were chief of very little and executive of even less."[22] And yet, though poor in "national leadership," the United States somehow became the richest and most productive nation in the world by century's end.

Unitarian Heresies

In the post-9/11 era, any discussion of the Framers' vision of the presidency—a constitutionally limited office that lacked the power to launch wars or otherwise revolutionize the existing political order—needs to address the very different theory of presidential power embraced by the modern conservative movement and, more importantly, by the men and women who controlled the executive branch from 2001 to 2008. Therefore, to set the stage, we'll need to spend a few pages outlining that theory before we return to 1787 and the quite different vision of the presidency the Framers settled upon at the Philadelphia Convention.

Devotees of the unitary executive theory—unitarians, for short—have long argued for expansive presidential prerogatives in foreign affairs. Even in peacetime, as the unitarians see it, the president has—and *should* have—broad power to shape American life.

"A Friendly Institution"

Unitary executive theory takes as its starting point the Constitution's so-called vesting clause, Article II, Section 1, which declares that "the executive Power shall be vested in a President of the United States of America."[23] The theory's narrowest and most plausible claim is that the vesting clause gives the president the authority to dismiss subordinate officers within the executive branch. The president can, for example, fire cabinet officers without asking the Senate for permission.[24]

Well before 9/11, however, many unitarians made more ambitious claims about the president's powers in foreign affairs. They denounced the 1973 War Powers Resolution as an unconstitutional attempt to limit the president's ability to engage in hostilities abroad and insisted that the Reagan administration had every right to secretly raise money for the Contras, despite a statute that clearly prohibited such activity.[25]

Though unitarians emphasize their doctrine's Hamiltonian pedigree, it really emerged as a coherent body of thought during the Reagan years, as attorneys in the administration's Office of Legal Counsel employed it to assert control over the federal bureaucracy and resist post-Watergate constraints on presidential power. The right's blossoming affection for the executive branch was a curious development. From the beginning of the modern conservative movement, with the founding of William F. Buckley's *National Review* in 1955, conservatives had been the leading critics of expansive theories of presidential power, seeing them as schemes to empower activist liberalism.[26] But by the time of Reagan's ascendancy, a different view prevailed. As Steven Calabresi, one of the leading unitarians, and a special assistant to Reagan's attorney general Edwin Meese, explained recently, "Conservatives who came of age in the '70s and '80s viewed the presidency as a friendly institution."[27] A generation of conservative lawyers associated with the Federalist Society, which Calabresi helped found, has been raised unitarian, and many of them have gone on to positions within the executive branch and federal judiciary.

After 9/11, unitary executive theory took on new urgency and expanded in new directions. Unitarians within and without the Bush administration argued that the president had the power to start preventive wars; to order torture, even where prohibited by treaty and statute; to arrest terrorist suspects—even Americans captured on American soil—and hold them without legal process; and to engage in domestic surveillance outside the statutory framework set up by Congress.

John Yoo and the 9/11 Constitution

The most prominent figure behind this radical version of "energy in the executive" is John Yoo, the wunderkind law professor who served as the legal craftsman for some of the administration's most controversial policies in the war on terror.

Despite his soft voice and mild manners, Yoo doesn't shy from conflict. A right-wing legal academic at the University of California, Berkeley's Boalt Hall, Yoo is married to the daughter of liberal, antiwar broadcaster Peter Arnett, which must make the holiday season interesting.

Yoo joined Boalt's faculty in 1993, a year out of law school. Shortly thereafter, he took a sabbatical to clerk for Justice Clarence Thomas. Yoo's coclerks often teased him about his ability to "channel" the Framers. One recalls ribbing: "John, break out the crystal ball and tell us what the Framers thought," with Yoo playing along: "Yes, I consulted the Framers. You're all wrong, and I'm right."[28]

What did Professor Yoo discover while "channeling" the Framers throughout the 1990s? Something counterintuitive, to say the least: the Framers' model for the war powers of the chief executive turns out to be none other than George III and his predecessors. The Framers, Yoo argued, understood "the executive power" in light of the British constitutional tradition, and in that tradition, taking the country into war was a royal prerogative. Though Article I, Section 8, of the Constitution gives Congress the power "to declare War," that power, Yoo argued, was far narrower than most modern scholars understood it to be, and it did not limit the president's ability to wage war at the time of his choosing.[29]

Given the boldness of Yoo's thesis, and the impressive depth of his scholarship, by the late 1990s, Yoo had become a Federalist Society favorite. After George W. Bush took office in 2001, Professor Yoo took another leave of absence from Berkeley to serve as deputy assistant attorney general in the Justice Department's Office of Legal Counsel. Two months after he joined OLC, the twin towers came down, and the 34-year-old Yoo was well placed to be of service to the Bush team. He soon garnered influence well beyond what his youth or position in the OLC hierarchy would ordinarily warrant.

In large part, that was because of Yoo's inclination to tell the administration that no treaty, no statute, and no coordinate branch of government could stand in the president's way when he acts in the name of American national security. That's not to suggest that Yoo was a pliable opportunist, willing to tailor his legal opinions for the sake of bureaucratic advancement. What Yoo argued at OLC was consistent with what he had published as a legal scholar and with what he's argued since leaving the government. As Georgetown University's David Cole has put it, Yoo "was the right person in the right place at the right time. . . . Here was someone who had made his career developing arguments for unchecked power, who could cut-and-paste from his law review articles into memos that essentially told the president, 'You can do what you want.'"[30]

Since leaving OLC in 2003, the architect of the "9/11 Constitution" hasn't backed down from the positions he took while working for the government. In his books, op-eds, and journal articles defending untrammeled executive authority, Yoo drifts easily from a discussion of the constitutional text and structure to the policy reasons that we might celebrate a system that places vast unchecked power in the president's hands. Because of the proliferation of weapons of mass destruction (WMDs), the "emergence of rogue nations," and the rise of stateless terror networks, Yoo argues, "the optimal level of war for the United States may no longer be zero, but may actually be dramatically higher than before." Given these new threats, Yoo contends, "we should not, at the very least, adopt a warmaking process that contains a built-in presumption *against* using force abroad."[31]

Presidents who break free from legal restraints may make us safer; in the process, Yoo suggests, they may also achieve greatness. Yoo is an enthusiastic advocate of the "Heroic Presidency" view reflected in modern scholars' presidential rankings. In a 2005 article reviewing a book on presidential leadership, Yoo and his coauthor, former OLC colleague Robert Delahunty, write, "A 'great' President may be one who does not stay within carefully chalked lines of acknowledged presidential and congressional authority, but one who, to surmount a crisis, revolutionizes the accepted understanding of his powers."[32]

Yoo's theory of crisis constitutionalism could be characterized as revolutionary, yet it's probably better understood as *counter* revolutionary. There's little in it that reflects the Spirit of '76. In his scholarship and his legal memorandums for the administration, Yoo states explicitly that the Framers based the commander in chief's powers on the prerogatives of the British king. Citing the Anti-Federalist "Cato," who charged that the proposed Constitution contemplated royal powers for the president, Yoo writes in his 2005 book *The Powers of War and Peace* that, "Cato correctly concluded that in the realm of practical politics, the president's authority under the Constitution did not differ in important measure from that of the king."[33]

No Man a King

Is Professor Yoo right about that? Had men who had risked their lives to throw off a king decided a decade later that kings were no longer to be feared? James Wilson, the Framer with perhaps the best claim to being the architect of the presidency, took a different view. After the "considerable pause" that followed Wilson's motion for a single executive, the convention delegates launched into debate. In that debate, Wilson made clear that he

did not consider the prerogatives of the British monarch as a proper guide in defining the Executive powers. Some of these prerogatives were of Legislative nature. Among others that of war & peace &c. The only powers he conceived strictly Executive were those of executing the laws, and appointing officers, not appertaining to and appointed by the Legislature.

Wilson emphasized that "he was not governed by the British model, which was inapplicable to the situation of this Country."[34] And it would have been surprising had he felt otherwise. Wilson's signature can also be found at the bottom of the Declaration of Independence, underneath the extensive train of executive abuses that makes up the bulk of the declaration's complaints.

Nor can support for Yoo's notion be found in the *Federalist Papers*. Indeed, the very pseudonym adopted by the authors of the *Federalist* says something about how unwilling their audience would have been to accept the notion that a republic's chief executive ought to be invested with monarchical powers. The 85 essays that make up the *Federalist* ran under the name "Publius," for Publius Valerius Poplicola, one of the founders of the Roman Republic. After the Romans expelled the tyrant Tarquin, and Publius's coconsul died, Publius became sole consul of Rome, and many citizens suspected him of coveting kingship. To reassure them, Publius enacted a law stipulating that anyone attempting to make himself a king could be summarily killed.[35]

Alexander Hamilton wrote the *Federalist's* principal essays on presidential powers, and in them, he took great pains to refute those Anti-Federalists who compared the chief magistrate with an elected king. He no more resembles a king, Hamilton wrote indignantly in *Federalist* no. 69, than he resembles "the man of the seven mountains."[36]

Was Hamilton entirely sincere? Perhaps not. After all, at the convention, he was the most zealous advocate for a strong presidency, arguing on June 18 that what America needed was a "supreme Executive" who would serve "during good behavior," in other words, possibly for life. And throughout the rest of his career, Hamilton steadily pushed to expand executive power. Yet, it's worth noting that even at his most zealous, Hamilton stopped well short of what Professor Yoo argues.[37] Even in the president-for-life speech, Hamilton made clear that his model chief executive would not have the power to initiate wars; he'd merely have "the direction of war when authorized or begun."[38] During his bitter fights with Madison and Jefferson in the 1790s over presidential foreign affairs authority, Hamilton held firm to that view.[39]

And for the purposes of determining the Constitution's allocation of powers, Hamilton's sincerity—or lack thereof—hardly matters. In the ratification conventions, Americans approved the constitutional *text*, not the secret desires of Alexander Hamilton or any other Framer. On the last day of the convention, Hamilton conceded that "no man's ideas were more remote from the plan than his were known to be."[40] Still, the Constitution was an improvement over the Articles of Confederation in Hamilton's view, and he wanted to help convince his countrymen to ratify it.

Thus, the assurances Hamilton gave in the *Federalist* were the sorts of assurances the document was sold on. They helped form the understanding on which the Constitution was ratified. And the political culture in which ratification took place was not one that looked fondly on kings.

A Constitution Founded on Distrust

That culture was steeped in the Radical Whig tradition born in the English Civil War and spread by colonial pamphleteers in the years leading up to the American Revolution. At the core of that tradition was the view of man as a fallen being—one who could not be trusted with unchecked authority over his fellows. As Bernard Bailyn writes in his classic study of Founding political thought, *The Ideological Origins of the American Revolution*, for the early Americans, "what turned power into a malignant force, was not its own nature so much as the nature of man—his susceptibility to corruption and his lust for self-aggrandizement. On this there was absolute agreement."[41] That skeptical view of human nature pervades the *Federalist*. As one scholar has put it, "A considerable portion of the book might be said to be a development of Lord Acton's aphorism: 'Power corrupts and absolute power corrupts absolutely.'"[42]

By 1789, according to Bailyn, the Framers had "scotched the fear of an effective national executive, showed its necessity and benignity in the American situation. But they continued to believe, as deeply as any of the militants of '76, that power corrupts; . . . that any release of the constraints on the executive—any executive—was an invitation to disaster."[43] Given man's innate lust for power, though, how could such constraints be maintained? How could Americans prevent the "accumulation of all powers, legislative, executive, and judiciary, in the same hands," a situation Madison pronounced "the very definition of tyranny"?[44] The answer was to design a constitution in keeping with David Hume's maxim: "In constructing any system of government . . . every man ought to be supposed a knave: and have no other end in all his actions but private interest"—a constitution that would channel ambition and self-interest *against* the unification of power.[45] "The great security against a gradual concentration of the several powers in the same department," Madison wrote, "consists in giving to those who administer each department the necessary constitutional means and personal motives to resist encroachments of the others. . . . Ambition must be made to counteract ambition."[46]

The principal danger of encroachment, Madison supposed, would come from a powerful Congress drawing all power into its "impetuous vortex." The American situation would be fundamentally different from one in which "a government where numerous and extensive prerogatives are placed in the hands of a hereditary monarch" and where the gravest threats to liberty could therefore be expected to come from the executive. In the American Constitution, "where the executive magistracy is carefully limited, both in the extent and the duration of its power," *legislative* encroachment was more to be feared.[47]

"In America, the Law Is King"

Today's unitarians share Madison's fear of legislative encroachment; but few seem to share his view that executive power under the Constitution is "carefully limited" or his horror at the idea of concentrating legislative, executive, and judicial authority in one branch. Since 9/11, unitarians have argued that when it comes to wiretapping or detaining terrorist suspects, the president can set the rules, carry out the policy, and serve as the sole reviewer of his own actions.

Where in the Constitution can such powers be found? Calabresi, Yoo, and other adherents to unitary executive theory place great weight on the differences between the first clauses of Article I and Article II. Article I, outlining Congress's powers, reads "all legislative Powers *herein granted*" (emphasis added); Article II, outlining the powers of the president, begins simply: "The executive Power shall be vested in a President of the United States of America." As then judge, now justice

Samuel Alito put it in a November 2000 speech before the Federalist Society, that language indicates that the president has "not just some executive power, but *the* executive power—the whole thing."[48]

Well, perhaps. But there are a number of hurdles to jump before one can conclude that the president has plenary power over foreign affairs— and domestic affairs as well, to the extent that his actions can plausibly be characterized as serving the end of national security. First, one has to establish that the constitutional text indicates a general grant of power to the executive—that the president's powers go beyond those specifically enumerated in Sections 2 and 3 of Article II. Second, if "the executive Power" *is* a general grant of power, one still has to unpack what that power contains. What is "the whole thing"? Is it broad enough, as many unitarians suggest, to allow domestic surveillance and imprisonment without trial, so long as those activities are incident to the president's wartime goals?

Is the vesting clause, namely, the first sentence of Article II, a general grant of "executive" power? If it is, then the enumeration of specific executive powers that follows in Article II, Sections 2 and 3, is largely redundant. If the president has the "whole thing," whatever it is, surely it must be broad enough to include requiring "the Opinion, in writing," of the heads of each executive department, or to allow him to "receive Ambassadors."

Further, if the vesting clause is a general grant of power—a font of significant "residual" authority not contained in the specifically enumerated Article II powers—it's surprising that so little of the discussion at the Philadelphia Convention, in the *Federalist*, and at the ratification conventions appears to reflect that. It's worth noting that, for all the emphasis unitarians put on the difference in wording between the introductory clauses of Article I (applicable to Congress) and Article II (applicable to the president), at the convention, few, if any, of the delegates noted the difference. The "herein granted" language was added to Article I by the Committee of Style, which had no official power to make substantive changes.[49] At no point during the Constitutional Convention did any participant argue that the vesting clause constituted a general grant of power.[50]

Hamilton's defense of the office in the *Federalist* centers on the powers listed in Article II, Sections 2 and 3, rather than addressing the clause that the unitarians claim would have been understood by 18th-century Americans to include broad powers over war and peace. Historian Jack Rakove notes that the proponents of the vesting clause thesis have failed to provide evidence that any participant in the extensive debates over the Constitution's ratification understood the clause in that way:

> If we know anything about the public discussions of 1787–1788, it was that when it came to identifying potential sources of tyranny and misrule in the Constitution's numerous clauses, Anti-Federalists wrote with promiscuous abandon. Here is one case where the inability to produce a single source positively falsifies the claim being made.[51]

Finally, the vesting clause thesis—at least in its broadest incarnations—fits uneasily with the principle that our Constitution is one of enumerated, and thus limited, powers. Madison's assurance in *Federalist* no. 45 that "the powers delegated by the proposed Constitution to the federal government are few and defined," was also the key argument the Federalists presented against a Bill of Rights.[52] Since no power had been granted that could threaten private rights, Hamilton asked, "why declare that things shall not be done which there is no power to do?"[53]

"The executive Power shall be vested in a President of the United States of America": enormous powers flow from that one unassuming sentence, according to Professor Yoo and other radical unitarians. It is a sentence, they say, that gives the wartime president authority to ignore nearly every provision of the Bill of Rights, from the Fifth Amendment's due process clause to the Fourth Amendment's guarantee against unreasonable searches and seizures.[54] If 18th-century Americans understood that all this flowed from "the executive Power," then it's odd, to say the least, that no one thought to raise the issue during the ratification debates, and odder still that they went through the apparently useless exercise of demanding a Bill of Rights.

There's good reason, then, to reject the versions of unitary executive theory that would make the president an elected king. Indeed, some prominent scholars reject even the narrower versions of the theory. As they see it, "vesting clause" is a misnomer: Article II, Section 1, merely identifies the officeholder who will exercise the powers outlined in the following two sections of Article II.[55]

That claim is hard to reconcile with the first sentence of Article II, which appears to grant a "power." The question is, what sort of power? If one agrees with the unitarians that the president has the power to fire his secretary of defense, must one also conclude, with John Yoo, that the president can invade Syria without so much as a courtesy call to Congress? Of course not.[56] The "executive Power," as understood by the Founding Generation, was hardly the bottomless fount of royal prerogative radical unitarians envision. Instead, it consisted of the power to execute the laws, to administer the government, and "to protect the personnel, property, and instrumentalities" of that government.[57] It carried with it no general power to invade private rights, absent prior legislative authority. And it did not give the president a Magic Scepter of Inherent Authority, placing him beyond the reach of the law.

Chaining the Dog of War

Acutely aware of man's weakness and power's temptations, the Framers rejected the idea that war-making power should reside entirely in the hands of the executive. Accordingly, the Constitution they drafted separates the power to authorize war from the power to direct it once initiated.

Naturally, Professor Yoo has a different interpretation of the Framers' handiwork. He stresses the Framers' familiarity with the 18th-century English jurist William Blackstone, who described the king as "the generalissimo, or the first in military command, within the kingdom. The great end of society is to protect the weakness of individuals by the united strength of the community: . . . [thus] in a monarchy the military power must be trusted in the hands of the prince."[58]

In the fourth *Federalist*, John Jay offers a less sympathetic take on monarchical control of military power: "absolute monarchs will often make war when their nations are to get nothing by it, but for the purposes and objects merely personal, such as thirst for military glory, revenge for personal affronts, ambition, or private compacts to aggrandize or support their particular families or partisans."[59] Nor did the Framers imagine that republican forms of government cured all the defects in human nature, making concentration of the war power in one man's hands less to be feared. Madison warned in 1793 that war unleashes "the strongest passions and most dangerous weaknesses of the human breast; ambition, avarice, vanity, the honourable or venial love of fame, are all in conspiracy against the desire and duty of peace." For that reason, he wrote, "in no part of the constitution is more wisdom to be found, than in the clause which confides the question of war or peace to the legislature, and not to the executive department. Beside the objection to such a mixture of heterogeneous powers: the trust and the temptation would be too great for any one man."[60]

War Powers at the Philadelphia Convention

The delegates to the Constitutional Convention were well aware of those temptations, and sought to minimize them by limiting the president's war powers. At the start of the June 1 debates over the shape of the executive, Charles Pinckney of South Carolina supported "a vigorous executive," but worried that "the Executive powers of the existing Congress might extend to peace & war &c., which would render the Executive a monarchy, of the worst kind, to wit an elective one."[61] His colleague John Rutledge, also from South Carolina, agreed that the executive should not have the powers of war and peace, as, of course, did Madison, who noted that the executive powers "do not include the Rights of war & peace &c, but the powers shd. be confined and defined—if large we shall have the Evils of elective monarchies."[62]

On August 17, the convention turned to the Committee of Detail's proposed language giving the legislature the power "to make war." Charles Pinckney again opened the debate, noting that the House of Representatives was too large and unwieldy, and met too infrequently, to properly manage a war; he suggested that the power be lodged in the Senate alone. South Carolina's Pierce Butler, alone among the delegates, argued for giving the president the powers of war and peace: "he was . . . for vesting the power in the president, who will have all the requisite qualities, and will not make war but when the nation will support it." As Madison's notes from the convention tell us, that idea was not warmly received. "Mr. [Elbridge] Gerry [of Massachusetts said he] never expected to hear in a republic a motion to empower the Executive alone to declare war." For his part, George Mason of Virginia "was agst. giving the power of war to the Executive, because not to be trusted with it. . . . He was for clogging rather than facilitating war."

The text the delegates settled on reflects Pinckney's objections to leaving the direction of war making in the hands of the legislature as a whole. But instead of vesting the full powers of war in the Senate, the Framers left the management of war, once authorized, to the executive. Madison and Gerry "moved to insert '*declare*,' striking out '*make*' war; leaving to the Executive the power to repel sudden attacks." The motion passed.[63]

War Powers in the Constitution's Text and Structure

The document that emerged from the convention vests the bulk of war-related powers with Congress, among them, the powers "to declare War, grant Letters of Marque and Reprisal, and make Rules concerning Captures on Land and Water."[64] The chief executive's military powers appear slender by comparison: "The President shall be Commander in Chief of the Army and Navy of the United States, and of the Militia of the several States, when called into the actual Service of the United States."

Significantly, several of the enumerated powers allocated to Congress involve the decision to initiate military action. For example, with its power to "grant Letters of Marque and Reprisal," Congress could authorize private citizens to harass and capture enemy ships. Since such actions might well lead to full-scale war, the Constitution vests the power to authorize them in Congress. Similarly, the power "to provide for calling forth the Militia" in cases of domestic unrest, leaves it to Congress to decide when domestic unrest has reached the point at which military action is required.

In contrast, the authority granted in the commander-in-chief clause is managerial and defensive. Just as the president will command the militia to suppress rebellions, should it be "called into the actual Service of the United States," he can command the army and the navy, should Congress pass the necessary appropriations, and he can lead the army and navy into battle, should Congress choose to declare war. As "first General" of the United States, in Hamilton's phrase, the president has an important role, but generals do not have the power to decide whether and when we go to war.[65]

In Professor Yoo's view, however, the president is the sole decider in matters of war and peace. He has, as Yoo puts it, the "right to start wars."[66] Yoo arrives at that position by interpreting Congress's power "to declare War" narrowly enough almost to read it out of existence.

As Yoo points out, the constitutional text does not say that Congress has the power to "'make,' 'begin,' 'authorize,' or 'wage' war." It merely has the power to "declare war."[67] According to Yoo, in the 18th century that language would have indicated the power to issue a formal proclamation of war, which, as Hamilton notes in the *Federalist*, was a practice that had "of late, fallen into disuse."[68] Such proclamations served two main purposes. First, they put the enemy nation on notice that a state of war existed, and that the declaring nation intended to invoke the protections of international law for its combatants and their actions. Second, declarations "informed citizens of their new relationship with the enemy state, and informed them that they could take hostile actions against the enemy without fear of sanction."[69] Though formal declarations served those functions, they were not a necessary prerequisite for war. As Yoo sees it, the president need not wait on Congress to act: he has "the executive power," which, according to Blackstone and other sources familiar to the Framers, included the monarch's power to undertake hostilities. In Yoo's version of the original understanding, then, the president can embroil the country in a war, and Congress can, if it chooses, make war official.

Was the constitutional power "to declare war" so narrowly understood by 18th-century Americans? In a 2002 exchange with Yoo, Professor Michael D. Ramsey showed that it was not. Rather, the Founding Generation understood the phrase "declare war" to mean initiating war by a public act: "not just a formal proclamation, but also an act (typically a hostile attack) that marked the beginning of a state of war."[70] As John Locke—a writer at least as familiar to the Framers as Blackstone—recognized in the *Second Treatise*, war can be declared "by Word or Action."[71] That's consistent with the way we use the phrase even today: "Japan declared war on the United States when it bombed Pearl Harbor." Or, as George W. Bush put it in his "mission accomplished" speech aboard the *USS Lincoln* in May 2003: "After the chaos and carnage of September the 11th, it is not enough to serve our enemies with legal papers. The terrorists and their supporters declared war on the United States, and war is what they got."[72]

That Congress, and not the president, has the constitutional power "to declare war" means that it is up to *Congress* to decide whether to take the nation into war, whether by making a formal proclamation or by authorizing the president to attack. As Ramsey argues, the narrower interpretation makes little sense; it "essentially ends up meaning that the President can initiate a state of war but cannot formally say anything about it."[73] If that's how the clause was understood, it's odd that participants in the ratification debates spoke about it as if it conveyed a significant power.[74]

War Powers in the Early Republic

Yoo's narrow reading of the constitutional text cannot be squared with the way prominent figures in the ratification debates described the constitutional allocation of war powers.[75] James Wilson told the Pennsylvania ratifying convention that "this system will not hurry us into war; it is calculated to guard against it. It will not be in the power of a single man, or a single body of men, to involve us in such distress; for the important power in declaring war is vested in the legislature at large."[76] Pierce Butler, like Wilson a delegate to the Philadelphia Convention, assured the South Carolina legislature that the proposed constitution prevented the president from starting wars: "Some gentlemen [i.e., Butler himself] were inclined to give this power to the President; but it was objected to, as throwing into his hands the influence of a monarch, having an opportunity of involving his country in a war whenever he wished to promote her destruction."[77]

That the president lacked such power was the understanding upon which the Constitution was ratified, and it was the understanding that prevailed throughout the first generation after the Founding. Indeed, our first president doubted he had the power to order preemptive strikes against hostile Indians, unless, as he wrote in 1793, Congress "shall have deliberated on the subject, and authorized such a measure."[78]

Today, one often hears the argument that the president needs broad war powers because the survival of the nation is at stake. But is our survival as a nation *really* more tenuous today than it was in the late

18th century, when the United States was a small frontier republic on the edge of a continent occupied by periodically hostile great powers and Indian marauders? In that dangerous environment, the Framers drafted, and the country ratified, a Constitution that sharply limited emergency powers and rejected the idea that the president was above the law.

And early presidents understood that. In his four-book series *The Constitution in Congress*, the University of Chicago's David Currie exhaustively examined congressional and presidential interpretations of the Constitution in the young Republic. With regard to the Constitution's allocation of war powers, Currie concluded that

> despite the usual line-drawing and factual difficulties the express position of every President to address the subject during the first forty years of the present Constitution was entirely in line with that proclaimed by Congress in the celebrated War Powers Resolution in 1973: The President may introduce troops into hostilities only pursuant to a congressional declaration of war or other legislative authorization, or in response to an attack on the United States.[79]

It's little wonder, then, that John Yoo's book *The Powers of War and Peace* skips directly from the Founding period to the post–World War II era. What happened (or *didn't* happen) in between doesn't help his thesis.

The Chief Magistrate on the Home Front

Thus, even in the realm of foreign affairs, where one might imagine that his powers are at their apex, the Constitution limited the president's freedom of action. On the home front, the president's powers were even more sharply limited. The Constitution gave him little or no independent power to coerce citizens. The president's veto power allowed him to check legislative abuses, but he was not expected to act as America's leader in domestic affairs.

Indeed, the term "leader," which appears repeatedly in Madison, Hamilton, and Jay's essays in defense of the Constitution, is nearly always used negatively, save for one positive reference to the leaders of the American Revolution.[80] The *Federalist* is bookended by warnings about the perils of popular leadership: the first essay warns that "of those men who have overturned the liberties of republics, the greatest number have begun their career by paying obsequious court to the people, commencing demagogues and ending tyrants." The last essay raises the specter of disunion and civil war, ending with the "military despotism of a victorious demagogue."[81] For the Framers, the ability to "move the masses" wasn't a desirable quality in a president—it was a threat.

Not the "Voice of the People"

By the mid-1950s, when Clinton Rossiter was writing *The American Presidency*, the president had become "a kind of magnificent lion who can roam widely and do great deeds so long as he does not try to break free from his broad reservation."[82] He was, Rossiter wrote, the true "Voice of the People," the supreme national leader charged with shaping the popular will. But in the early Republic, that notion of a "Plebiscitary Presidency" was anathema to Federalists and Anti-Federalists, Hamiltonians and Jeffersonians alike. As Yale's Robert A. Dahl has put it,

> [The Framers] did not wish an executive who would be a tribune of the people, a champion of popular majorities . . . who as a consequence of his popular election would claim a mandate for his policies; who in order to mobilize popular support for his policies would appeal directly to the people; who would shape the language, style, and delivery of his appeals so as best to create a public opinion favorable to his ambitions; and who whenever it seemed expedient would by-pass the members of the deliberative body in order to mobilize public opinion and thereby induce a reluctant Congress to enact his policies.[83]

When it came to constraining demagogic appeals, during the first century of the Republic, the informal mores that governed presidential behavior were as important as formal, constitutional checks. In his influential study of presidential speechcraft, 1987's *The Rhetorical Presidency*, Jeffrey K. Tulis notes that early American political culture proscribed popular appeals by the president: "very few [early presidential addresses] were domestic 'policy speeches' of the sort so common now, and attempts to move the nation by moral suasion in the absence of war were almost unknown."[84]

Early presidents often acknowledged the impropriety of popular appeals. Thus, in 1827, turning down an opportunity to make a speech at the opening of the Pennsylvania Canal, President John Quincy Adams declared "this mode of electioneering is . . . unsuitable to my personal character and the station in which I am placed."[85] In the first decades under the Constitution, presidents spoke to the public only rarely. Presidents from Washington to Jackson averaged little over three speeches a year, with those mostly limited to ceremonial addresses, thin on policy.[86] In his first year in office, President Clinton gave 600.[87]

The Deferential Executive

In part, that reticence reflected the public expectation that Congress would take the lead in domestic affairs. For Professor Rossiter, the modern president was inescapably America's "Chief Legislator," tasked with guiding Congress's legislative agenda by suasion or force. But here again, the constitutional culture of the young Republic prescribed a much more modest role for the chief executive.

In early presidents' annual messages—the speech we know today as the State of the Union—there was nothing that rang out like the 19th-century equivalent of "pass Social Security reform now!"[88] In his first annual message, in January 1790, Washington made sure to tread lightly: rather than proposing specific measures, he mostly confined himself to mentioning general areas deserving of Congress's attention.[89] After his third annual message, Washington wrote that "motives of delicacy" had deterred him "from introducing any topick which relates to legislative matters, lest it should be suspected that he wished to influence the question before it."[90] For instance, Washington firmly believed that the United States needed a national university and a federally funded system of canals. Yet, having made his preferences known, he would not proceed to browbeat Congress, or go "over their heads" by making direct appeals to the people. As he understood the Constitution, Congress steered the nation's course when it came to policy. The president could attempt to draw Congress's attention to areas that should be of legislative concern. But beyond that, if Congress chose not to act, it wasn't the president's place to insist. In a 1790 letter to a

European friend, Washington explained that though he supported a federal project to research improved agricultural methods, he would not go further than making a recommendation:

> I know not whether I can with propriety do any thing more at present than what I have already done. I have brought the subject in my speech, at the opening of the present Session of Congress, before the national Legislature. It rests with them to decide what measures ought afterwards to be adopted for promoting the success of the great objects, which I have recommended to their attention.[91]

Adams and Jefferson likewise tended in their annual messages to avoid specificity or anything that could be interpreted as a tone of command. More typical was Jefferson's approach in his first annual message: "I am happy in this opportunity of committing the arduous affairs of our government to the collected wisdom of the Union. Nothing shall be wanting on my part to inform, as far as in my power, the legislative judgment, nor to carry that judgment into faithful execution."[92]

Unlike his two predecessors, Jefferson delivered that message in writing, rather than in person before Congress assembled. Public delivery of the annual message reminded Jefferson of the British king's "Speech from the Throne," "an English habit, tending to familiarize the public with monarchical ideas."[93] The executive's conduct should be republican in form as well as substance: accordingly, Jefferson had his annual messages copied and hand-delivered to the Capitol. For 112 years, Jefferson's precedent held, until Woodrow Wilson, a man with a very different conception of the president's role, delivered his first State of the Union in person.[94]

Of course, early presidents, like later ones, had strong legislative preferences, and tried to influence developments on Capitol Hill. Despite Washington's reticent public posture, his treasury secretary Alexander Hamilton sent requests for appropriations to Congress, and worked doggedly to pass the administration's financial proposals. Jefferson operated behind the scenes as a party leader, through trusted allies in Congress. On occasion, he drafted proposed legislation for an allied representative to introduce—and then asked the member to burn the original.[95]

The public expectation was, as Madison put it in *Federalist* no. 51, that "in a republican government, the legislative authority necessarily predominates."[96] Though early presidents involved themselves in legislative affairs, republican ideology demanded that they publicly observe the forms. Indeed, it's difficult to imagine a modern president agreeing with President James Monroe's analysis of the relative importance of the three branches. In a message delivered to Congress on May 4, 1822, Monroe stated:

> Of these [branches] the legislative . . . is by far the most important. The whole system of the National Government may be said to rest essentially on the power granted to this branch. They mark the limit within which, with few exceptions, all the branches must move in the discharge of their respective functions.[97]

Monroe's words ably describe the constitutional structure of the early Republic: Congress, not the executive branch, was to be the prime mover in setting national policy. As in war, so too on the home front: the chief magistrate's role was mainly defensive. He could interpose himself between Congress and the people when Congress acted beyond its authority, but he was neither Tribune of the People nor Chief Legislator. His true role at home was at once more humble and more important: Constitutional Guardian. Modest but firm, dignified but not regal: this was the president as the Framers envisioned him.

A Note on "Framer Worship"

At this point, after having invoked "the Framers" and "the Founders" so frequently and so favorably, a cautionary note may be in order. Recent decades have seen a revitalization of interest in the nation's Founders. The bestseller lists are crowded with high-quality popular biographies of Washington, Hamilton, Adams, Jefferson, and their contemporaries. And that's all to the good: we have much to learn from the men who fought the Revolution and forged the Constitution. One can appreciate what moved Jefferson, who was not a member of the Philadelphia Convention, to call the delegates "an assembly of demigods." But hero worship can cloud our vision even when we only revere the dead.

The *Federalist* itself warns against a "blind veneration for antiquity."[98] And a clear-eyed look at the heroes of the young Republic reveals that, remarkable though they were, they were men nonetheless, subject to all the temptations to which flesh is heir. Like all men who seek and wield power, they could abuse it, and even the best among them violated their principles. To take just one example, as president, Jefferson flagrantly violated the Fourth Amendment and the republican proscription against military law enforcement by using army regulars to enforce the embargo acts; "on a prolonged, widespread, and systematic basis, in some places lasting nearly a year, the armed forces harried and beleaguered the citizenry."[99]

When we "consult the Founders," then, we ought not to revere them as gods or look to them as oracles. We can examine their writings to discern how the Constitution's text should be interpreted, and to better understand the principles that undergird their constitutional handiwork. Chief among those principles was the belief that human nature was ill suited to the exercise of unchecked power. If even those who understood that the best could abuse power, then that in itself is a reminder of the importance of maintaining constitutional checks.

The "Myth" of the Modern Presidency?

Despite occasional departures from principle, the Framers' vision of the president as a limited, constitutional officer held firm for most of the century that followed. At the Constitutional Convention, when James Wilson moved to place the executive power in the hands of a single officeholder, Virginia's Edmund Randolph worried that the delegates were creating "the foetus of monarchy." If so, it took a long time to be born. For most of the 19th century, as historian James T. Patterson has noted, the presidency was "an insignificant institution."[100]

In 1838, three years before his inauguration as the ninth president of the United States, William Henry Harrison outlined what he took to be "the principles proper to be adopted by any executive sincerely desirous to restore the administration to its original simplicity and purity," among them, "confin[ing] his service to a single term," "disclaim[ing] all right of control over the public treasure," and that "he should never attempt to influence the elections, either by the people or the state legislatures."[101] In an act of supreme deference, Harrison passed away a month into his term.

As a member of the Whig Party that had formed in opposition to the perceived abuses of "King Andrew" Jackson, Harrison's view of the presidential role was somewhat narrower than the "median" 19th-century president. Still, nothing like the modern vision of presidential power and responsibility had yet taken hold. The two-term precedent set by Washington had evolved, by accident or design, into a one-term tradition. Between Jackson and Lincoln, no president was elected for more than a single term, and Van Buren was the only president during that period to be renominated.

Of course, even in the 19th century, there were hints of the Imperial Presidency to come—in Jackson's claim to popular leadership, in Polk's abuse of his authority as commander in chief, and in Lincoln's dramatic expansion of presidential power throughout the cataclysm of the Civil War. Some scholars have employed such examples to argue that the concept of the modern presidency is a "myth," that the so-called modern president—an officer claiming a democratic mandate and boldly exercising unilateral power in its name—has been with us almost from the start.[102]

There's certainly something to that view. We should not lose sight of the fact that on a number of occasions, 19th-century presidents took independent action of enormous consequence. Jefferson carried out the Louisiana Purchase without being able to point to any constitutional power that would justify it; Madison seized West Florida in 1810, claiming it was part of the territory purchased from France.[103] Other significant examples include the proclamation of the Monroe Doctrine, and Jackson's vigorous response to the Nullification Crisis.

Yet, taken as a whole, the 19th-century presidency still appears a pale shadow of the plebiscitary office it would become in the 20th, when soaring appeals from the bully pulpit and bold executive action became the norm. Even the most aggressive 19th-century presidents are better understood as departures from the constitutional traditions that prevailed through most of that century.

Neither Jackson nor Polk revolutionized the office they held. And though Lincoln exercised wartime powers to rival any president in American history, whatever precedent he set had no immediate effect on the powers of the presidency. After Lincoln's passage, the country entered into another long era of congressional dominance.

True, Andrew Jackson's assertiveness as president prompted a good deal of apocalyptic rhetoric. Henry Clay warned in 1833 that Jackson's rule threatened to bring about "a total change of the pure republican character of the Government, and . . . the concentration of all power in the hands of one man."[104] The occasion was the fight over the Second Bank of the United States. When Jackson vetoed the bank's reauthorization, he cited policy objections as well as constitutional ones, thus violating a shared understanding that the president had no business using the veto to enforce his legislative preferences. Yet, the Constitution contains no such limitation, and the *Federalist* suggests the veto was designed as a weapon not just against unconstitutional laws but also misguided ones, passed "through haste, inadvertence, or design."[105]

Jackson's other offenses included removing executive officers without consulting Congress and advancing the theory that the president, as "direct representative of the people," "elected by the people and responsible to them" enjoys a unique democratic mandate.[106] The idea that the president had the power unilaterally to fire his subordinates was hardly revolutionary.[107] On the other hand, Jackson's claim that the president enjoyed a special mandate was significant, and potentially dangerous. It sat uneasily with the Framers' distrust of popular leadership, and later presidents would invoke Jackson's reasoning to expand the powers of the office.

However, Jackson's behavior did not conform to the vision of the plebiscitary presidency that animated 20th-century Progressives. Though Jackson enjoyed public speaking, as president he didn't do it often, constrained by the governing norms disfavoring popular appeals.[108] It's difficult to be a really effective demagogue while giving only a handful of speeches a year. And unlike modern presidents, when Jackson claimed to act as the people's tribune, he often did so to *decentralize* power, not to concentrate it in the federal government and the executive branch.

Combative though Jackson was, even he deferred to Congress far more than modern presidents. Faced with the question of whether to recognize the Republic of Texas, which had just won its independence from Mexico, Jackson demurred. "Consistent with the spirit of the Constitution," he advised Congress, the power of recognition "should be exercised, when probably leading to war, with a previous under-standing with that body by whom war alone can be declared."[109]

James K. Polk was far less deferential when it came to taking actions that could lead to war. In 1846, when he sent troops into territory that both Mexico and the United States claimed, he revealed the possibilities for executive mischief inherent in the Constitution's separation of army command from the legal authority to initiate war. When Mexican forces attacked an American detachment serving under General Zachary Taylor, Polk got the conflict he sought: Congress declared war.

Yet, Polk's behavior was widely recognized at the time as an abuse of the commander-in-chief power. In 1848, the House censured Polk, declaring that the war had been "unnecessarily and unconstitutionally begun by the President of the United States."[110] Writing to his law part-ner in Illinois, Abraham Lincoln noted the constitutional difficulty:

> Allow the President to invade a neighboring nation whenever he shall deem it necessary to repel an invasion, and you allow him to do so whenever he may choose to say he deems it necessary for such purpose, and you allow him to make war at pleasure. . . . The provision of the Constitution giving the war-making power to Congress was dictated, as I understand it, by the following rea-sons: kings had always been involving and impoverishing their people in wars, pretending generally, if not always, that the good of the people was the object. This our convention understood to be the most oppressive of all kingly oppressions, and they resolved to so frame the Constitution that no one man should hold the power of bringing this oppression upon us.[111]

Thirteen years later, as a war president, Lincoln would begin to ex-ercise the sorts of powers he would once have considered "kingly op-pressions." With Congress out of session in April 1861, he responded to the Deep South's secession by unilaterally ordering the blockade of Southern ports and suspending habeas corpus. The initial suspension of habeas rights rested on a claim of necessity: without it, the rail line to Washington through Baltimore might have been cut off, leaving the city with insufficient troops and vulnerable to attack. Yet, in Septem-ber of 1862, to put down resistance to the draft, Lincoln extended the suspension of habeas corpus throughout the North, far from any theater of war. During the war, Lincoln imprisoned at least 14,000 civilians without due process, and his administration ordered the shutdown, temporary or permanent, of over 300 newspapers. At one point, Secretary of State William Seward was said to have boasted to the British ambassador, "I can touch a bell ... and order the imprisonment of a citizen of New York, and no power on earth, except that of the President of the United States can release [him]. Can the Queen of England do as much?"[112]

There's no denying that during the Civil War Lincoln exercised powers equal to or greater than most modern presidents. And with the Emancipation Proclamation, he provided a powerful example of executive power being used for tremendous good. Supporters of expanded executive power and activist government would invoke Lincoln's example repeatedly throughout the 20th century, in cases far less compelling. But Lincoln's legacy had no immediately visible effect on the powers or prestige of the presidency.

Minimum Leader

What's remarkable is how resilient the old customs and limits remained, even after the war. When the Civil War crisis had passed, America returned to limited, congressionally led government. Despite the impressive whiskers sported by several of the office's occupants, it was hard to discern Clinton Rossiter's "magnificent lion" in the series of wonderfully forgettable presidents who passed through between Lincoln and McKinley. Looking back on the broad sweep of the 19th century, it is clear that the chief executive had nothing like the broad responsibilities and vast powers Rossiter described in *The American Presidency*.

War Powers after Lincoln

In that book, Rossiter noted approvingly that the 20th-century president's powers as commander in chief went far beyond tactical command of congressionally authorized wars. Congress's power "to declare War" notwithstanding, the modern president had acquired the power to unilaterally decide the question of war or peace. Here again, the 19th-century president cut a less imposing figure.

Lincoln's invocation of unilateral executive war powers set no immediate precedent with regard to foreign affairs. Even as it ratified his authority to impose a naval blockade on the South—an act of war under international law—the Supreme Court limited its ruling to the unusual circumstances of secession; the president, Justice Robert Grier wrote, "has no power to initiate or declare a war" against a foreign nation.[113]

True enough, as the 19th century progressed, presidents repeatedly engaged in small-scale interventions without congressional authorization. Throughout the 20th century, those incidents were repeatedly invoked in service of a supposed presidential right to launch wars. But as constitutional scholar Edward S. Corwin noted during the Korean War, the vast majority of those episodes consisted of "fights with pirates, landings of small naval contingents on barbarous or semi-barbarous coasts, the dispatch of small bodies of troops to chase bandits or cattle rustlers across the Mexican border, and the like," many of which were undertaken to protect American citizens, and virtually none of which presented any risk of full-scale war.[114] By the end of the 19th century, the constitutional allocation of war powers for the most part remained where the Framers had left it. The question of war or peace remained a question for Congress.

"She Goes Not Abroad in Search of Monsters to Destroy"

In his Helvidius letters, Madison had warned that war was the "true nurse of executive aggrandizement." It was

> the parent of armies; from these proceed debts and taxes; and armies, and debts, and taxes are the known instruments for bringing the many under the domination of the few. In war, too, the discretionary power of the Executive is extended; its influence in dealing out offices, honors and emoluments is multiplied; and all the means of seducing the minds, are added to those of subduing the force, of the people.[115]

Early American foreign policy helped avoid those evils and preserve the constitutional balance of power by disclaiming any grand mission to promote liberty abroad through force of arms. The president was not yet the World Leader described by Rossiter, a man responsible not just for the common defense of the United States, but for the defense of freedom worldwide. Instead, America followed the "Great Rule" of conduct set out by George Washington in his Farewell Address, that "in extending our commercial relations" with other nations, we should "have with them as little political connection as possible." The speech, on which Hamilton was the principal draftsman, contained passages, such as the warnings against "passionate attachments" for particular nations and "the insidious wiles of foreign influence," that clearly referred to republican affection for France. But as diplomatic historian Walter McDougall has noted, Washington's Farewell Address "laid down principles that virtually all the Founding Fathers endorsed."[116] That the Great Rule was bipartisan could be seen in Jefferson's first inaugural, proclaiming the advantages of "peace, commerce, and honest friendship with all nations, entangling alliances with none."[117]

When Hungarian patriot Louis Kossuth visited the United States in 1852, seeking support for Hungary's independence from the Austro-Hungarian Empire, Sen. Henry Clay of Kentucky told him that America's true mission was to keep her "lamp burning brightly on this Western Shore, as a light to all nations, [rather] than to hazard its utter extinction, amid the ruins of fallen or falling republics in Europe."[118] On the cusp of the 20th century, as America was gripped by war fever, former president Grover Cleveland still held fast to the old doctrine; to abandon the Great Rule in the name of spreading liberty would, he warned, be "to follow the lights of monarchical hazards."[119]

No Tribune of the People

The late 19th-century president was no more imposing at home than he was abroad. Despite Lincoln's unmatched eloquence, the post–Civil War president did not become Rossiter's Voice of the People. True, Lincoln's successor, the hapless Andrew Johnson, fancied the role, proclaiming that "your president is now the Tribune of the people, and thank God I am." That attitude helped get Johnson impeached in 1868. The main charges against Johnson centered on his removal of Secretary of War Edwin Stanton, a favorite of the Radical Republicans in Congress.[120] However, the 10th article of impeachment focused exclusively on Johnson's intemperate, populist rhetoric attacking Congress. It read, in part:

That said Andrew Johnson, President of the United States, unmindful of the high duties of his office and the dignity and proprieties thereof, and of the harmony and courtesies which ought to exist and be maintained between the executive and legislative branches of the Government of the United States . . . did attempt to bring into disgrace, ridicule, hatred, contempt and reproach the Congress of the United States . . . and to excite the odium and resentment of all good people of the United States against Congress.[121]

What did Johnson say that moved Congress to seek the ultimate constitutional sanction? Among the passages quoted in the bill of impeachment was a speech in which the president had charged, "We have seen Congress gradually encroach, step by step, upon constitutional rights, and violate day after day, and month after month, fundamental principles of the government." To be sure, some of Johnson's statements would be considered improper even today: comparing himself to Christ, accusing Congress of fomenting domestic violence, and the like. But the bulk of what's quoted in the 10th article isn't much worse than "give 'em hell Harry" Truman's stemwinders against the "do nothing" 80th Congress. More than anything, it was, Tulis notes, the *purpose* of Johnson's speeches—"to rouse public opinion in support of his policy initiatives"—that was considered illegitimate.[122]

Johnson was an anomaly. For three decades after his impeachment, no president saw himself as the people's tribune, and none engaged in an extended campaign to mobilize the public behind his favored policies.

Nor had the post–Civil War president become the Chief Legislator Rossiter described in 1956. With the exception of Johnson, the old forms of deference and respect survived the secession crisis. As George Hoar, a Massachusetts senator from 1877 to 1904, put it in his memoirs, Gilded Age senators and congressmen "would have received as a personal affront a private message from the White House expressing a desire that they should adopt any course in the discharge of their legislative duties that they did not approve. If they visited the White House, it was to give, not to receive advice."[123] That balance of power was reflected in the daily newspapers throughout the 19th century. In their coverage of national affairs, the print media devoted more attention to Congress than the president.[124]

Why didn't late 19th-century presidents use the "bully pulpit" to appeal to the public and expand presidential power? The most obvious explanation for early presidential reticence is a technological one. Modern presidents have radio, television, and other mass media at their disposal, and thus far more opportunities than 19th-century presidents to appeal to the masses. In *The Rhetorical Presidency*, Tulis considers that explanation and finds it incomplete. He notes that presidents could have made use of the radio and TV equivalents of their day: speeches printed in party newspapers—to make direct rhetorical appeals to "the People." For the most part, they did not.[125] What restrained them, Tulis suggests, was republican ideology and public mores that had been formed by it. The late 19th century saw some slippage in the old norms, but the arrival of the president as dynamic popular leader would have to await the new century.

And so, late 19th-century America prospered in an era of presidential anonymity. Few among us, without aid of a mnemonic device, could name everyone who held the office between Lincoln and McKinley. Yet, with a series of nobody presidents—Harrisons and Arthurs, broken up by an occasional Grant or Cleveland—America overtook Great Britain in wealth and influence.[126]

In the last years of the 19th century, the presidency stood much as the Founding Generation had envisioned it. It remained a modest, constitutionally constrained office that held out little hope for social transformation and great national crusades, a role that presented few opportunities for political heroism. And those who saw politics as the arena of heroes were not at all happy with that arrangement.

Designing Men

One such was Woodrow Wilson, who, like many of our modern presidents, seems to have harbored an intense political ambition from puberty onward. As a young man, he worked halfheartedly as a lawyer, then as an academic, yet the final object always in his sights was political power. Wilson was heavily influenced by Thomas Carlyle's view of the great man in history. In his famous 1840 lecture "On Heroes," laying out his "great man" theory of history, Carlyle proclaimed, rather breath-lessly, that the Great Leader could set the very world ablaze (a good thing, as Carlyle saw it):

> I liken common languid Times . . . with their languid doubting characters and embarrassed circumstances, impotently crum-bling down into ever worse distress toward final ruin—all this I liken to dry dead fuel, waiting for the lightning out of Heaven that shall kindle it. The great man, with his free force direct out of God's own hand, is the lightning. His word is the wise healing word which all can believe in. All blazes round him now, when he has once struck on it, into fire like his own.[127]

Wilson too wanted to light a fire in the minds of men. In his notes on Carlyle, jotted down in a commonplace book in 1876, the young scholar wrote:

> The King the most important of Great Men; the summary of *all* the various figures of Heroism. To enthrone the Ablest Man, the true business of all Social procedure: the ideal of Constitu-tions. . . . The world's sad predicament; that of having its *Able-Man to seek*, and not knowing in what manner to proceed about it.[128]

As an undergraduate at Princeton, Wilson entered into a sort of mu-tual self-improvement pact with Charles Talcott, a student he consid-ered a great orator. They pledged, as Wilson put it, that they "would school all our powers and passions for the work of establishing the principles we held in common; that we would acquire knowledge that we might have power."[129]

In 1884, as a 28-year-old graduate student at Johns Hopkins Univer-sity, Wilson finished writing *Congressional Government*, laying out what he saw as the defects in the Framers' design. "We are the first Americans," he wrote, "to hear our own countrymen ask whether the Constitution is still adapted to serve the purposes for which it was in-tended; the first to entertain any serious doubts about the superiority of our institutions as compared with the systems of Europe."[130] Chief among the ills Wilson diagnosed was the separation of powers. He spoke ruefully of "the piecing of authority, the cutting of it up into small bits, which is contrived in our constitutional system."[131] For Wilson, unity of power and action was essential to strong government; obstacles to that unity damned the United States to weak and vacillating policies, and kept it from becoming a truly great nation.

Wilson saw clearly what modern advocates of the Imperial Presidency do not: that the original Constitution would have to be overturned to open a path for the transformational exercise of power. And yet, at this stage, Wilson did not see the presidency as the vehicle for constitutional transformation. His greatest dream at this time was to be a senator from Virginia. It was perhaps a testament to the persistence of the original constitutional forms that even those with visions of political grandeur thought the legislature was where those visions must be realized. For an ambitious man, the Senate was still where the action was.

While Wilson was writing *Congressional Government*, another ambitious young man, Theodore Roosevelt, had begun his career in politics as a reform-minded New York state assemblyman. Through the last decades of the 19th century, he'd try his hand as a rancher and dilettante lawman, become a successful historian, serve as an activist police commissioner, and finally become William McKinley's assistant secretary of the navy. Through it all, he remained a loud advocate for the "strenuous life" and the martial virtues. "In strict confidence . . . I should welcome almost any war, for I think this country needs one," Roosevelt said in 1897.[132] He did his best to push for war with Spain, and when it came, he resigned to organize the Rough Riders and lead the famous charge up San Juan Hill.

Professor Wilson didn't feel any need to be *that* sort of hero, but the war with Spain awoke him to the possibilities of expanded presidential power. In the introduction to the August 1900 printing of *Congressional Government*, he wrote:

When foreign affairs play a prominent part in the politics and policy of a nation, its Executive must of necessity be its guide. . . . The President of the United States is now, as of course, at the front of affairs, as no president, except Lincoln, has been since the first quarter of the 19th century. . . . Upon his choice, his character, his experience hang some of the most weighty issues of the future. The government of dependencies must be largely in his hands. Interesting things may come out of the singular change.[133]

So they did, and in the years to come, both Wilson and TR would be a part of them, each playing a central role in transforming the presidency.

2

"PROGRESS" AND THE PRESIDENCY

If we are to go forward, we must move as a trained and
loyal army willing to sacrifice for the good of a common
discipline, because without such discipline no progress is
made, no leadership becomes effective. We are, I know,
ready and willing to submit our lives and property to such
discipline, because it makes possible a leadership which
aims at a larger good.
—Franklin Delano Roosevelt, First Inaugural Address
(March 4, 1933)

By the first decade of the 20th century, Woodrow Wilson had a national platform as president of Princeton University, and a new book, *Constitutional Government in the United States.* "Our life has undergone radical changes since 1787," he noted. Those changes had been especially rapid since the young Wilson had first confessed his dreams of power to his private journal in 1876.[1] In the last decades of the 19th century, unfettered American enterprise had transformed a continent, filling up the frontier, building vast new cities, and bringing forth new challenges and new problems.

The population of the United States had doubled between 1870 and 1900, the urban population more than tripled, as new immigrants streamed to America's booming cities.[2] During those years, America experienced the fastest rate of per capita gross national product growth in its history up to that point.[3] Increasing concentration of industry was both a result and a cause of American prosperity, with corporate behemoths like Standard Oil, U.S. Steel, and the Northern Securities railway company bringing lower prices and giving rise to concern over corporate power. Finley Peter Dunne, the Irish American humorist who wrote a popular column as the character "Mr. Dooley," a thick-brogued barkeep, summed up Americans' ambivalent attitudes toward progress at the dawn of the 20th century:

> I have seen America spread out from th' Atlantic to th' Pacific, with a branch office iv th' Standard Ile Compn'y in ivry hamlet. I've seen th' shackles dropped fr'm th' slave, so' he cud by lynched in Ohio. . . . An' th' invintions . . . th' cottongin an' th' gin sour an' th' bicycle an' th' flyin'-machine an'th' nickel-in-th'-slot machine . . . an' th' sody-fountain, an'crownin' wurruk iv our civilization—th' cash raygister.[4]

The Progressives' Intellectual Revolution

Growing concern over materialism was itself a reflection of material progress. The economic dynamism of the late 19th and early 20th century led to an intellectual revolution of rising expectations. Americans who had grown up amid the creative destruction of the Gilded Age had little patience for addressing the problems of growth within a framework of laissez faire and limited government; they wanted action. Progressivism's distinguishing characteristic was activism, Richard Hofstadter explains, and its ethos one of intense optimism.[5] American ingenuity had tamed the frontier; surely it could tame the trusts, vanquish machine politics, and alleviate urban squalor.

Toward those ends, the Progressives sought to both democratize power and centralize it. They supported allowing citizens to vote directly on legislative measures through initiatives and referendums, direct primaries for party nominations, direct election of U.S. senators, and other measures designed to weaken the hold of party bosses on the democratic process. To diminish the power of corporate elites and better the lot of the American laborer, Progressives favored increased regulation of trusts and working conditions, as well as giving professional administrators the power to rationalize the productive chaos of an unplanned economy. All this required enhanced executive authority. As constitutional scholar M. J. C. Vile has observed, "Legislatures were more suspect in Progressive eyes than executive officers, and the best solution for the problems of modern government was seen to be the strengthening of executive power at State and Federal levels."[6]

If the Constitution stood in the way of necessary reforms, then so much the worse for the Constitution. For the activists of the new century, power wielded in righteousness was benign, checks on such power, perverse. And they had little use for the hoary republican traditions that kept presidents from appealing directly to the public. The Progressives worked to undermine those traditions, the better to mobilize the public and concentrate power in the service of reform. Progressive activism at home was matched by activism abroad, with many reformers embracing America's rise to world power status, and hoping imperial adventures overseas could serve as a catalyst for domestic restructuring.

Modern conservatives don't typically think of themselves as ideological fellow travelers with the left-leaning reformers of the early 20th century. Yet, few Progressives would have found anything to argue with in the account of presidential greatness John Yoo offered to an audience of Federalist Society lawyers in 2006:

> the greatest presidents . . . have been the ones that have drawn most deeply upon this reservoir of [inherent] constitutional power, [they] have made at times what people at the time thought were dictatorial, extraordinary claims of executive power, but did so to protect the country. And because of that, history has viewed them often as quite successful not because they drew just on the power but because they matched the power to great emergencies. Some of our worst presidents have been of a set that felt constrained by the understanding of constitutional law held at that time and felt that as President, they could not do much.[7]

Twenty-first century conservatives may not share the Progressives' zeal for regulatory solutions or their desire for economic regimentation. Yet, in their theory of crisis constitutionalism and their notion of the presidency as a necessary unifying force in American life, they've embraced essential elements of the Progressives' vision for the chief executive. Indeed, one of Progressivism's leading theorists of the presidency, Henry Jones Ford, heralded the coming of John Yoo by stressing the British model and proclaiming in 1898 that "American democracy [had] revived the oldest political institution of the race, the elective kingship."[8]

The Progressives were "the nearest to presidential absolutists of any theorists and practitioners of the presidency," Raymond Tatalovich and Thomas S. Engeman write in their intellectual history of the office, *The Presidency and Political Science*. In Progressive ideology, the president was "*the* agent of modern revolution," and his powers needed to be "greatly invigorated to complete the herculean tasks" that revolution required. "To create a rational, egalitarian society," Tatelovich and Engeman explain, "the Progressive president marshals public opinion while forcefully leading the political and social agencies of scientific progress. For both tasks he needs the great rhetorical power provided by the Progressives' intellectual vision."[9]

How important was that vision to the creation of the powerful and all-consuming presidency we have today? It's a difficult question to answer. Certainly there's a strong argument that underlying material conditions and technological change made the development of the modern presidency inescapable. The problems that late 19th-century economic growth brought to the surface gave rise to demands for increased federal power, and new technologies of mass communication made it easier for activist presidents to claim the bulk of that power. Radio and television enhanced the president's emerging plebiscitary role, making him the center of public attention and the locus of government action.

Yet, the deterministic account of a presidency reshaped solely by changing material conditions slights the importance of ideas. And in some important respects, it gets the chronology backward. Two scholars who have tracked the relative prominence of Congress and the presidency in the 19th-century press note that

> presidential primacy in the news is not a recent development, but in fact predates the emergence of broadcast technology. . . .

Presidential dominance of news from Washington appears to have arisen from the transformation of Congress and the presidency during the early decades of the twentieth century. Presidents in the grip of progressivism became national tribunes.[10]

There's no doubt that technological change and changed economic conditions played central roles in the transformation of the office. But the story of the presidency's growth is not one of Marxian inevitability—it's one of ideology meeting opportunity in the form of successive national emergencies. The most astute among the Progressives recognized that given the American public's latent resistance to centralized rule, a sustained atmosphere of crisis might be necessary before the presidency's promise could be fully realized. Two world wars and the Great Depression made the Progressive dream a reality, transforming the president into the focus of national aspirations, a heroic figure charged with curing the ills of modern life.

This chapter will trace that transformation through the Progressive presidencies of TR, Wilson, and FDR. Each would embrace the plebiscitary role. Each would work to expand executive power and eliminate obstacles to its use. Each would recognize that war is the health of the presidency, though only Wilson and FDR would reign during conflicts that allowed revolutionary expansions of presidential power. Yet, with each we can see the modern presidency begin to take shape.

We'll pause along the way to wonder why historians have given short shrift to less dramatic figures like Taft, Harding, and Coolidge. Like the forgotten presidents of the late 19th century, these three were modest men, as presidents go, with limited and realistic goals for the office—the sorts of presidents that high school history teachers feel obliged to apologize for, because, well, they're just so *boring*. And so they were, in a sense. Other presidents aspired to Carlylean "great man" status, setting "the common languid times" ablaze with fire from God's own lightning. But Taft, Harding, and Coolidge thought "common languid times"—otherwise known as "peace and prosperity"—had much to recommend them.

No doubt many readers will sympathize with the bold activism of TR, Wilson, and FDR, the three presidential giants who dominated the first half of the 20th century. Many will find their innovations laudable—in some cases unavoidable. So be it. It's not my purpose here to show, for example, that each element of TR's Square Deal and FDR's New Deal was unnecessary, or that America might have safely sat out the Second World War. My goal is far more modest. It is to make clear that the problems of the modern presidency did not begin when George W. Bush emerged victorious from 2000's seemingly interminable Battle of the Chads.

Today, ever-increasing numbers of Americans resent President Bush's arrogant insistence that he is the sole "decider" on all matters relating to national security. Many see his repeated appeals to the war metaphor as a cynical attempt to concentrate power and eliminate checks and balances. But none of this is new. The Imperial Presidency has been a regularly recurring feature of American life for nearly a century. George W. Bush has followed a path marked out by history's "great" presidents. TR, Wilson, and FDR make the top 10 in nearly every scholarly survey ever conducted. If we worry about civil liberties abuses and extravagant claims of presidential power, then perhaps we should rethink how we measure presidential greatness.

Though we've grown up with a larger-than-life presidency, few of us embrace it without reservations. Many liberals—and some conservatives—fear that the modern president has accumulated far too much power in foreign affairs, power that can be used to start unnecessary wars and undermine civil liberties on the home front. Many conservatives—and some liberals—worry that the modern president has too much power over domestic affairs, power that can be used—or misused—to work dramatic changes in American life. In this chapter, we'll examine the intellectual revolution that gave us the presidency as we know it today, for better, and too often, for worse.

"As Big a Man as He Can"

In the 20-odd years between the publication of his first book and 1908's *Constitutional Government*, Woodrow Wilson's constitutional views had changed substantially. Where the young Wilson had seen the amendment process as perhaps the only legitimate means by which reformers could correct the Framers' errors, the Wilson of *Constitutional Government* celebrated the modern notion of the "Living

Constitution." No mere "lawyer's document," the Constitution, Wilson argued, should instead be understood as "a vehicle of life," and reinterpreted according to "Darwinian principles," the better to serve the living.[11]

The Framers, according to Wilson, thought as Newtonians, and constructed a "mechanical" theory of government, in which power was set against power, frustrating unified action. "The trouble with this theory," Wilson wrote, "is that government is not a machine, but a living thing. It falls, not under the theory of the universe, but under the theory of organic life. It is accountable to Darwin, not to Newton." Checks and balances might be appropriate in a machine, wrote Wilson, but government is the living agent of the people's will, and "no living thing can have its organs offset against each other as checks, and live."[12]

In this theory of government-as-human-body, it is the chief executive's role to direct the limbs. He alone has been selected by the nation as a whole, and therefore his, rightfully, "is the only national voice in affairs." If he can draw upon that position to shape and enact the national will: "The President is at liberty, both in law and conscience, to be as big a man as he can."[13] Political scientist Gary L. Gregg II notes that "it might not be terribly far from the mark to liken Wilson's doctrine of presidential government to the reversal of the Whig revolution of 1689." Where that revolution had repudiated royal absolutism, Professor Wilson's doctrine would restore it, in the form of executive supremacy based on "the people's direct and exclusive link to the single man in the White House as their only national representative."[14]

A year after Wilson released *Constitutional Government*, journalist Herbert Croly published *The Promise of American Life*, which quickly became known as the Progressive "bible." *Promise* echoed and amplified Wilson's view of the presidency. In it, Croly famously called for using Hamiltonian means to achieve Jeffersonian ends. The Hamiltonian part of the program was a strong central state; the Jeffersonian element, a focus on democracy and equal regard for citizens.

For the most part, though, Croly's vision was a self-conscious repudiation of Jefferson's. For Jefferson, the pursuit of happiness was an individual enterprise, secured by a government that protected private rights. For Croly's Progressives, private rights were America's "golden calf," a false idol that sapped the energy necessary for social progress.

The pursuit of happiness, properly understood, was a collective enterprise that could only be realized through increased central direction. And where the Founding Generation, Federalist and Anti-Federalist alike, shared a pessimistic view of human nature—especially where it intersected with political power—the Progressives believed with Croly that "democracy must stand or fall on a platform of possible human perfectibility."[15]

The Progressives' vision of perfection wasn't one of bourgeois complacency, with each man under his own vine and fig tree, at peace with the world. It was decidedly more martial. In his follow-up to *Promise*, 1914's *Progressive Democracy*, Croly envisioned an American economy made up of regulated "workplace democracies." "The morale of the scientifically managed industries," he wrote, "will be superior to that of the business autocracies, just as the morale of an army of patriots, who are fighting on behalf of a genuinely national cause, is superior to that of an army of merely mercenary or drafted soldiers." To direct this worker's army, the federal commander in chief would employ "a general staff for a modern progressive state . . . [which will] have much more to do than the general staff of an army."[16] Of course, the army itself would have plenty to do as well. As Croly saw it, "peace will prevail in international relations, just as order prevails within a nation, because of the righteous use of superior force."[17]

Even those Progressives who opposed military activism abroad, like Harvard philosopher William James, sought to harness the war spirit of the collective in support of national reform. Professor James was a prominent member of the Anti-Imperialist League formed around opposition to the Spanish-American War and an early critic of his former student Theodore Roosevelt's "adolescent" fascination with militarism. But James understood war's appeal. In a famous speech delivered at Stanford University in 1906, he expressed his sympathy with those Progressive militarists who condemned "a world of clerks and teachers, of co-education and zo-ophily, of 'consumer's leagues' and 'associated charities,' of industrialism unlimited, and feminism unabashed. No scorn, no hardness, no valor any more!" "Fie upon such a cattleyard of a planet!" Progressives should stand for peace, he argued, but they should also recognize that only "the Moral Equivalent of War" could tear Americans away from private pursuits and enlist them in a Progressive "army" devoted to national greatness:

> A permanently successful peace-economy cannot be a simple pleasure-economy. In the more or less socialistic future toward which mankind seems drifting we must still subject ourselves collectively to those severities which answer to our real position upon this only partly hospitable globe. We must make new energies and hardihoods continue the manliness to which the military mind so faithfully clings. Martial virtues must be the enduring cement; intrepidity, contempt of softness, surrender of private interest, obedience to command, must still remain the rock upon which states are built.

Compulsory national service—a favorite policy of Progressives then and now—could, James argued, put the martial virtues to work conquering poverty and backwardness, with American youths drafted off to coal mines, freight trains, and fishing fleets, "to get the childishness knocked out of them, and to come back into society with healthier sympathies and soberer ideas."[18]

Other Progressives doubted that anything short of a *real* war could get Americans to accept the regimentation the Progressive vision required. Colonel Edward Mandell House, Woodrow Wilson's White House consigliere, was one of them, judging by his 1912 novel *Philip Dru: Administrator.* In the book, the title character emerges victorious in a second American Civil War and uses the crisis to establish a benevolent dictatorship and effect a comprehensive restructuring of the laws, extending as far as "Burial Reform" (only cremation was properly Progressive, it seems).[19]

Herbert Croly sided with the opportunistic militarists among the Progressives: what was needed was *war*, not its mere "moral equivalent." "It is entirely possible," Croly wrote in *Promise*, "that hereafter the United States will be forced into the adoption of a really national domestic policy because of the dangers and duties incurred through her relations with foreign countries."[20]

Among those excited by Croly's *Promise of American Life* was our 26th president, Theodore Roosevelt. Two years after leaving office,

TR wrote to Croly: "I do not know when I have read a book which I felt profited me as much as your book on American life. . . . I shall use your ideas freely in speeches I intend to make."[21] The admiration was mutual. In *Promise*, Croly had described TR as a "Thor wielding with power and effect a sledge-hammer in the cause of national righteousness," a demigod capable of "emancipat[ing] American democracy from its Jeffersonian bondage."[22]

TR and the Joy of Power

What had inspired Croly inspired many others as well, then and now. "Roosevelt bit me and I went mad," is how Progressive journalist William Allen White explained his rabid support of TR's run for a third term in 1912.[23] Intellectuals and political leaders from Roosevelt's time to ours have found something intoxicating in TR's irrepressible personality.

Yet, Roosevelt's enduring appeal is a mystery. One might dismiss TR's creepy racial Darwinism and obsession with "race suicide" as an unfortunate product of the times.[24] More perplexing are the qualities TR is still admired for today. What is it, after all, that's so attractive about his political philosophy, such as it was: a loudmouthed cult of manliness; a warped belief that war can be a wonderful pick-me-up for whatever ails the national spirit; and a contemptuous attitude toward limits on presidential power?

TR in the White House

Love or hate him, though, TR cut a figure that was hard to ignore. He would become our first celebrity president, and the first to be known by his initials.[25] More than any of his predecessors, Roosevelt sensed the latent power in the office and reveled in it. Progressive journalist Lincoln Steffens described the atmosphere in TR's White House in the days following McKinley's assassination and Roosevelt's ascension to office:

the whole country was in mourning, and no doubt the president felt that he should hold himself down; he didn't; he tried to, but his joy showed in every word and movement. . . . With his feet, his fists, his face and with free words he laughed at his luck. He laughed . . . with glee at the power and place that had come to him.[26]

In his exercise of power, TR found himself held back somewhat by the absence of crisis and the remnants of 19th-century political culture. The office of the presidency was not yet the "sledgehammer" it would become. However, Roosevelt did expand executive authority in significant ways both at home and abroad.

Like Andrew Jackson, TR viewed himself as enjoying a special mandate as the sole representative of the people as a whole. Far more than Jackson, though, he used the "bully pulpit" to go "over the heads of the Senate and House leaders to the people" with direct appeals.[27] By publicly stumping for the Hepburn Act of 1906, which strengthened the Interstate Commerce Commission's control over railroad rates, TR helped push it through, despite vigorous opposition from Nelson Aldrich, the Senate majority leader and a member of the president's own party.[28]

TR also helped initiate the modern method of rule by executive order, a practice colorfully described by President Clinton's adviser Paul Begala as "Stroke of the pen. Law of the land. Kinda cool."[29] In his seven years in office, TR alone issued 1,081, nearly as many as all prior presidents combined.[30] One of TR's executive orders set aside 16 million acres of public land just before a bill passed by Congress restricted his authority to make such grants.[31] Another seemed to reflect the view that the president had dominion over the English language itself: Roosevelt attempted to revolutionize American spelling by shifting the federal government to a system of "Simplified Spelling." Under that system, "kissed" would read "kist"; "through," "thru"; "enough," "enuf"; and so on. The *Baltimore Sun* cracked that perhaps Roosevelt's last name should be spelled "Butt-in-sky." The House of Representatives voted 142–24 to get TR to rescind the order, which he did.[32]

TR's promiscuous use of executive orders followed from his expansive theory of presidential prerogatives; as he'd later explain, he believed that the president had a broad general power to do good. He put that theory to work in May 1902, when 125,000 coal miners walked off their jobs in Pennsylvania. Roosevelt vowed that he would bring an end to the strike before winter, despite the fact that, by his own admission, he lacked any constitutional authority to do so.[33] Faced with intransigence on the part of the mine owners, he resolved to use the army to "dispossess the operators and run the mines as a receiver" until the strike could be settled.[34] By October, Elihu Root, TR's secretary of war, had put a force of 10,000 soldiers on alert, ready to go into Pennsylvania. House Republican Whip James E. Watson, upon hearing of the plan, demanded, "What about the Constitution of the United States? What about seizing private property without due process of law?" TR seized Watson by the shoulder and wailed, "The Constitution was made for the people and not the people for the Constitution!"[35]

Roosevelt expanded executive authority in foreign affairs as well, perhaps most famously by using American military might to secure U.S. rights to the Panama Canal project. When the Colombian Senate rejected the Hay-Herrán treaty granting American rights to the Canal Zone, TR refused further negotiation with Colombia, choosing instead to bank on a Panamanian secession movement financed by canal interests. Ordered to the harbor of Colón by Roosevelt, the USS Nashville ensured the success of the Panamanian rebels by preventing Colombian forces from putting down the secession. "I took the canal zone and let Congress debate," TR said later, "and while the debate goes on the canal does also."[36] In 1907, when Roosevelt decided to send all 16 U.S. battleships around the world in a demonstration of American power, he informed skeptical congressmen that he had enough funds to get them halfway, and the choice was theirs as to whether to provide funding for the Great White Fleet's return.[37] That pattern—with the commander in chief ordering the U.S. military wherever he pleased, and daring Congress to cut off funds—would be repeated many times throughout the century.

Despite all his flexing, TR did not completely revolutionize the office of the presidency. Political conditions—domestic tranquility and the absence of war—would not allow it. Roosevelt recognized this, and, perversely, complained that the relative happiness of his countrymen had denied him a proper shot at greatness. As he put it in 1910: "A man has to take advantage of his opportunities, but the opportunities have to come. If there is not the war, you don't get the great general; if there is not the great occasion, you don't get the great statesman; if Lincoln had lived in times of peace, no one would know his name now." TR would later come to envy Woodrow Wilson because Wilson got to fight the European war TR himself had pushed for.[38]

"Even a Rat in a Corner Will Fight"

Having pledged in 1904 not to seek election to another full term (a pledge he'd come greatly to regret), Roosevelt picked his good friend and second-term secretary of war, William Howard Taft, to succeed him, a choice quickly ratified at the Republican National Convention in 1908. Taft went on to win easily over William Jennings Bryan in the general election.

Unlike Roosevelt, Taft hated politics. He was where he was due to intellect, ability, and the incessant prodding of an ambitious wife. But on the whole, he'd rather have been on the Supreme Court (a wish fulfilled in 1921 when President Harding named him chief justice).

For the most part, Taft governed as a Progressive: he greatly accelerated trustbusting and lent his support to the Sixteenth and Seventeenth Amendments to the Constitution, providing for an income tax and direct election of senators. Yet, history does not remember Taft as a heroic, reformist president. In fact, since he did not start any major wars or offer any Deals, Square or New, Taft is now best known for being shaped like a zeppelin—he weighed in at 355 pounds on the eve of his inauguration.

Taft's 1910 decision to remove conservationist Gifford Pinchot as the Interior Department's chief forester began the cooling of the Taft-TR relationship, a process that would eventually result in Roosevelt's challenging Taft for the Republican nomination in 1912, then bolting for the Progressive Party when the nomination was denied him.

The 1912 campaign revealed Roosevelt's increasingly radical view of the president's role—as well as a growing tendency toward public deification of the presidency. At a Carnegie Hall rally in March, Roosevelt took a page from Carlyle and declaimed, "In order to succeed we need leaders of inspired idealism, leaders to whom are granted great visions, who dream greatly and strive to make their dreams come true;

who can kindle the people with the fire from their own burning souls." At the Progressive Party Convention in Chicago in August, delegates sang "Onward, Christian Soldiers" and a reworked version of the revivalist hymn "Follow, Follow, We Will Follow Jesus," where "Roosevelt" replaced the Son of God, making it "Follow, Follow, We Will Follow Roosevelt."[39] TR spoke at Castro-like length, building to his peroration: "*We stand at Armageddon, and we battle for the Lord!*"

"I am a man of peace, and I don't want to fight," Taft protested at one point, summing up with a characteristically inept turn of phrase: "but even a rat in a corner will fight."[40] In September 1912, Taft temporarily overcame his reluctance to make campaign speeches, and denounced Roosevelt's view of government power at a gathering of Republicans in Beverly, Massachusetts, which included his son Robert, the future senator from Ohio, presidential aspirant, and critic of executive aggrandizement.

Without mentioning TR by name, President Taft denounced the Rooseveltian conception of the office: the president as tribune of the people, alone elected by the whole country and therefore justified in using the "bully pulpit" to arouse the electorate and pressure Congress. As Taft saw it, the people "have not any of them given into the hands of any *one* the mandate to speak for them peculiarly as the people's representatives."[41]

Roosevelt attacked that view in his 1913 autobiography, carrying on the debate well after both men had lost the election. In that book, TR articulated his "Stewardship Doctrine" of presidential power. The president, Roosevelt declared,

> was a steward of the people bound actively and affirmatively to do all he could for the people, and [was] not to content himself with the negative merit of keeping his talents undamaged in a napkin. . . . My belief was that it was not only his right but his duty to do anything that the needs of the nation demanded unless such action was forbidden by the Constitution or the laws.[42]

In a series of lectures delivered at Columbia University in 1915 and 1916, Taft fired back. He likened TR's self-congratulatory assessment of his own presidency to a precocious little girl's bragging to her father that she was the best scholar in the class: "the teacher didn't tell me—I just noticed it myself." The Stewardship Doctrine disturbed Taft, especially when combined with TR's vision of the chief executive as fiery soul-kindler. In the book that grew out of his Columbia lectures, *Our Chief Magistrate and His Powers*, Taft warned:

> Ascribing an undefined residuum of power to the President is an unsafe doctrine and . . . it might lead under emergencies to results of an arbitrary character, doing irremediable injustice to private right. The mainspring of such a view is that the executive is charged with responsibility for the welfare of all the people in a general way, that he is to play the part of a universal Providence and set all things right, and that anything that in his judgment will help the people he ought to do, unless he is expressly forbidden not to do it. The wide field of action that this would give to the executive, one can hardly limit.[43]

Yet, by that point the debate was truly academic. At the height of the Progressive Era's romance of government activism, Taft's gospel of self-restraint was a losing position politically. Americans were increasingly coming to think of the president in modern terms, as a dynamic national leader whose task it was to provide benefits, institute reforms, and fulfill the national destiny, whatever that might be.

The winner of the 1912 race, Woodrow Wilson, would in his first term continue to expand presidential power along the lines suggested by Roosevelt's Stewardship Doctrine. In his second term, with American entry into the Great War, Wilson would go on to wield powers of which even TR hardly dared dream.

Warrior-Priest

Something of Wilson's staggering self-regard can be seen in his comment the day after his election, when he met with the Democratic Party chairman to discuss appointments: "Before we proceed, I want it understood that I owe you nothing. Remember that God *ordained that I should be the next President of the United States.*"[44] That attitude carried Wilson throughout his presidency and the war that helped reshape the office. According to British prime minister David Lloyd George, at the Paris Peace Conference, Wilson asked him and French premier

Georges Clemenceau: "Why has Jesus Christ so far not succeeded in inducing the world to follow his teachings in these matters? It is because he taught the ideal without devising any practical means of attaining it. That is the reason why I am proposing a practical scheme to carry out His aims."[45] (Lloyd George later cracked that he hadn't done too badly in the negotiations, "seated as I was between Jesus Christ and Napoleon Bonaparte.")[46]

Wilson in Peace

From the start of his administration, Wilson set out to fulfill the promise of *Constitutional Government*, and become "as big a man" as he could. "I have been smashing precedents almost daily ever since I got here," Wilson bragged to a friend in 1913.

One of the precedents that Wilson smashed was the Jeffersonian tradition that the president's annual message would be delivered in writing. Jefferson believed that appearing before Congress to deliver the message was anti-republican; like the king's "Speech from the Throne," it left the impression that it was the executive's role to tell Congress what to do. Wilson had no such qualms: he delivered his first State of the Union in person to Congress assembled. One senator decried the change in pointed terms: "I am sorry to see revived the old Federalistic custom of speeches from the throne. . . . I regret this cheap and tawdry imitation of English royalty." On the way home after the speech, the first lady remarked that she bet TR wished he had thought of trying that first; "Yes," Woodrow chuckled, "I think I put one over on Teddy."[47]

The new practice was in keeping with Wilson's view that the president ought to act as "prime minister, as much concerned with the guidance of legislation as with the just and orderly execution of law."[48] Wilson drafted a key clause of the Clayton Antitrust Act, and according to Rep. Carter Glass (D-VA), he "dominated" the debate over the shape of the Federal Reserve Act.

Still, many Progressives remained unsatisfied with Wilson's leadership. Many condemned his initial reluctance to involve the United States in the conflict that began raging across Europe early in his first term.[49] After the sinking of the *Lusitania* in May 1915, prominent Progressives led the "preparedness" movement, urging Americans to get ready for war. "We should in all humility," Roosevelt declared in 1915, "imitate not a little of the spirit so in evidence among the Germans and the Japanese, the two nations which in modern times have shown the most practical type of patriotism . . . and the greatest farsightedness in safeguarding the country from without."[50] The 1916 Progressive Party platform blasted Wilson's alleged timidity and called for a larger army and universal compulsory military training to, as one historian has described it, heal "the divisiveness and flabbiness of the body politic."[51]

Just as it would nearly eight decades later in the run-up to the Iraq adventure, the Progressive journal the *New Republic* played a key role in mobilizing liberal elites' support for war. Four months after the assassination of Archduke Franz Ferdinand in Sarajevo, Herbert Croly founded *TNR* with financial backing from the Willard Straight family of New York (Straight was a banker with J. P. Morgan and Company, and his wife an heiress to the Standard Oil fortune).[52]

TNR's writers pushed tirelessly for war, seeing it as a means to shock America out of its soporific bourgeois contentment and bring about what one editorialist described as "the substitution of national and social and organic forces for the more or less mechanical private forces operative in peace."[53] For Croly, war would give the United States what it desperately needed: "the tonic of a serious moral adventure."[54] And for philosopher John Dewey, a *TNR* contributor, it would provide the "immense impetus to reorganization" long sought by the Progressives.[55]

Randolph Bourne, Dewey's onetime student at Columbia, described the same phenomenon in pithier and more pessimistic terms: "War is the Health of the State." Bourne, a contributing editor for the *New Republic* in its early years, was one of the few associated with the magazine who vehemently opposed American entry into the Great War. Bourne appears in John Dos Passos's bitter anti-war novel *Nineteen Nineteen* as a "little sparrowlike man," "poor and twisted in body" but bursting with enthusiasm for "pretty girls and good food and evenings of talk." "In the crazy spring of 1917," Dos Passos wrote, Bourne "began to get unpopular where his bread was buttered at *The New Republic*," because he saw clearly and would not tolerate cant: "for *New Freedom*, read *Conscription*, for *Democracy*, *Win the War* . . . Buy a Liberty Bond, Strafe the Hun, Jail the Objectors."

At the end, only the magazine *Seven Arts* would publish Bourne's writings against the war. Dos Passos wrote, "Friends didn't like to be seen with Bourne. His father wrote him begging him not to disgrace the family name. The rainbowtinted future of reformed democracy went pop like a pricked soapbubble."[56] Hounded by police on suspicion of espionage and disloyalty, Bourne died in the 1918 flu epidemic that was one of the Great War's many gifts to America.[57]

In the posthumously published, fragmentary essay that contains his famous aphorism, Bourne warned that

> the moment war is declared . . . the mass of the people, through some spiritual alchemy, become convinced that they have willed and executed the deed themselves. They then, with the exception of a few malcontents, proceed to allow themselves to be regimented, coerced, deranged in all the environments of their lives, and turned into a solid manufactory of destruction toward whatever other people may have, in the appointed scheme of things, come within the range of the Government's disapprobation. The citizen throws off his contempt and indifference to Government, identifies himself with its purposes, revives all his military memories and symbols, and the State once more walks, an august presence, through the imaginations of men.[58]

"The Spirit of Ruthless Brutality"

At first, Wilson resisted the growing war fever. But before long, his initial policy of neutrality became neutral in name only. German and English war policies both violated international law, with the British imposing a blockade designed to starve Germany into submission, and the Germans adopting unrestricted submarine warfare to cut off supplies to the U.K.; yet Wilson condemned German abuses of neutral rights while tolerating British violations. Why, Secretary of State William Jennings Bryan asked in April 1915, shortly before the sinking of the *Lusitania*, "do Americans take the risk" of traveling on British ships carrying munitions in a war zone despite German warnings, and why should they "be shocked at the drowning of a few people, if there is no objection to starving a nation?"[59] Bryan resigned in June, after Wilson rejected his advice to pursue a more evenhanded policy.

Once reluctant to risk American blood and treasure in the carnage of the Great War, Wilson came to see intervention as a way to realize what he'd earlier described as America's God-ordained destiny: "that we are chosen and prominently chosen to show the way to the nations of the world how they shall walk in the paths of liberty."[60] He shifted to a policy of armed "neutrality" that brought American involvement ever closer. Wilson had earlier shown how little respect he had for constitutional limits on his power, unilaterally ordering interventions in Mexico, Haiti, and the Dominican Republic.[61] And though Congress formally declared war on Germany in 1917, "it was Wilson," constitutional scholar Louis Fisher writes, "who made the basic policy decision to move from neutrality to armed neutrality and finally to a state of war."[62]

The result of the war, Randolph Bourne had earlier predicted, would be a "semi-military State-socialism" at home.[63] Bourne was right: wartime legislation gave the president enormous power to direct the economy, including power to seize all U.S. railroads, to license and control food and fuel production throughout the United States, and unilaterally to restructure the executive branch and create new agencies. Among the agencies Wilson created was the War Industries Board. Headed by financier Bernard Baruch, the WIB took control of all war-related production, backing up its dictates with the ultimate sanction: the power to seize production facilities.[64]

The federal assault on the rights of property and contract was matched by attacks on the freedoms of speech and assembly. At the start of the war, Wilson had warned, "to fight, you must be brutal . . . and the spirit of ruthless brutality will enter into the very fiber of our national life. . . . Conformity will be the only virtue. And every man who refuses to conform will have to pay the penalty."[65] If Wilson sounded worried about that prospect, he soon overcame his reservations. His administration would carry out the most brutal campaign against dissent in American history.

Concerns about German saboteurs led to unrestrained domestic spying by U.S. Army intelligence operatives. During the war, army spies had free rein to gather information on potential subversives, and were often empowered to make arrests as special police officers. To enforce uniformity at home, the Wilson administration relied heavily on quasi-private volunteer organizations of self-styled patriots eager to inform on their fellow citizens. Such groups included the colorfully named "Boy Spies of America," the "Sedition Slammers," and the "Terrible Threateners," but the largest and most important was the "American Protective League," over 200,000 strong.[66] At the War Department's request, APL volunteers harassed labor organizers, intimidated and arrested opponents of the draft, and investigated such potential subversives as Mexican-American leaders in Los Angeles, pacifist groups, and anti-war religious sects. By the end of the war, the APL had carried out some six million investigations.[67] Through it all, the army caught exactly one German spy.[68]

The Espionage Act and the Sedition Act were the Wilson administration's two key legal tools for the suppression of dissent. The former criminalized attempts to cause insubordination in the armed forces or to "obstruct the recruiting or enlistment service of the United States." The Sedition Act went even further, proscribing "disloyal" and "abusive" statements about the U.S. Army or the American form of government, and making it criminal to "by word or act oppose the cause of the United States."[69] During the course of the war, there were over 2,000 prosecutions under the Espionage Act alone. All told, over 30 people received 20-year sentences and 70 got 10-year terms. Among them were Socialist Party leader and perennial presidential candidate Eugene V. Debs, for making a speech praising three Socialists imprisoned under the act, and movie producer Robert Goldstein, for "sowing . . . animosity [and] want of confidence between us and our allies."[70] The offending film, *The Spirit of '76*, celebrated the American Revolution and showed British soldiers bayoneting women and children.[71]

The campaign against dissent inspired a good deal of regret among the Progressives, yet on the whole they welcomed the growth of the president's power to direct American life. In an unsigned editorial that ran on November 16, 1918, *TNR* sang the praises of wartime centralization:

> The whole issue hinges on social control. For forty years we have been widening the sphere of this control, subordinating the individual to the group and the group to society. Without such control, vastly magnified, we should not have been able to carry on

the war. . . . We conscripted lives, property and services; we took over railroads, telegraphs and other economic instruments. We fixed wages, prices, the quantity of coal, power, labor or transportation a man might command, and the quantity of food he might consume. . . . All this we did on the narrowest of legal bases, for no one dared question our power.[72]

TNR favored the continuation of such controls, hoping to fulfill the promise of American life through expert direction of the economy. That was not to be—at least not immediately.

The Presidency in the Era of Normalcy

The postwar era saw a return to earlier traditions of American governance: a more restrained presidency, one that spoke more softly and shunned grand schemes to remake American society. That era, nicely captured by President Warren G. Harding's neologism "normalcy," was one that brought middle-class prosperity to more and more Americans as the decade progressed. By 1923, the unemployment rate stood at 3 percent, and by 1929 manufacturing output had nearly doubled from its level in 1921.[73] Prohibition, lazily enforced as it was by Harding, did little to spoil the party.[74]

Harding took office after the Senate rejected the Treaty of Versailles, in part over concerns that participation in the League of Nations would require an unconstitutional delegation of Congress's power to declare war to the president.[75] "I shall consent to nothing," Wilson told reporters who asked about reservations to the treaty, "the Senate must take its medicine."[76] Wilson's relentless cross-country campaign to force Congress to ratify the treaty ended when he suffered a massive stroke in September 1919. Though he'd cling to life for another four years, it was Wilson's devotion to the plebiscitary presidency that wrecked his health and, perhaps, eventually killed him.

Yet, Wilson's burning ambition continued even after the stroke. Half-paralyzed, wheelchair-bound, and only intermittently lucid, in the summer of 1920 he waited eagerly, hoping to hear that the Democratic Convention would nominate him for an unprecedented third term. The news that the convention had settled on James M. Cox and Franklin

Roosevelt as the nominees "produced a string of curses from the president that left his valet in a state of shock."[77]

In his first State of the Union, Warren Harding expressed regret over the "excessive grants of authority" and "extraordinary concentration of powers in the Chief Executive" that had taken place during the war. The arrival of peace and repeal of much of the wartime legislation had started to right the balance, Harding said, "but I have wish to go further than that," restoring "mutuality of confidence and respect" among the branches, and renouncing "encroachment upon the functions of Congress or attempted dictation of its policy."[78]

Harding gets rough treatment from presidential scholars, finishing last or next-to-last in most presidential rankings. Most cite the Teapot Dome scandal, in which Harding's secretary of the interior took kickbacks in exchange for oil leases on public lands. But it's hard to believe that's the only reason for Harding's abysmal ranking: Harding wasn't personally corrupt, after all, and he never profited from his cronies' misdeeds. His sins were sins of omission: negligent supervision and unmerited trust in his appointees.

Place those faults against Harding's great merits: he presided over the dismantling of Wilson's draconian wartime controls, ushering in an era of prosperous normalcy. (Is it the normalcy that presidential scholars hold against him?) In 2001, two Ohio University economists developed an alternative presidential ranking scheme, based on reductions in size of government and ability to control inflation. Harding came in first.[79] By 1924, federal spending had been cut nearly in half, leading to large government surpluses.[80] And Harding's good nature and liberal instincts led him to overrule his political advisers and pardon 25 nonviolent protesters that Wilson had locked up, including Eugene Debs. "I want him to eat his Christmas dinner with his wife," Harding said.[81]

History remembers Harding's successor, Calvin Coolidge, mostly for his reticence and for fiscal policies that combined Yankee parsimony with generous tax cuts. Less well known is Coolidge's admirable record on civil liberties. Coolidge ordered the release of Wilson's remaining political prisoners, and his attorney general, Harlan Fiske Stone, put an end to political surveillance by the Federal Bureau of Investigation, abolishing the FBI's General Intelligence Division.[82] "The Bureau of

Investigation," Stone declared, "is not concerned with political or other opinions of individuals. It is concerned only with their conduct and then only with such conduct as is forbidden by the laws of the United States. When a police system passes beyond these limits, it is dangerous to the proper administration of justice and to human liberty."[83]

Coolidge kept things entirely too cool for historians who like presidential drama: he slept too much, didn't do enough, and didn't talk enough. There was method to his muteness, however. As Coolidge told his commerce secretary and successor, Herbert Hoover, "Nine-tenths of [visitors to the White House] want something they ought not to have. If you keep dead still, they will run down in three or four minutes."[84]

The Coolidge theory of the presidency was far more restrained than Teddy Roosevelt's swaggering Stewardship Doctrine. Where TR saw it as his "duty to do anything the needs of the nation demanded," upon ascending to office, Coolidge remarked that he did not intend "to surrender to every emotional movement" seeking remedies for problems better handled by state, local, or private actors.[85] Thus, Coolidge was the last president to resist the growing expectation that the president should serve as Rossiter's Protector of the Peace, providing federal aid and comfort to Americans afflicted by natural disasters. When the Mississippi River overflowed its banks in April 1927, killing hundreds and devastating surrounding communities, he appointed Herbert Hoover to coordinate appeals for private donations, but resisted the pressure to take on a more public role and fought congressional efforts to promote a large federal role in relief. The governor of Mississippi urged the president to visit the flood area, to "center the eyes of the nation" on the disaster and unite the country behind relief efforts, but Coolidge refused, just as he refused a request by NBC to broadcast a nationwide radio appeal. One editorialist charged that Coolidge had either "the coldest heart in America or the dullest imagination." Yet here again, Coolidge's reticence reflected a fear that careless use of the bully pulpit would inflame public demands for federal action in areas properly reserved to the states and the people.[86]

Presidents in the decade of normalcy pounded that pulpit far less than either TR or Wilson. For the most part, they declined to follow Wilson's practice of delivering the State of the Union in person to

Congress. Harding appeared in person twice, Coolidge once, and Hoover reverted entirely to the Jeffersonian practice.[87] Neither Harding nor Coolidge was quite as reticent or retiring as some of their 19th-century predecessors—Harding put the first professional presidential speechwriter on staff, while Coolidge made good use of the opportunities afforded by radio broadcasts.[88] Yet, neither sought to light fires in the minds of men. Upon Silent Cal's passing, H. L. Mencken eulogized that as president, Coolidge "had no ideas, and he was not a nuisance."[89] For Mencken, this was praise. It would be quite some time before that could fairly be said of another president.

War as Metaphor and Reality

Because "the sources of resistance to state-building are so strong" in American culture, writes Aaron L. Friedberg, the history of government growth in the United States has necessarily been a history of crisis: "periods of accelerated state-building have generally been preceded by the anticipation or the actual onset of war, or by a growing sense of impending domestic economic and social crisis."[90]

"We Must Move as a Trained and Loyal Army"

In late 1929, America faced an economic crisis of historic proportions. At the Depression's depth, unemployment approached a quarter of the labor force, and real GNP per capita fell by more than 30 percent.[91] Franklin Delano Roosevelt, elected in a landslide in 1932, wasn't the only political figure to analogize America's economic collapse to an attack by a hostile power; his predecessor Hoover had made the comparison regularly. FDR employed the war metaphor far more effectively, however. Roosevelt's first inaugural address tends to be remembered as an attempt to calm the public, a warning against "fear itself." The martial metaphors that appear throughout the speech make clear, though, that FDR wanted fear replaced by collectivist ardor. Americans were to move forward as "a trained and loyal army," with "a unity of duty hitherto evoked only in time of armed strife." Should the normal balance of legislative and executive powers prove insufficient, Roosevelt concluded, "I shall ask the Congress for the one remaining instrument to meet the crisis—broad Executive power to wage a war against the emergency, as great as the power that would be given to me if we were in fact invaded by a foreign foe."[92]

Two days after his inauguration, Roosevelt used the Trading with the Enemy Act to order the closure of all American banks. Passed during World War I, the act was designed to restrict trade with hostile foreign powers "during the time of war." Ignoring that limitation, Roosevelt wielded it in peacetime against Americans. It would not be the last time his administration would invoke powers forged in the Great War to battle the Depression. "Progressives turned instinctively to the war mobilization as a design for recovery," wrote historian William Leuchtenburg in his essay "The New Deal and the Analogue of War," "There was scarcely a New Deal act or agency that did not owe something to the experience of World War I."[93]

That was certainly the case with the centerpiece of the first New Deal, the National Recovery Administration, modeled on the War Industries Board under Wilson. To head up the NRA, Roosevelt appointed General Hugh Johnson, a WIB official in World War I. The National Industrial Recovery Act that created Johnson's agency empowered the president to approve or prescribe "codes of fair competition" for trades and industries throughout the United States, setting wages and prices and regulating labor practices. The NIRA essentially made the president commander in chief of the entire economy, allowing him to control the working conditions of 95 percent of industrial employees in the United States.[94] Upon hearing of the NIRA, Benito Mussolini exclaimed, "*Ecco un ditatore!*" ("Behold a dictator!")[95]

The Roosevelt administration encouraged loyal soldiers in the New Deal Army to display the NRA's "Blue Eagle." "In war, in the gloom of night attack," Roosevelt explained, "soldiers wear a bright badge on their shoulders to be sure that comrades do not fire on comrades."[96] General Johnson organized mass rallies to denounce the "slackers" and "chiselers" who resisted regimentation, declaring that "those who are not with us are against us."[97]

In "The Moral Equivalent of War," William James had envisioned a Progressive "army enlisted against Nature."[98] FDR's Civilian Conservation Corps, the vast work relief program created during his first 100 days, hewed closely to that vision. Over two and a half million men would eventually serve in the CCC.[99] They'd report to army-run camps, and awake in their tents or barracks every morning to the sound of "Reveille."[100] CCC enlistees were, as the assistant secretary of war put it in 1934, America's "economic storm troops."[101] As the decade progressed, and the possibility of another world war loomed, the CCC gave the army valuable experience in organizing and regimenting large numbers of young men.

War Itself

The Second World War, like the First, was formally declared by Congress. But like Wilson before him, FDR made many of the key decisions for American involvement unilaterally.[102] One lasting effect of the war was the development of an internal security apparatus that would spy on Americans without restraint for nearly four decades. Three years before the outbreak of war in Europe, FDR reversed the proscription on FBI intelligence gathering laid down by Coolidge's attorney general Harlan Fiske Stone. At a meeting with J. Edgar Hoover in August 1936, Roosevelt authorized the FBI director to monitor "subversive activities in the United States, particularly Fascism and Communism."[103] Interpreting his instructions broadly, Hoover authorized the bureau to gather information from "all possible sources," and defined "subversive activities" to include "the distribution of literature . . . opposed to the American way of life."[104] In a 1939 press release, Roosevelt urged local law enforcement agencies to turn over information related to espionage and subversion.[105] That same year, Hoover ordered the preparation of a detention list compiled mostly from subscribers to German, Italian, and Communist periodicals.[106] In 1940, FDR authorized the use of warrantless wiretaps against those suspected of subversive tendencies.[107]

It was a short step from investigating potential saboteurs to investigating presidential critics. FDR ordered wiretaps on associates he suspected of leaking damaging information, just as Richard Nixon would decades later. And when Roosevelt received letters especially critical of his foreign policy, he had the FBI open files on the Americans who wrote them. "The President thought you might like to look [these letters] over, noting the names and addresses of the senders," Roosevelt's secretary wrote to Hoover in 1940. Hoover sent what information he had on the president's critics and ordered surveillance of those that were unfamiliar—a practice he carried out repeatedly for FDR and his successors.[108]

The Presidency Transformed

By war's end, the presidency's dominance had been firmly established. The successive crises of World War I, the Great Depression, and World War II had given rise to a new constitutional regime. In 1946, constitutional scholar Edward Corwin described that regime's characteristics, which included

> the attribution to Congress of a legislative power of indefinite scope; the attribution to the President of the power and duty to stimulate constantly the positive exercise of this indefinite power for enlarged social objectives; [and] the right of Congress to delegate its powers *ad libitum* to the President for the achievement of such enlarged social objectives.[109]

In the 45th *Federalist*, Madison had explained that the powers of the federal government were "few and defined," those of the states, "numerous and indefinite." That distinction no longer held. FDR's 12-year reign saw the realization of the Progressives' dream of a federal government unrestrained by archaic checks and balances, and boldly directed by the people's tribune. The general welfare and commerce clauses of the Constitution's Article I, Section 8, had once served as checks on federal power, but after Roosevelt's abortive attempt to pack the Court in 1937, the judicial branch would no longer stand in the way of unbridled congressional power to spend and regulate.[110]

Ironically, the removal of restraints on legislative power had, in many ways, *weakened* Congress's authority relative to that of the president. That was in large part because, as Corwin noted, the new regime's foundation was the delegation of legislative power to the executive branch. Article I, Section 1, of the Constitution tells us that "all legislative powers" are vested in the Congress; Article II, Section 3, stipulates that it is the president's duty to "take care that the laws be faithfully executed." Yet, the constitutional revolution ushered in by the New Deal combined both functions within the executive branch, with Congress passing broad general statutes and leaving it to the president or other executive branch officials to determine the rules that would bind private conduct.[111] The National Industrial Recovery Act, which allowed the president to dictate wages, prices, and labor practices throughout the economy, was perhaps the starkest example of how unrestrained delegation allowed the executive to both make and enforce the law.

As recently as 1935, the Court had served as a bulwark against delegation.[112] But by 1944, the Court recognized few if any limits on Congress's ability to transfer its power to the executive branch. That year, in *Yakus v. United States*, the Court held that Congress could delegate to an executive agent the power to set maximum prices for virtually all goods throughout the economy.[113] By the postwar era, Congress had long been out of practice when it came to taking responsibility for the laws Americans lived under.

FDR's presidency was the culmination of tendencies visible in TR's and Wilson's before him. TR's activist, celebrity presidency had heralded the coming of a new sort of chief executive, one who would evermore be the center of national attention, the motive force behind American government. Woodrow Wilson had proved what the Progressives had hypothesized: that soaring rhetoric combined with the panicked atmosphere of war could concentrate massive social power in the hands of the president. But it took FDR's constitutional revolution to eliminate the vestiges of the old regime and usher in the modern presidency.

Under the original constitutional regime, the federal government was Congress centered and patronage based, that is, concerned with distribution of government jobs, public lands, and other benefits (tariff protection, internal improvements, and the like). In the main, it left social welfare policy and direct policing of citizens to the states.

But atop the federal "patronage state" of the original regime, the second Roosevelt grafted a "regulatory state" and a "redistributive state." Under FDR, "for the first time," Theodore Lowi writes, "the national government *established a direct and coercive relationship between itself and individual citizens.*"[114] The post–New Deal state had also pledged itself to the constant delivery of goods and benefits, with the public looking most of all to the president to meet the key test of the new regime's legitimacy: "service delivery."[115] The emerging "Second Republic of the United States" was one in which, as Lowi sums up, "the system of government had become an inverted pyramid, with everything coming to rest on a presidential pinpoint."[116]

The legendary "100 Days" of legislative activity that kicked off FDR's first term brought to fruition Woodrow Wilson's vision of the president as prime minister. The "100 Days" phrase had originated with Napoleon, describing the period beginning with his post-Elba return to Paris in 1815 and ending with the failure of his last attempt to defeat the coalition of European forces arrayed against him.[117] But there would be no Waterloo for executive power after FDR.

As Corwin had noted, by the Second World War, Americans had become accustomed to the idea of the president using the bully pulpit to demand further delegations of legislative power to the executive branch, to fulfill goals that the Constitution had reserved to the states or the people. In his 1944 State of the Union address, FDR conjured a "second Bill of Rights" into existence. Among the new rights were

> the right to a useful and remunerative job. . . . The right to earn enough to provide adequate food and clothing and recreation; The right of every farmer to raise and sell his products at a return which will give him and his family a decent living; . . . The right of every family to a decent home; The right to adequate medical care and the opportunity to achieve and enjoy good health; The right to adequate protection from the economic fears of old age, sickness, accident, and unemployment; [and] The right to a good education.[118]

The president would provide all this and more.

In fact, well before the war, it had become clear that increasing numbers of Americans looked to the president for personal help in a way that would have seemed peculiar—even dishonorable—to their fathers and grandfathers. Before the advent of the modern presidency, few Americans had bothered to write to the president, who was, after all, a distant official in Washington with duties that only rarely had a direct impact on ordinary people. FDR's revolutionary presidency changed all that. "Tell me your troubles," he urged listeners in one fireside chat—and they did.[119] William Howard Taft got only about 200 letters a week, but FDR's first inaugural address prompted nearly half a million. Ira Smith, head of the White House mail service for five decades starting with the McKinley administration, had handled the mail all by himself until FDR's first term. But soon after Roosevelt's ascension, Smith would require a staff of 50.[120] FDR averaged 5,000 letters a day, and the flood never stopped. Presidents received over a million letters a year through the 1970s.[121]

A remarkable film produced in 1932 and released shortly after FDR's election captured the changes in the public's orientation toward the presidency. Financed by William Randolph Hearst and starring Walter Huston, *Gabriel over the White House* depicts a president literally touched by an angel and empowered to heal the country and the world. The movie's fictional president, Judson C. Hammond, begins as an unflattering amalgam of Harding and Coolidge, a party hack more interested in bedding his comely assistant than in dealing with his country's ongoing economic woes.

After Hammond is gravely injured in a car crash, the archangel Gabriel visits him in the hospital. Gabriel imbues the comatose Hammond with the Holy Spirit of presidential activism. Hammond awakens from the coma, declares a state of emergency, and threatens Congress with a declaration of martial law should they refuse to pass his legislative program, which includes federally subsidized agriculture, a ban on mortgage foreclosures, and a CCC-style "Army of Construction" that will give a job to every unemployed man in America. To eradicate organized crime, Hammond authorizes a special army unit to fight gangsters, several of whom are convicted via military tribunal, then executed with the Statue of Liberty visible in the background. Toward the end of the movie, President Hammond uses a demonstration of American air power to force other world leaders to disarm, thereby ending the scourge of war. Then, with his work on Earth done, the president ascends into Heaven.

3

THE AGE OF THE HEROIC PRESIDENCY

First and foremost, I think there's the concept that many
of us acquire as students of the Presidency. . . . *This is the
belief*—it certainly was dominant in academic circles
when I was a student—*that a strong Presidency was a
good Presidency.* We looked at and rated the American
presidents in terms of their ability to accumulate power in
the oval office.

—Then Rep. Dick Cheney, speaking to college students
studying the presidency (March 23, 1984)

By the postwar era, Washington's humble term "chief magistrate"
could no longer adequately describe an office that in power and
responsibility had expanded far beyond Hamiltonian hopes or
Jeffersonian fears. The president was now the great leader of the Progressives' dreams, Herbert Croly's "Thor wielding with power and
effect a sledge-hammer in the cause of national righteousness"—or
perhaps, with the arrival of the atomic age, a figure better described
as a Zeus, capable of launching city-flattening thunderbolts. God
metaphors abound in midcentury scholars' descriptions of the presidency. In 1960, the University of Chicago's Herman Finer declared that
the presidency was "the incarnation of the American people in a sac-
rament resembling that in which the wafer and the wine are seen to be

the body and blood of Christ," the office rightly belonging "to the off-spring of a titan and Minerva husbanded by Mars."[1]

Superman Comes to the Supermarket

In a remarkable speech given not two weeks after he'd announced for the presidency, Sen. John F. Kennedy captured the prevailing mood:

> The history of this Nation—its brightest and its bleakest pages—has been written largely in terms of the different views our Presidents have had of the Presidency itself. This history ought to tell us that the American people in 1960 have an imperative right to know what any man bidding for the Presidency thinks about the place he is bidding for, whether he is aware of and willing to use the powerful resources of that office; whether his model will be Taft or Roosevelt, Wilson or Harding.

In case it needs explaining, for JFK, Taft and Harding were the patsies, Roosevelt and Wilson, history's winners. Kennedy went on to quote Wilson's line in *Constitutional Government*, "The President is at liberty, both in law and conscience, to be as big a man as he can," and complain that "President Woodrow Wilson discovered that to be a big man in the White House inevitably brings cries of dictatorship." (Perhaps that had something to do with Wilson's tendency to incarcerate people who opposed his policies.)

After a few digs at Eisenhower's placidity, JFK maintained that the country could no longer afford "a Chief Executive who is praised primarily for what he did not do, the disasters he prevented, the bills he vetoed." Rather, the presidency required "extraordinary strength and vision," because it was

> the center of moral leadership—a "bully pulpit," as Theodore Roosevelt described it. For only the President represents the national interest. And upon him alone converge all the needs and aspirations of all parts of the country, all departments of the Government, all nations of the world.[2]

The public agreed; midcentury Americans placed enormous faith in the federal government. For five decades, researchers associated with the University of Michigan have been asking Americans: "How much of the time do you think you can trust the government in Washington to do what is right—just about always, most of the time or only some of the time?" In 1958, the first year of the survey, 73 percent of respondents said "most of the time" or "just about always"; by 1964, over three-quarters placed themselves in the most trusting categories.[3]

Above all, Americans trusted the president. In a 1959 national poll, researchers posed the following question: "Some people say the president is in the best position to see what the country needs. Other people think the president may have good ideas about what the country needs, but it is up to the Congress to decide what ought to be done. How do you feel about this?" Only 17 percent picked Congress—61 percent of Americans said the president should decide.[4]

Their children, adolescents and undergraduates, studied textbooks that described the president in terms more appropriate for the bulletproof son of Krypton who, as fans of the George Reeves television series heard weekly throughout the 1950s, "fights a never-ending battle for Truth, Justice, and the American Way." In his 1970 essay, "Superman: Our Textbook President," presidential scholar Thomas Cronin surveyed political science textbooks for college students from 1955 to 1970 and found a near-uniform portrayal of "presidential omnipotence" and "moralistic-benevolence," in which "by symbolizing the past and future greatness of America and radiating inspirational confidence, a president can pull the nation together while directing us toward the fulfillment of the American dream." Moreover, "if, and only if, the right man is placed in the White House, all will be well, and, somehow, whoever is in the White House is the right man."[5]

Little wonder, then, that small children raised in that environment imbibed the view that those wielding political power were almost invariably benevolent, and none more benevolent, or more powerful, than the president. In 1960, political scientist Fred Greenstein reported on the results of his extensive survey research on the political socialization of children. Greenstein found children's view of political authority "strikingly favorable," especially with regard to the presidency. He found it almost impossible to elicit any skepticism from the children he interviewed, despite "a variety of attempts to evoke such responses."

Far more typical were statements like "he [the president] has the right to stop bad things before they start."[6]

This pattern of "juvenile idealization of the President" persisted in subsequent studies of children throughout the 1960s.[7] One such study quoted a Houston mother, who said that after JFK's assassination, "When my little girl came out of school she told me someone killed the President, and her thoughts were—since the President was dead, where would we get our food and clothes from?"[8]

As with children, so too with leading scholars of the era. Clinton Rossiter's veneration for the presidency was utterly typical among postwar academics, few of whom had major qualms about the powers the modern president had commandeered. In 1960, Richard E. Neustadt, who would go on to found Harvard's Kennedy School of Government, declared, "What is good for the country is good for the president and *vice versa*." Arthur Schlesinger Sr., who helped establish the national pastime of ranking presidents, wrote in 1962 that "every one" of the great presidents "left the Executive branch stronger and more influential than he found it."[9] Pulitzer Prize–winning presidential biographer James MacGregor Burns echoed that view in his 1963 book *The Deadlock of Democracy*, urging Americans to get beyond the "Madisonian dread of a man on horseback."[10] Much like the young Woodrow Wilson, Burns understood the Constitution to have established an "anti-leadership system," and Burns was no happier with that fact than Wilson had been.[11] Checks on presidential power had to be broken down because, Burns said, "The stronger we make the Presidency, the more we strengthen democratic procedures."[12]

Human nature being what it is—what the Founders said it was—disappointments were in store for those who had made the office the focus of national hopes and dreams. Presidential romantics awoke in the 1970s with throbbing headaches, smeared lipstick, and no small sense of shame. Presidential lies, a disastrous war, and serial abuses of authority stretching across several administrations made many Americans rue the loss of republican virtue.

This chapter and the next trace that arc of disillusionment. We begin with a discussion of the midcentury president's imposing job description, then turn to the enormous unilateral powers that the president had accrued in hopes of meeting the job's ever-increasing demands.

Here, as before, war was the health of the presidency. "There is considerable political advantage to the administration in its battle with the Kremlin," wrote Truman advisers Clark Clifford and James Rowe in a 1948 memo to the president, "The worse matters get up to a fairly certain point—real danger of imminent war—the more is there a sense of crisis. In times of crisis, the American citizen tends to back up his president."[13]

Up, Up, and Away

Yet, even in areas far removed from foreign policy, the midcentury president had amassed powers and responsibilities largely unknown to his 19th-century predecessors. Again, Clinton Rossiter's 1956 book *The American Presidency* is a good starting point for exploring several of the modern president's expanded roles.

"Chief Legislator"

We saw in Chapter 1 that the Founding-era norm was one of presidential deference. It was Congress's job to set the national direction in terms of policy; the president's role was to inform, suggest, and, when necessary, defend the Constitution from legislative overreaching. In contrast, as Rossiter noted, by the middle of the 20th century, Americans expected the president to guide Congress—and to use the "bully pulpit" to appeal directly to the people if Congress refused to go along.

In the early part of the 20th century, some presidents resisted the growing expectation that the president should twist arms and pound podiums unceasingly until Congress capitulated. Characteristically, Calvin Coolidge commented that he "never felt it was my duty to attempt to coerce Senators or Representatives, or to make reprisals. The people sent them to Washington. I felt I had discharged my duty when I had done the best I could with them."[14] But after FDR's historic "100 Days," there was no escaping the Chief Legislator's burden. During his first year in office, President Eisenhower declined to submit a legislative program, and got pilloried for it in the press.[15] Ike learned a lesson from that, and included a detailed legislative agenda in his 1954 State of the Union.[16] Yielding to the reality that Coolidge-style restraint was no longer politically feasible, Eisenhower also created the White House Office of Legislative Affairs, dedicated to moving legislation on the Hill.

As the president became increasingly responsible for setting the nation's policy direction, the Executive Office of the Presidency metastasized; from FDR's second term to Ike's, it quintupled in size, passing 2,500 employees by the late 1950s. By the end of Nixon's first term, the EOP employed over 5,500 people, with some 660 on the White House office staff alone.[17]

"Manager of Prosperity"

One of the core responsibilities of the president and his new army of functionaries was "managing" the economy. The Employment Act of 1946 played a key role in the growth of that responsibility. That act created the president's Council of Economic Advisers, required the president to submit an annual economic report, and committed the government to "promot[ing] maximum employment, production, and purchasing power." The original version of the bill, the Full Employment Act, came close to guaranteeing a job to every American who wanted one, codifying Keynesian economic management by commanding the federal government to make "such volume of federal investment and expenditure as may be needed . . . to assure continuing full employment." Conservative Democrats and Republicans helped kill that bill, fearing enhanced presidential power over the economy and a continuation of wartime regimentation.[18] Yet, the bill that passed still stoked the growing public belief that the president was responsible for protecting Americans from the fluctuations of economic life.

From the post–World War II era on, national discourse has often proceeded on the implicit view that the president sits in the cockpit of the national economy, pulling levers and adjusting dials to produce "maximum employment," minimum inflation, and rollicking growth. It is now nearly impossible to picture a modern president behaving as Ulysses Grant did, when in the teeth of the panic of 1873, he declared, "It is the duty of Congress to devise the method of correcting the evils which are acknowledged to exist, and not mine."[19]

"Protector of the Peace"

The Constitution empowers the president to keep the country secure from insurrections and invasions (when Congress has called up the militia) and the states secure from "domestic violence" (when requested to do so by the state legislature, or the governor when the legislature cannot be convened).[20] But by the mid-20th century, the president's obligations had expanded far beyond putting down occasional bursts of lawlessness or rebellion. "Is Maine scourged by forest fires? Is Texas parched with drought? Is Kansas invaded by grasshoppers?" Clinton Rossiter wrote, "then in every instance, the President must take the lead to restore the normal pattern of existence."[21]

Earlier presidents periodically resisted the notion that it was their job to protect Americans from the hazards of bad luck. Vetoing a bill to relieve Texas farmers suffering from the drought of 1887, President Grover Cleveland declared, "I can find no warrant for such an appropriation in the Constitution; and I do not believe that the power and duty of the General government ought to be extended to the relief of individual suffering which is in no manner properly related to the public service or benefit. A prevalent tendency to disregard the limited mission of this power and duty should, I think, be steadily resisted."[22]

But with the advent of the modern presidency, resistance was useless. Coolidge was the last president to show any real reluctance to provide federal relief for the perils of bad weather. Authority for disaster relief became increasingly centralized and governed by executive whim. The Disaster Relief Act of 1950 authorized federal agencies "[i]n any major disaster . . . when directed by the President, to provide assistance," making what had been an ad hoc, congressionally driven process into a matter of presidential responsibility.[23]

Throughout the second half of the 20th century, the president's role as Protector of the Peace would expand still further. In response to Sen. Barry Goldwater's attempt to make "violence in our streets" a major campaign issue, President Lyndon Baines Johnson told reporters that "the Constitution provides that responsibility for law and order should be vested in the States and in the local communities." But after trouncing Goldwater in the 1964 election, LBJ inaugurated what has been a four-decade drive to expand the federal criminal code, supporting and signing, among other bills, the Drug Abuse and Control Act (1965), the Law Enforcement Assistance Act (1965), and the Omnibus Crime Control and Safe Streets Act (1968).[24] Here too the war metaphor played a central role in presidential rhetoric, as when LBJ, upon signing the latter act, urged support for "the law enforcement officers, and the men who wage the war on crime day after day in all the streets and roads and alleys in America."[25]

"World Leader"

By Professor Rossiter's era, the modern president had become protector of the peace abroad as well as at home. In his famous oration on the Fourth of July, 1821, proclaiming that America "goes not abroad in search of monsters to destroy," John Quincy Adams expressed what was the consensus foreign policy in the early Republic: America was "the well-wisher to the freedom and independence of all," but she would be "champion and vindicator only of her own."[26]

No longer. The reserve of the Old Republic had given way to the bold promises of the New Frontier: "Let every nation know, whether it wishes us well or ill, that we shall pay any price, bear any burden, meet any hardship, support any friend, oppose any foe, in order to assure the survival and the success of liberty. This much we pledge—and more."[27] (And *more*?) As Rossiter recognized in *The American Presidency*, the modern president had become "President of the West" as well as president of the United States.[28] That perceived responsibility for the freedom of man would make it easier to mistake a setback for liberty anywhere for a threat to freedom everywhere. It would make it harder to define American interests soberly, and to refrain from battle where it was prudent to refrain.

"Voice of the People"

In their public rhetoric, postwar presidents embraced all four roles—Chief Legislator, Manager of Prosperity, Protector of the Peace, World Leader—and more. By loudly and incessantly promising great things, they encouraged the view that the president is responsible for most of the good or ill that befalls the nation. Talk may be cheap, but in the modern era, talk is central to the president's job.

After FDR's revolutionary presidency, the chief executive had become, in Rossiter's words, "the Voice of the People, the leading formulator and expounder of public opinion in the United States." From his perch at Princeton in 1908, Woodrow Wilson had foreseen this development, and rejoiced at the promise it held, for the country and, no doubt, for himself. "If [the president] rightly interpret the national thought and boldly insist upon it," Wilson wrote in *Constitutional Government*, "he is irresistible; and the country never feels the zest for action so much as when its President is of such insight and caliber."[29]

Constrained by the "rhetorical common law" of the time, the 19th century president spoke only rarely, and even more rarely on specific policy matters. But by the 1960s, the president couldn't manage to keep quiet for very long.[30] He was as uncomfortable with silence as his predecessors were with speechifying.

With the erosion of the Founding's rhetorical tradition, the president's major forms of public address, the inaugural address and the State of the Union, had changed dramatically from their earlier incarnations. The Framers had seen the State of the Union as a means of communicating useful information to the legislature; but modern presidents, responding to and shaping public expectations, made it yet another means of direct communication with the American people. Woodrow Wilson's decision to deliver the address in person moved the 20th-century State of the Union closer to the plebiscitary model, and Harry S. Truman changed the nature of the address still more fundamentally by delivering it via television in 1947. In 1966, Lyndon Johnson moved the speech to prime-time viewing hours, the better to reach a national audience.

Changes in the form of the address (from written to spoken—and televised) and its intended audience (from Congress to the American public at large) had significant effects on the State of the Union's content. By the second half of the 20th century, the SOTU had become the speech we know today: a passel of promises and demands on the public fisc, greeted with repeated standing ovations from members of a coordinate branch. The policy agenda outlined therein had become both more specific and far more ambitious, with presidents promising to do such things as educate the nation's children, heal the sick, and bring democracy to the world.

In the journal *Presidential Studies Quarterly* in 2002, political scientist Elvin T. Lim tracked the evolution of presidential rhetoric through two centuries of State of the Union and inaugural addresses. Lim found that the substance and the tone of presidential rhetoric had shifted radically. The content of modern public addresses reflects the president's growing role as national father-protector, responsible for the well-being of the dependents in his charge. The word "help" first appeared in the State of the Union in 1859, and the inaugural in 1889, but "it appears 110 times in the two genres between 1859 and 1932, and 784 times after." During the period before 1932, when the United States was, by contemporary standards, a poor country, the word poverty appeared only 17 times in the two categories of address, but it has appeared 95 times since then, reflecting the president's increased responsibility to provide for the poor.[31]

Early inaugural addresses often took the form of meditations on the oath of office and the constitutional role of the president. That too has declined over time. Fourteen of the first 19 inaugurals contain promises to defend the Constitution, the Union, or both. Only 1 of the last 18 does so.[32] References to the Constitution and "constitutional" have declined significantly; likewise, republican rhetoric—including terms such as "republic" and "citizen"—has nearly vanished, and references to "leader," "people," and "reform" have soared.[33]

In keeping with the activist orientation of the modern executive, Professor Lim noted "an increasing lack of humility" on the part of the president. The words "providence" and "fate," so prevalent in 19th-century presidential speeches, had essentially disappeared by the late 20th century, replaced by assertive, "can-do" rhetoric. For a president to publicly agonize about his fitness for the job, as Washington did in his first inaugural, noting at the outset that "no event could have filled me with greater anxieties than that of [assuming the presidency]," would be unthinkable in the modern era. FDR's bold "I assume unhesitatingly the leadership of this great army of our people" is more in keeping with the contemporary spirit.[34]

Interestingly, references to "God" became far more prevalent in the supposedly more secular 20th century than they were in the 19th. In the rhetoric of the 19th-century presidency, God appears, but He's less often invoked by name. Instead, He plays the role of a "providence" whose blessings are humbly sought, rather than demanded as of right.[35]

In their rhetoric and public behavior, modern presidents encouraged (and still encourage) this grandiose view of presidential capabilities by promising to protect Americans from economic dislocation, to shield them from natural disasters and all manner of hazards, and, increasingly, even to provide the moral leadership that could deliver them from spiritual malaise. By midcentury, thanks in part to soaring presidential oratory, public visions of presidential responsibility had become too great for a constitutionally constrained office to meet. And so constraints fell, to make way for the presidency unbound.

The postwar president had accumulated vast powers at home and abroad. Abroad, the decision to go to war was now his, and his alone. He could topple governments, bomb cities, and launch full-scale land invasions of other countries—he might even launch a war that could destroy the world—all without ever having to seek congressional authorization. At home, the president had amassed enormous unilateral authority to make law via executive order, and his ability to gather intelligence on Americans was virtually unchecked.

Truman's advisers were right when they told him that the American citizen could be counted on to back up his president in times of crisis. With the Cold War as a backdrop, Professor Rossiter could state, "We have placed a shocking amount of military power in the President's keeping, but where else, we may ask, could it possibly have been placed?"[36] The amount of military power commandeered by the modern president was indeed shocking, and the events of the latter half of the 20th century would lead many Americans to an assessment much less sanguine than Rossiter's.

Unilateral Powers Abroad

By the middle of the 20th century, through a combination of presidential aggrandizement and congressional acquiescence, the question of war and peace was entirely in the hands of the executive. Though prior presidents had stretched their commander-in-chief authority, when it came to major wars, they still observed the constitutional forms. But the Korean War marked a constitutional Rubicon—the first major conflict in which a U.S. president explicitly took the position that he did not need congressional authorization to launch a full-scale war.

The Korean War

Before dawn on June 25, 1950, without warning, North Korean forces began artillery bombardment of Seoul. Over 130,000 troops crossed the 38th parallel, aiming to unify Korea under the communist dictatorship of General Secretary Kim Il-Sung. On June 27, President Truman announced that he had committed American air and sea forces to support the embattled Republic of Korea, with land forces to follow. Two days later, at a press conference, Truman maintained "we are not at war," preferring to adopt a reporter's suggestion that it was "a police action under the United Nations."[37] By August, ROK troops and the U.S. Eighth Army were trapped in the "Pusan Perimeter," in the southeastern corner of the Korean peninsula.

Congress almost certainly would have authorized the use of force, but Truman refused to ask. Secretary of State Dean Acheson assured the president he had the authority to commit U.S. forces anywhere in the world without permission from Congress, and ordered the State Department to prepare a legal memorandum to that effect. The Truman administration seemed to believe that securing United Nations approval was far more important than getting approval from Congress. Yet, the Security Council's sign-off could not substitute for congressional authorization either under the terms of the UN Charter or, more importantly, the U.S. Constitution.[38]

Though he supported military action in Korea, Sen. Robert A. Taft, President Taft's son, had serious qualms about the precedent being set for executive-initiated war. In a June 28 speech on the Senate floor, Taft called Truman's action "a complete usurpation by the President of the authority to use the Armed Forces of this country." "If the President can intervene in Korea without Congressional approval," Taft argued, "he can go to war in Malaya or Indonesia or Iran or South America." If the principle advanced by the president were allowed to stand, Taft concluded, "we would have finally terminated for all time the right of Congress to declare war."[39]

Some five months later, with the war in Korea going poorly and Truman preparing to send more troops to bolster NATO forces in Europe, Taft objected again to the president's usurpation of congressional authority. Arthur Schlesinger Jr., the man who later popularized the phrase "Imperial Presidency," and who, throughout his long career had a recurring romance with that institution, jumped into the debate. In a letter to the *New York Times*, Schlesinger called Taft's complaints about presidential war "demonstrably irresponsible," and defended the (Democratic) president's prerogative to put troops in a war zone and start wars without authorization. This was Situational Constitutionalism at its worst. But 22 years later, during the Nixon administration, Schlesinger apologized. Taft, it turned out, had a point.[40]

Yet, the principle Taft feared was allowed to stand, completing the reduction of Congress to the status of advisory body at best on matters of war and peace. At a press conference in March 1951, Truman generously allowed that Congress had the right to express itself on the Korean War question: "I don't mind their talking about anything they want to. This is a free country. They can make any number of speeches they want . . . but that does not mean that it helps the relations with the rest of the world."[41] Talk all you want, Truman said, but the ultimate decision would rest with the president.

In the end, after a terribly unpopular war that on several occasions nearly escalated into a broader land war in Asia, the United States managed to restore the pre-1950 status quo on the Korean peninsula. Over 33,000 American soldiers, conscripts and volunteers, died without the courtesy of an up-or-down vote on the war from their representatives in Congress. And, in a sense, what was left of Congress's power to declare war died with them.

The Vietnam War

Lyndon Johnson's attitude toward Congress echoed Truman's imperiousness. As LBJ told an audience in Omaha, Nebraska, in 1966: "Now there are many, many who can recommend, advise, and sometimes a few of them consent. But there is only one that has been chosen by the American people to decide."[42] That appeared to be Congress's attitude as well, even as it authorized the use of force in Vietnam.

On August 5, 1964, in response to what he described as two unprovoked attacks on U.S. naval vessels operating off the North Vietnamese coast, President Johnson asked Congress for a resolution approving military action. Two days later, Congress passed the Gulf of Tonkin Resolution, stating that "Congress approves and supports the determination of the President, as Commander in Chief, to take all necessary measures to repel any armed attack against the forces of the United States and to prevent further aggression."[43]

Many in Congress denied that they were voting for full-scale war. Sen. J. William Fulbright, who would come to rue his vote for the resolution and would become a key critic of our Vietnam policy, shepherded the resolution to passage. Asked on the floor of the Senate whether the proposed resolution could be construed to "authorize or recommend or approve the landing of large American armies in Vietnam," Fulbright declared that a full-scale land war in Asia was "the last thing we would want to do. However, the language of the resolution would not prevent it. It would authorize whatever the Commander in Chief feels is necessary." The Gulf of Tonkin Resolution passed with less than nine hours of debate in the Senate, most before a chamber only two-thirds full. The House took only 40 minutes to approve the measure.[44]

The Johnson administration secured the resolution under false pretenses—not the first or last time that would occur in the modern practice of presidential war making. Defense Secretary Robert McNamara assured Congress that the attack was "unprovoked": "Our Navy played absolutely no part in, was not associated with, was not aware of, any South Vietnamese actions, if there were any."[45] In fact, the destroyer USS *Maddox* had been in the Gulf of Tonkin as part of a coordinated effort to gather intelligence on North Vietnamese defenses. South Vietnamese naval commandos, using boats provided by the U.S. Navy, would hit coastal targets selected by the Central Intelligence Agency, to "light up" North Vietnamese radar for the *Maddox*. The *Maddox* did come under fire from NVA torpedo boats on August 2, but its damage was limited to a single half-inch bullethole.[46] And despite Secretary McNamara's assertion that there was "unequivocal proof" of another attack two days later, no such proof existed, and it's now clear that the second attack never happened.[47] LBJ suspected as much at the time, telling Undersecretary of State George Ball a few days after the resolution's passage: "Hell, those dumb, stupid sailors were just shooting at flying fish!"[48] Nonetheless, Johnson seized on the opportunity to secure congressional approval for any action he deemed necessary in Southeast Asia.

The Gulf of Tonkin Resolution was broadly worded enough to allow the president alone to make the final decision about war. Johnson compared it to "grandma's nightshirt" because it "covered everything."[49] The president did not immediately use the authority granted him. But six months later, after he defeated Goldwater in the November election,

LBJ ramped up the war with the "Rolling Thunder" bombing campaign in North Vietnam and the introduction of large numbers of American ground troops in the south.

The principal rationale behind the Vietnam War was containment of communist aggression. Yet, in a larger sense, it was a Progressive war, reflecting an exalted view of the president's role and America's historic mission. In it, we can see something of the sentiments of Progressive senator Albert J. Beveridge, who told his colleagues in 1900 that "God has marked the American people as his chosen Nation to finally lead in the regeneration of the world."[50] In his book *Promised Land, Crusader State*, Walter McDougall calls Vietnam the "Great Society War." McDougall wasn't the first to make the connection: as Vice President Hubert Humphrey put it in a 1966 television interview, "There is a tremendous new opening here for realizing the dream of a great society in Asia, not just here at home."[51]

With his legislative blitzkrieg on the home front—pushing through bills on health care, civil rights, and poverty—Johnson exhibited the Progressive's boundless faith in government's ability to solve complex social problems. "We have the power to shape the civilization that we want," Johnson declared in his May 1964 Great Society speech at the University of Michigan.[52]

That faith applied abroad as well as at home: the daunting task of nation-building in South Vietnam could be achieved by setting loose the social workers, planners, and social scientists: "McNamara put more than a hundred sociologists, ethnologists, and psychologists to work 'modeling' South Vietnamese society and seeking data sufficient 'to describe it quantitatively' and simulate its behavior on a computer." McDougall quotes soldier and military analyst Colonel Harry Summers: "[Vietnam was] the international version of our domestic Great Society programs where we presumed that we knew what was best for the world in terms of social, political and economic development and saw it as our duty to force the world into the American mold—to act not so much as the World's Policeman as the World's Nanny."[53]

"Dammit," Johnson exclaimed to aide Jack Valenti in 1966, "we need to exhibit more compassion for the Vietnamese plain people.... We've got to see that the South Vietnamese government wins the battle ... of crops and hearts and caring."[54] Crops and hearts and caring—and massive civilian loss of life. Though estimates of civilian casualties are murky, they range from 195,000 to 430,000 in South Vietnam alone from 1965 to 1974. In North Vietnam, the numbers are even less certain, but given that the volume of bombing in Vietnam surpassed the 2.7 million tons dropped by all Allied forces in all of World War II, "high civilian casualties were an inevitable feature of the nature of the war and the sheer volume of firepower used by the American military."[55] As for the costs to America, Vietnam became our longest and second most expensive war, and one of our bloodiest, with some 58,000 killed.

A Close-Run Thing

Despite the tragedy of Vietnam, Americans tend to associate the Cold War with some of the modern presidency's greatest triumphs. But with nearly two decades' distance from the fall of the Soviet Union, it's difficult to appreciate what a close-run thing the Cold War was, how much worse it could have gone.

During that "long twilight struggle," the president's control of the powers of war and peace extended well beyond cases of open warfare employing U.S. troops. He also claimed broad powers to force regime change through covert action. As General James Doolittle put it in a top-secret report to President Eisenhower in 1954,

> If the United States is to survive, long-standing American concepts of "fair play" must be reconsidered. We must develop effective espionage and counterespionage services and must learn to subvert, sabotage and destroy our enemies by more clever, more sophisticated, and more effective methods than those used against us. It may become necessary that the American people be made acquainted with, understand and support this fundamentally repugnant philosophy.[56]

Under Eisenhower's direction, the CIA toppled the democratically elected leftist governments of Mohammed Mossadegh in Iran and Jacobo Arbenz Guzman in Guatemala. The agency also began training Cuban exiles for an invasion of Cuba aimed at removing the Castro regime.

The Cuban operation, planned under the Eisenhower administration and carried out under Kennedy, did not go nearly as smoothly as its predecessors. Lacking promised U.S. air support, the invasion force never got off the beach, and the bulk of the 1,500 exiles were captured by Cuban forces.

After the Bay of Pigs debacle, top military officials developed a plan to foment a war with Cuba by blaming Cuba for attacks on Americans that the military itself would stage. On March 13, 1962, Army general Lyman L. Lemnitzer, chairman of the Joint Chiefs of Staff, presented Robert McNamara, President Kennedy's defense secretary, with a memo detailing "Operation Northwoods": a plan to covertly engineer various "pretexts which would provide justification for US military intervention in Cuba."[57] Those pretexts would include "a 'Remember the Maine' incident"—staging the explosion and sinking of a U.S. ship in Guantanamo Bay. Though no U.S. personnel were to be killed in the incident, phony casualty lists would be supplied, which "in US newspapers would cause a helpful wave of national indignation."[58] The memo also contemplated faking a Cuban attack on "a chartered civil airliner enroute from the United States to Jamaica, Guatemala, Panama or Venezuela," and staging a phony

> Communist Cuban terror campaign in the Miami area, in other Florida cities and even in Washington. The terror campaign could be pointed at Cuban refugees seeking haven in the United States. We could sink a boatload of Cubans enroute to Florida (real or simulated). We could foster attempts on lives of Cuban refugees in the United States even to the point of wounding in instances to be widely publicized. Exploding a few plastic bombs in carefully chosen spots, the arrest of Cuban agents and the release of prepared documents substantiating Cuban involvement also would be helpful in projecting the idea of an irresponsible [Cuban] government.[59]

The plan, signed off on by all of the Joint Chiefs of Staff, was apparently vetoed by Defense Secretary McNamara.[60]

The short-term effect of the botched landing at the Bay of Pigs— combined with repeated CIA-sponsored attempts to assassinate

Castro—helped make the Cuban dictator receptive to the Soviet offer to place medium- and intermediate-range missiles on Cuban soil. That in turn led to the Cuban Missile Crisis, the closest the world ever came to thermonuclear war.

John Yoo, the Imperial Presidency's most prominent modern defender, sees the Cuban Missile Crisis as one of executive unilateralism's finest hours. In a debate at the Federalist Society's 2006 Lawyers' Convention, Yoo argued that

> in the Cold War period, presidents often used their authority unilaterally in ways that we have come to admire and praise. . . . We put up a blockade around Cuba, which is an act of war, in order to forestall a serious change in the balance of power. President Kennedy not only put up a blockade unilaterally, but he determined all of the rules of engagement, he made all the tactical and strategic decisions, as a commander-in-chief would, and we all think of this as the greatest moment of Kennedy's leadership in his presidency.[61]

It's astonishing that Yoo can be so upbeat about the standoff that brought the United States and the Soviet Union close to a nuclear exchange. In fact, the missiles did *not* represent "a serious change in the balance of power." Defense Secretary Robert McNamara noted as much at the first meeting of the Executive Committee set up by Kennedy to explore possible responses to the Soviet action. "A missile is a missile." Placing missiles in Cuba did nothing to change the United States' overwhelming nuclear deterrent to a Soviet first strike.[62] Nonetheless, in large part because of domestic political considerations, Kennedy rejected out of hand any option that involved leaving the missiles in place, even if doing so could avoid the risk of nuclear war.

If there's anything to praise about JFK's leadership during the crisis, it's that he resisted efforts to get him to escalate the conflict still further. Thomas Power, head of the Strategic Air Command, and Curtis LeMay, the air force chief of staff, both tried to push the Cuban Missile Crisis into a full-scale war with the Soviets. Both men, like much of the military establishment at the time, were enamored with the concept of preventive war, in which the United States would kill off its superpower rivals before they grew too strong. When LeMay had served as head of SAC from 1948 to 1957, he hoped to provoke an incident that would allow him to deliver his "Sunday Punch," 750 nuclear bombs in a few hours, leading to an estimated 60 million Russian dead. Without authorization, in 1954 LeMay ordered B-45 overflights of the Soviet Union, commenting to his aides, "Well, maybe if we do this overflight right, we can get World War III started."[63] General Power, LeMay's successor at SAC, and a man that even LeMay considered "a sadist," chastised a colleague at a 1960 briefing on nuclear strategy, yelling, "Restraint! Why are you so concerned with saving *their* lives? The whole idea is to *kill* the bastards. . . . Look: at the end of the war, if there are two Americans and one Russian, we win!" The colleague replied, "Well, you'd better make sure that they're a man and a woman."[64]

At the height of the Missile Crisis, Power allowed the prescheduled test launch of an Atlas ICBM, in an apparent attempt to spook the Soviets into action.[65] LeMay in turn repeatedly challenged Kennedy's courage, urging the president to approve air strikes on the missile installations. That action would likely have led to the nuclear exchange LeMay had long lusted after. As we later learned, during the crisis, the Soviets had 20 operational, nuclear-armed medium-range ballistic missiles in Cuba, as well as nine tactical nuclear weapons that Russian field commanders had been authorized to use in the event of an attack.[66] In his book *Dark Sun: The Making of the Hydrogen Bomb*, historian Richard Rhodes writes, "If John Kennedy had followed LeMay's advice, history would have forgotten the Nazis and their terrible Holocaust. Ours would have been the historic omnicide."[67]

That presidents advised by such men had in their hands the means to kill millions should be unsettling to people of normal human sensibilities. That presidents showed restraint while in possession of such power gives us cause for thanks, but it is, at best, an uneasy source of comfort.

Unilateral Powers at Home

Presidential arrogance and deception, congressional cowardice, highminded rhetoric in the service of disastrous wars—the pattern established in the Cold War may seem all too familiar from a post-9/11 vantage point. And as with the war on terror, the communist threat led to enhanced secrecy and greatly increased executive power at home.

"Who in this year 1948," Professor Rossiter asked in his book *Constitutional Dictatorship*, "would be so blind as to assert that the people of the United States, or of any other constitutional democracy, can afford again to be weak and divided and jealous of the power of their elected representatives?" "If the crisis history of the modern democracies teaches us anything," Rossiter continued, "it teaches us that power can be responsible, that strong government can be democratic government, that dictatorship can be constitutional."[68] The 26-year-old William F. Buckley Jr. echoed that sentiment when he wrote in 1952 that "we have got to accept Big Government for the duration—for neither an offensive nor a defensive war can be waged . . . except through the instrumentality of a totalitarian bureaucracy within our shores."[69]

"Totalitarian bureaucracy"? "Dictatorship"? If it never came to that, we have our congenital anti-statism to thank. Even during an uncharacteristic period of high trust in government, Americans proved resistant to the idea of a garrison state.[70] Not resistant enough, however, to prevent disturbing abuses of power. Some of the worst would be carried out in secret, but even in the open, presidents pressed extraordinary theories of executive power and were checked only intermittently and imperfectly by Congress and the Court.

In fact, more than once Congress forced on a president powers he'd rather not have, as in 1950, when Congress passed the McCarran Internal Security Act. The emergency detention provisions of that act allowed the president, during an "internal security emergency," to incarcerate anyone he believed likely to engage in "acts of espionage or sabotage." To his credit, President Truman vetoed the act, but Congress overrode his veto.[71] The government readied six detention camps, including one at Tule Lake, California, which had been used to imprison Japanese Americans during World War II. Altogether the camps could hold up to 15,000 people, and the Federal Bureau of Investigation maintained lists of potential subversives, totaling close to 40,000 names, who might be confined in the event an emergency was declared.[72] Though the camps were never used, they were maintained by the government until the 1960s.[73]

The McCarran Act veto was an uncharacteristic display of self-control by President Truman, who rarely shrank from authoritarian methods. In May 1946, nearly a year after V-J Day, in the midst of a nationwide railroad strike, Truman announced that he would use the military to break the strike, and went to Congress for authority to draft the strikers into the army if they refused to return to work; "We'll draft them and think about the law later," Truman snapped when his attorney general brought up the Constitution. Not surprisingly, the strike was settled on the president's terms.[74]

In 1952, two years into the Korean War, Truman took a similarly hard line facing down a nationwide steelworkers' strike. With Executive Order 10340, he ordered Secretary of Commerce Charles Sawyer to seize the steel mills and operate them for the government.[75] This time, however, the Supreme Court pushed back.

In an April 8 radio and television address, Truman characterized his action as a war measure: "If steel production stops, we will have to stop making the shells and bombs that are going directly to our soldiers at the front in Korea." This was TR's Stewardship Theory on steroids. Citing his powers as president and authority as commander in chief of the U.S. Army, Truman announced that the steel companies would be nationalized and production continued until the strike could be settled. At an April 17 press conference, a reporter asked the president whether his theory would allow a president to "seize the newspapers and/or the radio stations." Truman would say only that "under similar circumstances, the President of the United States has to act for whatever is for the best of the country."[76]

The steel companies sought a preliminary injunction on the grounds that the president had acted without legal authority. Assistant Attorney General Holmes Baldridge fought the injunction with arguments as sweeping as any that the Bush administration's legal team has employed in the post-9/11 legal environment:

JUDGE PINE: So you contend the Executive has unlimited power in time of an emergency?

BALDRIDGE: He has the power to take such action as is necessary to meet the emergency.

JUDGE PINE: If the emergency is great, it is unlimited, is it?

BALDRIDGE: I suppose if you carry it to its logical conclusion, that is true . . .

JUDGE PINE: And that the Executive determines the emergencies and the courts cannot even review whether it is an emergency.

BALDRIDGE: That is correct.

Later, Pine asked Baldridge: "So, when the sovereign people adopted the Constitution, it enumerated the powers set up in the Constitution, but limited the powers of the Congress and limited the powers of the judiciary, but it did not limit the powers of the Executive. Is that what you say?" Baldridge replied, "That is the way we read Article II of the Constitution."

The Supreme Court, however, disagreed with the proposition that the Constitution granted unlimited power to the chief executive. In *Youngstown Sheet & Tube Co. v. Sawyer*, by a 6–3 vote, the Court affirmed Judge Pine's ruling and held the seizure invalid. Justice Black's majority opinion categorically rejected the Truman theory of executive power, noting that "in the framework of our Constitution, the President's power to see that the laws are faithfully executed refutes the idea that he is to be a lawmaker."[77] Justice Robert Jackson's influential concurrence evaluated claims of presidential power through the lens of congressional authorization: with such authorization, the president's authority was at its maximum; but when he acts against the express or implied will of Congress, it is at its "lowest ebb"—as it was in this case, Congress having considered and rejected property seizure as a means of settling labor disputes. According to Jackson, the expansive emergency authority the president claimed had no constitutional basis. The Framers "knew what emergencies were" and "knew how they afford a ready pretext for usurpation." Other than allowing Congress to suspend the writ of habeas corpus in times of rebellion or invasion, they did not provide emergency powers allowing the suspension of liberties. "I do not think we rightfully may so amend their work," Jackson wrote.[78]

Executive Orders

But *Youngstown* did not appreciably reduce the growing practice of rule by executive order. In the first century of the Republic, with Congress still serving as the country's principal lawmaker, presidents issued only about 300 executive orders. Yet, as the president's responsibilities expanded, so too did his power to make public policy unilaterally, with TR, Wilson, and FDR combined issuing over 6,500. Though no successor came close to FDR's record of 3,723, presidents from Truman through Nixon issued over 2,400 such orders.[79] Moreover, during this period, executive orders became increasingly indistinguishable from legislative acts. Where most of the executive orders issued by Coolidge and Hoover related to administrative matters such as civil service rules, with no more than 10 percent "policy-specific," by the 1960s, executive orders making national policy and affecting private rights "reached 50% and never declined."[80] As the president's responsibility for the welfare of the nation grew, his power grew accordingly.

When carried out pursuant to legislative or constitutional authority, executive orders are unobjectionable. Thus, when President Truman desegregated the armed forces with the stroke of a pen in 1948, he acted pursuant to his powers as commander in chief and corrected an offense that violated constitutional equality before the law.[81] Yet, many of the orders issued by modern presidents lack such authority and justification. By combining legislative and executive powers, they put the president in the constitutionally dubious position of both making and enforcing the law. Such orders cannot be squared with the Madisonian scheme of separation of powers. Montesquieu, who was for Madison "the oracle who is always consulted" on separation of powers, maintained that "there can be no liberty where the legislative and executive powers are united in the same person, or body of magistrates."[82]

The most infamous example of that dynamic occurred when FDR authorized the mass internment of over 110,000 innocent Japanese Americans via Executive Order 9066. A less notorious example, but one that did lasting damage, was Truman's 1951 Executive Order 10290, which greatly expanded federal officials' ability to classify information they deemed "necessary . . . to protect the security of the United States." Where before classification powers had rarely extended to nonmilitary agencies, Truman's order extended the authority to all civilian federal agencies and did not limit its exercise to wartime.[83] Truman declined to cite any specific legislative authority as the basis for the order, resting simply on "the authority vested in me by the Constitution and statutes, and as President of the United States."[84]

President Eisenhower tightened the criteria for classification somewhat, but not enough to prevent some hideous abuses. Among the worst were the government-sponsored radiation tests carried out until the mid-1970s, often without the consent of the subjects. In one study, federal researchers irradiated prison inmates' testicles to test the effects of radiation exposure. In 1994 the *Los Angeles Times* obtained a 1963 memorandum detailing the proposed study. On it, one scientist had written, "I'm for support at the requested level, as long as we are not liable. I worry about possible carcinogenic effects of such treatments."[85]

Even where executive orders affect citizens' rights less directly, they place vast power in the president's hands, power that can be used to shape public policy without the inconvenient and messy process of convincing a majority of the people's representatives that legislative action is necessary. One man makes the decision to establish a new agency, implement an affirmative action plan, or impose a new regulation on private conduct, and then, should legislators object, it is up to them to change the law.

That turns the Constitution on its head: the Framers erected significant barriers to the passage of legislation in an attempt to curb "the facility and excess of lawmaking."[86] Under the Constitution, a law must meet with the approval of the representatives of three different constituencies: the House, the Senate, and the president. But when the executive branch makes the law, those constitutional hurdles then obstruct legislative efforts to repeal it. For that reason, executive orders have proved especially popular at the end of presidents' terms. As two leading scholars of executive orders note: "When presidential command over the legislative process reaches its low point, presidents regularly strike out on their own, set vitally important public policies, and leave it up to Congress and an incoming administration to try and recover an old status quo."[87] That Congress is most often unable to do so points to the enormous unchecked power commandeered by the modern president.

One of the most significant—and least constrained—powers the post-war president exercised was the power to spy on American citizens. Under the rubric of national security, postwar presidents of both parties routinely gathered intelligence on their political adversaries. Presidents and their aides used the FBI to investigate and wiretap presidential critics and anyone they viewed as possibly threatening to their interests. Despite some qualms, the FBI complied "unquestioningly" with the requests.[88]

John F. Kennedy was among the most zealous of the modern presidents in his abuse of wiretap powers. JFK's attorney general, brother Bobby, ordered wiretaps on *New York Times* and *Newsweek* reporters, along with various congressmen and lobbyists.[89] In 1962, when U.S. Steel and other steel corporations raised prices by some $6 a ton, JFK invoked the crises in Berlin and Southeast Asia, and accused the companies of "a wholly unjustifiable and irresponsible defiance of the public interest."[90] Privately, Kennedy was more colorful: the steel executives "fucked us, and now we've got to fuck them."[91] To that end, JFK and RFK ordered wiretaps on the heads of the companies and had FBI agents carry out dawn raids on the steel executives' homes.

At a 1962 dinner party attended by the *Washington Post's* Benjamin Bradlee, who would later, as executive editor, help bring down the Nixon presidency, the Kennedys felt free to joke about their abuse of wiretapping authority in the dispute over steel prices. Toasting Bobby, President Kennedy recounted a conversation with Thomas F. Patton, the president of Republic Steel, who complained that the attorney general had wiretapped the steel executives and enlisted the Internal Revenue Service to bully them. "Of course," JFK said, "Patton was right." RFK stood up and cracked, "They were mean to my brother. They can't do that to my brother!"[92]

Later that year, when JFK celebrated his 45th birthday in a little ceremony at Madison Square Garden with 15,000 in attendance, Marilyn Monroe, clad in a flesh-colored, rhinestone-bedazzled dress she'd had to be sewn into, closed her steamy version of "Happy Birthday" with a couple of lines sung to the tune of "Thanks for the Memories":

Thanks, Mr. President
For all the things you've done
The battles that you've won
The way you deal with U.S. Steel
And our problems by the ton
We thank you so much.

Respected federal judge Laurence H. Silberman didn't sew himself into a rhinestone-studded dress when he addressed a conservative gathering at Washington's University Club in October 2005. Yet, he managed to unsettle the audience nonetheless. That night, Silberman recounted his experiences as a deputy attorney general in 1974, when the House Judiciary Committee asked him to review secret files kept by J. Edgar Hoover. Silberman discovered a scandalmonger's treasure trove of "nasty bits of information on various political figures—some still active." According to Silberman, "Lyndon Johnson was the most demanding" when it came to requisitioning FBI political intelligence.[93] In 1964, after D.C. police arrested LBJ aide Walter Jenkins for homosexual conduct in a YMCA bathroom, special assistant to the president Bill Moyers ordered Hoover to find something similar on Goldwater's campaign staff.

During the 1964 contest, the Johnson administration also used the CIA to keep Goldwater campaign officials under surveillance and to procure advance copies of the candidate's speeches.[94] And at Johnson's request, the FBI bugged Goldwater's campaign plane. In a 1971 conversation with Robert Mardian, an assistant attorney general under Nixon, Hoover admitted having the plane bugged. Why did he do it? Hoover explained to Mardian that "you do what the President of the United States orders you to do."[95]

In Richard Nixon's view, there were very few things that a president couldn't order his subordinates to do. "When the President does it, that means it is not illegal," he told David Frost in a 1977 interview.[96] That put it pretty starkly, but Nixon's constitutional theory wasn't dramatically more imperial than any postwar president's, save possibly Eisenhower's. And there was some truth to the conservative complaint that Nixon was deposed for attempting what JFK and LBJ got away with with some regularity—that is, using federal intelligence agencies against the president's political enemies.

That point is usually offered as a defense of Nixon, as in conservative historian Paul Johnson's *History of the American People*, in which he writes, hilariously, that Nixon's impeachment

> was an ugly moment in America's story and one which future historians, who will have no personal knowledge of any of the individuals concerned and whose emotions will not be engaged either way, are likely to judge *a dark hour in the history of a republic which prides itself in its love of order and its patient submission to the rule of law*.[97]

But the "everybody does it" defense offered by Johnson and other conservatives merely pointed to the systematic erosion of checks and balances and the abuses it made possible. In the early 1970s, Americans were learning a lot about those abuses, and what they learned reawakened their native skepticism about power.

4

HERO TAKES A FALL

Out of the gobbledygook, comes a very clear thing: . . .
you can't trust the government; you can't believe what
they say; and you can't rely on their judgment; and
the—the implicit infallibility of presidents, which has
been an accepted thing in America, is badly hurt by
this, because it shows that people do things the President
wants to do even though it's wrong, and the President
can be wrong.
> —H. R. Haldeman to Richard Nixon (June 14, 1971)

"Our long national nightmare is over," President Gerald Ford declared upon Nixon's resignation. The metaphor didn't quite fit.
Nightmares can be disturbing, but they're not real, and parents
are right to tell their children to forget all about them. In a sense, the
country *was* asleep during the era of the Heroic Presidency, but the
abuses of that period actually happened, and, rather than forget them,
most Americans wanted to prevent their repetition.

During the 1970s, what Americans learned about the presidency
would lead to a resurgence of checks and balances and a political culture
that would no longer take claims of executive benevolence on faith.
Resurgent distrust manifested itself in a newly adversarial press, and,

perhaps most importantly, in a Congress and a judiciary now willing to challenge presidential power.

The period of executive retrenchment was short lived, unfortunately. The Heroic Presidency had fallen. But it would in time be replaced by an office less grand but no less menacing. By the Clinton years, if not well before, the presidency was as imperial as ever, even if lacking entirely the glamour of Camelot. By century's end, Americans had recovered much of their historic skepticism about power. And yet, even as faith in power has waned, power endures.

Therapeutic Regicide

Like his heroic-era predecessors, Richard Nixon had a view of executive power that was vast indeed. The president held total control of the power to make war; he could wiretap at will, without court approval; he could withhold from Congress and the public any information he chose; and he was virtually immune from judicial process aimed at correcting abuses.[1] As Nixon saw it, the president also had a sweeping power to impound congressionally appropriated funds, zeroing out whole programs because he disagreed with them or found them wasteful. As one federal court noted, the president's theory would allow him to "ignor[e] any and all Congressional authorizations if he deemed them . . . contrary to the needs of the nation."[2]

Even before Watergate unfolded, Nixon's legal theories began to look uncomfortably like claims that the president was above the law. Yet, Americans had tolerated—even applauded—similar claims from presidents in the past. Nor was Nixon the first president to wiretap his enemies and attempt to subvert the Federal Bureau of Investigation and Central Intelligence Agency for political purposes. How then, could a "third-rate burglary"—what John Wayne termed a "glorified panty raid"—bring down a president?[3]

Context was everything. By the time Watergate happened, public trust in the presidency had already begun to erode, due to the widening "credibility gap" associated with the Vietnam War and serial revelations of past executive abuses, many of which had little to do with Nixon himself. What Americans learned about those abuses punctured the myth of presidential infallibility.

An article released in the decade's first month gave a hint of things to come. In the January 1970 issue of the *Washington Monthly*, former army intelligence officer Christopher Pyle exposed an ongoing program of military surveillance dating from President Johnson's decision to use the army to quell the 1967 race riots in Detroit. As Pyle put it, "the Army had assembled the essential apparatus of a police state."[4] Under pressure from the White House and the Justice Department, the U.S. military became deeply involved in monitoring the peaceful political activities of civilians. By the fall of 1968, more military intelligence officials were monitoring domestic protest groups than were assigned to any foreign theater, including Vietnam.[5] In addition to infiltrating peaceful protest groups, the army kept files on over 100,000 citizens, including such dangerous national security threats as child psychologist Dr. Benjamin Spock and folk singers Arlo Guthrie and Joan Baez.[6] The Pyle article spurred Senate Judiciary Committee hearings chaired by Sen. Sam Ervin, in which the senators learned that "comments about the financial affairs, sex lives, and psychiatric histories of persons unaffiliated with the armed forces appear throughout the various records systems."[7]

Then, on March 8, 1971, anti-war activists calling themselves "the Citizen's Commission to Investigate the FBI" broke into an FBI field office in Pennsylvania and stole reams of files on agency "black ops" at home. What they found, they leaked to various media outlets, and soon Americans became familiar with the ungainly term "COINTELPRO." COINTELPRO, for "Counterintelligence Program," went far beyond intelligence gathering—embracing burglaries, wiretaps, attempts to provoke street violence between members of targeted groups, and covert actions designed to topple movement leaders by, among other things, tagging them with "snitch jackets"—forged documents containing trumped-up evidence of cooperation with the FBI and police.

The program had begun in 1956 with a focus on the U.S. Communist Party, but soon broadened to include white and black nationalist groups, and eventually "New Left" organizations. The bureau had an expansive definition of "subversive." Among its targets were liberal Antioch College and Martin Luther King's Southern Christian Leadership Conference, which the FBI termed a black nationalist "hate group."[8]

Some of the FBI's actions during this period had the flavor of high school pranks, albeit potentially murderous ones. In "Operation

Hoodwink," carried out between the fall of 1966 and the summer of 1968, agents purporting to be Communist Party members sent insulting letters to mob figures Carlo Gambino and Santo Trafficante, among others, hoping to "provoke a dispute between La Cosa Nostra and the Communist Party, USA."[9] Other schemes were less amusing. On one occasion, FBI agents kidnapped an anti-war activist to intimidate him into silence.[10] On another, agents bugged Martin Luther King's hotel rooms and sent him a tape containing evidence of his extramarital affairs. With the tape was a letter saying "King, there is one thing left for you to do. You know what it is"—that is, commit suicide.[11] King was only the most famous of the FBI targets on whom this sort of gutter tactic was employed.

A few months after COINTELPRO became a household word, former Defense Department analyst Daniel Ellsberg began leaking to the *New York Times* and the *Washington Post* portions of a classified DOD history of the Vietnam War. Prepared at the behest of then Defense secretary Robert McNamara after he'd begun to lose faith in the war, the Pentagon Papers included details of sordid behavior on the part of the Kennedy and Johnson administrations. Among other revelations, the papers showed that JFK was complicit in the military coup that ended in South Vietnamese president Ngo Dinh Diem's assassination, and that the Johnson administration had lied about the Gulf of Tonkin incident to get congressional authorization for the war.

Nothing in the Pentagon Papers directly implicated Nixon. Yet, the Nixon team feared such leaks would undermine their efforts to secure "peace with honor" in Vietnam.[12] And so the White House "Plumbers" were born. Ex-CIA operative E. Howard Hunt and former FBI agent G. Gordon Liddy warmed up by breaking into Ellsberg's psychiatrist's office, hoping to find dirt on the former defense analyst. Then on June 17, 1972, the Plumbers, led by Liddy, botched a burglary of the Democratic National Committee's headquarters at the Watergate office complex. Over the next two years, the story behind that break-in gradually emerged from the courts, congressional hearings, and the press— leading to Nixon's resignation.

Along the way, the fight over Nixon's presidency kicked up still more dirt, sullying Nixon's image, and that of the presidency as a whole. When it came to light in 1973 that Nixon and White House Counsel

John Dean contemplated ordering Internal Revenue Service audits of Democratic contributors (in Dean's words, "the use of the available federal machinery to screw our political enemies"[13]), *Time* magazine revealed that this had been common practice in the Kennedy and Johnson administrations. At Kennedy's instigation in 1961, the IRS had set up a "strike force" aimed at groups opposing the administration.[14] Perhaps it was not mere bad luck that led to Nixon himself getting audited three times during the Kennedy-Johnson years.[15]

And as the House Judiciary Committee geared up for impeachment proceedings, it had yet another revelation to consider. In 1973, Air Force major Hal Knight came forward with information that he had helped President Nixon conceal a 14-month bombing campaign against neutral Cambodia in 1969 and 1970. Without any authorization to expand the war, in March 1969, Nixon ordered U.S. planes to target North Vietnamese base camps in Cambodian territory along the border with Vietnam. The campaign, which included nearly 4,000 sorties dropping over 100,000 tons of bombs between March 1969 and May 1970, was code-named "Operation Menu," with the various phases of the campaign going by the monikers "Breakfast," "Lunch," "Snack," "Dinner," and "Dessert." The high-altitude, indiscriminate bombing runs caused massive civilian casualties among Cambodian farmers.[16] The president kept the bombing secret not only from Congress and the public, but even from Secretary of State William Rogers, the secretary of the air force, and the air force chief of staff.[17] Even the classified records of targets selected were falsified. Nixon repeatedly ordered Chairman of the Joint Chiefs of Staff Earle Wheeler not to reveal the campaign "to any member of Congress." When the facts about the secret bombing became public, Nixon was unapologetic; there had been no secrecy with regard to anyone "who had any right to know or need to know."[18]

Rep. John Conyers (D-MI) drafted an article of impeachment based on concealment of the bombing "in derogation of the power of the Congress to declare war." That article failed to make it into the final bill of particulars, which focused on obstruction of justice and attempting to misuse the CIA to interfere with the Watergate investigation.

Ironically, Nixon had on the whole proved less successful than Kennedy and Johnson at bending federal intelligence agencies to his will.

The CIA had provided false identification, disguises, and cameras for the burglary of Ellsberg's psychiatrist's office; but the agency balked at the administration's request that it lean on the FBI to quash the Watergate investigation for "national security" reasons. The recording of Nixon and Haldeman plotting to involve the CIA became the "smoking gun" that led to the president's resignation when the Supreme Court forced him to turn over the tape.

Three Branches, After All

That case, *U.S. v. Nixon*, was one of three key cases in which the Court stood up against unconstrained presidential power. A newly assertive Court would be joined by a newly assertive Congress, in a halting attempt to right the constitutional balance.

Judicial Pushback

First, in *New York Times Co. v. United States*, the Court rebuffed Nixon's attempt to stop publication of the Pentagon Papers.[19] Invoking "the constitutional power of the President over the conduct of foreign affairs and his authority as Commander-in-Chief," the administration argued that the president had the power to suppress "publication of information whose disclosure would endanger the national security."[20] On June 30, 1971, barely two weeks after the first Pentagon Papers excerpts were published, the Court held that the government had not met the heavy burden the First Amendment imposes on attempted prior restraints of political speech.

The Nixon team feared that exposure of the papers would undermine the war effort and threaten the president's ability to prevent damaging national security leaks. Worse, the papers' release was a threat to the presidency itself. In an Oval Office meeting discussing what to do about the leak, White House Chief of Staff H. R. Haldeman warned Nixon, in the passage quoted at the beginning of this chapter, that the release of the papers would undermine the public's perception of "the implicit infallibility of presidents."[21] Haldeman was right: the Court's decision helped clear the way for increased public scrutiny of the executive branch and provided a valuable lesson in the perils of trusting government too much.

A year later, in *United States v. United States District Court* (the *"Keith"* case), the Court rejected another claim of limitless executive power.[22] In *Keith*, three left-wing radicals charged with conspiracy to destroy government property sought disclosure of information on electronic surveillance that the attorney general had ordered without a warrant. The administration claimed the surveillance was lawful, asserting a presidential power to order warrantless wiretaps on anyone he suspected of threatening national security. In oral argument before the Court, Assistant Attorney General Robert C. Mardian declared, "Now, certainly neither this President nor any prior President has authorized electronic surveillance to monitor the activities of an opposite political group." Similarly, in its brief, the administration suggested that any concerns about possible abuse of wiretap authority should be assuaged by the fact the attorney general would personally approve each wiretap application.[23] At the time, of course, the attorney general was John Mitchell, who was neck deep in political wiretapping and would, less than five months after the case was argued, approve G. Gordon Liddy's plan to bug Democratic National Committee headquarters at the Watergate Hotel.

In fact, the Watergate burglars were arrested the same week the Court handed down the *Keith* decision, which rejected the administration's claim of unchecked surveillance powers. In *Keith*, the Court left open the question of warrantless wiretapping in cases involving a foreign power—that question would later be addressed by Congress with the Foreign Intelligence Surveillance Act. As for surveillance of homegrown security threats, the Court noted, with more wisdom than perhaps it recognized at the time, that "the Fourth Amendment does not contemplate the executive officers of government as neutral and disinterested magistrates."[24] Preservation of Fourth Amendment freedoms demanded prior judicial approval.

But it was the third case, *U.S. v. Nixon*, that would bring the age of the Heroic Presidency to a close.[25] In the spring of 1974, Nixon had refused to release selected Oval Office audiotapes to special prosecutor Leon Jaworski, who sought them as evidence against the Watergate conspirators (Nixon himself being named as an "unindicted co-conspirator" in the case). Resisting discovery of the tapes, Nixon claimed "absolute privilege." He could decide for himself what to disclose and what to withhold:

"The president is answerable to the Nation, but not to the courts."[26] In earlier testimony before a Senate committee, Attorney General Richard Kleindienst (Mitchell had by then resigned) asserted that the privilege attached to all 2.5 million employees of the executive branch and could be invoked even against an impeachment inquiry.[27]

On July 24, 1974, a unanimous Court rejected Nixon's claim. Though it allowed for the existence of a qualified executive privilege and recognized the need for deference in national security matters, it held that in this case, the need for evidence in a criminal trial outweighed the president's interest in confidentiality. Two weeks later, Nixon resigned.

But the release of the tapes had a broader effect still. In his memoirs, Nixon wrote that "the American myth that Presidents are always presidential, that they sit in the Oval Office talking in lofty and quotable phrases, will probably never die—and probably never should because it reflects an important aspect of the American character."[28] Yet, the Nixon tapes did much to kill that myth, showing that presidents can be foul-mouthed, petty, paranoid—and lawless. With that revelation, the heroic image of the presidency went down hissing like the Wicked Witch of the West.

A Resurgent Congress

Congress joined the Court in its attempt to confine presidential power. The legislative reforms of the Watergate era and its aftermath fell into two broad categories: those that restricted the president's unilateral powers and those that imposed on the executive branch obligations of openness and disclosure.

Even before Watergate, Congress had begun restoring important legal protections. In 1971, Congress passed, and Nixon signed, the Non-Detention Act, which repealed the emergency detention provisions of the McCarran Internal Security Act. That act, passed over Truman's veto in 1950, gave the president authority, in "an internal security emergency," to lock up subversives. After the McCarran act passed, FBI Director J. Edgar Hoover sent the White House a plan contemplating the "permanent detention" of 12,000 suspects, almost all of them American citizens.[29]

In Nixon's first term, Japanese American groups, civil libertarians, and, surprisingly enough, Nixon's own Justice Department, pushed for a repeal of the detention law. The new law provided that "no citizen shall be imprisoned or otherwise detained by the United States except pursuant to an Act of Congress."[30] In that case, Congress acted with the support of the Nixon administration; not so with most of the other reforms of the period.

In 1973, a Senate special committee identified 470 statutory provisions that delegated broad authority to the president in times of national emergency. With four open-ended presidential declarations of national emergency dating back to 1933 still in effect, most of those provisions remained at the president's disposal.[31] The National Emergencies Act of 1974 decreed that all the statutory delegations of emergency power would expire by 1976, and it provided a one-year limit to all future emergency powers—shorter, if Congress ended the state of emergency by joint resolution. With the Impoundment Control Act, passed the same year, Congress moved to reassert its power of the purse, putting curbs on the president's ability to override congressional spending decisions.

Congress also took a number of measures to reassert control over the power to go to war, most importantly with the War Powers Resolution. Passed in 1973 over Nixon's veto, the WPR attempted "to fulfill the intent of the framers of the Constitution of the United States and insure that the collective judgment of both the Congress and the President will apply to the introduction of United States Armed Forces into hostilities."[32] In essence, the WPR provides that if the president introduces U.S. armed forces into hostilities or "situations where imminent involvement in hostilities is clearly indicated by the circumstances," he must remove those forces within 60 days (90, if necessary to ensure safe withdrawal) absent a congressional declaration of war, specific statutory authorization for the action, or a situation in which Congress is physically unable to meet because of an armed attack on the United States.[33] The Hughes-Ryan Act, passed the next year, sought to rein in the president's ability to order covert actions unilaterally, requiring notification to select committees of Congress when such actions were undertaken.[34]

Congress had also moved to limit the president's powers to classify information. In this, it faced strong opposition from two young Ford administration aides, Chief of Staff Donald Rumsfeld and his deputy Dick Cheney. In 1966, Congress had passed a Freedom of Information Act that was essentially toothless: through a variety of tactics, executive branch officials managed to withhold vast amounts of material that the act required to be provided at citizens' request. In 1974, Congress passed amendments to the act designed to overcome executive intransigence, most importantly, strengthening judicial review of executive branch determinations that records are properly classified. At Rumsfeld and Cheney's urging, President Ford vetoed the bill on October 17, 1974.[35] A month later, Congress overrode Ford's veto.

Finally, with the Foreign Intelligence Surveillance Act of 1978, Congress took up the Supreme Court's invitation, in the *Keith* case, to set up a framework for national security surveillance involving Americans at home.[36] Under FISA, such surveillance would require the executive branch to secure a warrant from a special court. The standard for granting FISA warrants was a lenient one, but since it at least required the approval of an independent branch of government, FISA put an important check on the executive's ability to conduct domestic spying under the rubric of national security.

Like most periods of reformist fervor, the post-Watergate era generated its share of ill-considered schemes.[37] In some cases, Congress and the courts went too far, in others not far enough, to right the constitutional balance. Yet, by the mid-1970s, for the first time in decades, the country had a Congress and a judiciary awake to the problem of unchecked executive power.

A Culture of (Justified) Distrust

Important though they were, the legislative and judicial reforms of the 1970s were only a reflection of broader changes in the American attitude toward executive power. In *How We Got Here*, his cultural history of the 1970s, David Frum describes the public mood after the last decade of the Heroic Presidency:

> Of the three presidents after 1960, the first stood exposed as a womanizing rogue who abused the FBI and IRS, who was implicated in assassinations and attempted assassinations, and who wiretapped Martin Luther King, Jr. The second owed his political career to stuffed ballot boxes, had corruptly enriched himself, had lied the country into Vietnam, and had also wiretapped King. The

third had orchestrated a campaign of lies to cover up multiple crimes, had chiseled on his income tax, had chosen a corrupt governor as his vice president, and had bankrolled his campaigns with illegal corporate gifts. "I am not a crook"? It was looking like a good working assumption that everybody was a crook.[38]

New Revelations

Even after Nixon's departure, there was no respite from the horror show of continuing disclosures. In 1974, investigative reporter Seymour Hersh revealed in the *New York Times* that under pressure from presidents Johnson and Nixon, the CIA had been running something called Operation CHAOS, a domestic surveillance and espionage program aimed at anti-war groups.[39] Despite the fact that the agency itself had concluded that the New Left and Black Power groups it targeted were not controlled or manipulated by foreign governments—and that the program violated the CIA's charter—Operation CHAOS continued until it was publicly exposed.[40]

The disclosure of the CHAOS program, coming as it did after the steady stream of early 1970s reports of federal abuses, prompted the formation of the Senate Select Committee to Study Governmental Operations with Respect to Intelligence Activities, chaired by Idaho senator Frank Church.[41] In 1975 and 1976, the Church Committee published 14 reports on CIA and FBI abuses. The committee uncovered new details on everything from army and National Security Agency spying, to the wiretapping of Martin Luther King, to the Kennedy administration's attempts to get the Mafia to assassinate Castro. In a report published in April of America's bicentennial year, the committee concluded:

> For decades Congress and the courts as well as the press and the public have accepted the notion that the control of intelligence activities was the exclusive prerogative of the Chief Executive and his surrogates. The exercise of this power was not questioned or even inquired into by outsiders. Indeed, at times the power was seen as flowing not from the law, but as inherent in the Presidency. Whatever the theory, the fact was that intelligence activities were essentially exempted from the normal system of checks and balances.

Such Executive power, not founded in law or checked by Congress or the courts, contained the seeds of abuse and its growth was to be expected.[42]

All told, this did not make for a political environment that encouraged confidence in government. By the mid-1970s, it had become clear that trust in government was a sucker's game, and there were far fewer suckers around.

Just Because You're Paranoid . . .

In 1964, 62 percent of respondents to the University of Michigan's National Election Studies survey affirmed that they trusted the federal government to do what was right "most of the time." That number dropped to 34 during the year of Nixon's resignation, and bottomed out at 23 percent at the tail end of the 1970s.[43] Asked to pick their poison as to who should take the lead on policy matters, in the 1970s Americans answered, Congress. Where 61 percent had agreed in 1959 that "the president is in the best position to see what the country needs," by 1977 the numbers had nearly reversed: 58 percent of Americans agreed that "it is up to Congress to decide what is to be done" and only 26 percent stubbornly remained presidentialists. By 1975, even children had begun to display a grown-up attitude toward presidential power. Grade-schoolers of the 1970s no longer viewed the president as an unambiguously benevolent leader.[44]

In popular entertainment, distrust often manifested itself as ridicule. Previously, in the age of the Heroic Presidency, even comedians had felt obliged to portray the president positively. Comedian Eddie Cantor asked FDR's approval for a woefully tame 1934 radio bit where "Dr. Roosevelt" heals "Mrs. America."[45] Vietnam and Watergate put an end to that sort of deference. "Final Days," a skit from *Saturday Night Live*'s first season, portrayed Richard Nixon as a raving loon. A drunk Nixon, played by Dan Aykroyd, wanders the White House, calling Kissinger a "Christ-killer," praying for a heart attack, and shouting to JFK's portrait: "They're gonna find out about you, too. The president! Having sex with women within these very walls. That *never* happened when Dick Nixon was in the White House! Never! Never! Never!"

Now presidents would seek entertainers' favor, instead of the other way around. In April 1976, Gerald Ford's press secretary, Ron Nessen, hosted *SNL*, with the president himself contributing the opening line: "Live from New York, it's Saturday Night!" To embarrass the administration, *SNL's* writers kicked the vulgarity up a notch, including parody commercials featuring a douche called "Autumn Fizz" and a jam called "Painful Rectal Itch."[46]

Pop culture increasingly reflected an anti-government sensibility that at times verged on the paranoid. Thrillers like *The Parallax View* (1974), *Three Days of the Condor* (1975), and *Capricorn One* (1978)—in which federal officials fake a Mars landing and then attempt to cover it up by killing the astronauts—all portrayed a common enemy: the U.S. government. In a 2000 study called "Government Goes Down the Tube," researchers at the Center for Media and Public Affairs looked at portrayals of public officials over four decades of American television. "Television increasingly focused on the dark side of political life after the mid-1970s," they wrote; from 1975 to 2005, "not a single show presented the political system as functioning to uphold the public good rather than private interests."[47]

A Newly Empowered Press

Vietnam and Watergate wrought equally significant changes in American journalism. Bob Woodward and Carl Bernstein, the reporters who helped break the Watergate story, showed a rising generation of journalists that exposing abuses of power could turn reporters into movie stars (If you were lucky, Robert Redford; not so lucky, Dustin Hoffman). The inflated self-regard some journalists displayed was irritating, to be sure—as when *Washington Post* executive editor Ben Bradlee boasted that "the press won on Watergate."[48] Yet, it was, in a way, Madison's theory of ambition counteracting ambition applied to the so-called fourth estate. By serving their own interests, fame-hungry reporters would serve the public's as well.

Recall Bradlee's behavior some 10 years earlier. Chummy with the Kennedys, intoxicated by Camelot, the *Post* reporter refrained from writing up the information he had on illegal wiretaps of steel executives. The brothers viewed "Benjy" as reliable enough to feel safe joking about it in front of him. Reporters in the White House press corps were also willing to hush up Kennedy's womanizing, which reflected a sexual appetite that rivaled Motley Crüe on world tour. One could argue that Kennedy's affairs were his own affair, but given that the president shared a mistress with Chicago mob boss Sam Giancana, it's hard to maintain that no issues of public concern were involved.[49]

After Vietnam and Watergate, few reporters would follow Kennedy pal Bradlee and sit on a scoop, regardless of which party it would hurt. Aided by the FOIA, post-Watergate investigative reporters would make it harder for presidents to hide corruption, incompetence, and abuses of power. The press's changed attitude could be seen in the sorts of questions that the White House press corps put to the president. A 2006 study sampling presidential press conferences from Eisenhower through Clinton finds that "the Nixon era marks the beginning of an extended period of increasingly vigorous questioning," with deference declining and reporters growing more assertive and adversarial.[50]

Like the declining trust numbers, the newly adversarial journalism gave rise to much handwringing on the part of those earnest souls who saw muckraking as an impediment to government doing great works. In books with titles like *Feeding Frenzy: How Attack Journalism Has Transformed American Politics*, and *Spiral of Cynicism: The Press and the Public Good*, we continue to hear complaints that the cynicism stoked by scandal-driven journalism has made it "impossible to govern."

The governing class tends to agree. When Bob Woodward requested an interview with George H. W. Bush in 1998, Bush declined, writing, "I think Watergate and the Vietnam War are the two things that moved beltway journalism into this aggressive, intrusive, 'take no prisoners' kind of reporting that I can now say I find offensive."[51] No doubt that kind of reporting *was* offensive to people in power; but it helped expose and deter presidential abuses.

How Conservatives Learned to Stop Worrying and Love the Imperial Presidency

In a 1984 speech, looking back on his experience as a top Ford administration official, Dick Cheney complained that during the 1970s legislators no longer wanted "to help presidents accrue power in the White House—so that they could achieve good works in the society." Instead,

Congress sought "to limit future presidents so that they would not abuse power the way it was alleged some had abused power in the past."[52] "Alleged" was a nice touch.

Cheney's remarks reflected the enormous ideological shift that had occurred in the Nixon years. In the 1970s, while liberals were having second thoughts about the need for a powerful, activist presidency, conservatives were warming up to the idea. Nixon had hardly governed as a conservative, but in some ways—serving as "tribune" of the "silent majority," aggressively impounding funds and asserting control over administrative agencies—he showed conservatives how the office could be used to serve their political ends.

Still, the right's growing affinity for presidential power was at odds with the movement's political heritage. It was conservatives, after all, who, troubled by the growth of presidential power during FDR's 12-year reign, had led the fight for the Twenty-Second Amendment, limiting presidential terms.[53] And it was conservatives who had the best claim to be heirs to the Founders' views on human nature and concentrated power. Russell Kirk, whose 1953 book *The Conservative Mind* helped galvanize the postwar right, insisted that "the need for prudent restraints upon power and upon human passions" was a core conservative principle:

> The conservative endeavors to so limit and balance political power that anarchy or tyranny may not arise. In every age, nevertheless, men and women are tempted to overthrow the limitations upon power, for the sake of some fancied temporary advantage. It is characteristic of the radical that he thinks of power as a force for good—so long as the power falls into his hands. . . .
>
> Knowing human nature for a mixture of good and evil, the conservative does not put his trust in mere benevolence. Constitutional restrictions, political checks and balances, adequate enforcement of the laws, the old intricate web of restraints upon will and appetite—these the conservative approves as instruments of freedom and order.[54]

Almost to a man, the intellectuals who had coalesced around William F. Buckley's *National Review* associated presidential power with liberal activism and saw Congress as the "conservative" branch. In 1960 *NR* senior editor Willmoore Kendall, who had been one of Buckley's professors at Yale, made the case for Congress in an article titled "The Two Majorities." Kendall viewed Congress's deliberative and incrementalist character as "a highly necessary corrective against the bias toward quixotism inherent in our presidential elections."[55] In 1967, Russell Kirk and coauthor James McClellan praised the late Robert A. Taft, "Mr. Conservative," for insisting that war had to be a last resort, threatening as it did to "make the American President a virtual dictator, diminish the constitutional powers of Congress, contract civil liberties, injure the habitual self-reliance and self-government of the American people, distort the economy, sink the federal government in debt, [and] break in upon private and public morality."[56] Even so ardent a cold warrior as *NR*'s James Burnham wrote a book, *Congress and the American Tradition*, warning that the erosion of congressional power risked bringing about "plebiscitary despotism for the United States in place of constitutional government, and thus the end of political liberty."[57]

Senator Goldwater, who represented postwar conservatives' highest hopes for political success, could sound as extremist in opposition to presidential power as he did on other matters involving the defense of liberty. In his 1964 campaign manifesto "My Case for the Republican Party," Goldwater wrote:

We hear praise of a power-wielding, arm-twisting President who "gets his program through Congress" by knowing the use of power. Throughout the course of history, there have been many other such wielders of power. There have even been dictators who regularly held plebiscites, in which their dictatorships were approved by an Ivory-soap-like percentage of the electorate. But their countries were not free, nor can any country remain free under such despotic power. Some of the current worship of powerful executives may come from those who admire strength and accomplishment of any sort. Others hail the display of Presidential strength . . . simply because they approve of the *result* reached by the use of power. This is nothing less than the totalitarian philosophy that the end justifies the means. . . . If ever there was a philosophy of government totally at war with that of the Founding Fathers, it is this one.[58]

Goldwater's 1964 bid for the presidency failed disastrously, but out of the wreckage emerged a new conservative hero. In Ronald Reagan's famous televised speech supporting Goldwater, Reagan identified a number of political figures who would "trade freedom for security" and whose philosophy threatened to take America "down to the antheap of totalitarianism." Among them was "Senator Fulbright [who] has said at Stanford University that the Constitution is outmoded. He referred to the president as our moral teacher and our leader, and he said he is hobbled in his task by the restrictions in power imposed on him by this antiquated document. He must be freed so that he can do for us what he knows is best."[59]

Of course, Reagan and Goldwater also advocated a hyperaggressive posture in the struggle against the Soviet Union, a position that sat uneasily with their distrust of presidential power.[60] Rollback of communist gains demanded presidential activism abroad, and those demands began to weaken conservative opposition to powerful presidents. In an article examining congressional voting patterns on presidential power, political scientist J. Richard Piper found that "what erosion occurred in conservative support for a congressionally-centered federal system [from 1937 to 1968] occurred most frequently on foreign policy matters and among interventionist antiCommunists."[61] Even so, Piper noted, congressional conservatives of the period "were more likely to favor curbing presidential powers than were moderates or liberals."[62]

In 1966, conservative opposition to the activist presidency remained strong enough that Willmoore Kendall and George W. Carey could write that "the two camps [i.e., conservatives and liberals] appear to have made permanent and well-nigh irreversible commitments on the President-versus-Congress issue." What would happen, Kendall and Carey wondered, if the future brought a changed political alignment: conservative presidents and liberal Congresses? "Would liberal and conservative spokesmen . . . be able to switch sides? That, we may content ourselves with saying, would now take some doing!"[63]

In fact, the two camps did switch sides not long after Kendall and Carey wrote those words. The 1970s brought increasing tension over foreign policy and, perhaps more importantly, the emergence of what political analyst Kevin Phillips called "the Emerging Republican Majority" in the Electoral College. Right-wing *ressentiment* over Nixon's downfall helped drive the shift; as right-wing writer M. Stanton Evans later quipped, "I didn't like Nixon *until* Watergate."[64] By the 1970s, prominent conservatives had begun to see the *executive* as the conservative branch, and they set to work developing a case for the Imperial Presidency.

Three months after Nixon resigned, *National Review* featured a cover story by Jeffrey Hart, "The Presidency: Shifting Conservative Perspectives?" Hart began by noting the "settled and received view" among American conservatives, who "have been all but unanimously opposed to a strong and activist presidency." It was time, Hart argued, to rethink that view. Foreshadowing the conservative embrace of unitary executive theory in the 1980s, Hart suggested that the growth of the regulatory state demanded a powerful president who could hold the bureaucracy in check. Even more important, according to Hart, was the emergence of a "fourth branch of government" in the form of an activist, left-leaning press. Only a centrist or conservative president willing to use the bully pulpit could compete with the liberal media in the fight for American public opinion.[65]

While right-wing intellectuals made the case for presidential dominance, conservatives in Congress worked to defend and enhance the president's powers. As Piper noted, of "thirty-seven major roll call [votes] concerning presidential powers of greatest long-term significance [from 1968 to 1986] conservatives took the most propresidential power position . . . often (as on the item veto, impoundment, and war powers) contradicting conservative positions of the past."[66]

Another factor in the ideological shift was the growing influence of the neoconservatives, zealous cold warriors who came over from the left and "took many of their conceptions of presidential government with them when they left the liberal fold."[67] In 1974, the "godfather" of the neocons, Irving Kristol, charged (not without reason) that much of the ongoing liberal hostility toward the strong presidency should be understood as distrust of strong *Republican* presidents. In any event, Kristol wrote, the Imperial Presidency was "here to stay," and there was "no reason why this latest version of the democratic republic shouldn't be a reasonably decent form of government."[68]

By the Reagan era, prominent conservatives were calling for a repeal of presidential term limits, and for scrapping various post-Watergate reforms that they believed had neutered the executive branch. The new conventional wisdom on the right held that the real threat to separation of powers lay not in an Imperial Presidency, but in an Imperial *Congress*.[69] In 1988, Rep. Newt Gingrich (R-GA), then a mere backbencher with a gleam in his eye, contributed a foreword to the Heritage Foundation book of that name. In it, Gingrich quoted the Founders on the dangers of concentrating all powers within a single branch, and declared, "The 100th Congress approaches the despotic institution about which James Madison and Thomas Jefferson wrote."[70]

The Post-Imperial Presidency?

Whatever one thought of the trend toward congressional assertiveness, conservatives were right that in the immediate post-Watergate era, the presidency appeared much diminished. It was hard to maintain reverence for the office with Chevy Chase's Gerald Ford stapling his ear, stabbing himself with a letter opener, and pratfalling all over the set of *Saturday Night Live* every week. Pundits and political scientists began to speak of the "post-imperial presidency."[71]

Even after Ronald Reagan restored an air of competence and command to the office, many continued to lament the state of the American presidency—and conservatives still led the lamenters. After 1986, much of the right's ire focused on the separation-of-powers fight forced by the Iran-Contra affair. The Reagan administration provoked a constitutional crisis when it sold weapons to Iran in exchange for the release of hostages and then diverted some of the proceeds to the Nicaraguan Contras. In the process, the administration violated a clear statutory ban on "supporting, directly or indirectly, military or paramilitary operations in Nicaragua by any nation, group, organization, movement, or individual."[72] However desirable it might have been to combat communist influence in the Western Hemisphere, defending the administration's behavior was an odd stance for self-described constitutionalists to take. In Iran-Contra, the administration had attempted in secret to combine purse and sword within the executive branch, in defiance of the Framers' insistence that those powers should never fall into the same hands.

Conservatives also decried the War Powers Resolution as another instance of an "Imperial Congress" tying the president's hands. Yet, it's hard to understand why the WPR upset them so. By implicitly allowing the president the ability to launch a war and prosecute it for at least 60 days, the resolution cedes more power to the president than the Constitution allows. Nor has any president felt much constrained by the law. Since its passage, the WPR has run aground on presidential intransigence and judicial unwillingness to enforce it.[73]

Indeed, throughout the 1980s and 1990s, presidents made war more or less at will. On October 25, 1983, 48 hours after the truck bombing that killed 241 marines stationed in Lebanon, President Reagan ordered some 2,000 U.S. troops into the tiny island nation of Grenada, to overthrow a communist-aligned military government.[74] In December 1989, his successor, George H. W. Bush, overthrew the Noriega government in Panama without congressional authorization, in the rather defensively titled "Operation Just Cause."

President Bush did secure congressional authorization for the 1991 Gulf War, yet for all intents and purposes, that authorization merely ratified the president's unilateral decision. The president alone had made the decision to send U.S. troops into Saudi Arabia after Saddam Hussein's invasion of Kuwait. He alone decided that Iraqi aggression would not stand, and insisted that no authorization was needed to send half a million Americans into battle. Dick Cheney, who had returned to the executive branch to serve as Bush's secretary of defense, told the Senate Armed Services Committee in December 1990 that the president had all the constitutional power he required to expel Iraqi forces from Kuwait. In private, Cheney advised Bush that even asking for support conceded too much to Congress. (Years later, Cheney confirmed that even if Congress refused to authorize the war, he would have advised the president to go ahead anyway.)[75] Cheney's Pentagon fed the war fever with disinformation, warning that a quarter of a million Iraqi troops and 1,500 tanks were massed at the Saudi border, ready to invade. Yet, contemporaneous commercial satellite photos of the region purchased by the *St. Petersburg Times* told a different story. They showed nothing but desert in the areas where the Iraqi buildup was supposedly taking place.[76]

Given the crisis atmosphere promoted by the administration, it's surprising that the Gulf War vote was as close as it was; Congress authorized the use of force by votes of 250 to 183 in the House and 52 to 47 in the Senate. Following the passage of the use-of-force resolution, the president declared that "as a democracy, we've debated this issue openly and in good faith."[77] The extent of that good faith can be judged by the president's behavior on the campaign trail in 1992. At one appearance, he told a Texas audience, "I didn't have to get permission from some old goat in Congress to kick Saddam Hussein out of Kuwait."[78] As his successor's behavior would show, that attitude was a bipartisan one.

The Clinton Years: Arrogance of Power Redux

Strange as it might now seem, opponents of the Imperial Presidency had reasons for cautious optimism upon Bill Clinton's accession to the presidency in January 1993. As the first Democrat elected to the nation's highest office in 16 years, the new president belonged to the political party that had since Watergate and Vietnam sought to rein in the executive's ability to conduct foreign policy without congressional authorization and oversight. Clinton had come of age during Vietnam, a war he vehemently opposed, in part because it was undeclared. He began his political life working on the Senate Foreign Relations Committee for Senator Fulbright, who by then had become one of the Imperial Presidency's sharpest critics.[79]

Grandiose Visions of Leadership

By the time Clinton took office in 1993, the prevailing rationale for the Imperial Presidency had vanished with the collapse of Soviet communism. Conditions were ideal for a more modest approach to presidential leadership, one that recognized constitutional limits to unilateral action.

Of course, the Clintons retained the Progressive Era fascination with the executive branch as the catalyst of moral leadership. On the campaign trail, Governor Clinton promised a "New Covenant" between the government and the governed—a metaphor that had the state stepping in for Yahweh. First Lady Hillary Rodham Clinton proclaimed that America suffered from "a sleeping sickness of the soul," a deep existential angst stemming from our inability to redefine "who we are as human beings in this postmodern age." To heal our spiritual wounds, we'd need "a new politics of meaning" engendered by bold executive action.[80]

After the collapse of the Clinton Health Security Act and the Republican sweep of Congress in 1994, the "politics of meaning" gave way to the politics of the poll-tested microinitiative, courtesy of presidential adviser Dick Morris. Faced with a legislative majority opposed to most of his policies, President Clinton also relied on executive orders to work his will. In 1998, after tobacco control legislation failed in the Senate, Clinton laid the groundwork for successful prosecution of the industry by ordering federal agencies to gather data on teen smoking habits. Later, he nationalized millions of acres of western land by executive fiat, over the objections of Congress and the state governors.[81]

Arrogance Abroad

In foreign affairs, President Clinton was able to operate with still fewer checks on his power. And if he had learned anything from his mentor Senator Fulbright's critique of foreign policy crusades led by "high-minded men bent on the regeneration of the human race," it didn't show.[82] In mid-1994, Clinton prepared to invade Haiti to restore ousted president Bertrand Aristide to power. He did so while asserting that he was not "constitutionally mandated" to get congressional approval for a 20,000-troop invasion of a tiny island nation that represented no threat, imminent or otherwise, to America's security.[83] Likewise, in 1994 Clinton unilaterally ordered air strikes in Bosnia and in 1995 ordered 20,000 troops there to enforce a peacekeeping agreement.

Though some Republicans objected to Clinton's usurpation of congressional prerogatives, their leadership, for the most part, did not. On June 7, 1995, the House narrowly voted down a bill introduced by Rep. Henry Hyde (R-IL) that would have repealed the War Powers Resolution. In endorsing the measure, then Speaker Newt Gingrich urged the

House Republicans to "increase the power of President Clinton. . . . I want to strengthen the current Democratic President because he is President of the United States."[84]

But President Clinton had all the power he needed to conduct presidential wars. Operation Allied Force, the air war carried out over Serbia in 1999, was the largest commitment of American fighting forces and material since the Gulf War. As the first war since Vietnam to continue beyond 60 days without statutory authorization, it also demonstrated that repealing the War Powers Resolution would have been entirely superfluous.[85]

U.S.-led NATO air forces flew over 37,000 sorties during the conflict, an average of 486 missions per day. But, echoing Harry Truman's "police action" word games, administration officials refused to characterize U.S. actions as war.

Given that the United States was dropping bombs on Serbia and its people, how could we be said not to be at war? White House spokesman Joe Lockhart explained that, much like the president's definition of the word "is," before the Starr grand jury, it all depended on what your definition of the word "war" was:

Q: Is the President ready to call this a low-grade war?

LOCKHART: No. Next question.

Q: Why not?

LOCKHART: Because we view it as a conflict.

Q: How can you say that it's not war?

LOCKHART: Because it doesn't meet the definition as we
    define it.[86]

However you defined it, this large-scale application of military force wasn't authorized by Congress. On April 28, 1999, the House voted no on declaring war, 427 to 2; no on authorizing the use of ground troops, 249 to 180; and no on authorizing the president to continue airstrikes, 213 to 213. Because the House voted down legislation that would have authorized the air war, this was not simply another war carried out amid congressional silence. Congress had considered and *rejected* authorization—but Clinton continued in defiance of congressional will.[87] As National Security Council spokesman David Leavy put it:

"There's broad support for this campaign among the American people, so we sort of just blew by" the House votes.[88]

The end of the Cold War should have brought the era of crisis government to a close. Yet, it did not end the president's incentive to gin up emergencies when he finds himself in political trouble. President Clinton's behavior during the Starr investigation and the impeachment debates makes that clear. On the day the president's testimony before the Starr grand jury was released to the public, Clinton gave a speech—in the midst of a booming economy—proclaiming that the United States faced the greatest economic crisis in 50 years.[89]

Wagging the Dog?

Far more troubling were what some have called the "Wag the Dog" bombings, after the 1997 film starring Robert De Niro and Dustin Hoffman. In the movie, the Dick Morrisesque spin doctor played by De Niro diverts attention from a presidential sex scandal by enlisting a Hollywood producer (played by Dustin Hoffman) to create a fake war. Unlike the Hollywood version, though, the Washington production used real missiles.

The third week of August 1998 was a tumultuous one for President Clinton. On Monday, he went on national television to admit his affair with Monica Lewinsky; the president's nonapology wasn't well received. On Thursday, with the media reporting that independent counsel Kenneth Starr had obtained a DNA sample from the president, and Lewinsky starting her second round of testimony before the grand jury, President Clinton ordered surprise missile strikes on Sudan and Afghanistan.

The Sudan strike soon proved to be an early case of missing WMDs. The administration refused to release the evidence it claimed to have relied on for its assertion that the Sudanese pharmaceutical plant targeted in the strike manufactured nerve gas. Independent tests conducted by the head of Boston University's chemistry department confirmed, contrary to the administration's claims, that no nerve gas precursors could be found in the soil surrounding the factory.[90] The Clinton administration later issued an order unfreezing the plant owner's assets, rather than coming forward with evidence supporting the owner's purported connection to Osama bin Laden.

Absent the dubious timing, one might, with post-9/11 hindsight, see the missile strike as a laudable attempt to do something about a gathering threat. As it was, apart from shifting the news cycle toward less prurient matters, the administration managed only to knock over some empty tents in Afghanistan and wipe out an important source of medicine in a desperately poor country.

If the timing of the Afghanistan and Sudan strikes was suspicious, the timing of the "Desert Fox" airstrikes on Iraq could hardly have been more so. The Desert Fox operation began on the eve of the House impeachment debate. President Clinton asserted that "we had to act and act now [because] without a strong inspections system, Iraq would be free to retain and begin to rebuild its chemical, biological, and nuclear weapons programs—in months, not years."[91] However, as a direct result of the president's action, we went nearly four years without *any* weapons inspection system, strong or otherwise. The inspectors withdrew shortly before the bombing and did not return until November 2002. The urgent need to reestablish inspections seemed to have vanished as soon as the threat of impeachment did.

The timing of President Clinton's actions inevitably gave rise to suspicion about his motives. Some pundits found those suspicions distressingly cynical. *Washington Post* columnist David Broder professed to be shocked that then Senate majority leader Trent Lott would question the timing of President Clinton's attack on Iraq,[92] and former Nixon speechwriter William Safire could not "bring [him]self to think" that a U.S. president would "stoop to risking lives to cling to power."[93]

Is it really so cynical to suppose that embattled presidents might be tempted to distract the public by waging war abroad? Perhaps so, but only in the sense offered by Ambrose Bierce in his *Devil's Dictionary*: "Cynic, n.: a blackguard whose faulty vision sees things as they are, not as they ought to be."[94]

In 1995, the *American Economic Review* published an article examining the relationship between military conflict, national economic health, and the presidential election cycle from Eisenhower through Reagan. The authors postulated that conflict initiation or escalation would be more likely in the case of a first-term president up for reelection in the midst of a weak economy, then tested that prediction using data on military conflict and the business cycle. Their results were robust, to say the least; based on the data from 1953 to 1988, "the probability of conflict initiation or escalation exceeds 60 percent in years in which a president is up for reelection and the economy is doing poorly. By contrast, the probability is only about 30 percent in years in which either the economy is healthy or a president is not up for reelection."[95] Beleaguered first-term presidents are about twice as likely to resort to the sword as second termers or boomtime leaders. The erosion of Congress's power "to declare War" means that nothing stands in their way.

The Framers, too, were cynics in the Biercean sense. They saw human nature for what it is, and rejected unchecked war power for that reason. As Madison put it, the power to start a war had been lodged in Congress because otherwise "the trust and the temptation would be too great for any one man."[96]

Our Modern Dilemma

By the last years of the 20th century, Americans were not a particularly trusting bunch. The long decline in confidence in government that started during the Vietnam era and bottomed out during Watergate had become a permanent feature of the political landscape. The numbers on the University of Michigan's Trust in Government Index never came close to recovering their Camelot-era vigor; the trust-the-feds "most of the time" answer hit a new low of 19 percent in 1994 before the Republican takeover of Congress.[97] Trust in the presidency saw a similar decline; those Americans investing "a great deal" of confidence in the executive branch fell from 42 percent in 1966 to 12 percent in 1997.[98]

Some among the cognoscenti watched the trust indicators as if they were fading vital signs on a body politic in critical condition. Concern over low levels of faith in government periodically gave rise to solemn conferences at places like the Brookings Institution, the think tank that the Nixon administration had considered firebombing and burglarizing in an attempt to recover classified documents related to Vietnam.[99]

Yet, it's never been clear why a healthy—and, by the 1970s, manifestly justified—distrust of unchecked power should be cause for so much angst. That sort of distrust, after all, is the core of our political heritage. If their fellow citizens' lack of faith in their leaders troubled late-20th-century *bien pensants*, one wonders what they would have made of the Founding Generation's killjoy attitude. As Bernard Bailyn explains in *The Ideological Origins of the American Revolution*, "Federalists and antifederalists both agreed that man in his deepest nature was selfish and corrupt; that blind ambition most often overcomes even the most clear-eyed rationality; and that the lust for power was so overwhelming that no one should ever be trusted with unqualified authority."[100]

Americans' drift away from that perspective in the early postwar era served as a presidential enabler. Unwarranted trust had allowed unrestrained spying at home and disastrous presidential adventurism abroad. The recovery of our native skepticism helped restrain the former, even if it has not, as yet, had much effect on the latter.

What's problematic is that this resurgent skepticism exists side by side with inordinately high expectations for the office. None of Rossiter's roles has passed to any other institutional actor or been abandoned as beyond the proper scope or competence of government.

Father–Protector and National Nursemaid

The post-Watergate president remained Rossiter's Protector of the Peace, America's guardian against everything from natural disasters to ordinary street crime. Despite the collapse of public trust, the president's authority over disaster relief and crime continued to grow throughout the last three decades of the 20th century.

In 1979, President Carter further centralized authority for responding to natural disasters, creating the Federal Emergency Management Agency by executive order, combining the responsibilities of various federal agencies under one heading on the bureaucratic chart. President Clinton bumped FEMA up to cabinet status in 1993, but the most significant change in presidential responsibility for natural disasters occurred in 1988 with the passage of the Stafford Act, which gave the president enormous discretion to issue disaster declarations and award federal aid as he pleases.[101]

Demand for such aid is virtually limitless—"In Texas they want a declaration every time a cow pisses on a flat rock," one FEMA official groused in the mid-1990s.[102] So it's not surprising that unfettered presidential discretion has led to some dubious expenditures, as in 1996, when President Clinton funneled federal funds to 16 states affected by unseasonably heavy snow.[103] Presidents have made liberal use of their Stafford Act powers to bolster their political support in electorally significant states. Political scientist Andrew Reeves studied disaster declarations from 1981 to 2004 and found that "a highly competitive state can expect to receive over 60% more presidential disaster declarations than an uncompetitive state, holding all else constant including the damage caused by the disaster."[104]

The FEMA pork barrel allowed presidents to use the public purse as their personal campaign war chest; but it did not represent a threat to civil liberties. In contrast, the burgeoning war on crime, stoked by presidential promises to keep America's streets safe, had by the last decades of the 20th century seriously undermined the rule of law. As the American Bar Association's Task Force on the Federalization of Criminal Law put it in 1998, "So large is the present body of federal criminal law that there is no conveniently accessible, complete list of federal crimes."[105] By the turn of the 21st century, there were over 4,000 federal crimes, an increase of one-third since 1980.[106] As a result, even teams of legal researchers—let alone ordinary citizens—cannot reliably ascertain what federal law prohibits. Though the Constitution mentions only three federal crimes, in the 1970s, 1980s, and 1990s, presidential races increasingly focused on "law and order," and presidential candidates promised new federal initiatives to keep America safe.

And even after the shame of Watergate, presidents continued to view themselves as the Voice of the People, using the bully pulpit to stimulate demand for executive action on all matters of public concern. Anyone searching for limits to presidential power or responsibility would be hard pressed to find them in the speeches of post-Watergate presidents. As Elvin T. Lim noted in his 2002 study of presidential rhetoric, by the late 20th century, it was "all about the children," with "Presidents Carter, Reagan, Bush, and Clinton [making] 260 of the 508 references to children in the entire speech database, invoking the government's responsibility to and concern for children in practically every public policy area." Granted, George Washington had mentioned children in his seventh annual message, protesting "the frequent destruction of innocent women and children" by Indian marauders.[107] But in the modern State of the Union address, references to children have a different tenor, as when George H. W. Bush told the country in 1992 that "when Barbara [Bush] holds an AIDS baby in her arms and reads to children, she's saying to every person in this country, 'Family Matters,'" or when Bill Clinton used his 1997 State of the Union to declare, "We must also protect our children by standing firm in our determination to ban the advertising and marketing of cigarettes that endanger their lives."[108]

I Hate You; Don't Leave Me

Vietnam, Watergate, and the revelations of the Church Committee had reminded Americans about power's corrupting tendencies. Yet, as the 20th century drew to a close, Americans still seemed to want a president who promised all things to all people. Declining trust had not caused the public to demand less from government as a whole. As the Pew Research Center noted in a 1998 survey, "Public desire for government services and activism has remained nearly steady over the past 30 years."[109] The Pew study featured intensive polling carried out between the Republican takeover of Congress and the Clinton impeachment, and it revealed some puzzling tensions in Americans' attitudes toward government. Sixty-four percent of respondents agreed that "government controls too much of our daily lives."[110] Yet, 65 percent also said the government did not pay enough attention to poor people, and 54 percent complained that even the middle class got less attention than it deserved.[111] Overwhelming majorities also said that government did not place a high enough priority on "ensuring access to affordable health care," "providing the elderly a decent standard of living," "reducing poverty," or "reducing juvenile delinquency."[112] How such responsibilities could be fulfilled without further extension of government controls is a mystery beyond the ken of any pollster.

Wail to the Chief

The demand for presidential salvation hit its rhetorical nadir in the 1992 presidential debates, when a ponytailed social worker named Denton Walthall rose to ask Ross Perot, Bill Clinton, and President Bush the following question:

> The focus of my work as a domestic mediator is meeting the needs of the children that I work with, by way of their parents, and not

the wants of their parents. And I ask the three of you, how can we, *as symbolically the children of the future president*, expect the two of you, the three of you to meet our needs, the needs in housing and in crime and you name it. . . .

"You name it," indeed. Walthall followed up by asking,

Could we cross our hearts; it sounds silly here, but could we make a commitment? You know, we're not under oath at this point, but could you make a commitment to the citizens of the United States to meet our needs, and we have many, and not yours. Again, I have to repeat that, it's a real need, I think, that we all have.[113]

Denton Walthall came in for a fair amount of criticism on the op-ed pages and talk-radio airwaves.[114] Yet, under the hot lights, none of the candidates risked chastising him, however gently, for having an overly capacious view of presidential responsibility. Instead, they accepted his premise. Ross Perot said he'd take Walthall's pledge, "no hedges, no ifs, ands and buts." Governor Clinton argued with Perot about who was more authentic and less dependent on "spin doctors," and noted that as governor, he'd "worked 12 years very hard . . . on the real problems of real people." "It depends on how you define it," President George H. W. Bush stammered his reply to Walthall,

. . . I mean I—I think, in general, let's talk about these—let's talk about these issues; let's talk about the programs, but in the Presidency a lot goes into it. Caring is—goes into it; that's not particularly specific; strength goes into it, that's not specific; standing up against aggression, that's not specific in terms of a program. So I, in principle, I'll take your point and think we ought to discuss child care, or whatever else it is.[115]

Indeed, Walthall's formulation of the American people as "symbolically the children of the future president" is not far off from how presidents and presidential aspirants—whether of the "mommy party" or "daddy party" variety—in their franker moments describe the relationship between the government and the governed. "The average American is just like the child in the family," Richard Nixon told an interviewer in 1972, "you give him some responsibility and he is going to amount to something."[116] In 1997, then vice president Al Gore told an audience at George Washington University that the federal government should act "like grandparents in the sense that grandparents perform a nurturing role."[117]

One has difficulty imagining a Grover Cleveland or a Calvin Coolidge in a late-20th-century town hall–style debate, perched awkwardly on a stool, trying to look relaxed and amicable. But forced into such an undignified posture, if they restrained themselves from insulting the ponytailed fellow burbling about national needs and likening Americans to children, one can picture a Cleveland or a Coolidge giving a far more modest description of the president's constitutional responsibilities: execute the laws, defend the Constitution, protect the country from foreign attack and domestic insurrection—and little else.

In the context of the modern presidency, though, such an answer would make little sense. President Bush's halting reply to Denton Walthall can't be blamed merely on the pressure of the moment or on the Bush family's notorious difficulty with words. Presidential responsibility in the modern era really *is* that diffuse and unconfined. "Caring," "standing up against aggression," "child care and whatever else it is," are a decent approximation of the modern president's job description. The president, as Clinton Rossiter put it in *The American Presidency*, is expected "to watch like a mother hen over all the eggs in all our baskets," and perhaps, as presidential responsibility has expanded over the four decades since Rossiter's observation, to provide us with still more eggs.[118] Chief Legislator, Manager of Prosperity, shield against disaster, defender of the free world, living embodiment of the general will—the burden of these expanded functions, Rossiter noted, "is monstrous."[119]

With Great Responsibility Comes Great Power

Monstrous, yes—and dangerous. No one man, however powerful, can meet responsibilities so vast. Thus, we should not be surprised that presidential approval ratings have been in a steady 40-year decline.[120] The office, as it has evolved, is set up to fail. Worse, the incentives for the officeholder are to seek still more power as a result of the failure.

Surveying the pedagogical materials of the late 1960s, political scientist Thomas Cronin announced that the president described in America's textbooks was "Superman." Nearly 40 years later, Americans no longer fully believe in the heroic president. Yet, the president's job description still requires a superhero. And to reverse the credo of another comic book hero: with great responsibility comes great power. If the president is charged with righting all the country's and the world's wrongs, he's going to seek the vast power needed to discharge those responsibilities. In peacetime, he'll ask for that power; faced with an emergency, he may seize it.

"War is the health of the state," wrote Randolph Bourne as the Great War raged across Europe, and America slipped toward entanglement in that vast continental tragedy. Throughout the 20th century, real wars and ersatz wars on various social maladies—crime, domestic subversion, poverty, drugs—validated Bourne's dictum, delivering enormous power to government in general and the presidency in particular. In time of crisis, real or imagined, presidential responsibility has relentlessly expanded, as Americans have turned to the president for deliverance.

Crisis was far from the public mind in the bright early fall of 2001. Americans followed the hunt for Chandra Levy, wondered about Rep. Gary Condit (D-CA), and watched their new president's difficulties with a Senate that had recently lost its Republican majority. Politics had rarely seemed so pleasantly inconsequential.

In one terrible morning, all that would change.

5

SUPERMAN RETURNS

We stand strongly united behind the President as *our* commander in chief.
—Joint statement by congressional leaders of both parties
(September 11, 2001)

O n the afternoon of September 10, 2001, talking with a *U.S. News* reporter, a senior White House adviser ruminated on the connection between crisis and presidential greatness. "Abraham Lincoln would have been judged a hayseed if not for the Civil War," he said, "Franklin Roosevelt would have been just another politician from New York without the Depression and World War II."[1]

At 7:00 a.m. the next morning, CNN led with 38-year-old Michael Jordan's impending announcement that he would come out of retirement to play for the Washington Wizards. The front page of the *Washington Post* featured a story on the Environmental Protection Agency's decision to issue stricter arsenic standards for drinking water, backing off the administration's earlier position on the issue. The *New York Times's* lead editorial that morning decried "The Politics of Panic," by which it meant the Republican push for capital gains tax cuts in the face of a worsening budget outlook. And the president was in Sarasota, Florida, for a series of photo ops pushing his No Child Left Behind education bill.

Shortly after Bush's arrival at Emma E. Booker Elementary School on the morning of September 11, Chief of Staff Andy Card told the president about the first plane. "There's one terrible pilot," Bush remarked a few minutes later on the phone with then national security adviser Condoleezza Rice, before being led into Sandra Kay Daniels's second-grade classroom so the cameras could capture him reading along with the children.[2]

In the film clip made famous by Michael Moore's movie *Fahrenheit 9/11*, we can see the president's reaction just after he learned that the second tower had been hit. Bush sits at the front of the class on a child's wooden chair as Card approaches to tell him that the country is under attack. At that point, everything in the president's demeanor shifts. His eyes widen, his lips tighten, his color seems to fade. His movements—shifting in his chair, looking around the room, pretending to follow along in the children's book—become painfully deliberate and self-conscious—as if any sudden twitch might ignite the very air around him.

How surreal it all must have seemed from Bush's perch on that undersized chair. As Card walked away, the children read in unison, "But-the-goat-did-some-things-that-made-the-girl's-dad-mad." Bush later told the *Washington Times'* Bill Sammon that as he sat there, "Victory clicked into my mind."[3] But the tape projects a very different image. The president looks as though every cell in his body would, if it could, melt into the blackboard behind him.

Subtlety has never been Michael Moore's strong suit; so in the movie, rather than letting the tape speak for itself, he adds a sarcastic voice-over asking, "Was [Bush] wondering if maybe he should have shown up for work more often?" But if you shut out Moore's voice, you may come away with a different take on what was going through the president's mind that morning.

Through the first nine months of his tenure, George W. Bush seemed an unlikely candidate to restore the heroic conception of the presidency. An unremarkable man, as presidents go, he'd never seemed as hungry for the job as most others who'd sought it. And in those seven minutes, struggling to appear guarded and in control before the students and the cameras, Bush had never looked so vulnerable and helpless—overwhelmed by the enormity of what he'd signed up for and realizing that there was no place to hide.

September 11 shook nearly every American to the core. But only one American would be the focus of national attention through it all. One more than any other would be held responsible for framing our response. As Professor Rossiter noted, the burden of the modern presidency is "monstrous," and never more monstrous than on that horrific September morning.

For hours that day, the president seemed as much swept along by events as were the rest of us. His first public statement, scribbled on typing paper and delivered from the school library, was halting and awkward, announcing his intention to "hunt down and to find those folks who committed this act."[4] "Folks" didn't seem remotely the right word. The president said he was headed straight back to Washington, but he would not return to the White House for over eight hours.

After Bush delivered his remarks, the Secret Service swept him off to the Sarasota airport and on board *Air Force One*. When the south tower of the World Trade Center collapsed at 9:59 a.m., followed by the north 29 minutes later, *Air Force One* was flying in wide, aimless circles, which it did for two hours before heading toward Barksdale Air Force Base in Louisiana. At Barksdale, Bush taped another short statement and, under pressure from Vice President Cheney and the Secret Service, flew to yet another military installation, Offutt Air Force Base, near Omaha, Nebraska. White House aides, concerned with the political ramifications of the president's absence, fought with the Secret Service, who wanted to keep the president at the base overnight, or perhaps even longer. Finally, around 4:00 p.m., Bush ordered that *Air Force One* be readied to fly to Washington.[5]

Bush began the day as a prisoner, paralyzed by the enormous expectations surrounding the office and trapped by the security apparatus built to enclose and protect its occupant. But by the evening of the 11th, he would begin to assert control. Over the next several days, he would use the bully pulpit to shape Americans' view of the conflict, describing it as a war, and then defining that war in the broadest terms possible.

By 7:00 p.m., the president was back at the White House. That night, in a nationally televised address, he declared that we would "go forward to defend freedom and all that is good and just in our world."[6] Three days later, the bully pulpit was the actual pulpit at Washington's National Cathedral. From it, President Bush declared that America's "responsibility to history is already clear: to answer these attacks and rid the world of evil." The service concluded with the singing of "The Battle Hymn of the Republic." Americans were used to hearing it in its softer, post-1950 version, with the line "As He died to make men holy, let us live to make men free." But on this day, the congregation went back to the starker 1862 original: "As He died to make men holy, let us *die* to make men free."[7]

That evening found the president addressing rescue workers from atop a crushed fire truck at Ground Zero in lower Manhattan. All the scripted photo ops of presidents past paled before that one spontaneous moment with a bullhorn. Even the most incorrigible of political cynics had to believe in the Heroic Presidency, however briefly. One arm draped over a soot-covered firefighter, the other clutching the megaphone, the president told the crowd: "I can hear you. The rest of the world hears you. And the people—and the people who knocked these buildings down will hear all of us soon!"

Everyone was listening when the president gave an address to a joint session of Congress on September 20. At a Flyers-Rangers game in Philadelphia, 19,000 hockey fans roared their disapproval when stadium officials cut away from video feed of the speech to resume play. The stadium stayed with the speech and canceled the rest of the game, to a standing ovation.[8]

Again, the president described the conflict as a war—and not simply a war with Osama bin Laden and his agents: "Our war on terror begins with al Qaeda, but it does not end there. It will not end until every terrorist group of global reach has been found, stopped and defeated."[9] In his postspeech commentary, ABC's guest historian Michael Beschloss gushed, "The imperial presidency is back. We just saw it"—momentarily forgetting that the phrase was supposed to be pejorative.[10]

The coming years would validate Beschloss's assessment, though perhaps not his celebratory tone. Now more than ever, the president was Professor Rossiter's Protector of the Peace, Voice of the People, and World Leader. Bush would use the bully pulpit forcefully, to frame the debate over the response to 9/11. We were at war, the president declared, and that war demanded an extraordinary concentration of power in the hands of the commander in chief. Congress's capitulation to those demands would raise serious questions about the vitality of separation of powers in the early 21st century.

In Government We Trust

If the Imperial Presidency was back, so were the levels of trust in government that prevailed at its height. The *Washington Post* took a national poll on September 25–27 using the same question as the perennial National Election Studies polls: "How much of the time do you trust the government in Washington to do what is right?" Sixty-four percent of respondents answered "just about always" or "most of the time." That was a 34-point increase from the most recent, pre-9/11 numbers—and the highest level in 35 years.[11] Americans also showed an increasing willingness to trade constitutional protections for security, with 74 percent of respondents to a CBS/*New York Times* poll agreeing that "Americans will have to give up some of their personal freedoms in order to make the country safe from terrorist attacks."[12]

Trust in the president soared as well. Presidential approval ratings cracked 90 percent in some polls in the week after the attacks. Those numbers would prove more durable than the trust in government numbers, with George W. Bush enjoying the longest period of above–60 percent approval of any president since Eisenhower.[13] Bush's post-9/11 boost was bigger and lasted longer even than FDR's approval bump after Pearl Harbor.[14]

That's Not Funny

In the immediate aftermath of 9/11, American irreverence was suspended, at least where the presidency was concerned. In *Time* magazine, Roger Rosenblatt predicted "the end of the age of irony" and the dawn of a more serious age.[15] For a time at least, he seemed to be right. In 2001 before 9/11, President Bush had been the most frequent butt of late-night talk-show host jokes: 32 percent of the time, according to the Center for Media and Public Affairs, the research organization that keeps the tally. Between September 11 and November 15, that number went down to 4 percent.[16] Jacob Weisberg, the compiler of presidential malapropisms for *Slate*'s "Bushisms" feature, suspended the column from September 12 until March 2002. It no longer seemed appropriate to poke fun at the president's periodic difficulties with syntax. Likewise, Comedy Central canceled reruns of *That's My Bush!* the 2001 presidential sitcom produced by *South Park* creators Trey Parker and Matt Stone, in which George W. Bush accidentally takes ecstasy, gets a job as a masked wrestler, and breaks Jack Kevorkian out of prison to euthanize the presidential cat (though not all in the same episode). Two years later, the star of *That's My Bush!* Timothy Bottoms would play Bush again—this time as a hero, not a clown—in Showtime's hagiographic docudrama *DC 9/11*. Neoconservative pundits Fred Barnes and Charles Krauthammer got to vet the script.[17]

The Rock of Our Salvation

In the aftershock of 9/11, Americans wanted a hero, and the plainspoken man with the bullhorn seemed to fit the part. On the op-ed pages and the talk shows, some pundits thought that even "hero" didn't quite capture Bush's greatness. "I find myself thinking in mystical terms of President Bush's speech to Congress and the country," former Reagan speechwriter Peggy Noonan wrote in the *Wall Street Journal* about Bush's September 20 address, "It seemed to me a God-touched moment and a God-touched speech."[18] "This war happens to be the reason he is president: because something big and bad and dark was coming, and he was the man to lead us through it," she wrote a few weeks later.[19]

Perhaps Noonan was temperamentally more inclined to mysticism than most, having seen the Hand of God at work in the dolphins that surrounded Cuban refugee Elian Gonzales in his passage to Florida.[20] But in the weeks after the terror attacks, she wasn't the only pundit to see the president as God touched. On October 8, the *Weekly Standard*'s Fred Barnes described a meeting that the president had with various religious leaders on the afternoon before his September 20 speech before Congress. At the meeting, the leader of the Southern Baptist Convention told Bush: "I believe you are God's man for this hour. God's hand is upon you." "The stage was set for Bush to be God's agent of wrath," Barnes noted approvingly.[21]

Centrist and liberal commentators went much lighter on the presidential idolatry. But many welcomed the resurgence of trust in government and celebrated the possible emergence of another "Greatest Generation," dedicated to reform at home and the promotion of American ideals abroad.

In a way, it wasn't surprising that center-left intellectuals saw promise in wartime unity. Post-Vietnam liberals tended to be less bellicose than their conservative counterparts; even so, they'd never entirely abandoned their Progressive forebears' romanticism about the spirit of collective purpose inculcated by a "Good War." In a 1995 interview with the *New York Times*, former New York governor Mario Cuomo waxed nostalgic about the grand global conflict that killed some 50 million people from 1939 to 1945:

> The biggest event in my lifetime was the Second World War and we have never been able to recreate it. Some people say thank God, but there's something we lose by not recreating what happened in the Second World War. The Second World War was the last time that this country believed in anything profoundly, any great single cause. What was it? They were evil; we were good. . . . Let's all get together, we said, and we creamed them. We started from way behind. We found strength in this common commitment, this commonality, community, family, the idea of coming together was best served in my lifetime in the Second World War.[22]

In his widely discussed 2000 book *Bowling Alone*, Harvard political scientist Robert Putnam had written that restoring America's sense of common purpose "would be eased by a palpable national crisis, like war or depression or natural disaster, but for better and for worse, America at the dawn of the new century faces no such galvanizing crisis."[23] After 9/11, Putnam revisited the subject in the left-wing magazine the *American Prospect*, welcoming the togetherness that terrorism brought. "As 2001 ended," he wrote, "Americans were more united, readier for collective sacrifice, and more attuned to public purpose than we have been for several decades."[24]

Liberal hawks joined neoconservatives in urging the president to make the war on terror a Wilsonian crusade worthy of a great nation. True to its Progressive heritage, the post-9/11 *New Republic* championed a bellicose liberalism—what editor Peter Beinart, borrowing a term from Arthur Schlesinger Jr., called "a fighting faith."[25] Writers in *TNR* periodically complained that the president hadn't demanded more sacrifices from Americans at home: taxes, national service, perhaps scrap-metal drives and war on terror bond rallies.[26] Many latter-day Progressives saw 9/11 as a historic opportunity to realize William James's vision of universal national service.[27] National crisis brought with it the opportunity for a new politics of meaning, a chance to redirect American life in accordance with "the common good." War was a terrible thing, of course, but war could also be "a force that gives us meaning," as *New York Times* foreign correspondent Chris Hedges put it in his 2002 book lamenting the romanticization of combat.[28]

The Ascendancy of National Greatness Conservatism

Some on the right also saw war as a wonderful tonic for the national soul. Like their hero Teddy Roosevelt, the writers associated with William Kristol's *Weekly Standard* had long believed that Americans needed grand federal crusades to pull them away from private, parochial concerns and invest their lives with meaning.[29] Invoking TR in his 1997 *Weekly Standard* cover story "A Return to National Greatness: A Manifesto for a Lost Creed," then senior editor David Brooks decried limited-government conservatives who "have become besotted with localism, local communities, and the devolution of power to the localities." "We have," he warned, "replaced high public aspiration with the narrower concerns of private life."[30]

The question the self-styled "National Greatness Conservatives" put to us is, how can a nation be truly great if it is devoted to minding its own business at home and abroad? As Kristol and Brooks saw it, government should have loftier goals than protecting life, liberty, and property: "Wishing to be left alone isn't a governing doctrine," they declared.[31] Then *Reason* editor Virginia Postrel heard echoes of Herbert Croly in Kristol and Brooks's belief that the "Promise of

American Life" could only be fulfilled collectively. Like Croly, Postrel wrote, the National Greatness Conservatives "view America as a rotten society, whose very creativity and exuberance is a cause for dismay."[32]

At the core of National Greatness Conservatism lies the belief that "ultimately, American purpose can find its voice only in Washington."[33] And Washington is never louder or more powerful than when it has a war to fight. Brooks, Kristol, and their fellow travelers had spent the 1990s searching for an enemy, at times sounding distinctly unsettled by the fact that the United States didn't have anyone to fight. In a 1996 article in *Foreign Affairs*, Bill Kristol and Robert Kagan argued that "the ubiquitous post–Cold War question—where is the threat?—is thus misconceived. In a world in which peace and American security depend on American power and the will to use it, the main threat the United States faces now and in the future is its own weakness."[34] In the spring of 2000, reviewing the book *Present Dangers*, in which Kristol and Kagan presented the foreign policy prescriptions of an all-star cast of neoconservatives, Jonathan Clarke wrote:

> Far from looking for ways to take the toxicity out of international problems, the authors purposefully seek out trouble spots (the Taiwan Strait, North Korea, Iraq) and then reach for the gas can. "Quiet diplomacy" or "keeping one's powder dry" are anathema. "Steely resolve" is the watchword, with the emphasis on steel. Indeed, it is hardly an exaggeration to say that if the book's combined recommendations were implemented all at once, the United States would risk unilaterally fighting at least a five-front war.[35]

September 11 brought the grand crusade that National Greatness Conservatives had hungered for. Less than a month after people jumped from the World Trade Center's north tower to avoid burning to death, David Brooks asked, "Does anybody but me feel upbeat, and guilty about it?" "I feel upbeat because the country seems to be a better place than it was a month ago," Brooks explained, "I feel guilty about it because I should be feeling pain and horror and anger about the recent events. But there's so much to cheer one up."[36]

"We Are at War"

For most Americans, however, the garrison-state atmosphere that prevailed in the days immediately following 9/11 hardly promoted good cheer. With armed soldiers on the streets, in the airports, and guarding national landmarks, the war on terror looked anything but metaphorical. At President Bush's request, state governors called up some 6,000 national guardsmen for duty at the nation's airports. Troops carrying M-16s became a common sight for holiday travelers. In February 2002, as Salt Lake City prepared for the 2002 Winter Games, Black Hawk helicopters and F-16s circled the skies while thousands of troops patrolled the streets. Defense Secretary Donald Rumsfeld observed, "The largest theater for the United States is not Afghanistan today. It is in fact Salt Lake City and the environs. We have more people in the area around Salt Lake City for the Olympics than we do in Afghanistan."[37]

"Our" Commander in Chief

In the newly militarized America, all eyes turned to the commander in chief. Congressional leaders and political figures of both parties looked to Bush for leadership, and repeatedly referred to him by his military title, as if the U.S. Congress and even the nation as a whole were under his command. In the 1952 steel seizure case, Justice Jackson had reminded the president and the country that "the Constitution did not contemplate that the title Commander in Chief of the Army and Navy will constitute him also Commander in Chief of the country, its industries and its inhabitants."[38] In the fear-charged environment of late 2001, many found it hard to recall that distinction.

Again and again, prominent pols echoed the formulation offered by Sen. Dick Durbin (D-IL) on October 7: "He is our commander in chief. He is our leader."[39] The leadership of both houses of Congress used the phrase in a bipartisan statement issued on September 11: "We stand strongly united behind the President as our commander in chief."[40] And even former vice president Al Gore declared, before an audience of Democrats, that "George W. Bush is my commander in chief."[41]

In this, they joined the president—and just about everyone else—in defining the conflict as "war" and the solution as military. That the president would characterize the conflict as a war was to be expected, both because of the nature of the attacks and because the war metaphor has long been the president's most powerful rhetorical weapon for motivating Americans and securing new powers. The metaphor doesn't always sell: it didn't work for President Carter in the 1977 energy crisis, and it failed President Ford in his abortive "war on inflation." (The latter campaign featured ad agency–designed "WIN" buttons, for "Whip Inflation Now"; some slackers and smart alecks started wearing them upside down: "NIM," for "No Immediate Miracles.")[42] But with a sufficient atmosphere of crisis as a background, the war metaphor can be enormously effective in framing public debate and justifying government action.

Unlike the artificial wars of the past, there was little that felt forced about the war metaphor as applied to 9/11, and nothing sinister in the president's employment of it. Here, we had a devastating physical attack by a real, if elusive, enemy. With a gaping hole in the west side of the Pentagon and a national landmark reduced to a smoking crater, "war" suggested itself to just about every American on September 11. Among the president's first remarks to his aides before leaving Booker Elementary School was, "We are at war."[43]

But was war the *right* metaphor? In some ways, yes. In the case of Afghanistan, we had a government defiantly harboring the group that had killed nearly 3,000 people on American soil. If, as the left-wing bumper sticker of the time had it, "War is not the answer" here, it's difficult to envision circumstances in which it would be.

In other ways, though, the war paradigm clouded more than it revealed. The enemy in this "war" was not a nation-state, and it would not politely arrange itself into an army that could be smashed in set-piece battles with the world's most formidable military. As defense analyst Colin S. Gray put it, the fight against al Qaeda "bears more resemblance to a protracted hunt than it does to what most people understandably call a war."[44] The important work of rounding up anti-American jihadis would, of necessity, depend more on cooperation with foreign intelligence services and law enforcement officials than it would on tanks and planes.

But arresting terrorist suspects in Germany or Pakistan is not what people think of when they think of war. A "war" on terrorism seemed to promise further battles against enemy states, even if, after the destruction of the Taliban government, state support was no longer a significant component of the al Qaeda threat. And the president stayed true to the metaphor. Having toppled the one state that lent significant support to al Qaeda, President Bush padded the enemies list with three additional states that did not. In his 2002 State of the Union address, he described Iran, Iraq, and North Korea as "an axis of evil, arming to threaten the peace of the world."[45]

The war paradigm also presented a conceptual challenge to the American constitutional order, especially since, as the president acknowledged from the start, this was "a different kind of war." Conventional wars have a relatively fixed theater (usually abroad) and a foreseeable endpoint. Neither was the case here. Given the decentralized nature of the enemy—a loose, clandestine network of terrorists determined to strike again on American soil—this war lacked a geographically defined frontline. Rather, as administration officials would repeatedly suggest, the frontline was everywhere, and that might require militarization of the home front. Nor would the war announced by the president conclude like other wars, with a peace treaty signed across a diplomat's table. This war might go on for as long as terrorists were willing to kill themselves to kill Americans.

America the Battlefield

In a war without frontlines, administration officials could argue that the laws of war applied to the home front. Tapping Americans' phones in New Jersey could be recast as "gathering battlefield intelligence." Seizing an American citizen on American soil and holding him indefinitely in a military brig, without charges or access to counsel, became "capturing an enemy combatant." During oral argument at one stage of the José Padilla case, federal judge J. Michael Luttig told Deputy Solicitor General Paul Clement that accusations that Padilla was an enemy combatant "don't get you very far, unless you're prepared to boldly say the United States is a battlefield in the war on terror."

Clement replied, "I can say that, and I can say it boldly."[46] If the fight against al Qaeda was a war, and the United States was a battlefield, certain constitutional protections would have to be suspended. And given that the war had no foreseeable endpoint, those protections might well have to be suspended permanently.

Untroubled by their framework's implications, the administration embraced the war paradigm without reservation. That was apparent on every page of the administration's National Security Strategy, released in September 2002. The NSS reaffirmed that the enemy was no longer merely al Qaeda: "The enemy is terrorism—premeditated, politically motivated violence perpetrated against innocents."[47] But not just terrorism; as the president suggested in his 2002 State of the Union, the enemy was also "rogue states." Under the preventive war doctrine formalized in the NSS, rogue nations in the process of developing nuclear, chemical, or biological weapons would be vulnerable at any time to preemptive attacks by the United States.

And judging by the NSS, President Bush's Wilsonian promise to "history" on September 14 was no mere rhetorical flourish. The strategy paper begins by quoting the president's vow from the pulpit at the National Cathedral to "rid the world of evil." In the war against evil, America would go on the offensive, taking the war to the enemy, however broadly that enemy was defined.

But if war it was, what role would Congress play? That war inevitably empowers the executive should not mean that legislative authority becomes irrelevant. And as framed by the president, the war on terror raised significant questions for Congress. Would the preventive war doctrine, with its emphasis on quick, unilateral action, be used to cut Congress out of the decision to go to war against "axis" members? Would the president be given as free a hand to fight terrorism at home as he enjoyed abroad? What legal framework was appropriate for handling "enemy combatants" in a war against an international conspiracy acting independently of any enemy state?

Congress has the constitutional power—and had the constitutional duty—to address these questions. As commander in chief, the president has broad authority over battlefield tactics, but the bulk of constitutional war powers are left to the Congress. Through its power to declare war, Congress could set the strategic direction of the fight against al

Qaeda and any nations that harbor or support it. Using its powers "to define and punish . . . Offenses against the Law of Nations" and "to make Rules concerning Captures on Land and Water," it could establish the framework for the apprehension and punishment of enemy prisoners. And surely Congress would have a role in determining how far the war metaphor would be allowed to reshape American law.

Yet, given how Congress had evolved through the course of the 20th century, there were ample reasons to doubt the institution was up to the task. In the months after September 11, Congress would repeatedly confirm those doubts.

The *New* "Least Dangerous Branch"

On April 23, 2002, a point roughly midway between September 11 and the congressional vote on the Iraq War, Congress heard testimony from a distinguished guest: Elmo the Muppet, of "Tickle Me Elmo" fame. The furry red creature, beloved by children everywhere, had been invited to testify before the House Education Appropriations Subcommittee to urge more federal spending on musical instruments for school programs. And so he did, declaring: "Elmo knows that there is music in Elmo's friends all over the country, but some of them just don't know it yet. They don't know how to find their music. So that's why Elmo needs Congress to help."[48]

In between trying to eat the microphone and interrupting his fellow witness, Elmo engaged in this informative colloquy with subcommittee chair Ralph Regula (R-OH):

ELMO: Please, Congress, help Elmo's friends find the music in them. I love you, Congress.

REGULA: And my grandchildren love you too, Elmo.[49]

True, the 107th Congress had better days. And perhaps it's unfair to judge the state of the institution by focusing on its most embarrassing moments. But there are other reasons to believe that Congress today is not serious, sober, or responsible enough to properly carry out the duties the Constitution charges it with.

In *The Imperial Presidency*, Arthur Schlesinger Jr. noted that the 20th-century trend toward an increasingly autocratic executive "was as much a matter of congressional abdication as of presidential usurpation."[50] How did Congress become so pliable, so willing to cede its constitutional authority to the executive branch? Schlesinger, an inveterate New Dealer and a periodic supporter of strong (Democratic) presidents, would have disagreed, but the problem has its roots in the Roosevelt Revolution.

Since the New Deal era, Congress has only intermittently fulfilled the central duty imposed on it by the Constitution: making the law. The Court's post-1937 refusal to strike down broad delegations of legislative authority helped give rise to what Theodore Lowi has called the "Second Republic" of the United States, in which most of the day-to-day business of governance is conducted by administrative agencies rather than Congress itself. Instead of making the final decision on the rules that most Americans live under, Congress routinely delegates lawmaking authority to the executive branch. In America today, most of the federal rules governing private conduct are generated as follows: Congress passes a statute endorsing a high-minded goal—accommodation of the handicapped, safe drinking water, protection of wildlife—and leaves it to the relevant executive branch agency to issue and enforce the regulations governing individual behavior. That process results in some 75,000 new pages added to the *Federal Register* every year. Given the judiciary's deferential posture toward agencies' interpretations of their own statutory authority, once issued, those rules are exceptionally difficult to revise or repeal.[51]

Despite the fact that "All legislative Powers" granted by the Constitution are vested in Congress—and that the executive branch is supposed to *execute*, not *make*, the laws—the post–New Deal administrative state leaves most actual lawmaking power in the hands of the executive. Legal scholar Gary Lawson has compared the current legal regime with one governed by "a statute creating the Goodness and Niceness Commission and giving it power 'to promulgate rules for the promotion of goodness and niceness in all areas within the power of Congress under the Constitution.'" In Lawson's example, the executive branch, clearly, would both make and enforce the law. The myriad "Goodness and Niceness" commissions of the modern administrative state go by different names and have narrower purviews individually, but collectively, they're hard to distinguish from Lawson's *reductio ad absurdum*.[52]

That system may be constitutionally suspect, but it's certainly convenient if you're a representative or senator running for reelection. Delegation is a "political shell game," says New York Law School's David Schoenbrod, allowing legislators to simultaneously support the benefits and oppose the costs of regulation. By passing a vague, expansive statement in favor of environmental protection, such as the Endangered Species Act, Congress curries favor with the broad swathe of Americans who favor conservation. Then, when the Fish and Wildlife Service restricts logging throughout the Pacific Northwest to preserve habitat for the spotted owl, legislators get to rail against the bureaucracy for abuse of the authority delegated to it. In the words of former EPA deputy administrator John Quarles, delegation provides "a handy set of mirrors . . . by which politicians can appear to kiss both sides of the apple."[53] Which, of course, is how politicians prefer it.

"I Didn't Realize What All Was in It"

Whether it is directly enacting rules of private conduct or delegating authority to the executive branch to do so, Congress pays little attention to what it enacts. It's less a dirty little secret than a well-known fact that Congress does not read the bulk of the bills it passes. In 1994, as Congress was preparing to consider President Clinton's health care plan, a Manhattan Institute analyst had a huge effect on the debate simply by sitting down and reading the 1,364-page bill and reporting what she found in the *New Republic*.[54] At the end of the article, when she wrote, "Members of Congress should read this bill, instead of relying on what they hear," it was offered more in the spirit of an earnest plea than as a reproof.

More recently, in February 2003, the *New York Times* reported that the Democratic and Republican party organizations had hired high-priced lawyers and consultants to run seminars teaching legislators about the requirements of the McCain-Feingold campaign finance law they had just passed. "I didn't realize what all was in it," Rep. Robert

Matsui (D-CA) said. "It's a real education process," echoed Rep. Thomas M. Reynolds of New York, chair of the National Republican Congressional Committee.[55]

Given how little attention legislators paid to a statute that directly affected their livelihoods, it's not surprising to find that they're less than meticulous with the laws that affect everyone else. In many cases, though, it would be physically impossible for a conscientious legislator to perform that most basic of duties: reading the bills. Even though modern Congresses delegate most of their lawmaking authority to the executive, statutes have continued to get longer and more complex. In the 80th Congress (1947–1948), the average bill was two and a half pages long. By the 104th Congress, it was over 19 pages.[56]

But averages don't quite capture the heft of the megastatutes that modern Congresses regularly pass. In President Lincoln's first annual message to Congress in 1861, he complained about the growing complexity of federal law. Even so, he noted that with modest legislative effort to revise and simplify the federal code, "all the acts of Congress now in force might [be contained in] one or two volumes of ordinary and convenient size."[57] Not so today. Some of the most important statutes passed by modern Congresses would take up half that space by themselves.

Nor is it merely the length of the laws that keeps the lawmakers from reading what they pass. Quite often in recent years, congressional leaders have deliberately scheduled votes to keep the bills from being read. The final bills that issue from House-Senate conference committees are often significantly different from what each house approved, and it has become common practice to schedule floor votes to prevent careful review of legislative language.[58]

That means that some of the most significant legislation Congress considers—laws with sweeping fiscal effects and social consequences, like the president's 2003 medicare prescription drug plan—passes into law unread.[59] Through a combination of fearmongering and strategic scheduling by its allies on the Hill, the Bush administration managed to push through the Patriot Act in October 2001 without allowing any member of Congress to read the bill and raise informed objections. The week before the vote, Attorney General Ashcroft suggested that Congress would be held responsible if al Qaeda struck again before the act passed: "Talk won't prevent terrorism," he warned.[60] Anyone who wanted to understand the enormous changes in federal surveillance laws contained in the bill could not even perform the basic duty of sitting down and reading it, because the bill was not available to members before the vote.[61]

In the civics book ideal, Congress is a deliberative body in which members carefully review proposed legislation, debate its merits, and, if a majority, in their considered judgment, support it, pass the bill, and send it to the president for his review. As always in life, political reality departs from the civics book ideal—but rarely this dramatically and with regard to such vital matters.

The most vital matter the Constitution empowers Congress to decide is, of course, the question of war or peace. Yet, having accustomed itself to avoiding responsibility by delegating away much of its legislative authority and refusing to read the laws it passes, the modern Congress was ill prepared to reassert itself in the debates over military action after September 11.

War and Irresponsibility

In those debates, members at least got to read what they were ratifying. But Congress as an institution showed little inclination to take responsibility for the wars we were about to fight.

Power without Accountability

The administration led off the post-9/11 war powers debate by seeking a resolution that authorized the use of military force "to deter and preempt any future acts of terrorism or aggression against the United States."[62] That formulation would have amounted to a wholesale, perpetual delegation of the war power—giving the president authority to launch a war against whomever he wanted, whenever he wanted.

Congress rejected that language. But the joint resolution it passed, known as the Authorization for the Use of Military Force or AUMF, contained an unusually broad delegation of authority to the president, authorizing him to make war on "those nations, organizations, or persons *he determines* planned, authorized, committed, or aided the terrorist attacks that occurred on Sept. 11, 2001, or harbored such organizations or persons."[63]

Congress held only a perfunctory debate on September 18 before ceding enormous power to the president. That debate was particularly brief in the Senate, where only two senators spoke before members voted and got on the buses that were waiting to take them to a memorial service at the National Cathedral. It was left to Sen. Robert Byrd (D-WV), weeks after the resolution's passage, to express his "qualms" over the broad grant of authority to the president.

On its face, the AUMF appears to leave it to the president to decide who, where, and when to attack. President Bush never pressed that authority as far as he might have. During the Iraq War debate, for instance, he declined to argue that the flimsy evidence of a Saddam–al Qaeda connection permitted him to invade Iraq under the AUMF. Yet, he took advantage of the AUMF's broad language in other contexts, arguing that in the resolution Congress by implication amended both the Foreign Intelligence Surveillance Act—to allow warrantless wiretaps—and the Non-Detention Act—to authorize the internment of suspected enemy combatants on American soil.

Indeed, with regard to terrorist suspects, from the very beginning of the conflict, the president made clear that he, not Congress, would set the rules. On November 13, 2001, President Bush issued a "Military Order" on the "Detention, Treatment, and Trial of Certain Non-Citizens in the War Against Terrorism." Under the order, the president could detain any noncitizen he suspected of terrorist involvement, and even if that person was a legal resident of the United States, he or she would be barred from American courts and tried before a military court whose rules would be determined at the discretion of the president and could be unilaterally altered at any time.[64]

If the challenge of international terrorism demanded different rules from those that prevail in ordinary criminal proceedings or even courts-martial, it was up to Congress to decide what those rules would be. But the post-9/11 Congress showed little interest in asserting its constitutional authority to formulate the rules for 21st-century warfare.[65]

"Debating" the Iraq War

If the September 2001 debate over war powers left a lot to be desired, the following year's debate over war with Iraq was an unmitigated disgrace. The Bush administration pushed a limitless view of executive authority, and intimated that if Congress didn't ratify that view—and quickly—its irrelevance as an institution would be apparent to all when the president launched the invasion anyway. In August 2002, White House press secretary Ari Fleischer allowed, somewhat charitably, that Congress "has an important role to play" in the debate over war with Iraq.[66] But it was clear that the Bush team conceived of that role in terms of ratifying the administration's stunningly broad view of its own authority. In one of John Yoo's first post-9/11 Office of Legal Counsel memos, he maintained that the Constitution gave the president "plenary power to use military force," and that the president's decisions in that regard "are for him alone and are unreviewable." Congress could not "place any limits on the President's determinations as to any terrorist threat, the amount of military force to be used in response, or the method, timing, and nature of the response. These decisions, under our Constitution, are for the President alone to make."[67]

Well before Congress took any action on Iraq, in the summer of 2002, the administration had begun secretly to fund 21 military projects in Kuwait, Qatar, and Oman—projects that were necessary for prosecution of the war in Iraq and served no other defense-related purpose.[68] The administration secretly spent anywhere from $178 million to $700 million laying the groundwork for war with Iraq—without any congressional appropriation authorizing such action.[69] By so doing, President Bush usurped Congress's power of the purse, violating the Constitution's command, in Article I, Section 9, that "no Money shall be drawn from the Treasury, but in Consequence of Appropriations made by Law."

While preparations for war went on in secret, the president opened the public debate on Iraq by asserting, through administration lawyers, that he didn't need any congressional authorization for launching a massive ground war half a world away. A senior administration official told the *Washington Post* in August 2002, "We don't want to be in the legal position of asking Congress to authorize the use of force when the President already has that full authority."[70] The next month the *New York Times* reported that "White House officials have said that their patience with Congress would not extend much past the current session."[71]

In addition to the Justice Department's apparently limitless view of the president's constitutional power, the administration had an equally brazen statutory claim. That same month, the White House counsel's office floated the argument that an earlier Congress—the 102nd Congress that had voted to go to war with Iraq in 1991—had already authorized the upcoming war. As the Bush team saw it, the congressional resolution that authorized Bush the father to expel Saddam Hussein from Kuwait still had enough life left in it to allow Bush the son to take Baghdad 11 years later.[72]

That was an argument that might—barely—be appropriate for a trial lawyer zealously pressing his client's interest. But the president isn't DOJ's sole client; the department has a legal obligation to the American people as well. And surely, American soldiers asked to risk their lives in battle deserve what the Constitution demands: an up-or-down vote from the people's representatives.

Most members of Congress were in no mood to conduct the serious debate that the Constitution required before embroiling the country in war. In a July 2002 press conference, Senate minority leader Trent Lott (R-MS) called the push for a vote on authorization "a blatant political move that's not helpful." He sarcastically elaborated: "Oh, Mr. Saddam Hussein, we're coming, we're coming! Get ready! You can expect us, you know, two weeks after election day. And by the way, here's the way we're coming. But before we do that we'll have a huge debate so you'll know full well exactly what's going on. Give me a break!"[73] (Was Senator Lott under the impression that we'd attach detailed battle plans and launch dates as an appendix to the war resolution?)

Whether "Bush lied" in making the case for war is a debate that will never end, and one best not covered at length here. Suffice it to say that administration officials, including the president, made numerous misrepresentations about the supposed threat presented by the Iraqi regime.[74]

Shortly before the vote on the use-of-force resolution, for example, President Bush gave a speech making the transparently silly claim that Iraq could threaten the U.S. homeland with unmanned aerial vehicles that had less than a 300-mile range. (Perhaps after ferrying them most of the way across the Atlantic so they could get within striking distance?)[75] At that point, it should have been obvious to any member of Congress paying attention that the alleged Iraqi threat was being inflated dramatically.

But whether or not one wants to call such misrepresentations "lies" hardly matters. To consider them material, you'd have to have a Congress that showed some inclination to discover the facts for itself; the 107th Congress showed no such inclination. In the rush to war, most members couldn't even be bothered to do the most basic due diligence on the question of war with Iraq—to examine the available intelligence and decide for themselves whether they thought a serious threat existed.

When the war debate started, U.S. intelligence agencies had not put together a National Intelligence Estimate (NIE), the formal document representing the intelligence community's best judgment on a given national security question. Nor were they planning to until four senators requested one in September 2002.[76] That didn't mean, however, that their colleagues would be interested in reading the NIE. From late September on, copies of the 92-page NIE on the Iraq threat were kept in two guarded vaults on Capitol Hill—available to any member of the House or Senate who wanted to review it. Only six senators and a handful of representatives found it worth the effort to go and read the whole document. Sen. John Kerry (D-MA), the 2004 Democratic nominee, wasn't one of them, though that didn't stop the Kerry campaign from criticizing Bush for not having read it either.[77] Nor were senators and 2008 candidates John Edwards (D-NC) or Hillary Clinton (D-NY) among the six who took the time to read the report before voting for war.[78]

Why did so few members sit down with the NIE? Sen. Jay Rockefeller (D-WV) explained that, when you're a senator, "everyone in the world wants to come see you" in your office and getting away to the secure room—a short walk away across the Capitol grounds—is "not easy to do." He added that intelligence briefings tend to be "extremely dense reading."[79]

Though the NIE on Iraq was designed to further the case for war, it still contained plenty to support doubts about the alleged Iraqi threat. Any representative or senator who read it could have discovered that the evidence for active WMD programs in Iraq was not nearly as solid as the administration publicly asserted.[80] Yet, few were interested in the afternoon of heavy reading that would have required.

The Buck Stops There

In the subsequent national debate over whether the Iraq War was justified, the war's opponents frequently floated analogies to the Vietnam War. Sometimes those analogies were less than persuasive. But in one respect at least, the comparison holds: in both Vietnam and Iraq, Congress structured its authorization in a way that left the final decision to the president and allowed members to deny that they had voted for war.

The administration initially pushed for broad legislative language that, as Sen. Russ Feingold (D-WI) put it, "appear[ed] to actually authorize the president to do virtually anything anywhere in the Middle East."[81] Congress stopped short of that wholesale delegation; but the resolution that passed gave the president all the authority he needed to initiate war. True, there is some boilerplate, bedecked with "whereases," about exhausting other options. But the resolution's key clause reads, "The President is authorized to use the Armed Forces of the United States as he determines to be necessary and appropriate in order to (1) defend the national security of the United States against the continuing threat posed by Iraq; and (2) enforce all relevant United Nations Security Council resolutions regarding Iraq."[82] As Senator Byrd said at the time, the resolution was a "blank check."[83]

Yet, so determined was Congress to pass the war resolution and put the Iraq question behind it, that it could not be stayed even by the evaporation of a key aspect of the administration's rationale for war right in the middle of the congressional debates. On October 8, 2002, in a letter read before a joint House and Senate Intelligence Committee hearing, CIA director George Tenet declared that "Baghdad for now appears to be drawing a line short of conducting terrorist attacks with conventional or chemical or biological weapons." Tenet went on to say that should Saddam conclude that a U.S.-led attack was imminent, "he probably would become much less constrained in adopting terrorist action." The letter also quoted a newly declassified exchange between Sen. Carl Levin (D-MI) and an unnamed "senior intelligence witness" at a closed-door congressional hearing the previous Wednesday. The witness told Levin that, in the absence of an imminent U.S. invasion, "My judgment would be that the probability of [Saddam Hussein] initiating an attack—let me put a time frame on it—in the foreseeable future given the conditions we understand now, the likelihood would be low."[84]

Thus, on the eve of the Iraq vote, the administration's own intelligence officials were telling Congress that a key element of the Bush team's public rationale for war was bankrupt. The risk of an unprovoked attack or aid to terrorists by Saddam Hussein—the risk the administration sought war to avoid—was low; but that risk would be increased precipitously if the United States sought to overthrow the regime. One might have thought this would have some effect on the debate. But it wasn't even a speed bump in the drive to war. Despite Senator Byrd's failed attempt at a last-minute filibuster, three days after Tenet's letter, Congress overwhelmingly passed the resolution, 77–23 in the Senate and 296–133 in the House.

After voting for the resolution, which gave the president all the authority he needed to attack Iraq when and if he decided to, prominent members of Congress insisted they hadn't really voted to use force. That was for the president to decide. Sen. Thomas Daschle (D-SD) said, "Regardless of how one may have voted on the resolution last night, I think there is an overwhelming consensus . . . that while [war] may be necessary, we're not there yet."[85] Senator Kerry explained his vote by saying, "On the question of how best to hold Saddam Hussein accountable, the administration, including the president, recognizes that war must be our last option to address this threat, not the first."[86] In 2007, Hillary Clinton's campaign chair Terry McAuliffe explained that Senator Clinton never voted for the Iraq War: instead, she voted "to give the president the authority to negotiate and to have a stick to go over there and negotiate with Saddam Hussein."[87]

The parallels with Vietnam were striking. As with the Gulf of Tonkin Resolution that authorized the Vietnam War, the Iraq War resolution was broadly worded enough to allow the president to make the final decision about war all by himself. And, like LBJ before him, the president did not immediately use the authority granted him. It would be six months and one presidential election later before Johnson would escalate the war with the Operation Rolling Thunder bombing campaign and the introduction of large numbers of ground forces. President Bush waited until four months after the fall elections to launch Operation Iraqi Freedom. In each case, Congress left the final decision to the president.

If such broad delegations of legislative authority are constitutionally suspect in the domestic arena, they are even more troubling when it comes to questions of war and peace. As Madison put it:

> Those who are to *conduct* a war cannot in the nature of things, be proper or safe judges, whether a war ought to be commenced, continued, or *concluded.* They are barred from the latter functions by a great principle in free government, analogous to that which separates the sword from the purse, or the power of executing from the power of enacting laws.[88]

Early practice by the Founding Generation reflected that distrust of delegated war powers. In 1799, during the Quasi-War with France, Hamilton had proposed that Congress authorize the president to "declare that a state of war exists," if negotiations with France did not succeed. The proposal went nowhere. In 1810, the Senate passed a resolution authorizing the president, if and when he felt it necessary, to order the navy to protect American shipping against the British and French. Madison objected that this would transfer congressional war powers to the president, and the House rejected the measure. Later, President Andrew Jackson, seeking redress from France for damage to American shipping, asked Congress to pass a law authorizing reprisals "in case provision shall not be made for the payment of the debt." Albert Gallatin argued against the "proposed transfer by Congress of its constitutional powers to the Executive, in a case which necessarily embraces the question of war or no war," which, he said, "was entirely inconsistent with the letter and spirit of our Constitution." The measure was rejected.[89]

The letter and the spirit of the Constitution wasn't Congress's foremost concern in October 2002, however. Cowed by the resurgent Heroic Presidency, most members preferred to rush past their most solemn responsibility and get back to the pleasant business of constituent service. After letting the president know they wouldn't stop him from waging the war he wanted, the Senate got back to business, focusing on such matters as compensating "agricultural producers in the State of New Mexico that suffered crop losses as a result of use of a herbicide by the Bureau of Land Management" and strengthening "enforcement of provisions of the Animal Welfare Act relating to animal fighting." There was also some discussion of the Jobs for Veterans Act; perhaps, having ceded to the president the authority to launch the war, some members felt compensation was in order for the men and women who would have to fight it.[90]

Two weeks before the authorization vote, Senator Edwards commented, "In a short time Congress will have dealt with Iraq and then we'll be on to other issues."[91] Senator Kerry echoed Edwards in terms that gave the lie to his later protestations that he didn't know the president was determined to go to war: "We will have done our vote.... You're not going to see anything happen in Iraq until December, January, February, sometime later.... And we will go back to the real issues."[92]

What were the "real issues" Senator Kerry wanted to focus on? Well, there were the campaign issues surrounding Enron, health care, and the economy, of course. But as far as legislative action goes, immediately after the Iraq vote, Kerry turned his attention to bailing out telecom companies and passing out loans through the Small Business Administration.[93] The "real issues," apparently, were those that allowed senators to reward contributors and constituents at little political risk.

But the question of war *is* a "real issue," if anything is. It is the most important issue the Constitution requires Congress to decide. That prominent senators—and presidential candidates—squirmed to avoid responsibility for it doesn't bode well for the future health of either branch.

Institutional Irrelevance

After 9/11, faced with a wartime president asserting unilateral power to launch hostilities, Congress surrendered. When war was justified—as it was in Afghanistan and against al Qaeda—the 107th Congress passed a broad resolution that stood as an open invitation to presidential mischief. When the need for war was debatable—as it surely was with Iraq—the 108th Congress lacked the courage to debate. It passed a resolution that passed the buck to the president—saying, in essence, "This is hard. You decide."

In the post-9/11 world it was predictable, and perhaps inevitable, that the president would assume more power. Yet, the growth in executive power demanded supervision and, where appropriate, checks from the coordinate branches. Lacking purse and sword, the judiciary could not be expected to serve as the sole barrier to presidential aggrandizement. Congress had a historic responsibility to ensure that a newly emboldened executive would not abuse his power or use it unwisely. What we got instead was a headlong flight from accountability.

In the Madisonian vision, separation of powers was supposed to be largely self-executing, driven by each branch's ambition to maintain its status in the constitutional order. "The interest of the man"—that is, the ambitions of individual representatives, judges, and presidents— would lead each to defend "the constitutional rights of the place": the authority of the particular branch each occupied. The failure of that incentive structure since the New Deal is in large part a result of the divergence between the interests of individual legislators and the interests of Congress as a whole in maintaining its constitutional prerogatives. "Congress" is an abstraction. Members of Congress are not, and their most basic interest is in getting reelected.[94]

Domestic delegation of lawmaking authority allows representatives to position themselves on both sides of any given issue: they can take credit for reform when they pass a high-minded, broadly worded bill, and they can please their constituents by railing against executive agencies that use that broad language to impose unpopular costs. So too with delegation of the decision to go to war: by leaving the final decision to the president, Congress gets "to kiss both sides of the apple"— taking credit if the war goes well and blaming the president if things go badly, as they have in Iraq. "It's his war," as Sen. Dianne Feinstein (D-CA) put it in 2004, and though she didn't vote to authorize the use of force, most who did shared that sentiment.[95]

In his landmark study of congressional abdication of war powers, *War and Responsibility*, Stanford's John Hart Ely noted that the usual solution offered by opponents of presidential wars is an ineffectual "halftime pep-talk imploring [Congress] to pull up its socks and reclaim its rightful authority."[96] Or in the case of this chapter, a postgame harangue decrying the worthlessness of the players. It's hard to avoid the language of moral condemnation when confronted with modern Congresses' denial of responsibility over matters of war and peace. And perhaps a little contempt is in order: incumbent members of Congress have reelection rates of over 95 percent most years.[97] Would it be asking too much that they consider "the constitutional rights of the place" and their constitutional responsibilities—even if doing so lowered reelection to a 75 percent proposition?

Whether the fault lies in individual members' cowardice or a flawed incentive structure—or both—it was clear that by the first presidential election after the terrorist attacks of 9/11, if not well before, Congress had completed the process of reducing itself to an advisory body. At the 2004 Republican National Convention, pro-Bush Democratic senator Zell Miller of Georgia wowed the delegates with a Huey Long–style stemwinder. This was one of the biggest applause lines:

> Senator Kerry has made it clear that he would use military force only if approved by the United Nations.
>
> Kerry would let Paris decide when America needs defending. *I want Bush to decide!* [98]

That there was a third option for making such decisions—one that involved senators like Miller and their counterparts in the House—seemed not to occur to anyone.

When it comes to matters of war and peace, Congress now occupies a position roughly analogous to that of the student council in university governance. It may be important for the administration to show pro forma respect and deference to it—but there can no longer be any doubt about where the real authority resides.

Flying High Again

By May 2003, when President Bush proclaimed the end of "major combat operations" in Iraq, he had reason to exult. Though the word "cakewalk," offered by Defense Policy Board member Ken Adelman, would later be much derided, Iraq *had* been a cakewalk: the United States overthrew the Iraqi regime with fewer than 150 American fatalities. The president's approval rating stood in the 70s. And in the 2002 elections, the GOP had recaptured the Senate and picked up seats in the House, partially as a result of the focus on national security and the coming war with Iraq. That victory defied the historical odds: since the Civil War, only two presidents had coattails large enough to pick up House seats midterm, and it had been over 100 years since another incumbent president's party had taken control of the Senate during a midterm election.[99]

President Bush capped his nearly-two-year period of legislative and popular dominance with another Heroic Presidency photo op, this one far less spontaneous than the bullhorn rally at Ground Zero. On May 1, 2003, the president swooped onto the deck of the USS *Abraham Lincoln* in a Lockheed S-3 Viking with "George W. Bush Commander-in-Chief" emblazoned below the cockpit window. He emerged wearing a Navy-issued olive-green flight suit, doffed his helmet outside the view of the cameras, then greeted the *Lincoln*'s crew on live television, slapping backs, and repeatedly saying, "'preciate it." Later, with the troops, an F-16, and a "Mission Accomplished" banner as a backdrop, he delivered a speech timed to capture the golden flush of the late afternoon sunlight. Reporters recognized the moment as the beginning of Bush's 2004 reelection campaign.

In the coming years, Iraq would deteriorate, and many Americans would be disgusted by the pictures from Abu Ghraib and disturbed by the absolutist theories of executive power contained in Justice Department memos leaked to the press. The landing and the banner would eventually become the stuff of bitter punch lines. At the time, however, the president's appearance aboard the USS *Lincoln* was a brilliant piece of presidential theater, one that could hardly be rivaled by C-SPAN speeches to empty seats on the Senate floor.

6

WAR PRESIDENT

This so-called war operates not on the usual battlefield,
geographically located. Here the war knows no bounds. . . .
An enemy activity may be both a violation of the laws of
war and of domestic law. The president may choose to
deal with it as law enforcement officer or as commander
in chief. The decision is his, and the commander in chief
has a significant function even in the United States.
                        —Justice Department official Viet Dinh (2003)

"I'm a war president," George W. Bush proclaimed on NBC's *Meet the
Press* in February 2004, "I make decisions here in the Oval Office in
foreign policy matters with war on my mind."[1] In a different era,
"foreign policy matters" might have been an important qualification.
But after the September 11 attacks, the distinction between foreign and
domestic policy had become uncomfortably blurry. America was a
battlefield, the administration insisted, and on that battlefield, there
could be only one commander in chief.

And since America was a battlefield, legal barriers to domestic use
of the military might well have to be removed. Soon after 9/11, Bush
officials suggested amending or repealing the Posse Comitatus Act, the

longstanding federal statute that restricts the use of standing armies to keep the peace at home. The administration's first post-9/11 *National Strategy for Homeland Security* called for a "thorough review of the laws permitting the military to act within the United States."[2] And in October 2002, the administration established the U.S. military's new Northern Command or NORTHCOM, placing all domestic military assets under one commander, and defining the continental United States as a theater of war. Shortly before assuming his post as the first head of NORTHCOM, General Ralph Eberhart announced, "My view has been that Posse Comitatus will constantly be under review as we mature this command."[3]

As General Eberhart saw it, fighting al Qaeda at home might require troops on the streets, and it would almost certainly require the military to resume domestic intelligence gathering, a practice it had largely abandoned after the abuses of the 1960s and 1970s. In September 2002, Eberhart told a group of National Guardsmen that the military needed to "change our radar scopes. . . . Not just look out, but we're also going to have to look in. We can't let culture and the way we've always done it stand in the way."[4]

Eberhart's comments neatly summed up the Bush team's approach to the fight against al Qaeda. The vast national security apparatus America had developed to project power abroad would have to be turned inward to win the war that had begun in lower Manhattan and Northern Virginia. And the wartime president needed to be free to fight that war as he saw fit; as the administration saw it, forcing the president to answer to Congress and the courts was as absurd as pulling a general off the battlefield so he could respond to a subpoena.

Under the wartime constitution envisioned by the Bush administration:

- Terrorist suspects—even Americans captured in the United States—could be held without trial in military prisons for the duration of the war on terror.
- Surveillance capabilities built up during the Cold War could be used to gather "battlefield intelligence," even where the battlefield was defined broadly enough to include the American homeland.

- The nature, and even the very existence, of domestic surveillance programs and other war on terror initiatives—even those that directly affected the home front—would be classified as military secrets and shielded from examination by the courts or Congress.
- Pre-9/11 restrictions on domestic use of the military would no longer apply. Should the president decide to use army regulars to fight the terrorist threat at home, no mere statute could stand in his way.

For the president, and for much of the country, the war metaphor had powerful explanatory power; it not only gave context and meaning to the carnage of September 11, it provided battle plans outlining the proper response to attacks on American soil. At home, as abroad, the al Qaeda threat demanded a ruthless response, and, often as not, a military one. Given the nature of the war on terror, however, George W. Bush would not be the last president to wield the limitless authority he claimed; these were potentially permanent powers in a perpetual war.

The American Heritage of Anti-Militarism

That America had been born amid fear of standing armies would have been hard to detect by observing the politics of the post–September 11 era, in which presidents and presidential aspirants did everything they could to bask in the reflected glory of the U.S. military. In his first two and a half years in office, George W. Bush spoke at military installations or to military audiences 45 times.[5] As November 2004 approached, Bush based his drive for reelection on his record as a "war president," making ample use of American soldiers in campaign photo ops.

The Democratic nominee, Senator Kerry, responded in kind. Trying to position himself as a battle-tested war leader, Kerry used his campaign literature, commercials, and speeches to emphasize his role as a Swift Boat commander during the Vietnam War. In the early 1970s, as spokesman for Vietnam Veterans against the War, Kerry had been rather less proud of his service, claiming that American soldiers had committed countless atrocities in Southeast Asia. But for the 2004 race, the theme was "I'm John Kerry and I'm reporting for duty."

Over its history, America had seen plenty of presidential campaigns focusing on candidates' war records. But the 2004 race went well beyond "Tippecanoe and Tyler Too."[6] By the time of the Democratic National Convention in Boston, one half-feared Senator Kerry would be lowered rock star–style to the stage in a mock Swift Boat, shooting at black-pajama-clad Viet Cong popping up from rice paddies set up around the dais. In fact, the Kerry campaign actually searched for a Vietnam-era Swift Boat to place on the convention floor in the Fleet Center.[7] Ultimately, his handlers opted for a less dramatic water-taxi ride into Boston's inner harbor, with the senator flanked by former crewmates and snapping salutes to the crowd.

In the first post-9/11 presidential race, it was vitally important to look "more military than thou." In his 2005 book *The New American Militarism*, Boston University's Andrew Bacevich, a Vietnam veteran and former lieutenant colonel in the U.S. Army, writes that in recent years, Americans have "come to accept the propriety of using neatly turned-out soldiers and sailors as extras" in presidential campaigns. They have also become accustomed to "their president donning military garb—usually a fighter jock's snappy leather jacket—when visiting the troops or huddling with his advisors at Camp David." Bush's flight-suited carrier-deck landing on the *USS Abraham Lincoln* in May 2003 was, as Bacevich saw it, the culmination of this trend, with "the president as warlord," merging his identity with the troops.[8]

The rhetoric of the American Revolution would have seemed bizarre—even treasonous—in the political environment conditioned by the war on terror. Yet at times, the Founding Fathers could sound much like the young John Kerry of the Winter Soldier hearings. In 1784, Benjamin Franklin decried the regimentation of military service, comparing it with chattel slavery. For him, the army was "a devouring monster." Benjamin Rush, surgeon general of the Continental Army and, like Franklin, a signer of the Declaration of Independence, proposed in 1792 that two captions be painted "over the portals of the Department of War": "An office for butchering the human species" and "A Widow and Orphan making office."[9]

Of course, most 18th-century Americans respected individual soldiers and revered General Washington, the unanimous choice of the electors as first president of the United States. Yet, Americans of the time were also extremely wary of the army as an institution. Their experience under British rule had taught them to distrust and fear permanent military establishments. As Bernard Bailyn explains:

> Their fear was not simply of armies, but of *standing armies,* a phrase that had distinctive connotations . . . the colonists universally agreed that "unhappy nations have lost that precious jewel *liberty* . . . [because] their necessities or indiscretion have permitted a standing army to be kept amongst them."[10]

"Princes, armies, and perpetual war defined Europe," Andrew Bacevich writes; "the *absence* of these things was to provide a point of departure for defining America." Founding Generation Americans believed that "military power was poison—one not without its occasional utility, but a poison all the same and never to be regarded otherwise."[11]

Indeed, James Madison warned in 1795 that because war was "the parent of Armies" and a relentless force for the concentration of power, "no nation could preserve its freedom in the midst of continual warfare."[12] Earlier, at the Constitutional Convention, Madison had described the evils that "incessant wars" could bring:

> In time of actual war, great discretionary powers are constantly given to the Executive Magistrate. Constant apprehension of War, has the same tendency to render the head too large for the body. A standing military force, with an overgrown Executive will not long be safe companions to liberty. The means of defense agst. foreign danger have always been the instruments of tyranny at home.[13]

Power without Limit

Nonetheless, "continual warfare" was the background assumption and "great discretionary powers" the overarching goal after September 11, when John Yoo, top Cheney aide David Addington, and other administration lawyers began developing the legal framework for the administration's response to terrorism. Speaking with a *U.S. News* reporter in 2006, a former Justice Department official described the social dynamic at work at DOJ in the months after the terror attacks: "You put Addington, Yoo, and [then White House Counsel Alberto] Gonzales in a room, and there was a race to see who was tougher than the rest and how expansive they could be with respect to presidential power. . . . If you suggested anything less, you were considered a wimp."[14]

The product of that intellectual Toughman Contest was a series of Office of Legal Counsel legal opinions reading restraints on executive power out of the Constitution. As the Bush legal team saw it, the wartime president's constitutional authority was so broad, his discretion so vast, he could ignore any and all federal statutes that he believed to impinge on his ability to fight terrorism.

The core of the Bush theory of executive power can be seen in the so-called torture memos, a series of internal legal opinions written in 2002 and 2003 and publicly revealed in 2004.[15] Much of the public discussion about the torture memos has focused on the narrowness of their definition of torture, and the question of whether the Geneva Conventions cover al Qaeda and Taliban prisoners. What's most disturbing about the memos, however, is their assertion that the president cannot be restrained by validly enacted laws.

In 1988, the United States signed the United Nations Convention against Torture; in 1994, the Senate ratified that agreement. Later that year, Congress passed a statute implementing the agreement by making acts of torture committed under color of law outside the United States a federal crime. (Acts of torture committed within the United States were already prohibited by federal law.)[16] Yet, according to the key torture memo, an August 1, 2002, OLC opinion drafted by Yoo, such laws cannot bind the commander in chief: "Congress can no more interfere with the president's conduct of the interrogation of enemy combatants than it can dictate strategic or tactical decisions on the battlefield."[17]

To make that argument, Yoo had to ignore several constitutional provisions that bear directly on Congress's power to regulate the treatment of enemy prisoners. In contrast with the British system, in which the king had "the sole power of raising and regulating fleets and armies," the Framers gave Congress the power "to make Rules for the Government and Regulation of the land and naval forces," a power that had long been understood to allow regulation of U.S. servicemen's conduct in wartime.[18] The Constitution also gives Congress the power to "define and punish ... Offenses against the Law of Nations," empowering it to proscribe violations of America's treaty obligations, such as the Geneva Conventions' restrictions on the treatment of prisoners and the requirements of the UN Convention against Torture.[19]

One can imagine statutes that might, by dictating battlefield tactics, encroach on the president's authority as commander in chief. A law that said "Take Baghdad from the north, using the Fourth Infantry Division" would give us war by committee, which is what the Framers wanted to avoid when they made one man, the president, "first General and admiral of the Confederacy."[20] In the administration's view, however, *any* law that gets in the way of *any* tactic the president wants to pursue falls into this category—whether that tactic is torture or wiretapping or locking up American citizens without charges. Thus, not only can the president disregard the federal laws banning torture, he can ignore the Non-Detention Act, which bars imprisonment of American citizens "except pursuant to an Act of Congress," and the Foreign Intelligence Surveillance Act governing electronic surveillance for the purposes of gathering foreign intelligence. The administration reads the commander in chief and executive power clauses roughly as, "Congress shall make no law abridging the freedom of the president to do whatever he thinks effective in fighting the war on terror."

Faith-Based Constitutionalism

Are there *any* limits to that theory? The theory's principal architect, John Yoo, suggests that there aren't. After leaving OLC in 2003, Yoo resumed his prior career as a public intellectual and an enthusiastic defender of executive power. And in a December 2005 debate in Chicago, Yoo's exchange with Notre Dame law professor Douglass Cassel had the audience squirming in its seats:

> CASSEL: If the president deems that he's got to torture somebody, including by *crushing the testicles of the person's child,* there is no law that can stop him?
> YOO: No treaty ...

CASSEL: Also no law by Congress—that is what you wrote in
the August 2002 memo . . .

Yoo's answer? "I think it depends on why the President thinks he needs to do that."[21]

Is that the president's view as well? In a January 2006 interview CBS's Bob Schieffer asked Bush about the legal limits, if any, to his power: "Do you believe that there is anything that a president cannot do, if he considers it necessary, in an emergency like this?" The president responded:

> That's a—that's a great question. You know, one of the—yeah, I don't think a president can tort—get—can order torture, for example. I don't think a president can order the assassination of a leader of another country with which we're not at war. Yes, there are clear red lines, and—it—you—you—you just asked a very interesting constitutional question.[22]

It's telling that neither of Bush's examples represents a case in which the president considers himself bound by law or by anything other than his own sense of self-restraint. It's not a *statute* that bars the president from assassinating foreign leaders, but an executive order that the president himself could change unilaterally.[23] As for torture, the administration has never repudiated the theory of uncheckable executive power outlined in the torture memos. Less than a month before sitting down with Schieffer, the president signed an appropriations bill that included an amendment by Sen. John McCain (R-AZ) reaffirming the statutory ban on torture. Though Bush had threatened to veto the legislation, faced with a veto-proof majority in Congress, he acquiesced. But upon signing the law, he issued a signing statement suggesting that he could ignore the law if he thought it necessary.[24]

"There are clear red lines," Bush told Schieffer in the interview. But if those lines exist at all, they reside in the president's mind, and, under the administration's theory, they vanish when the president changes his mind. Bush's answer to Schieffer was less direct—and less cringe inducing—than Yoo's answer to Cassel, but in substance, much the same. In the place of the Framers' constitutional theory, which rested on a deep pessimism about man's capacity to withstand the temptations of unchecked power, the Bush administration had constructed a new constitution that depended entirely on trust.

With their man in office, Bush partisans seemed unable to imagine that anyone other than the pure of heart would ever inherit the powers forged by the Bush Justice Department. That was ironic, given that many of President Bush's most ardent supporters had spent the 1990s trying to convince the country that the presidency had been seized by someone of extraordinary venality, an unindicted felon, a serial abuser of women, and a man who could not be trusted with unchecked power.

Just how short memories had become on the right was evident at the February 2006 Conservative Political Action Conference in Washington, D.C. One of the panels at CPAC's annual gathering of movement conservatives featured a debate between former Justice Department official Viet Dinh and former representative Bob Barr. Barr, one of the House impeachment managers in the effort to remove President Clinton, was once the sort of fellow conservative activists loved. But in recent years, he had become a prominent critic of President Bush's war on terror policies, and that made him far less popular with the true believers attending CPAC.

Barr warned the audience about the dangers of an increasingly imperial presidency, and got booed for his troubles. His opponent, the architect of the Patriot Act, was more of a crowd pleaser. Dinh told the CPAC attendees that "the conservative movement has a healthy skepticism of governmental power, but at times, unfortunately, that healthy skepticism needs to yield."[25]

Individualized Martial Law

And yield it has, judging by the enthusiasm with which most conservatives rallied behind the president's claim that he had the constitutional power to serve as judge, jury, and jailer for American citizens suspected of terrorist involvement.[26] If the Constitution restricts the president at all, surely it must prevent him from arresting American citizens without review and confining them in military prisons for as long as he thinks it's necessary. After all, as Justice Antonin Scalia has noted, "The very core of liberty secured by our Anglo-Saxon system of separated powers has been freedom from indefinite imprisonment at the will of the Executive."[27]

Yet, the power to imprison American citizens at will was exactly what the administration demanded in the José Padilla case. At Chicago's O'Hare Airport in May 2002, federal agents arrested Padilla, a Brooklyn-born American, and held him on a material witness warrant. Two days before a hearing in federal court on the validity of that warrant, the president declared Padilla an "enemy combatant" and ordered him transferred to a naval brig in South Carolina, hundreds of miles away from his lawyer. The Department of Defense held Padilla there for three and a half years without charges, until the administration, fearing a possible loss in the Supreme Court, transferred him to federal prison in January 2006.

Legal scholar and former military lawyer Eugene Fidell saw the administration's legal theory as a grotesque version of martial law. Martial law had traditionally been defined on a geographical basis—a temporary condition, necessitated by emergency, governing areas of the country where the civil law could not operate. Yet, the legal fiction the president's lawyers had devised for Padilla was, Fidell wrote, "an unprecedented form of *personal* martial law regime," under which the president could restrict civil liberties indefinitely, without an emergency, even while federal courts functioned quite normally.[28]

In the ensuing litigation, when asked to produce evidence justifying Padilla's confinement, the administration came forward with a five-and-a-half-page "Declaration" by Michael Mobbs, an obscure Pentagon bureaucrat who has never been cross-examined by Padilla's attorneys. In that document, Mobbs averred that Padilla had met with al Qaeda operatives in Afghanistan and Pakistan to plot the construction and detonation of a "'radiological dispersal device' . . . possibly in Washington, DC."

Sparse as it is, the Mobbs Declaration still gives one pause about the caliber of evidence offered as justification for permanently extinguishing the rights of an American citizen. Referring to the confidential informants who fingered Padilla, the declaration notes:

Some information provided by the sources remains uncorroborated and may be part of an effort to mislead or confuse U.S.

officials. One of the sources, for example, in a subsequent interview with a U.S. law enforcement official recanted some of the information that he had provided, but most of this information has been independently corroborated by other sources. In addition, at the time of being interviewed by U.S. officials, one of the sources was being treated with various types of drugs to treat medical conditions.[29]

Granted, there's little in José Padilla's background to suggest he's an innocent man wrongly accused—he's a violent ex-con with apparent ties to al Qaeda.[30] But "the innocent have nothing to fear" is cold comfort and poor constitutional argument. The very principle that imprisons the guilty can be used to seize the innocent. And the principle the Bush administration advanced to justify Padilla's detention was broad indeed. The Bush legal team maintained that the power to unilaterally declare American citizens enemy combatants and hold them for the duration of the war on terrorism was "a basic exercise of [the president's] authority as Commander in Chief."[31]

That theory prompted an interesting exchange when the administration argued the case before the Supreme Court. The justices pressed Deputy Solicitor General Paul Clement on whether there were limits to what the president could do to an American accused of al Qaeda involvement: could the prisoner be shot or tortured? Clement said no, "that violates our own conception of what's a war crime." Justice Ruth Bader Ginsburg pressed him further: suppose the executive says that torture will be useful: "some systems do that to get information." "Well," said Clement, "our executive doesn't." But "what's constraining?" Ginsburg asked, "Is it just up to the good will of the executive?" Here's Clement's reply:

> You have to recognize that in situations where there is a war—where the Government is on a war footing, that *you have to trust the executive* to make the kind of quintessential military judgments that are involved in things like that.[32]

"Trust the leader" isn't the sort of check on abuse of power that the Framers had in mind. Our Constitution provides firmer guarantees than that: in the limited powers it grants each branch of government, and in the restraints it places on them in the Bill of Rights. Nor does the Bill of Rights feature an asterisk reading "unenforceable during time of war." As the Supreme Court declared when it rejected the military trial of a civilian in 1866, "the Constitution of the United States is a law for rulers and people, equally in war and in peace, and covers with the shield of its protection all classes of men, at all times."[33]

In the last few years, it's become common, even trite, for civil libertarians to liken George W. Bush's theory of executive power to Richard Nixon's infamous statement in his 1977 interview with David Frost: "When the president does it that means it is not illegal."[34] But in one important respect, the comparison is unfair to Nixon. Richard Nixon never claimed inherent power to arrest American citizens on American soil and hold them indefinitely without review. When he signed the Non-Detention Act of 1971, which made clear that the president had no such power, Nixon emphasized that "our democracy is built upon the constitutional guarantee that every citizen will be afforded due process of law. There is no place in American life for the kind of anxiety—however unwarranted—which the Emergency Detention Act has evidently engendered."[35] Three decades later, in the *Padilla* case, George W. Bush's Justice Department would argue that the Non-Detention Act was null and void.[36] The president's Magic Scepter of Inherent Authority allowed him to ignore the act's constraints.

Military Surveillance at Home

If the wartime constitution allowed the president to confine citizens at will in military prisons, surely it allowed him to use the military to gather intelligence at home. But, as noted earlier, domestic surveillance by the military has had a long and sordid history in the United States. Woodrow Wilson had set military intelligence agents free to spy on and harass war protestors during World War I. In the 1960s, under pressure from Presidents Johnson and Nixon, the army got back into the domestic spying business. What had begun as an effort to better prepare for periodic riot control duties in American cities was soon afflicted by mission creep on a massive scale. The army amassed files on groups it viewed as potential threats, a category that, as one intelligence officer later testified, grew to include "virtually every group engaged in dissent in the United States," including the American Civil Liberties Union, Business Executives Move to End the War in Vietnam, the National Organization for Women, and "clergymen, teachers, journalists, editors, attorneys . . . business executives, and authors."[37]

In the months after 9/11, the Bush administration brushed aside that legacy of abuse, aggressively ramping up military intelligence gathering at home. First, there was the revelation in 2002 that, under the direction of former Reagan national security adviser John Poindexter, the Pentagon's Defense Advanced Research Projects Agency was developing a powerful data-mining system called "Total Information Awareness." Poindexter, then working as senior vice president of a defense technology firm, sold DARPA on the idea in October 2001 in a briefing titled "A Manhattan Project for Counter-Terrorism." The Pentagon hired Poindexter to run the program despite his 1988 conviction on seven felony counts arising out of the Iran-Contra scandal.[38]

Once developed, TIA could potentially allow the military—or whatever part of the government has access to the technology—to build a comprehensive data profile on, and track the activities of, any American it chooses. A TIA graphic featured on DARPA's website in 2003 envisioned use of "Transactional Data," including "Financial, Education, Travel, Medical, Veterinary, Country Entry, Place/Event Entry, Transportation, Housing . . . [and] Communications" data, as well as "Authentication Biometric Data," including "Face, Finger Prints, Gait, [and] Iris" identifiers.[39]

Poindexter maintained that TIA would not necessarily remain in the military's hands, but military officials showed a keen interest in its development. Major General Dale Meyerrose, then chief information technology officer for NORTHCOM, told a conference of military officials and civilian contractors in November 2002, "I've been to [visit] Admiral Poindexter; he and I are talking about TIA."[40]

That month, William Safire, who had been subject to illegal wiretapping as a Nixon speechwriter, drew attention to the program in a *New York Times* op-ed entitled "You Are a Suspect." The resulting public outcry led Congress in early 2003 to pass legislation restricting TIA's development or deployment until key questions about its uses and potential for abuse were answered.[41] But that bill didn't put an end to the program. Core elements of TIA migrated to the National Security

Agency. If it's any consolation, the TIA prototype no longer goes by its original Orwellian moniker. "We will be describing this new effort as 'Basketball,'" wrote one of the contractors in an email to others working on the program.[42]

Of course, the most controversial post-9/11 surveillance initiative was the National Security Agency program revealed by the *New York Times* in December 2005. As the *Times* reported, via a secret executive order issued in 2002, President Bush informed the Pentagon's key intelligence-gathering agency that it could ignore certain requirements of the Foreign Intelligence Surveillance Act.[43] The NSA would no longer need warrants to listen in on or read Americans' telephone calls, emails, and other communications, so long as one party to the communication was located outside the United States and there was reason to believe that it involved a person "affiliated with Al Qaeda or part of an organization or group that is supportive of Al Qaeda."[44]

Congress had passed FISA in 1978 to prevent a recurrence of the abuses documented by the Church Committee. Among them were two NSA programs that violated Americans' privacy rights on a massive scale. Under "Project Minaret," from the early 1960s until 1973, the NSA, in cooperation with other federal agencies, compiled watch lists of potentially subversive Americans, monitored their overseas calls and telegrams, and distributed information about them to other federal agencies. Watch-listed Americans "ranged from members of radical political groups, to celebrities, to ordinary citizens involved in protests against their Government."[45] "Project Shamrock," under which the NSA collected all telegraphic data entering or leaving the United States, was, according to Senator Church, "probably the largest government interception program affecting Americans ever undertaken."[46]

The Bush administration's secret end run around FISA raised the possibility that abuses like Minaret and Shamrock could recur. But the Bush Justice Department dismissed civil libertarian concerns and insisted that the program was perfectly legal. In support of its evasion of FISA, the administration offered a statutory argument based on the Authorization for the Use of Military Force that Congress passed the week after September 11. In that resolution, Congress authorized the president to use "all necessary and appropriate force" to fight al Qaeda.

According to DOJ, abrogating FISA was "necessary and appropriate" in a conflict that might, after all, be fought on American soil.

That argument ignored FISA's plain language, which (together with the Wiretap Act) makes FISA the "exclusive means" for conducting foreign intelligence surveillance. It also ignored the facts that FISA already included a provision for temporary wartime suspension of the warrant requirement for 15 days after war is declared, and that, as far as we know, no member of Congress believed he or she was amending FISA by authorizing war in Afghanistan. In fact, after 9/11, at the administration's request, Congress debated and passed legislation to loosen FISA's requirements, seemingly unaware that they'd already given the president the power to suspend the statute for as long as it might take to "rid the world of evil."[47]

To bolster its unimpressive statutory claim, the administration added the by-now-familiar constitutional argument. According to DOJ's white paper defending the NSA program, Congress was powerless to control the "war president," even when he invoked his war powers to listen in on Americans' voice and internet communications: "The NSA activities are supported by the President's well-recognized inherent constitutional authority as Commander in Chief and sole organ for the Nation in foreign affairs to conduct warrantless surveillance of enemy forces."[48]

The Justice Department initially claimed that the NSA program was limited to international communications. But the administration's limitless view of inherent executive authority raised the question: if the president's powers are that broad, don't they also allow him to monitor communications that are wholly domestic—calls and emails between two Americans located in the United States?

Attorney General Alberto Gonzales came close to endorsing that view in an appearance before the House Judiciary Committee. In response to questioning from the panel, Gonzales intimated that the president had inherent authority to wiretap Americans' *domestic* communications without a warrant: "I'm not going to rule it out," the attorney general said. Later that day, the Justice Department issued a Nixonian "nonclarification clarification" of Gonzales's remarks: "The attorney general's comments today should not be interpreted to suggest the existence or nonexistence of a domestic program or whether any such program would be lawful under the existing legal analysis."[49] Again, anyone looking for a straight answer as to the limits of presidential power would have to look elsewhere.

The Military and State Secrets Privilege

The administration didn't plan to be any more forthcoming with the courts than it had been with Congress or the public, however. Exposure of the NSA program spurred a number of civil suits by, among others, scholars, journalists, and ordinary citizens who believed that the government might be listening in on their overseas phone calls and emails. The administration's response was to request dismissal with prejudice of all cases involving the program:

> The United States submits that the actions authorized by the President are essential to meeting a continuing and grave foreign terrorist threat and are well within lawful bounds. To demonstrate this, however, would require evidence that must be excluded from consideration under the military and state secrets privilege.[50]

The privilege the administration invoked in the NSA cases is a powerful one; it has its roots in "crown privilege" in English law, which allowed executive officers "to keep the King's counsel secret."[51] In its modern incarnation, the military and state secrets privilege lets the government shield information from civil or criminal discovery when "compulsion of the evidence will expose military matters which, in the interest of national security, should not be divulged."[52] Courts accord "utmost deference" to executive assertions of privilege on national security grounds, and judicial review of any such claim is narrow.[53] As the Supreme Court explained in *United States v. Reynolds*, the landmark 1953 case recognizing the military and state secrets doctrine, if a court satisfies itself that national security secrets are at issue, "even the most compelling necessity [on the part of the litigant] cannot overcome the claim of privilege."[54] However great the harm to the citizen, however egregious the abuse he's suffered, a successful invocation of the privilege bars the courthouse door.

Typically, the judge will not even examine the documents sought to ensure that they actually contain privileged information, lest too much judicial inquiry "force disclosure of the thing the privilege was meant to protect."[55] In fact, in more than two-thirds of reported cases in which the privilege has been invoked, courts have simply taken the government at its word.[56]

Although the privilege appears in only six reported cases between 1953 and 1976, its use has increased significantly over the past three decades. From Carter through Clinton, presidents invoked it in 59 reported cases, and the Bush administration appears to be using the privilege with still greater frequency: it appears in 39 reported cases since 2001, more than twice as frequently as it did from 1976 to 2000.[57]

Before 9/11, presidents had most often claimed state secrets to limit discovery, rather than attempting to quash entire cases. In the last few years, however, the Bush administration has used the privilege to seek blanket dismissal of cases challenging warrantless surveillance and the practice of "extraordinary rendition": transferring terrorist suspects to countries where they may be tortured. In one recent case involving a challenge to the NSA wiretapping program, federal judge Vaughn Walker noted the unusual nature of the government's claim: in the history of the privilege, "No case dismissed because its 'very subject matter' was a state secret involved ongoing, widespread violations of individual constitutional rights."[58]

The administration has demanded extraordinary deference from the courts as it fights off challenges to various war on terror initiatives. But even well before 9/11, judicial deference toward the state secrets privilege was an invitation to abuse. There's no better illustration of that than *Reynolds*, the seminal Supreme Court case examining the doctrine. *Reynolds* arose out of the 1948 crash of a B-29 aircraft in Waycross, Georgia, on a flight to test electronic navigation equipment. Three widows of civilian observers killed in the crash brought a wrongful-death suit and sought discovery of the air force's accident report on the crash. The secretary of the air force refused to turn over the report, citing national security reasons, and the Supreme Court upheld the claim of privilege.

It now appears that the Court was hoodwinked. Five decades later, the report had been declassified, and Judy Loether, the daughter of one of the victims, ordered a copy. According to the declassified report, "the aircraft is not considered to have been safe for flight," because in violation of air force directives, a protective shield designed to prevent engine overheating had not been installed on the bomber. No genuine military secret was involved—instead the executive branch used "crown privilege" to shield evidence of its own negligence.[59] The Bush team's drive to expand the military and state secrets privilege would virtually ensure more such "successes," perhaps on matters far graver than mere negligence.

Deployed in the USA

While the Bush Justice Department was developing the legal theories necessary to excuse domestic surveillance by military agencies—and shield the very fact of that surveillance from discovery in the courts and Congress—the administration's lawyers were also working to clear the way for more direct participation by U.S. armed forces in the fight against terrorism on the home front. The legal barrier here was the Posse Comitatus Act.[60] Passed in 1878, the PCA makes it a crime to use federal troops to "execute the laws" in circumstances not "expressly authorized by the Constitution or Act of Congress."[61] Thanks to the PCA, any president who wants to use the U.S. military to arrest, search, or otherwise coerce citizens is prevented from doing so unless he can point to a statutory or constitutional exception to the act's requirement.

In the early days of the war on terror, administration officials wanted to get the act amended or repealed; but by 2003, they'd decided that no changes were necessary. But the reasoning that seems to lie behind that decision is anything but comforting. Apparently, the administration does not consider itself bound by the PCA if it decides to use the military domestically for any purpose related to the war on terror. In October 2001, John Yoo authored a memorandum invoking the president's inherent executive authority and powers as commander in chief to make the case that the PCA "does not forbid the use of military force for the military purpose of preventing and deterring terrorism within the United States."[62] A year after the attacks, Peter Verga, one of the Pentagon's top officials on homeland security, put it plainly: "As we have looked at Posse Comitatus and looked at the missions of the

Department of Defense and the potential missions of NORTHCOM, we do not see any conflicts between the two. . . . The president cannot order things that are inconsistent with Posse Comitatus, because one of the things that [it] provides for is [for] the president to essentially waive Posse Comitatus." The law constrains the president—except, apparently, when the president decides to waive the law.[63]

In the jittery aftermath of 9/11, public officials reached instinctively for the military option in the face of what seemed to be an enormous and ongoing threat. That reflex was understandable, even if it led to some bizarre policy prescriptions. In the weeks after the attacks, then Transportation secretary Norman Mineta repeatedly urged that U.S. special forces troops—including elite Delta Force members—be placed aboard civilian airliners to neutralize hijackers. Clearly Delta Force soldiers belonged abroad, hunting al Qaeda operatives—not racking up frequent-flier miles on transcontinental flights.[64] Reflexive militarism governed much of the response at the state level as well. Authorities in Florida stationed a tank outside Miami International Airport over the Thanksgiving holiday in 2001, as if the next terror attack would come in the form of an al Qaeda mechanized column, rather than a shoe bomb or a smuggled box cutter.[65]

Even after the initial wave of fear had passed, though, the Bush administration moved to keep its options open with regard to possible use of U.S. armed forces at home. In the summer of 2005, the *Washington Post* reported on classified military plans that envisioned rapid-reaction forces responding to various crisis scenarios with up to 3,000 soldiers per incident.[66]

But there was and is little reason to believe that a military response to the terrorist threat on the home front would prove effective. At its core task, defeating enemy regimes, the U.S. military has no equal. The further the theater of operations departs from set-piece battles against enemy armies, however, the further our armed forces find themselves from their core competence. Counterinsurgency warfare is difficult enough, as the Iraq War has demonstrated. The American "battlespace"—a disquieting concept in its own right—presents still greater difficulties for an institution designed to solve problems with overwhelming firepower. The military option won't work where constitutional rights apply, as they do—or should—at home, and the enemy knows better than to reveal itself and engage in a "fair fight." What, after all, is the military response to backpack explosives set off in a subway car or a bomb smuggled aboard an airplane? A show of force at home might create the illusion of security, but, like the tank stationed outside Miami International Airport after 9/11, it's a clumsy response to the sorts of threats we face.

Clumsy, and potentially dangerous. The history of domestic military intervention cautions against weakening those barriers that inhibit the use of standing armies at home. Repeatedly throughout American history, the executive branch has deployed troops against civilians, often with appalling results. In the years leading up to the Civil War, the federal government used U.S. armed forces to disperse abolitionist protestors and return escaped slaves to bondage, and in the late 19th century, federal officials periodically violated the act to crush labor movements.[67]

The PCA was designed to serve as a shield against such abuses. As one federal court has put it: "Military personnel must be trained to operate under circumstances where the protection of constitutional freedoms cannot receive the consideration needed in order to assure their preservation. The Posse Comitatus statute is intended to meet that danger."[68] Police officers, ideally, are trained to operate in an environment where constitutional rights apply, and to use force only as a last resort. But the soldier "is trained to vaporize, not Mirandize," as former assistant secretary of defense Lawrence Korb has put it.[69] The same training that makes U.S. soldiers outstanding warriors makes them extremely dangerous as cops.

A tragic incident in 1997 made that all too clear. On May 20 of that year, a Marine Corps anti-drug patrol shot and killed an 18-year-old high school student named Esequiel Hernandez. Hernandez was herding goats and carrying a .22-caliber rifle near his family's farm in Redford, Texas, when he ran into the marines, who were hidden in the brush, heavily camouflaged, with blackened faces and bodies covered in burlap and leaves. Shots were exchanged. Instead of identifying themselves or trying to defuse the situation, the marines hunted Hernandez for 20 minutes. When Hernandez raised his rifle again, one of the marines shot him, and let him bleed to death without attempting to administer first aid.[70]

An internal Pentagon investigation into the incident noted that the soldiers were ill prepared for contact with civilians, their military training having instilled "an aggressive spirit while teaching basic combat skills," an assessment echoed by a senior FBI agent involved with the case: "The Marines perceived a target-practicing shot as a threat to their safety. . . . From that point, their training and instincts took over to neutralize a threat."[71] The Justice Department ultimately paid out $1.9 million to the Hernandez family as settlement of a wrongful-death lawsuit.

As the Hernandez case shows, mixing war-fighting and policing functions puts civilians at risk. Reducing that risk requires retraining soldiers for interaction with American civilians. But that in turn undermines military readiness: because combat skills are perishable, the longer soldiers are deployed at home, the less effective they'll be in conventional warfare. In 2003, the General Accounting Office closely examined the post–September 11 deployments on the home front, and found, unsurprisingly, that walking around airports and sitting at border guard stations were poor ways to prepare for combat, and that homeland security demands could "significantly erode [U.S. soldiers'] readiness to perform combat missions and impact future personnel retention."[72]

A militarized approach to homeland security would weaken the U.S. military and increase the threat of collateral damage to civilians, without making them any safer from terrorism. Worst of all, it would undermine a bedrock principle of American liberty: that maintaining order at home is a job for civilian peace officers, not combat-trained soldiers. As we'll see later, that principle has been undermined even in areas that have nothing to do with terrorism, as when the Katrina fiasco helped the president gain new powers to put troops in policing roles during hurricanes and other natural disasters.

Mission Creep

From the first, the Bush administration viewed every aspect of the terrorist threat through the lens of the war paradigm, and, accordingly, crafted a homeland security strategy based on reflexive militarism and devotion to unchecked power. Troubling as that approach might be, no sober, fair-minded person would argue that George W. Bush has turned post-9/11 America into a police state. The process of getting on an airplane may have become a bit more degrading and far more annoying than it used to be, but the average American retains virtually every important civil liberty he had before September 2001.

Although the Bush team was completely unrestrained in court, arguing for the broadest possible interpretation of executive power, in practice the administration never pushed those powers as far as its underlying theory would allow. In its legal briefs and internal memorandums, the administration insisted that Article II of the Constitution gives it the power to use the army as it pleases, tap the phones and read the emails of whomever it chooses, and confine any American it suspects of terrorist involvement. At the same time, the administration was fairly restrained when it comes to using the vast powers it claims.[73]

But there's no guarantee that future presidents will continue to show such restraint. America has enjoyed relative peace and quiet since September 11, but if that calm is shattered by further attacks, the wartime constitution forged by the Bush Justice Department may be used to work drastic and permanent changes in American law.

The Future of Executive Detention

Consider President Bush's claim that his wartime powers allowed him to seize American citizens at home and subject them to indefinite military detention. Thus far, José Padilla remains the lone U.S. citizen to whom this extraconstitutional power has been applied.[74] But in 2002, the administration considered *routinely* locking up terrorist suspects without trial.

A year after 9/11, Vice President Dick Cheney and Defense Secretary Donald Rumsfeld wanted to use the "enemy combatant" concept to hold six Americans from Lackawanna, New York, in a military brig without access to the courts. "They are the enemy, and they're right here in the country," Cheney declared, according to an administration official. The administration also debated using that power against other Americans, including a group of suspected terrorists in Portland, Oregon. It was, surprisingly enough, then attorney general John Ashcroft who spoke up for civil liberties and the rule of law, convincing the administration to pursue the Lackawanna Six through ordinary constitutional processes.[75] Yet, the administration still clung to the constitutional theory it advanced in the *Padilla* case, and should a significant terrorist threat resurface at home, future presidents may find the idea of an executive arrest power quite tempting.

21st-Century Military Surveillance

The dangers of mission creep in domestic surveillance are already apparent, as recent experience with the Pentagon's TALON database shows. TALON, short for Threat and Local Observation Notice, was the military's version of Operation TIPS, the Bush administration's aborted 2002 attempt to deputize private citizens to report suspicious activity to federal law enforcement. From 2002 to 2007, the Pentagon encouraged military personnel and civilians working with the military to file TALON reports on suspicious activities, reports that could be sent to civilian law enforcement agencies for further investigation or action.

Federal intelligence operatives assigned to COINTELPRO, CHAOS, and other domestic spying programs in the 1950s, 1960s, and 1970s found little genuine evidence of communist subversion. Yet, it's the rare bureaucracy that closes up shop for lack of anything useful to do: instead, COINTELPRO and CHAOS agents began keeping files on law-abiding citizens who disagreed with their government. A similar dynamic seems to have been at work with the TALON program. In December 2005, NBC News obtained 400 pages worth of TALON reports, revealing that the Department of Defense had compiled information about scores of anti-war meetings, including a "war profiteering" protest outside the Houston headquarters of Halliburton, where a group of peace activists wore papier-mâché masks and handed out free peanut butter sandwiches.[76] In another case, the army's 902nd Military Intelligence Group warned the Akron, Ohio, police department about a March 2005 assembly of middle-aged peace activists organized by local Quakers. Responding to criticism about the army's interest in the Quaker gathering, a Pentagon spokesman declared, "The fact that the marches proceeded peacefully is irrelevant to leveling criticisms against the Army in this instance. Hindsight is always 20/20."[77]

Eventually, the DOD decided that whatever security benefits TALON provided weren't worth the public ridicule it brought; in early 2007, the Pentagon announced it would shut down the database. Yet, other domestic intelligence gathering efforts—TIA development, the NSA surveillance program, military cooperation with domestic law enforcement—continue apace.

Moore's law, coined by Intel cofounder Gordon E. Moore, stipulates that computer-processing power per unit cost—"bang for your buck"—doubles every two years. And in the three decades since the Church Committee and FISA reined in domestic spying, we've come very far technologically. Keeping tabs on dissenters was a low-tech affair during the age of the Heroic Presidency. FBI and CIA agents depended on paper files and index cards; they needed to physically open letters and individually review telegrams. Today, with modern processing power and data-mining technology, the possibilities for surveillance are staggering. And so is the potential for abuse.

Our history gives us little reason to hope that such powers won't be abused by future presidents. Defenders of the so-called Terrorist Surveillance Program like to reduce that history to one word, "Watergate." As we've seen, however, presidents misused federal intelligence agencies and spied on American citizens for decades before the "Plumbers'" unit was born. From FDR's ordering the FBI to monitor "subversives" and his political opponents, to JFK's wiretapping uncooperative businessmen, to LBJ's bugging Goldwater's campaign plane, the history of executive branch surveillance makes it clear that power unchecked will become power abused.

The Future of Posse Comitatus

There's also a serious danger that the war on terror will blur the line between civil and military functions. The U.S. military is becoming highly integrated with federal law enforcement: military personnel are stationed in all 56 FBI field offices around the country, and since 2002, federal law enforcement has been sharing information with NORTHCOM and vice versa.[78] And the U.S. military has technological assets and manpower that embattled civilian agencies will find tempting. In the heightened threat environment of the post–September 11 world, that temptation may lead to more military involvement at home.

The D.C. sniper incident from October 2002 shows how that might happen. For three weeks that fall, two men with a rifle terrorized the greater Washington area, killing 10 people and wounding 3. With local and federal law enforcement frustrated, Defense Secretary Donald Rumsfeld approved the use of Army RC-7 surveillance aircraft to find the sniper. The low-flying planes, crammed with $17 million worth of infrared sensors and other surveillance technologies, are typically used for tasks like monitoring troop movements around the demilitarized zone on the Korean peninsula, and federal officials thought they could help pinpoint the sniper's location.[79]

Of course, in the end, when the snipers were caught, it wasn't with high-tech military hardware, but through old-fashioned police work. However, law enforcement officials' eagerness to seek military help in the sniper case suggests that we may see more military involvement in high-profile investigations in the future. As Bob Barr asked during the sniper hunt, "If you use this as a precedent, where do you then draw the line?"[80]

Even where the military's role is limited to advice, training, and provision of equipment—none of which technically violates the PCA—the erosion of the civil-military line is troubling. After all, military involvement in the 1993 standoff between federal agents and the Branch Davidian community in Waco, Texas, contributed to one of the worst law enforcement disasters in American history. Federal law enforcement officials used false allegations of drug trafficking to obtain military hardware for the raid, including Bradley Fighting Vehicles and M1 Abrams tanks.[81] And it was U.S. Army Delta Force commanders who advised federal agents to launch a tank and CS gas assault against the Branch Davidians.[82] Though the military's role at Waco was apparently limited to providing equipment and advice, that involvement helped lead to a militarized assault that ended in the deaths of 80 civilians, including 27 children.

Waco's survivors had extraordinary difficulty getting the executive branch to provide information about the army's role in the raid; so did the parents of Esequiel Hernandez, the boy killed by the Marine Corps anti-drug patrol. In both cases, the executive branch tried to shield the soldiers from questioning and keep the details of military involvement from coming to light.[83] Americans injured by civilian police officers often run up against the so-called blue wall of silence, a misguided ethic that encourages police officers to shield brutality and corruption in the ranks. The militarization of homeland security threatens to erect a wall of silence that's even harder to breach. The more the executive branch turns the machinery of war inward to fight the war on terror at home, and the more it relies on aggressive use of the state secrets privilege, the greater the danger that any resulting "collateral damage" to American lives and liberty will go unexamined and future abuses, undeterred.

"Suicide Pact"?

The Framers designed a Constitution in which powers were carefully limited, cabined by specific constitutional guarantees, and those guarantees reinforced by each branch's desire to preserve its own power. After 9/11, the Bush administration propounded an alternative constitution—a "Neoconstitution" in which trust would take the place of checks and balances. Under the Neoconstitution, the president has the power to ignore the law, spy on citizens, lock them up without due process, put troops in the streets, and keep Americans from finding out what happened if they're harmed along the way. The vision that animates that document is as alien to the Framers' Constitution as was the Progressives' dream of a president unbound by law.

Yet, some say that removing restraints on the executive is necessary to meet the threats we face. As former Massachusetts governor and 2008 presidential candidate Mitt Romney put it, "Our most basic civil liberty is the right to be kept alive."[84] In the phrase that's become so common since September 11, "the Constitution is not a suicide pact."[85]

That phrase has become the "tell it to the hand" of constitutional debate, a means to bring discussion to a close before it has properly begun. Those who deploy the "suicide pact" sound bite rarely bother to provide evidence that protecting whichever constitutional liberty is currently in the cross hairs amounts to national "suicide"—or at least presents unacceptable risks.

But the "suicide pact" sound bite is no mere debater's trick; many Americans sincerely believe that al Qaeda represents an "existential threat" to our way of life. In his 2007 book *The Terror Presidency*, Jack Goldsmith recounts his experiences as head of the Justice Department's Office of Legal Counsel in 2003 and 2004, when he tried to distance the administration from the legal theories developed by John Yoo and others. "If you rule that way," Cheney lieutenant David Addington told Goldsmith when Goldsmith quarreled with one presidential initiative, "the blood of the hundred thousand people who die in the next attack will be on *your* hands."[86] Though Goldsmith thought some of Addington's judgments were "crazy," he agreed with Addington's assessment of the threat. President Bush may have "acted in such disregard of our constitutional traditions," Goldsmith writes in *The Terror Presidency*, but we ought to keep in mind that "no president [before George W. Bush] has faced such an imminent threat to the nation's existence."[87]

Is Islamic terrorism "an imminent threat to the nation's existence"? Evidence for that proposition is hard to find. As political scientist John Mueller points out, before 2001, more Americans were killed by lightning every year than died in terror attacks. Even after factoring in 9/11, year by year more Americans die from allergic reactions to peanuts than fall victim to jihad.[88] *True* "weapons of mass destruction," principally nuclear weapons and certain biological agents, are exceedingly hard to come by. The most spectacular terrorist use of so-called WMDs was the sarin-gas strike on the Tokyo subway by the Aum Shinrikyo cult. It killed 12 people.[89] If terrorists ever managed to kill 100,000 Americans, as Addington suggests they might, that would represent roughly 37 times the toll of the most destructive attack in the tactic's history, and nearly 17,000 times the average number of fatalities for individual terrorist attacks on Americans.[90]

It's hard to make such arguments without sounding like one has adopted a dangerously complacent attitude toward the terrorist threat. That's why such arguments rarely get made. All too often they're summarily dismissed, or used to indict the person making them. On the campaign trail in 2004, when Senator Kerry said we'd never eliminate terrorism, but he hoped we'd get to the point where it was simply a "nuisance," he spoke good sense. His reward was a Bush campaign commercial using the statement to portray him as soft on terror.[91]

Hoping to rekindle Americans' waning sense of urgency about the terrorist threat, in November 2007 the conservative Heritage Foundation released a study titled "U.S. Thwarts 19 Terrorist Attacks against America since 9/11." To get to 19, Heritage had to pad the numbers with cases that didn't involve threats to America, and several in which the would-be perpetrators hadn't yet come up with anything resembling a plan.[92] Some of those who had formulated plans seemed distinctly inept: would-be jihadi Iyman Faris schemed to cut down the Brooklyn Bridge with a blowtorch, whereas the Fort Dix plotters planned to launch an armed attack on a New Jersey military base, but were rounded up after they "asked a store clerk to copy a video of them firing assault weapons and screaming about jihad."[93]

Again, none of the above should be taken as a counsel of complacency. Of course federal law enforcement officials should vigorously pursue those who may be plotting terrorist attacks, and of course they shouldn't wait until an attack is imminent to arrest and prosecute those who would do us harm. But it's also worth entertaining the idea that perhaps we're *not* all going to die if we're old-fashioned enough to maintain constitutional checks on executive power. If there's a case to be made for abandoning Anglo-American liberties, like protection from arbitrary imprisonment, that date back to the Magna Carta, it ought to be made of more terrifying stuff.

"Situational Constitutionalism" and Executive Power

After 9/11, however, it became clear that most of the right shared David Addington's views on the magnitude of the threat and the need to remove restraints on the executive branch. Once an ideological bulwark against the concentration of power, the conservative movement had become a presidential enabler, and conservative opinion leaders seemed unable to understand how any patriotic American could, in good faith, oppose presidential wars or unrestricted surveillance.

Exhibit A was the *Wall Street Journal*, whose commentary pages had long been required daily reading for movement conservatives. In the 1990s, the *Journal*'s editorialists worked ceaselessly to convince the country that Bill and Hillary Clinton were crooks who could not be trusted with power. The *Journal* compiled enough dirt on the Whitewater scandal alone to fill a six-volume collection. On the op-ed page, the *Journal* ran columns intimating that, as governor of Arkansas, Bill Clinton was a drug runner and a rapist.[94]

September 11 really did "change everything" for the *Journal*'s opinion editors (though one suspects that Republican recapture of the executive branch played a part as well). George W. Bush's second term found the paper running encomiums to the Imperial Presidency that would test the skills of the archest satirist. In August 2007, Ion Mihai Pacepa, "the highest-ranking intelligence official ever to have defected from the Soviet Bloc," explored the ominous parallels between communist espionage and domestic criticism of George W. Bush, telling the *Journal*'s readers that "discrediting the president was one of the main tactics of the Soviet-bloc intelligence community." As Pacepa recounted, the Soviets would stop at nothing in their disinformation campaign, portraying "Nixon as a petty tyrant, Ford as a dimwitted football player and Jimmy Carter as a bumbling peanut farmer." (Just think of how close Americans came to believing those vicious lies.) "This same strategy is at work today," the former Soviet spy warned darkly, in places like the 2004 Democratic National Convention.[95] Some months earlier, the *Journal* gave the Harvard philosopher and self-styled expert on "manliness" Harvey Mansfield over 3,000 words to make "The Case for the Strong Executive," in which Mansfield asserted that "defects" in the rule of law "sugges[t] the need for one-man rule," especially in emergencies—temporary or otherwise.[96]

Indeed, conservatives seemed incapable of imagining that anyone other than George W. Bush would ever wield the new powers his administration was busily forging. Recall the debate between Viet Dinh and Bob Barr at 2006's Conservative Political Action Conference: while lauding the conservative movement's traditional skepticism toward government power, Dinh insisted that "at times, unfortunately, that healthy skepticism needs to yield." "At times" might have been more accurately reformulated as "from now on." After all, the war on terror will not end with a treaty in Paris and a ticker-tape parade. It is, in a phrase used repeatedly by Pentagon officials, "the Long War," one that may continue for as long as there are Islamic terrorists who want to do us harm.

And there's good reason to believe that future presidents will find George W. Bush's constitutional theories attractive as they wage the Long War. In December 2007, Charlie Savage, the *Boston Globe* reporter who won a Pulitzer Prize for his stories on the Bush administration's belligerent approach to signing statements, polled the presidential candidates on executive power. Of the Republicans who responded, only long shot Ron Paul gave consistently constitutionalist answers.

In contrast, the Democrats mostly renounced the Bush administration's constitutional theories in areas such as surveillance and detention of terrorist suspects.[97] But whatever their party, Bush's successors will face powerful incentives to revert to that doctrine and enhance their dominance. Each of those who follow him will assume the role of post-9/11 "Protector of the Peace," conscious that the public holds the president responsible for a vigorous response to the terrorist threat. As Jack Goldsmith put it in *The Terror Presidency*,

> For generations the Terror Presidency will be characterized by an unremitting fear of attack, an obsession with preventing the attack, and a proclivity to act aggressively and preemptively to do so. . . . If anything, the next Democratic President—having digested a few threat matrices, and acutely aware that he or she alone will be wholly responsible when thousands of Americans are killed in the next attack—will be even more anxious than the current President to thwart the threat.[98]

Goldsmith may be wrong about the magnitude of the threat, but he's very likely correct about the political dynamic at work.

Moreover, few presidential candidates make the sacrifices entailed in running for president hoping to *reduce* the powers of the office once they assume it. Capturing the presidency tends to imbue presidents and their supporters with a newfound appreciation of the advantages of unilateral control. Upon assuming power, the former out-party typically abandons its criticisms of unilateralism; the ability to make law by executive order, to order military action without congressional approval, to tap phones and read email without securing a warrant—all such powers seem far more enticing when one's friends are at the helm.

The record of the Clinton administration provides little reason to suppose that the next Democratic administration will take a timid attitude toward the unilateral exercise of executive power. Bill Clinton had no reservations about using the threat of terrorism to improve his political standing and amass power in the aftermath of the Oklahoma City bombing in April 1995. That bombing, until 9/11 the most devastating terror strike ever to occur on American soil, came less than 24 hours after the memorable prime-time news conference in which the president, visibly unsettled by a reporter's suggestion that the new

Republican Congress was in charge, sputtered: "The constitution gives me relevance. The power of our ideas gives me relevance. . . . The President is relevant."[99] After the destruction of the Alfred P. Murrah Federal Building, the president's relevance was immediately apparent. Rahm Emanuel, then a senior White House adviser, later commented that "Oklahoma is where [Clinton] finds the combination to the lock, in my view. He finds his voice as the president."[100]

Soon President Clinton used his newfound voice to describe Oklahoma City in terms of a "war against terrorism."[101] And in keeping with the historical pattern, Clinton moved to enhance his power, seeking new wiretapping authority and new powers to use the military at home.[102] Ironically enough, on some of the new proposals, the president faced resistance from civil liberties–minded Republicans.[103] After the Republican-dominated House of Representatives refused to pass several provisions Clinton had demanded to fight terrorism, the president denounced it angrily:

> The House also voted to let terrorists like Hamas continue to raise money in America by stripping the Justice Department's authority to designate organizations as terrorists. . . . The House voted against allowing us to deport foreigners who support terrorist activities more quickly, and it voted to cripple our ability to use high-tech surveillance to keep up with stealthy and fast-moving terrorists.[104]

Even in the longest period of peace and prosperity since the reign of Warren Harding and Calvin Coolidge, when it came to presidential prerogatives, Bill Clinton behaved little differently—and in some ways, more aggressively—than his Republican predecessors. "The Clinton administration was every bit as important as the Reagan and first Bush administrations in helping the current Bush administration formulate its attitude toward the unitary executive," writes political scientist Christopher S. Kelley.[105]

Walter Dellinger, head of the Office of Legal Counsel under Clinton, never pushed presidential power as far as Bush OLC head Jay Bybee and his deputy John Yoo; but, as Dellinger puts it, "I strongly upheld executive power and handed it on largely intact." In 1994, after President Clinton had publicly maintained that he was not "constitutionally mandated" to seek congressional authorization before a contemplated invasion of Haiti with some 20,000 American soldiers, Dellinger provided the (flimsy) legal justification for the president's claims.[106] After Dellinger left OLC, one of his successors drafted a legal opinion defending the legality of the 1999 Kosovo War, in which Congress, by voting down authorization for Operation Allied Force, denied Clinton the constitutional authority to wage war.[107] Unperturbed, President Clinton carried out the war without authorization.

Nor did then first lady Hillary Clinton worry much about congressional prerogatives during the last Clinton presidency. On a diplomatic trip in North Africa in 1999, while her husband was contemplating air strikes on Serbia, she called to offer him her advice: "I urged him to bomb," she later said. "I'm a strong believer in executive authority," she declared on the ABC Sunday morning program *This Week* in December 2003, "I wish that, when my husband was president, people in Congress had been more willing to recognize presidential authority."[108]

Congress was all too willing to recognize presidential authority in the Bush years, greatly strengthening the office. And, the next Democratic president is likely to find much to celebrate—however quietly—in the constitutional innovations devised by the Bush Justice Department. Law professors Jack Balkin and Sanford Levinson are both Democrats and civil libertarians, so they take no pleasure in their prediction that "the next Democratic President will likely retain significant aspects of what the Bush administration has done":

> By staking out such aggressive positions on executive power and by changing expectations about what Presidents can do and can keep secret, the Bush Administration has created a wide space for future Presidents of both parties. Future Presidents may find that they enjoy the discretion and lack of accountability created by Bush's unilateral gambits. . . . Moreover, if future Presidents appear to be even a little less aggressive than the press has portrayed Bush to be, they will appear quite moderate in comparison. . . . Indeed, Bush's reputation will be burnished by later presidents following his example.[109]

How will the conservative movement react to a liberal president forcefully wielding powers forged in a Republican administration? Will the *Wall Street Journal*'s editorial page return to its prior practice of condemning Democratic abuses of executive power after nearly a decade of stridently denouncing every attempt to restore checks on that power? It will be interesting—and perhaps grimly amusing—to find out.

Situational Constitutionalism may well be a permanent feature of modern American politics; so too, it seems, is the ebb and flow of presidential popularity. In that respect, our 43rd president followed the pre-9/11 historical pattern. George W. Bush's heroic stature, record-setting popularity, and near-total dominance of the political "battlespace" inevitably began to erode as his first term came to a close. A year after his reelection, Bush had become as deeply unpopular as any president of the modern era. Predictably, various figures in the commentariat began to agonize over the perils of a "weakened presidency."

The remarkable thing about Bush's second term, however, was that, even amid the near-total collapse of his public support, the president was able to accumulate vast new powers. One of the hoariest maxims of presidential scholarship is that "presidential power is the power to persuade."[110] After Iraq and Katrina, George W. Bush had lost the power to persuade 65 percent of the country. And yet, Congress acquiesced to virtually every attempt the increasingly unpopular president made to enhance his power. How that happened is the subject of the next chapter.

7

OMNIPOTENCE AND IMPOTENCE

> And this is the catch: There are built-in barriers to
> presidents' delivering on their promises, and the unlikely
> occasion of one doing so would only engender another
> round of new policies, with new responsibilities and new
> demands for help. . . . This is a pathology because it
> escalates the rhetoric at home, ratcheting expectations
> upward notch by notch, and fuels adventurism abroad, in
> a world where the cost of failure can be annihilation.
> —Theodore J. Lowi, *The Personal President* (1985)

A year into George W. Bush's second term, the brief post-9/11 resurgence of the Heroic Presidency seemed like something from a half-remembered dream. Was there really a time, just a few years before, when Americans would stop whatever they were doing to hear the commander in chief's new plans to vanquish terrorism—a time when even late-night comics thought it was their patriotic duty to go easy on the president? The twin disasters of Iraq and Katrina had swept away the president's aura of competence and command, turning him from superhero to bumbler in the public mind. The president responded with increasing rigidity, as if leadership could be reduced to a mere act of will. "I've never been more convinced that the decisions I made are the right decisions," he told a group of conservative journalists in

September 2006: "I firmly believe—I'm oftentimes asked about, well, you're stubborn and all this. If you believe in a strategy, in Washington, D.C., you've got to stick to that strategy, see. . . . It's tactics that shift, but the strategic vision has not, and will not, shift."[1] As if to emphasize the point, the president let a group of House Republicans know that, despite his plunging popularity, there would be no withdrawal from Iraq even "if Laura and Barney [Bush's Scottish Terrier] are the only ones who support me."[2]

The post-9/11 surge in political trust had started to ebb even earlier, while Bush still remained enormously popular. A May 2002 Brookings Institution study grieved for the faded "government moment" created by 9/11, one "for citizens to recognize and appreciate the services that government provides and the skill with which it performs"; alas, the authors noted, "clearly, the moment has passed."[3] Though three-quarters of Americans held a favorable view of the president's performance at the time the Brookings report was released, the percentage who trusted "the government in Washington to do what's right" "just about always" or "most of the time" had gone from its post-9/11 high of 57 down to 40. That was still 11 points higher than the figure registered the summer before 9/11, but by 2004 the familiar post-Watergate distrust had returned: the trust indicators measured by the University of Michigan's National Election Studies were back to their pre–September 11 levels.[4]

Bush's approval rating hit 90 percent shortly after 9/11—the highest number ever recorded by Gallup over seven decades of polling. By early 2004, however, the president's job approval numbers dipped below 50 percent for the first time. After April 2005, Bush never again rose above that mark.[5] Three times in the first two and a half years of his second term, Bush registered negatives of 65 percent, just a point less reviled than Richard Nixon had been in August 1974, right before resigning—and two points short of the record holder, Harry S. Truman, who hit 67 in January 1952.[6]

Bush preferred the Truman comparison. As his popularity plummeted, Bush repeatedly equated himself to HST, a favorite of historians, despite—or because of?—his bellicosity and aggressive view of executive power. In one speech alone, a May 2006 commencement address at West Point, Bush invoked Truman 17 times.[7] With Bush nearing record levels of unpopularity and the courts pushing back against his most ambitious claims of unchecked power, the Imperial Moment had passed—or so it seemed.

It Only *Looks* Dead

The week after the 2006 elections, in which the Democrats gained 30 House seats and 6 in the Senate, the *Economist* magazine led with a story on "The Incredible Shrinking Presidency." The cover featured a caricature of a dwarfish Bush, his head peeking above the top of a cowboy boot.[8] A few years before, the *Wall Street Journal* had run a piece by then Washington editor Al Hunt with virtually the same title, "The Incredible Shrinking President."[9] In it, Hunt noted that Bush seemed "on the defensive," unable to influence the political debate. Three days after Hunt's column appeared, the twin towers collapsed, and by the end of the week, the president no longer looked quite so small and ineffectual.

Hunt's was just one in a long line of premature eulogies for the Imperial Presidency. During the Clinton administration, even Arthur Schlesinger Jr. could be found announcing the institution's demise— and sounding almost despondent about it. In an August 1998 *New York Times* op-ed, "So Much for the Imperial Presidency," Schlesinger complained that independent counsel Ken Starr had left the executive branch "harried and enfeebled."[10]

Not three weeks after that op-ed ran, Bill Clinton bombed targets in Sudan and Afghanistan, airstrikes that providentially coincided with Monica Lewinsky's second round of testimony before the Starr grand jury. On the eve of impeachment some months later, Clinton suddenly concluded that the time was right to bomb Iraq for resisting cooperation with United Nations weapons inspectors. Shortly thereafter, the "harried and enfeebled" president carried out a 78-day air war over Kosovo despite Congress's refusal to authorize it.

In 2006, as in 1998, reports of the Imperial Presidency's death had been greatly exaggerated. Throughout his second term, Bush suffered several legal and political setbacks and made a number of tactical retreats on executive power. Many saw those retreats as evidence of a weakened presidency. But the administration never backed away from its claims that the wartime president could not be bound by law. And even amid the collapse of presidential approval and trust in government, the presidency continued to gain ground and accumulate vast new powers. Though Bush lost some battles in the courts and appeared to make some concessions on warrantless wiretapping and enemy combatant detention, Congress repeatedly ratified the president's limitless conception of his own authority.

George W. Bush's second term provided an object lesson in the resilience of presidential power. Part of that lesson is that determined ideologues in the executive branch can work their will on a compliant Congress. But the story does not end there. Hurricane Katrina's aftermath showed the enormous role that public expectations play in the growth of the Imperial Presidency. As counterintuitive as it may seem, the political fallout from Katrina actually made the president *more* powerful, even in areas where he had not initially sought power. Like the rest of us, presidents respond to incentives, and the incentives set up by the modern conception of the president as national savior encourage the officeholder to try to break free from legal restraints. Faced with irrational public expectations about their ability to solve large national problems, presidents have good reason to push for power commensurate with that responsibility. And that push may be successful even when the president is enormously unpopular and his political capital is at its lowest ebb.

Pushback and Partial Climb-Down

At first, as Bush's popularity waned, he faced challenges to his contention that the wartime president could not be restrained by law. As with the period of executive retrenchment that began in the Nixon administration, resistance to presidential power came first in the courts. In the spring of 2004, the Supreme Court heard *Hamdi v. Rumsfeld*, a case challenging the president's authority to detain American citizens without trial. *Hamdi* involved Yaser Esam Hamdi, an American citizen, born in Louisiana, who had moved to Saudi Arabia with his family as a child. In late 2001, Hamdi had been captured by Northern Alliance fighters on the battlefield in Afghanistan. American authorities transferred him to Guantanamo Bay, then, upon learning that he was a U.S.

citizen, to a naval brig in Norfolk, Virginia. When Hamdi's father filed a petition for a writ of habeas corpus on his son's behalf, the Bush administration responded as it had in the *Padilla* case, with another affidavit from Pentagon official Michael Mobbs asserting that the prisoner was an enemy combatant. This "Mobbs Declaration," two pages long, was even shorter than the one offered to justify Padilla's permanent confinement.

Few, if any, would dispute the president's power to capture American citizens found bearing arms against their country on an actual battlefield and hold those citizens at least until it becomes practical to bring charges against them. But in *Hamdi*, the administration made a far more ambitious claim: that the president's authority as commander in chief was expansive enough to allow him to detain Hamdi indefinitely, citizen or not, on the basis of two pages of unanswered assertion.

The Supreme Court declined to address the president's claim of inherent authority, upholding Hamdi's detention instead on the basis of the Authorization for the Use of Military Force, the September 2001 use-of-force resolution that Congress had passed to authorize war in Afghanistan. However, as Justice Sandra Day O'Connor warned in her plurality opinion, "A state of war is not a blank check for the President when it comes to the rights of the Nation's citizens."[11] The president could not permanently imprison an American citizen without affording that citizen the chance to refute the government's claims: "Due process demands that a citizen held in the United States as an enemy combatant be given a meaningful opportunity to contest the factual basis for that detention before a neutral decisionmaker." Though the process given could, O'Connor suggested, be quite a bit more flexible than that afforded to criminal defendants, permanent detention on the mere assertion of the executive could not meet the constitutional standard. Rather than battle in the lower courts over the contours of that standard (and risk losing), less than three months after the Court's decision, the administration released Yaser Hamdi to Saudi Arabia, on the conditions that he abandon his U.S. citizenship, abide by various travel restrictions, and agree not to sue the United States for civil rights violations.

The Court's resistance to the president's most aggressive claims of detention power helped lead to another climb-down in *Padilla*, despite the administration's victory at the court of appeals level in that case. On September 9, 2005, a Fourth Circuit Court of Appeals panel reversed the federal district court that had ordered the government to charge José Padilla with a crime, detain him as a material witness, or release him.[12] The Fourth Circuit opinion, written by Judge J. Michael Luttig, then said to be on the president's "short list" for the Supreme Court, rested, as did *Hamdi*, on the September 2001 AUMF. Though the court declined to rule on the administration's inherent executive power claim, Luttig in effect read the AUMF as a standing grant of emergency power to the president for the duration of the war on terror.

Padilla's attorneys appealed to the Supreme Court for a ruling on the merits. Two days before the government's response was due, the Bush administration requested that Padilla be transferred to Florida for trial in civilian court on charges unrelated to his alleged plot to set off a radioactive "dirty bomb" in the United States. Judge Luttig, who learned about the administration's decision while watching television, viewed the request as an attempt by the government to avoid Supreme Court review of the case, and issued a sharp rebuke. The administration's actions had, he wrote, "left not only the impression that Padilla may have been held for these years, even if justifiably, by mistake," but also that "the principle upon which [the government] detained Padilla for this time, that the President possesses the authority to detain enemy combatants . . . can, in the end, yield to expediency with little or no cost to its conduct of the war against terror." All that came, Judge Luttig suggested, "at what may ultimately prove to be substantial cost to the government's credibility before the courts."[13]

Though Luttig refused to transfer Padilla to the civilian court system, the Supreme Court granted the government's request in January. In Padilla's subsequent criminal trial, his lawyers filed papers charging that he was tortured during his three and a half years of military confinement. Among other things, Padilla claims that his captors subjected him to stress positions and forced hypothermia, and made him take hallucinogenic drugs.[14]

At an earlier stage of the case, when Deputy Solicitor General Paul Clement was asked whether, under the president's legal theory, it would be permissible for the government to torture Padilla, he equivocated, asserting that our executive doesn't torture. Padilla's 2007 trial raised the question: did the Bush theory of executive power lead to the federal government torturing an American citizen on American soil? We may never know the answer to that question; as Clement put it during his oral argument, in such situations, "you have to trust the executive."[15]

The Supreme Court thought "trust, but verify" was a sounder constitutional theory. Six months after the administration's retreat in the *Padilla* case, the Court handed the administration another defeat. In *Hamdan v. Rumsfeld*, the Court held that the president had exceeded his constitutional authority when he attempted to try an enemy prisoner under the system of military tribunals he'd created by executive fiat in November 2001. Since that system allowed the accused to be excluded from his own trial and denied access to the evidence against him, the tribunals violated the Uniform Code of Military Justice passed by Congress in 1950, which requires the procedures for military commissions to provide roughly the same protections afforded in courts-martial.[16]

Though the administration's legal team had argued, among other things, that both the AUMF and the president's inherent authority allowed the president to set up the tribunals as he saw fit, the Court rejected both arguments. Justice John Paul Stevens's opinion for the Court employed Justice Jackson's framework in the *Steel Seizure* case to argue that "whether or not the President has independent power, absent congressional authorization, to convene military commissions, he may not disregard limitations that Congress has, in proper exercise of its own war powers, placed on his powers."[17] The administration could prosecute Hamdan in civilian court, proceed in military court under the UCMJ, or get Congress to enact different rules. But the administration could not, absent congressional authorization, try Hamdan by military tribunal without protections equivalent to those available under the UCMJ.

Since the administration had also relied on the AUMF and inherent executive authority for its claim that the Foreign Intelligence Surveillance Act could not bind the president, *Hamdan* looked like an indirect rebuke of the legal theory behind the president's warrantless wiretapping program.[18] If Congress had sufficient constitutional power to regulate the treatment of alien enemy prisoners, then surely it could require judicial oversight when the president wanted to "gather battle-field intelligence" by tapping Americans' phones.

The Justice Department denied that *Hamdan* undermined the legal rationale for the National Security Agency program. But several months after the decision, the administration made what looked like yet another tactical retreat. In early 2007, Attorney General Gonzales informed Congress that the president had decided, as a result of a new accommodation reached with the FISA court, that "any electronic surveillance that was occurring as part of the Terrorist Surveillance Program will now be conducted subject to the approval" of that court.[19] Details, as usual, were murky, but it looked as though the program, conducted in secret for over five years, would now have its legality reviewed by members of a coordinate branch, in keeping with FISA's design. Early in his second term, under fire from the courts, the press, and much of the public, the embattled president appeared to be backing down.

The "Sixth-Year Curse"

September 11 worked radical changes in our politics; but it did not change Americans' tendency to weary of their presidents. George W. Bush's second-term political difficulties were part of a pattern seemingly endemic to the modern presidency. All two-term presidents in the modern era have been plagued by some form of the "Sixth-Year Curse," characterized by "scandals, weakened political coalitions, and mid-term electoral defeat."[20] Starting as it did in his fifth year, George W. Bush's curse came a little early, but it did not wane going into his sixth, and showed no signs of fading as his second term came to a close.

With few exceptions, the public has greeted each post–World War II president with an initial burst of enthusiasm, followed by dashed expectations and declining popularity. Thus, modern presidential approval graphs strung together look like an EKG on a patient being repeatedly shocked to life—"clear!"—and then fading out again. Just as popularity tends to fade within each president's tenure, average approval ratings have been in decline from one president to the next for most of the era of the modern presidency.[21]

Some political scientists attribute declining presidential popularity to the "expectations gap"—the vast distance between what the public expects of the president and what he can realistically deliver.[22] The office cannot bear the weight of the expectations placed upon it, nor, in most cases, can the officeholder, who often responds to the dilemma with behavior at once imperious and petulant. That behavior tends to worsen his predicament, and thus it's little wonder that we want most presidents' shows canceled by their sixth season, if not before.

But whether he's loved or hated at any given stage of the news cycle, the president remains "our perennial main character, occupying center stage during almost all dramas in national political life."[23] The president's dominance of the news coverage of nearly any large-scale national incident likely leads us to overestimate his control over events. The fact that the president is front and center on the nightly news whenever there's a significant economic downturn, a hurricane, or a terrorist attack reinforces the view that he is the man in charge—responsible for, and capable of dealing with the emergency of the week, whatever it may be.[24]

Daunting as meeting public expectations can be when it comes to events like natural disasters or national security threats, the president's responsibility goes beyond the merely corporeal; as some see it, he's also the steward of the national soul itself. As Thomas Cronin put it in his classic 1970 essay "Superman: Our Textbook President":

> On both sides of the presidential popularity equation [the president's] importance is inflated beyond reasonable bounds. On one side, there is a nearly blind faith that the president embodies national virtue and that any detractor must be an effete snob or a nervous Nellie. On the other side, the president becomes the cause of all personal maladies, the originator of poverty and racism, inventor of the establishment, and the party responsible for a choleric national disposition.[25]

The Buck Stops Here

Few presidents try to puncture the public's illusions about presidential competence to handle all national problems, however diffuse or intractable. Instead, most appear to welcome the new responsibilities that burgeoning public expectations continually add to the president's portfolio.

Omnipresident

Even Clinton Rossiter, the enumerator of all the modern president's impossible jobs, didn't think to mark down a role for the president as "Consoler in Chief." Yet, that too is one of the modern chief executive's core duties. After the April 2007 shooting rampage at Virginia Tech, President Bush traveled to Blacksburg, Virginia, to comfort the student body in front of the cameras. One can hardly blame the president for making the trip; it was what he was expected to do, and his presence probably made some of the students feel better, their suffering having been recognized and acknowledged by the most important figure in American life. But the way prominent public figures described Bush's visit said much about the presidency's progress from limited constitutional officer to savior and spiritual leader. Commenting to the *Washington Post*, David Gergen, adviser to three Republican and one Democratic president, said, "At times like this, [the president] takes off his cap as commander in chief and puts on the robes of consoler in chief." Leon Panetta, former chief of staff to President Clinton, went even further: "In many ways, [the president] is our national chaplain."[26]

Several weeks before donning the robes of national chaplain, Bush played the role of national fitness coach, meeting with executives from Kraft Foods, PepsiCo., and McDonald's, Inc., to urge them to emphasize the importance of exercise and healthy eating. "Childhood obesity is a costly problem for the country," the president told the press just before the meeting. "We believe it is necessary to come up with a coherent strategy to help folks all throughout our country cope with the issue."[27] Faithfully executing the laws, protecting the country from foreign attack—and helping Americans "cope" with their kids' Dorito cravings—the modern president's portfolio is vast indeed.

Of course, it's unlikely that the voting public holds the chief executive responsible for American children's girth. But political scientists have demonstrated that voters penalize the president for failure to solve many other problems "over which he has incomplete control, from economic performance to government corruption."[28] Two of Rossiter's roles, Manager of Prosperity and Protector of the Peace, show the difficulties the modern president faces as the "man in charge" of circumstances no one human being could possibly control.

Over the second half of the 20th century, Gallup polls showed that an average of 41 percent of Americans per year cited economic issues as the most important problems facing America.[29] Here, as usual, the buck stopped with the president, Rossiter's Manager of Prosperity, despite the fact that expecting any president to successfully "manage" a $13 trillion economy made up of some 150 million workers, each with his or her own plans and goals, is unrealistic, to put it mildly.

The only presidential candidate in recent years to echo William Howard Taft's 1912 admonition that "the national government cannot create good times," was a fictional one, Republican contender Arnold Vinick, played by Alan Alda on NBC's *West Wing*. In November 2005, the network aired a live "debate" between Vinick and his Democratic opponent, Jimmy Smits's Matt Santos. Asked "how many jobs will you create?" Vinick said, "None." "Entrepreneurs create jobs," he elaborated, "Business creates jobs. The president's job is to get out of the way."[30] Real-life contenders don't talk that way, nor do real-life presidents. (For what it's worth, Vinick lost.)

Granted, presidential policy can have significant effects on the economy. President Carter's appointment of Paul Volcker as head of the Federal Reserve helped, at the cost of serious short-term pain, to put an end to the runaway inflation of the 1970s. Many economists argue that President Reagan's successful campaign to reduce high marginal tax rates cleared the way for the boom times of the 1980s. The addition of tremendous new, unfunded obligations to federal entitlements in the form of President Bush's prescription drug benefit is sure to reduce future economic growth. Yet, in all those cases, the economic effects of presidential policy play out over periods far longer than voters' time horizons.

Those time horizons are, it turns out, remarkably short. In a 2004 study, Princeton's Christopher Achen and Larry Bartels demonstrated that short-term economic growth is a much better predictor of presidential election outcomes than economic performance over the incumbent's full term. Come election day, Achen and Bartels write, voters "forget most of their previous experience and vote solely on the basis of how they feel about what has happened lately."

Achen and Bartels draw on the work of social psychologist and Nobel laureate Daniel Kahneman to employ one of the more vivid metaphors in a recent political science paper. They compare American voters to "medical patients recalling colonoscopies." Like patients undergoing that unpleasant procedure, voters' "assessments of past pain and pleasure are significantly biased by 'duration neglect.'" That is, the duration of the pain does not figure heavily in the patient's assessment of his or her suffering—what the patient remembers more is the level of pain experienced just before the procedure ended.[31]

Likewise, when they step into the voting booth, voters focus on the here and now, heavily discounting the economic pain or pleasure of years past. Rather than evaluate their economic well-being over a president's full term, voters reward or penalize him based on the vagaries of the business cycle. Achen and Bartels compare voters with Egyptian serfs killing pharaoh when the Nile fails to rise: they "reward and punish for events no administration can control."[32]

Nonetheless, the view that it's the president's responsibility to "protect jobs" and "grow the economy"—however much in tension those two goals may be—remains a central feature of American political life. Presidents and presidential aspirants embrace the role of economic helmsman, guaranteeing prosperity for all. As part of his 2004 presidential campaign, Senator Kerry rode through the Rust Belt in a bus emblazoned "Jobs First Express," promising to "create a manufacturing sector that's once again the envy of the world" through "Manufacturing Business Investment Corporations," federal research and development, and college tax credits.[33] For the 2008 campaign, Hillary Clinton rode the "Middle Class Express," and it too was a magic bus, judging by the miracles Senator Clinton promised in her first big economic policy speech in October 2007. Not only would she end our dependence on oil, the lifeblood of the American economy, she'd make us rich while doing it, with new jobs in the alternative energy sector. In response to the ongoing mortgage crisis, Senator Clinton's "Save Our Homes Program" would "rescue families trapped in unworkable mortgages," while her "Realizing the Dream Program" would make more credit available to homebuyers—despite the fact that easy credit seems to have had something to do with rising foreclosures in the first place.[34]

Whether such initiatives can deliver what's promised is quite beside the point. The modern race for the presidency *demands* such promises from the candidates. And when something goes wrong with the economy, Americans will hold the president to account, even if that something involves long-term economic trends that no one person, however powerful, could possibly "manage."

"Where in the Hell Is the Cavalry?"

The public also holds the president responsible for responding quickly and effectively to any headline-dominating natural catastrophe. The president derives political benefits from that responsibility, but it's a mixed blessing at best.

As noted in Chapter 4, there's abundant evidence that presidents use their disaster-declaration authority under the Stafford Act to aid their own reelection prospects. Presidents direct more disaster relief to politically important states and declare more disasters in election years—and the average number of yearly disaster declarations has been increasing over time.[35] Bill Clinton still holds the election-year record, with 75 disaster declarations in 1996; George W. Bush came in a close second in 2004, and has declared disasters at a faster rate overall than Clinton.[36]

Though presidents welcome the opportunity to game the disaster relief system in election years, responsibility for bad weather cuts both ways—it can be a political liability as well. Our 41st president, George H. W. Bush, learned that lesson when Hurricane Andrew hit Florida in late August 1992. Bush visited Florida on the day Hurricane Andrew struck, but delays in the Federal Emergency Management Agency's response angered Dade County's director of emergency preparedness, leading her to call a press conference and unleash a politically damaging sound bite: "Where in the hell is the cavalry on this one? They keep saying we're going to get supplies. For God's sake, where are they?" A month before the 1992 election, Bush wound up having to devote considerable campaign resources to a state he'd won handily in 1988.[37] Thirteen summers later, his son would suffer a much greater political disaster in the aftermath of Hurricane Katrina.

In a March 2006 talk at the Heritage Foundation, Homeland Security Secretary Michael Chertoff noted that the DHS secretary, and by extension, the president, "are really part of the war on terror, as well as the *war against all hazards*."[38] "All hazards" is a FEMA term of art for the myriad crises—natural and otherwise—for which a federal response is expected.[39] Yet, given the scope of events for which the public holds the president accountable, one could be excused for taking the phrase literally. In the public mind, any major televised peril—from a terrorist attack to a tropical storm—calls for decisive presidential action. If presidential action fails to fix the problem, the public tends to be unforgiving.

In Search of Monsters, to Distract

In the BBC production of Robert Graves's *I, Claudius*, Emperor Augustus tells his wife Livia that the Senate had voted to make him a god in the Syrian city of Palmyra, and the people there had put a statue of him in the temple, to which they'd bring offerings in the hopes that the emperor would grant rain or cure their ailments. "Tell me, Livia," Augustus says, "If I'm a god, even in Palmyra, how do I cure *gout*?"[40]

Augustus's frustration is all too familiar to the modern president. He can no more "manage" the economy or provide seamless protection from all manner of hazards than Augustus could bring rain or cure gout. But given congressional abdication of the war power, the president *can* divert the public's attention from domestic problems to foreign affairs by using military force. Is it possible that presidents, held accountable for events they cannot possibly control, are tempted to change the subject by exaggerating foreign threats and even sending troops into battle? If exploring that possibility sounds cynical, then once again it's worth remembering that our Constitution is *based* on cynicism, if that's the right word for the desire to limit the power that can be exercised by fallible humans.

There's a fair amount of social science evidence justifying the Framers' cynicism. The "diversionary war" hypothesis—the scholarly moniker for "Wag the Dog"—predicts that a weak economy, eroding popularity, and impending elections all increase the chances that the president will send Americans into battle. A host of studies by economists and political scientists has repeatedly borne out that hypothesis.

As noted in Chapter 4, Gregory D. Hess and Athanasios Orphanides found that first-term presidents facing a recession were twice as likely to engage in military conflict as second-term presidents or first termers with a strong economy.[41] Other scholars have found that presidential use of force is more likely during an economic downturn.[42]

To be sure, such claims haven't gone unchallenged.[43] But other recent research provides support for the diversionary war theory. In their 2007 book *While Dangers Gather*, William G. Howell and Jon C. Pevehouse find that "presidents resort to force more quickly when their approval ratings decline."[44]

It's easy enough to caricature the diversionary war hypothesis as conspiratorial and paranoid. That's one reason the idea rarely surfaces in the mainstream press. So let's be clear: those who suspect that presidents sometimes engage in diversionary wars don't imagine the commander in chief twirling his (imaginary) mustache like a silent-movie villain and cackling to himself, "Ah! Here's my chance to distract the public!" Nothing about the diversionary war hypothesis requires venal presidents who consciously and deliberately decide to put Americans at risk and get innocent foreign civilians killed for the sake of managing the news cycle. It's unlikely that the motivation to use force is quite so stark. As World Leader and guarantor of international stability, the modern president is regularly briefed on potential threats, military options for dealing with those threats, and credible reasons for choosing those options. A commander in chief constantly presented with a plausible target list can easily convince himself that he's simply doing what's necessary to protect American interests around the world, regardless of politics.

Does it work, though? Does the decision to let slip the dogs of war restore the president to the public's good graces? Here the answer is a qualified yes: "reliance on foreign policy actions does appear to be a feasible, short-term strategy for influencing the pattern of public support."[45] The key word here is "short-term": "this support is often ephemeral and is likely to wane should the conflict become long-term."[46]

But even when the president stops short of sending Americans into combat, he may benefit simply by stimulating the public's fear of foreign threats. After the entire country watched the World Trade Center collapse on 9/11, that wasn't hard to do. The images Americans saw on television then and since were a forceful example of what psychologists call "mortality salience." For over 20 years, psychologist Sheldon Solomon and his colleagues have studied that phenomenon, examining how being reminded of our mortality affects our judgment. In their experiments, subjects are asked to describe what will happen after they die, provided with pictures of horrible accidents, or otherwise prompted to think about their own deaths, and then they're asked to make judgments on social or political matters. Again and again, the experiments showed that reminders of mortality triggered what Solomon and his colleagues call "cultural worldview defense," increasing the subjects' affinity for people with similar cultural beliefs and hostility toward those with different beliefs, as well as making them "more punitive toward moral transgressors and more benevolent to heroic individuals."[47] In one experiment, after being reminded of their mortality, judges gave more stringent sentences to hypothetical defendants convicted of nonviolent crimes.

In 2004, Mark J. Landau, Solomon, and others tested mortality salience's effect on presidential politics. They took a group of college undergraduates and made half of them write down how September 11 made them feel. Both groups were asked to evaluate an essay supporting George W. Bush's policies in the war on terror. The "death-prompted" group showed significantly more support for Bush than the control group in several variations of the experiment.[48]

A 2004 study by Berkeley's Robb Willer provided evidence of the real-world effects of mortality salience. It found "consistent evidence supporting the hypothesis that government-issued terror warnings led to increases in President Bush's approval levels," as well as evidence that "the threat of terror may lead to more positive evaluation of the president on a dimension largely irrelevant to terrorism, his handling of the economy."[49]

Willer's data show that the bump the president gets from reminding Americans that al Qaeda wants to kill them is fleeting at best, but an unpopular president may find it as attractive as an alcoholic finds the prospect of his next drink. And whatever its limitations in terms of enhancing long-term popularity, there's little doubt that waving the bloody flag of September 11 helped George W. Bush amass and retain power.

Power amid Collapse

Perhaps that's why President Bush rebuked any attempt to redefine the fight against al Qaeda in any terms other than "war." In late July 2005, both Defense Secretary Donald Rumsfeld and Joint Chiefs chairman General Richard Myers floated the idea of retiring the war paradigm. In a speech before a military audience in Annapolis, Rumsfeld tried out a new name for the fight against al Qaeda, offering "the global struggle against violent extremism" as a replacement for "the war on terror." General Myers told reporters at the National Press Club in D.C. that he objected to "the term 'war on terrorism' . . . because if you call it a war, then you think of people in uniform as being the solution."[50]

President Bush wasn't having it. A week after the Myers and Rumsfeld speeches, the president punctured their trial balloon: "Make no mistake about it, we are at war," Bush declared in a speech to the American Legislative Exchange Council. That speech focused largely on domestic policy, but still the president found occasion to use the phrase "war on terror" five times, and "war" 13 more: "We're at war with an enemy that attacked us on September the 11th, 2001. We're at war against an enemy that, since that day, has continued to kill."[51]

With his approval ratings dragging him under, Bush clutched the war metaphor like a life preserver. That strategy did little to boost his popularity, but it proved effective in fighting off challenges to executive authority. Despite the administration's apparent retreat on enemy combatant detention and NSA surveillance, the president's near-record unpopularity has not led to any significant checks on the powers he seized after 9/11.

"Reckless Justice"

In no small part, that's due to Congress's indifference to preserving its constitutional prerogatives. While the courts have resisted some of the administration's most extravagant constitutional claims, Congress has capitulated at almost every turn.

That, too, was consistent with modern trends. The Framers believed they had crafted a self-correcting constitutional order in which each branch would push back against the others to preserve their respective constitutional roles. Through much of the 20th century, the prevailing pattern of executive aggrandizement and congressional acquiescence repeatedly frustrated the Framers' expectations. Bush's second term brought more of the same.

The last week of May 2006 provided a particularly depressing illustration of Congress's indifference to its own institutional interests. Monday found members of both parties getting vocally indignant over the Federal Bureau of Investigation's Saturday raid of Rep. William Jefferson's (D-LA) office, seeking evidence for an ongoing corruption investigation (the summer before, FBI agents had videotaped Jefferson taking a $100,000 bribe and later found $90,000 in cash in Jefferson's freezer at his home in Northeast Washington). Here, apparently, was a true constitutional outrage. The raid on Representative Jefferson's office was the rare event that could get then Speaker Denny Hastert and then minority leader Nancy Pelosi singing from the same hymnbook, both decrying the alleged constitutional violations raised by the search.[52] House Judiciary Committee chairman James Sensenbrenner (R-WI) announced upcoming hearings under the title "Reckless Justice: Did the Saturday Night Raid of Congress Trample the Constitution?"

That Friday, the Senate voted 78 to 15 to confirm General Michael V. Hayden as director of the Central Intelligence Agency, despite the fact that in his prior job as head of the National Security Agency he had helped design and run the agency's illegal surveillance program. At a press conference after the *New York Times* exposed the program's existence, General Hayden explained his decision to implement it: "The lawfulness of the actual authorization was reviewed by lawyers at the Department of Justice and the White House and was approved by the attorney general. Now, you're looking at me up here, and I'm in a military uniform, and frankly, there's a certain sense of sufficiency here."[53]

In fact, just two weeks before his confirmation, *USA Today* broke the story that under General Hayden's leadership, the NSA had compiled a huge database of the telephone records of tens of millions of Americans, again in secret, and again, illegally.[54] And yet, the Senate barely hesitated to confirm him as head of the nation's principal intelligence agency, even though the Cold War–era CIA, under leaders with similar legal theories, had repeatedly and massively violated its own charter to spy on Americans at home.

General Hayden's confirmation was of a piece with the Senate's behavior a year before, when it voted to confirm Alberto Gonzales as attorney general. As White House Counsel, Gonzales had presided over the Office of Legal Counsel's efforts to rationalize presidential lawbreaking in the torture memos, the legal opinions justifying defiance of FISA, and elsewhere. But contempt for congressional authority apparently did not disqualify Gonzales from serving as the nation's highest-ranking law enforcement officer. True, the Gonzales confirmation was partisan—it occurred on a near party-line vote, with only six Democrats supporting Gonzales. But in Hayden's case, more than half the Democratic caucus voted to confirm the architect of the administration's warrantless wiretapping scheme.

As one of its last major acts, in October 2006 the 109th Congress responded to the Supreme Court's June 2005 *Hamdan* decision with legislation authorizing military commissions. Among other things, the Military Commissions Act of 2006 declared that the Geneva Conventions did not apply to noncitizen detainees, and that terrorist suspects could not challenge their detention in American courts.[55] In the administration's view, the latter provision applies even to legal residents of the United States, so long as they're not citizens. In fact, under the statute's definition of "unlawful enemy combatant," the president arguably has the power to seize American citizens (though they retain habeas corpus rights and cannot be tried before a military commission).[56]

A month after the MCA's passage, the voters elected a Democratic Congress, but the new majority proved utterly unable to prevent the president from sending more troops to fight a war that most Americans by then considered a disaster. In August 2007, eager to leave town for summer recess, Congress passed the Protect America Act, which effectively legalized the NSA surveillance program, removing the FISA court from individualized review of wiretaps of Americans' phone calls and emails when the government "reasonably believe[s]" that the targeted person on the other end is outside the United States.[57] That law left very little of FISA standing, and raised the possibility that the dragnet surveillance documented by the Church Committee could happen again, this time on a much larger scale.

As 2007 drew to a close and President Bush's would-be successors readied themselves for the Iowa caucuses and the New Hampshire primary, virtually all of the president's most ambitious claims of unchecked power remained intact. Having learned from hard experience not to expect much out of Congress, civil libertarians and constitutionalists looked to the courts to rein in the terror-enhanced presidency.

Though the courts had shown more independence than the legislative branch after September 11, there was little reason to believe that the judiciary alone had either the muscle or the inclination to put the executive back in its constitutional place. Even the Supreme Court's *Hamdi* decision, hailed by most civil libertarians as a constitutional victory, suggested that the president could imprison Americans on the basis of thin evidence and procedures stacked against the accused. In his dissent, Justice Scalia condemned the *Hamdi* plurality for "writing a new Constitution," one that included "an unheard-of system in which the citizen rather than the Government bears the burden of proof, testimony is by hearsay rather than live witnesses, and the presiding officer may well be a 'neutral' military officer rather than judge and jury."[58]

Three years later, the prospects for salvation via the Court didn't look any more promising. In October 2007, the Supreme Court signaled its reluctance to challenge the administration's expansive use of the state secrets privilege in the war on terror.

The case the Court declined to hear, *El-Masri v. United States*, contained some appalling claims of government abuses. Khaled el-Masri, a German citizen of Lebanese extraction, sought damages for his "unlawful abduction, arbitrary detention and torture by agents of the United States." Traveling to Macedonia for a vacation in late 2003, el-Masri, a car salesman, was arrested at the border on suspicion of terrorist involvement. After 23 days of questioning, Macedonian officials turned their prisoner over to American CIA operatives, who, el-Masri claims, stripped him, beat him, drugged him, gave him an enema, chained him spread-eagled to the floor of a plane, and flew him to Afghanistan, where he was interrogated for four months. CIA officials soon began to suspect that el-Masri's passport was genuine, and that they had confused him with a genuine terrorist suspect with a similar name. Following an order from Secretary of State Condoleezza Rice, the CIA finally released el-Masri in April 2004. But the method they chose was nearly as terrifying as el-Masri's confinement had been: they left him on a deserted road in Albania, fearing that his release was a ruse and he'd be shot at any moment.[59]

Despite that disturbing set of facts, on October 9, 2007, the Supreme Court declined to review the *El-Masri* case, instead letting stand a court of appeals ruling dismissing the case on state secrets grounds.[60] In its brief on behalf of el-Masri, the American Civil Liberties Union had maintained that the judiciary should not allow the "government to engage in torture, declare it a state secret and . . . avoid any judicial accountability."[61] Even conservatives who consider the civil liberties organization their bête noire might, in a quiet moment, find it troubling that the Court had done just that.

Many Americans find it comforting to believe that the judicial branch will always serve as a reliable bulwark against constitutional revolution. But however much we like the idea of federal courts standing athwart the tide of history, yelling "stop!"—history shows that they are an imperfect barrier to radical constitutional changes driven by the executive and legislative branches—or, in the post-9/11 era, pushed by the president and greeted with indifference by Congress.[62] When political actors are determined to reshape the constitutional order, the courts may resist at first, but, as Jack Balkin and Sanford Levinson argue, for good or for ill, "in the long run, [the courts] cooperate with [those efforts], shape their contours, and legitimate them through the development of constitutional doctrine." Through a process that Balkin and Levinson label "partisan entrenchment," Congress and the president "build new constitutional institutions, and the courts eventually rationalize them."[63] In part, that's because, given enough compliant senators, a determined president can shift the composition of the courts in the direction he seeks. It is partisan entrenchment, Balkin and Levinson argue, rather than FDR's court-packing scheme, that best explains the survival and flourishing of the New Deal constitutional revolution.[64]

Ratification of the administration's theories of limitless executive power appeared to be at least as central to George W. Bush's selection criteria for new justices as issues like abortion or gay marriage.[65] Then Republican National Committee chair Ken Mehlman suggested as much in an October 2005 conference call with conservative leaders. Seeking to rally support for the Harriet Miers nomination, Mehlman stressed "the need to confirm a justice who will not interfere with the administration's management of the war on terrorism."[66] Miers had to withdraw amid doubts about her qualifications, but in Samuel Alito the president got a defender of executive power at least as reliable as Miers, and far more formidable.[67]

In his second term, after George W. Bush became the most reviled president in a generation, some commentators noted the "irony" that an administration devoted to expanding executive power might leave the presidency weaker than it had found it.[68] Given the enormous powers President Bush had accumulated even after his approval rating dove below 50 percent, it was an irony that was hard to savor.

New Fronts in the War at Home

The Bush administration's post-9/11 power grab was, like Woodrow Wilson's in World War I, largely a case of ideology meeting opportunity. Though any president would have sought more power after September 11, the highest echelons of the Bush administration were dominated by people—including, most prominently, Vice President Dick Cheney—who had long believed that post-Watergate America had made terrible mistakes in restricting executive power. Like other Americans, top Bush administration officials were frightened, disgusted, and angered by the 9/11 attacks. But they also saw in those events a once-in-a-lifetime chance to attain the policy goals they'd long advocated. Former OLC head Jack Goldsmith recalls Cheney aide David Addington telling him in February 2004: "We're one bomb away from getting rid of that obnoxious [FISA] court."[69]

It's hard to fault critics of the Bush administration when they blame the post-9/11 growth of presidential power on George W. Bush and the band of militant ideologues that surrounds him. But Bush critics are wrong to suppose, as many seem to, that the growing centralization and militarization of executive power are an aberration, to be blamed on a stack of hanging chads and a cabal of neoconservative ideologues.

The political aftermath of Hurricane Katrina gives us reason to doubt that the conventional narrative explains all of our current predicament. Katrina suggests that, for a beleaguered president, seizing new powers can be an adaptive response. Though foreign threats have often provided the backdrop for the modern president's accumulation of power, the Katrina experience shows that crisis is the health of the presidency in areas far removed from the war on terror and other foreign threats.

In the fall of 2005, in the midst of public recriminations over the government's inept response to the disaster in New Orleans, President Bush turned once again to the option that shows a president is serious: the military option. Twice in a matter of weeks, Bush called for weakening the Posse Comitatus Act and giving the president more power to use the army at home. First, two weeks after Katrina made landfall, with his approval ratings at a then career low, the president proposed that the law be changed to allow him to take charge of disaster areas militarily and use federal troops to restore order. Shortly thereafter, he asked Congress for the power to order military quarantines in the event of an outbreak of avian flu. Despite public recriminations over Katrina and the president's near-Nixon-level unpopularity—and despite the lack of any evidence that calling in the troops would help save Americans from hurricanes or hypothetical plagues—in the end, the president got what he demanded.

A Federal War on Hurricanes?

On September 15, 2005, in a prime-time address from New Orleans's French Quarter, President Bush apologized for the federal government's ineffectual response to the disaster, and promised that "this government will learn the lessons of Hurricane Katrina. We are going to review every action and make necessary changes, so that we are better prepared for any challenge of nature, or act of evil men, that could threaten our people." Among the changes required, Bush suggested, was "a broader role for the armed forces."[70] What the president envisioned was legislation that would automatically give him the authority to take command in a disaster area, putting troops in policing roles if necessary. Explaining the administration's view, Pentagon spokesman Lawrence Di Rita identified the Posse Comitatus Act as one of a number of "very archaic laws" that hamper the executive's ability to respond to natural disasters.[71]

Yet, nothing about the Katrina fiasco suggested that fundamental legal changes were necessary. The Posse Comitatus Act doesn't prevent the army from providing logistical help during a natural disaster. Along with the other federal statutes governing military deployments at home, it merely sets a high bar to clear before the president can order federal troops into a policing role over the objection of a sitting state governor. Judging by their reaction, the state governors seemed to think that a high bar was appropriate. Even the president's brother, Florida Governor Jeb Bush, recoiled at the suggestion that the president should automatically become supreme military commander within any state suffering a severe hurricane.[72]

Besides the obvious federalism concerns, there are other reasons to worry about too readily militarizing disaster response, among them the dangers to life and liberty that come with giving combat-trained soldiers the authority to coerce citizens. Lt. Gen. Russel Honoré commander of the federal forces assembled for Katrina relief, seemed to recognize that danger upon his arrival in New Orleans, when he growled at his soldiers, "Keep your guns down. This isn't Iraq." Honoré's troops, serving under federal command and therefore subject to the Posse Comitatus Act, lacked arrest authority or the power to forcibly evacuate citizens—which was fine with Honoré: "That is not something for federal troops."[73] Television news coverage of Katrina's aftermath provided plenty of unsettling images as it was, but without Honoré's restraint and the legal barrier of the PCA, Americans might have turned on CNN to watch federal troops confiscating lawfully owned firearms and forcing citizens to evacuate at gunpoint.

That said, had the situation required it, President Bush could have authorized federal troops to assume policing duties. He could have invoked the 1807 Insurrection Act, which allows the president to deploy the army in cases of lawlessness or rebellion. That was what his father did in the 1992 Los Angeles riots, and what President Eisenhower did in 1957 to enforce desegregation in Little Rock, Arkansas. Had the stories about large-scale violence in New Orleans—a National Guardsman killed, a Guard helicopter fired upon, murder and mayhem in the streets and the shelters—proved true, there might have been a better argument for taking that drastic step.

But in the weeks after Katrina, it became clear that early reports of bloody anarchy in the Louisiana Superdome and elsewhere were little more than urban myths. In early September, FEMA officials pulled up to the Superdome in a refrigerated 18-wheeler, expecting to collect up to 200 corpses. They retrieved six, none of whom died of foul play, and none of whom actually died in the stadium.[74] Weeks after the levees broke, New Orleans police superintendent Edwin P. Compass III told the *New York Times*: "We have no official reports to document any murder. Not one official report of rape or sexual assault."[75]

There's no denying that Katrina's toll was enormous—nearly 1,500 fatalities in Louisiana alone.[76] But despite what early reports seemed to suggest, they weren't killed in the sort of civil unrest that the army has effectively put down in the past. According to Louisiana public health officials, over 99 percent of Katrina's fatalities came from "storm-related deaths," anything from drowning, to electrocution, to blunt-force trauma from falling tree limbs.[77]

Putting more troops in place earlier might have saved some of Katrina's victims. But it wasn't the Posse Comitatus Act that stood in the way. Many of the region's National Guardsmen were unavailable to help out at home because they'd been called up to help democratize the Middle East. When Katrina hit, there were 7,000 Louisiana and Mississippi Guard troops deployed in Iraq, among them 3,700 members of Louisiana's 256th Mechanized Infantry Brigade, who took with them high-water vehicles and other equipment that could have been put to better use in New Orleans.[78] The Guard personnel at home had only one satellite phone for the entire Mississippi Gulf Coast; the other phones were in Iraq. Lt. Gen. Steven Blum, chief of the National Guard Bureau, noted that had the Louisiana Guard "been at home and not in Iraq, their expertise and capabilities could have been brought to bear."[79]

Would that have been enough to provide an orderly exit for Katrina's refugees? Perhaps. But it's also possible that given the scale of the flooding in New Orleans, and the inevitable imperfections of public institutions, even the best response achievable wouldn't have looked pretty.

Still, the idea of flawless disaster response remains seductive, not least to those whose political fortunes are held hostage to the flaws of the existing system. In late September 2005, at Peterson Air Force Base in Colorado, the president anxiously watched the monitors at NORTHCOM's Joint Operations Center as the next Category 3 storm, Hurricane Rita, made landfall near the Texas-Louisiana border. The high-tech command center, lined with 120 computers and 18 video screens flashing aerial maps, wowed the president with a display rivaling the counterterrorism center on TV's 24. Rita turned out to be comparatively mild, and Bush left the base distinctly impressed with NORTHCOM's capabilities.[80]

The following week, the papers reported an official death toll of over 1,100 for Katrina, and a new House select committee convened to hold hearings, excoriating administration officials for incompetence and poor planning. And on October 4, President Bush came forward with yet another proposal for using military forces at home. This time the threat was the theoretical specter of an avian flu pandemic. At a press conference in the Rose Garden, Bush proposed new presidential powers to impose military quarantines, asking: "Who best to be able to effect a quarantine? One option is the use of a military that's able to plan and move. So that's why I put it on the table. I think it's an important debate for Congress to have."[81]

Granted, there was some reason to be concerned about avian flu: should any of the avian influenza viruses mutate to become readily transmittable from human to human, the result could be a severe public health crisis. Yet, few public health experts think military quarantines could be effective in curtailing the spread of a flu pandemic. Avian flu has an incubation period of three to five days before symptoms emerge; in a porous, highly mobile country of nearly 300 million people, that makes the army a poor bet for stopping its spread. Dr. Irwin Redlener, director of the National Center for Disaster Preparedness at Columbia University's School of Public Health, called Bush's proposal "unworkable," noting that the pathogen spreads too rapidly to be contained, and that relying on soldiers to restrict Americans' freedom of movement would "cause extraordinary disruption."[82]

In fact, even the executive branch's own public health experts saw no need for military quarantines. Less than a month after President Bush suggested fighting the flu with the military option, his own Department of Health and Human Services released its 396-page *Pandemic Influenza Plan*, the result of years of careful study. The HHS plan omits any role for the military in enforcing quarantines, relying instead on voluntary quarantines, except for "extreme situations . . . [when] community-level interventions may become necessary." Even then, the report notes, "Measures designed to increase social distance, such as 'snow days,' may be preferred alternatives to quarantine."[83]

If Bush's top public health experts didn't see a need for army involvement, then why had the president come forward with a scenario that seemed drawn from dystopian science fiction? Why would he propose drastic legal changes that raised the prospect of armed 19-year-old soldiers facing off against a panicked populace? And if nearly all the state governors and much of the military establishment itself rejected the idea of scrapping Posse Comitatus during bad weather, why did the president put *that* proposal on the table? The administration's conduct suggested that its reflexive response to any crisis—whether real or hypothetical—was the same: *we need more military power*. That is a dangerous reflex. But that drive for power won't disappear when George W. Bush heads back to the ranch in 2009. The motive force behind reflexive militarism is the American public, and our insatiable demand for executive action will remain long after Bush has gone.

Blaming Pharaoh

As Clinton Rossiter noted in 1956, in times of crisis "the people turn almost instinctively to the White House and its occupant for aid and comfort."[84] By the middle of the 20th century, the president had become "a one-man riot squad ready to muster up troops, experts, food, money, loans, equipment, medical supplies, and moral support," whenever catastrophes occur.[85] The aftermath of Hurricane Katrina made clear that in the five decades since Rossiter wrote those words, the president's responsibilities as Protector of the Peace had only increased.

But effective disaster response depends on decisions made by officials at all levels of government: municipal, state, and federal—most of whom the president does not command. Nonetheless, the president remains by far the most visible actor on the national stage, and the public holds him accountable when it thinks he has handled his responsibilities badly.

That was how the public assessed President Bush's response to the chaos in New Orleans. A week after Katrina, 58 percent of Americans disapproved of Bush's handling of the crisis, and 77 percent found the federal response inadequate.[86] By mid-September, Bush's approval rating stood at 40 percent—at that point, a career low.[87]

It was fair enough to blame the executive branch for its inept response to Katrina. FEMA blocked private parties who wanted to help, and marshaled its own resources with all the skill and enthusiasm of a clock-watching DMV teller approaching the end of his shift. In one widely reported example, truckers tasked with delivering ice to New Orleans were shuttled around according to mysterious bureaucratic imperatives that often left the ice hundreds of miles away from afflicted areas. Following FEMA's directives, one driver traveled through 22 states over a period of several weeks without delivering a single cube to the disaster area.[88]

But in this case, failure had many authors. Louisiana Governor Kathleen Blanco didn't call up her National Guard units until just days before Katrina hit, and together with Governor Haley Barbour of Mississippi, mustered only 8,000 troops for an incident that eventually required far more. And contrary to advice from federal disaster officials, New Orleans Mayor Ray Nagin delayed ordering mandatory evacuation until after Katrina hit New Orleans, and hadn't secured drivers for the buses that were available.[89]

With roughly 2,500 employees, FEMA isn't designed to serve as a national rescue squad, despite what seems to be a widespread public impression to the contrary. The agency is not a first responder, and it has no authority to command first responders on the ground. As Frank Cilluffo, head of the Homeland Security Policy Institute at George Washington University, put it, responsibility for disaster "starts at the local level and works its way up from the bottom. And unless you are willing to quickly federalize police, firefighters, and other first responders in a crisis, and re-examine the Constitution and the federalist system that has been embedded in our ethos since 1776, we may have to live with that fact."[90]

One almost had to feel sorry for former FEMA director Michael "Heckuva Job" Brown(ie) a month after the hurricane, when he reported for his mandatory grilling before the House committee investigating the response to Katrina. Brown had resigned in disgrace several weeks before, but as he sat down to testify, he seemed well aware that there would be more public humiliation to come.

There's little question that Brown, an undistinguished lawyer with no emergency management experience, did a poor job of coordinating disaster relief efforts in New Orleans. But much of the questioning seemed to hold the former FEMA director responsible for decisions that were never his to make. Rep. Chris Shays (R-CT) focused on mandatory evacuation, which Brown lacked the authority to order, and which came far too late to avoid stranding hundreds of thousands of people in a drowning city. Though FEMA was powerless to order evacuation, Shays blamed Brown and the administration for the delay. "I want to know how you coordinated the evacuation," Shays demanded; Brown answered, "By urging the governor and the mayor to order the mandatory evacuation."

SHAYS: And that's coordinating?

BROWN: What would you like for me to do, Congressman?

SHAYS: And that's why I'm happy you left, because that kind of, you know, look in the lights like a deer tells me that you weren't capable to do the job. I would have liked you to do. . . .

BROWN: I take great umbrage to that comment, Congressman. . . . I guess you want me to be this superhero that is going to step in there and suddenly take everybody out of New Orleans.

SHAYS: No, what I wanted you to do was do your job of coordinating. And I want to know what you did to coordinate. . . .

BROWN: And coordinating is talking to the governor and the mayor, and encouraging them to do their obligation to their citizens. I am not a dictator and I am not going and cannot go in there and force them to do that.

SHAYS: See, what I think that is just talk; that's not coordinating. Were you in contact with the military?[91]

Sweating under the hot lights, Brown found himself held accountable not only for his incompetent performance in delivering relief supplies to New Orleans, but also for what he lacked the power to accomplish.

So too with the president himself. The executive branch shouldn't be excused for bungling the tasks it was authorized to handle. But judging by the press and the polls, the administration took blame for failures well beyond its control. (By way of contrast, Mayor Nagin was reelected in May 2006, despite widely circulated news reports before the election that he still didn't have an emergency response plan in place that could help the city avoid the same mistakes made in Katrina.)[92]

In business or in politics, responsibility without authority is any chief executive's worst nightmare. That was the political nightmare that gripped the Bush administration in the weeks after Katrina. As the *National Post*'s Colby Cosh put it, "The 49 percent of Americans who have been complaining for five years about George W. Bush being a dictator are now vexed to the point of utter incoherence because for the last fortnight he has failed to do a sufficiently convincing impression of a dictator."[93] Small wonder, then, that President Bush promptly sought the authority to head off future political disasters by overriding the decisions of state and local officials and using the military at home.

Empowering Pharaoh

Though few in the media noticed, the president got that authority. On October 17, 2006, the same day he signed the Military Commissions Act, the president also signed the Defense Authorization Act for Fiscal Year 2007, Section 1076 of which covers the "Use of the Armed Forces in Major Public Emergencies." That provision amended the 1807 Insurrection Act and provided a new, gaping exception to the Posse Comitatus Act.

Where the Insurrection Act had limited the president's domestic use of the military to situations involving "insurrection, domestic violence, unlawful combination, or conspiracy," the new language allowed him to use the army to "restore public order and enforce the laws of the United States" in "natural disaster[s]," "epidemic[s]," "serious public health emergenc[ies]," and "other condition[s]"—a catchall phrase that greatly expanded the president's power to use troops against citizens. Under the new law, when the president decides—all by himself, apparently— that impending storms, spreading illness, or "other condition[s]" have "hinder[ed] the execution of the laws," he could declare himself supreme military commander within the afflicted state.[94]

In a move that underscored the benefits of divided government, in January 2008, Congress restored pre-Katrina checks on the president's powers.[95] Yet, Katrina's aftermath showed that when the public demands presidential protection from the hazards of bad weather, it creates the conditions for a large-scale executive power grab. And we cannot be sure that Congress will hold the line after future natural disasters.

Creeping Militarization

As Bush recognized, there can be no greater public display of serious-ness than a decision to send in the troops. No other American institu-tion is as widely respected and admired as the American military. In a Gallup poll from the summer of 2007, 69 percent of Americans professed "a great deal" or "quite a lot" of confidence in the military as an institution; the presidency got 25 percent in the same poll.[96] In a perceived emergency, when civilian institutions appear weak and vac-illating, calling in the military shows the public that the president is determined to get the job done.

To recognize the incentives under which the president operates is not to excuse his push for powers he should not have. But given those incentives, we should not be surprised that President Bush sought mil-itary power to match his seemingly boundless responsibilities.

Where will that dynamic lead? Despite the more lurid claims of some of Bush's detractors, it's quite unlikely to end in a military coup or a fascist dictatorship, whether with this president or future presidents. Experts on U.S. civil-military relations find the prospect of a military takeover absurd. "The notion of a cabal of U.S. military officers collud-ing to overthrow the government is almost unthinkable," says Brig. Gen. Charles G. Dunlap, staff judge advocate at Langley Air Force Base. Andrew Bacevich agrees: "The professional ethic within the military is firmly committed to the principle that they don't rule."[97]

Instead, military analysts like Dunlap and Bacevich warn of a creeping domestic militarization driven by the demands of the civilian political leadership. Both cite the increasing militarization of the war on drugs as an example of how that process works.

President Nixon was the first to begin framing the federal government's efforts to stamp out illegal narcotics in terms of a "war on drugs." But it wasn't until the Reagan administration that Congress and the president began taking the war metaphor seriously. In 1981, Congress passed the Military Cooperation with Law Enforcement Officials Act, directing the U.S. armed forces to provide training, equipment, and other forms of assistance to civilian police agencies fighting the drug trade.[98] In 1986, via executive order, President Reagan declared drug trafficking a "national security threat."[99]

Throughout the 1980s and 1990s, the war rhetoric ran hot. In a televised address to the nation in September 1986, Reagan referred to the fight against drugs as "a war for our freedom":

> My generation will remember how America swung into action when we were attacked in World War II. The war was not just fought by the fellows flying the planes or driving the tanks. It was fought at home by a mobilized nation—men and women alike—building planes and ships, clothing sailors and soldiers, feeding marines and airmen; and it was fought by children planting victory gardens and collecting cans. Well, now we're in another war for our freedom, and it's time for all of us to pull together again.

"We Americans have never been morally neutral against any form of tyranny," Reagan declared in closing, "Won't you join us in this great, new national crusade?"[100]

In his first prime-time speech to the country, Reagan's successor George H. W. Bush escalated the war rhetoric still further. Holding up a Baggie of crack, purchased "in a park just across the street from the White House,"[101] Bush warned, "If we fight this war as a divided nation, then the war is lost. But if we face this evil as a nation united," making "an assault on every front," then America would prevail. After all, "there is no match for a united America, a determined America, an angry America."[102]

An angry and determined America allowed Congress and the president to weaken the restrictions on military involvement in law enforcement. That led directly to the 1997 Esequiel Hernandez tragedy, in which marines on a drug war patrol killed an innocent American high school student. And over time, the militarization of the drug war fundamentally changed policing in America. Increased special forces training of civilian SWAT teams and transfer of military equipment to local police departments have led to a dangerous warrior ethos among civilian police forces and a considerable body count from wrong-door raids and other violent mistakes.[103] Calling in the troops in the drug war has blurred the line between crime control and war fighting to the point where most Americans can't see anything wrong with peace officers routinely serving warrants while clad in ninja gear and armed with submachine guns.

For all that, drug war paramilitarism still hasn't appreciably reduced either the supply of or demand for illegal narcotics. But militarization served its political purpose; when it counted, it showed that America's political leadership was deadly serious about fighting what the public perceived as a deadly scourge. Militarization of disaster response followed the same logic. A year after gaining the power to deal with bad weather as it would a foreign attack, the Bush administration made hurricane response a central part of its 2007 *National Strategy for Homeland Security*, reminding us that "threats come not only from terrorism, but also from nature."[104]

Toward a Garrison State?

If a war on an amorphous social ill could fuel domestic militarization as dramatically as the drug war did throughout the 1980s and 1990s—if a hurricane and a busted levee could empower the president to declare martial law virtually at will—then what of a war against terrorist enemies who, however elusive, are very real? Not all Americans think that saving their children from drug addiction is a core federal responsibility, and some even resist the idea that it's the president's job to save Americans from hurricanes. But virtually all of us expect a strong federal response to foreign enemies who can strike the American homeland.

The post-9/11 growth of presidential power, enormous as it is, has occurred despite the lack of any significant follow-up attacks on American soil since 2001. We have been very lucky in that regard. Yet after September 11, the potential for crisis became an ever-present feature of

American life: as the administration never ceased to remind the voters, an attack could come anywhere at any time. The public demanded protection and the president insisted that he alone could provide it. And with great responsibility comes great power. Former OLC head Jack Goldsmith, a dissenter from the Bush administration's absolutist theories of executive power, often clashed with Dick Cheney's deputy David Addington, the most unitary of unitarians. But Goldsmith understood why Addington was so unrelenting:

> He believed *presidential power was coextensive with presidential responsibility.* Since the president would be blamed for the next homeland attack, he must have the power under the Constitution to do what he deemed necessary to stop it, regardless of what Congress said.[105]

If the president is responsible for stopping any and all potential homeland attacks, and if he must have power as broad as that responsibility, then there can be no limits to his authority. But even if that theory is accepted, even if we concede the president's claim that he has the power to spy, arrest, and wage war whenever he pleases, he will never be able to seamlessly protect us against possible terrorist strikes. In America, as in any open society, "soft targets" are ubiquitous, and the president cannot realistically "terror-proof" the entire domestic United States. But he can, by reaching for the military option, signal his determination to do everything in his power to protect Americans.

As we've seen, there are good reasons to resist that option. Domestic employment of the standing army raises the risks of collateral damage to American life and liberty. It risks, in Jefferson's words, "overaw[ing] the public sentiment," and acclimating Americans to a militarized home front inconsistent with democratic life.

And, just as domestic militarization is unlikely to win the war on drugs or the war on hurricanes, it is unlikely to make America any safer from terrorism. After all, the military is a blunt instrument: effective for destroying enemy troops en masse, but ill-suited to homeland security, which requires subtler investigative and preventive skills. Put simply, you can't beat a shoe bomber with a tank column. Guardsmen at airports and subway stops are little more than "security theater," exercises that create the perception of security without the reality.[106]

From the perspective of the president, however—whether George W. Bush or his successors—that hardly matters. Perception is reality in politics. When confronted with impossible expectations, a militarized display of seriousness may be all that is available to the post-9/11 president, who finds his role as Protector of the Peace vastly expanded.

As the D.C. sniper incident showed, it will not always be clear at the beginning of a crisis whether what's going on is a crime or an act of war. Yet, what rationally self-interested chief executive would wait until all the facts emerge from the fog before ordering a federal response? After Katrina, what president would hesitate to centralize authority in anticipation of a potential crisis? Throughout the 20th century, more and more Americans looked to the central government to deal with highly visible public problems, from labor disputes to crime waves, to natural disasters. And as responsibility flowed to the center, power went with it. The political environment of post-9/11 America looks likely to escalate that trend dramatically. And as it does, the responses to matters of great public concern will be increasingly federal, increasingly executive, and increasingly military.

The militarized future to fear isn't one that ends in a coup or the imposition of martial law. It's far less cinematic. It's one in which the public, conditioned by events like Katrina and the ever-present possibility of terrorism, comes ever more fully to embrace the notion that civilian institutions are weak and messy, and that when you want the job done, you call in the boys in green.

From Superhero to Scapegoat

The image that best captured the Bush presidency at the height of its power was May 2003's dramatic "Top Gun" landing on the deck of the *USS Abraham Lincoln*. "We're history's actors," a senior adviser to President Bush had famously told reporter Ron Suskind the summer before, "and you, all of you, will be left to just study what we do."[107] As the president strutted the deck of the *USS Lincoln*, clad in a naval aviator's flight suit and bathed in the adulation of the assembled troops, he looked more than ever like History's Actor—a man at the helm of national and global destiny. Three weeks before, the world had watched as U.S. Marines pulled down a Stalinesque statue of Saddam Hussein in central Baghdad. Now we watched the man whose decision brought that statue down celebrating his triumph.

In his 1970 essay "Superman: Our Textbook President," Thomas Cronin deplored the then dominant view of the president as a figure of unmatched power and benevolence, who, "by attacking problems frontally and aggressively, and interpreting his power expansively, can be the engine of change to move this nation forward."[108] If ever there was a president-as-superhero moment, the carrier-deck landing was it. In September 2003, KB Toys introduced a flight-suited Bush action figure, the "Elite Force Aviator," celebrating "George Dubya himself in all his glory and flight equipment." No doubt the doll became an ironic Christmas gift for many a smartass blue-state hipster, but the conservative websites marketing it embraced it with zeal.[109]

Two years after the flight-deck photo op, a quite different snapshot captured the Bush presidency's decline. On August 31, 2005, as the extent of Katrina's toll was becoming clear, President Bush knew he had to leave his ranch in Crawford, Texas, to fly back to the White House. En route to Washington, the president had the pilot circle low over the remains of a once-great American city. During the 35-minute tour, the presidential plane descended to 3,000 feet, where Bush could see the flooded streets of New Orleans and Katrina's survivors sitting on rooftops, waving flags. The next day's papers featured a photograph of the president grimacing as he looked out the window of *Air Force One* at the wreckage below.

Almost immediately, pundits and pols seized on the image as emblematic of the president's distance—his disconnection—from the struggles of ordinary Americans trapped on the ground. Perhaps—but it showed something else as well. Here was the other side of the superhero presidency.

In the Saturday morning cartoons of my youth, the assembled heroes of the Superfriends watched the monitor at their headquarters for news of crime or distress in the world at large. When a Trouble Alert appeared, they'd swoop off to do battle with evil and rescue the innocent from villainy or disaster. Something about the image of President Bush leaving the Ranch of Justice to survey the scene in his Superplane made me wonder if our expectations of the presidency had evolved much past the cartoonish perspective Cronin had skewered 35 years before.

Here then was the image that captured the modern presidency: an office at once omnipotent and impotent. Here, with his face pressed up against *Air Force One*'s window, was a man with the power to topple tyrants, to launch weapons that could destroy life on Earth: a man invested with the hopes and fears of a country and the wider world. Yet, with all the vast powers at his disposal, he was helpless to part the waters below, to undo the damage done. As George W. Bush stared out the window, he watched his presidency brought low by a poorly designed levee and a trick of the weather.

In the weeks to come, President Bush would twice propose dramatic changes in American law that would allow him to employ troops against civilians. In the year that followed, he'd get those powers and more, convincing Congress to codify his long-asserted authority to wiretap at will and arrest anyone anywhere on Earth whom he suspected of terrorist involvement.

Some of those powers might, if used properly, somewhat reduce the risks of a future terrorist attack, albeit at great cost to our constitutional order and American standing in the world. Others, like the proposed abandonment of Posse Comitatus, were exercises in security theater at its worst. But each new power sought was in large part a response to the dilemma of the modern presidency and the boundless public expectations that created that dilemma. When crisis looms, all eyes turn to the man at the center. What is he doing to keep us safe? What more is he prepared to do?

It would take enormous virtue, enormous self-restraint, for any president carrying the burden of such expectations to resist seeking vast new powers. To suffer the inevitable political blowback from events that may, in the end, be unpreventable—without chafing against the constitutional safeguards that limit presidential power. And yet the system we've adopted to select presidents, and the environment they enter once they get there, make self-restraint among the least likely of presidential virtues.

8

WHY THE WORST GET ON TOP . . . AND GET WORSE

> I pray Heaven to bestow the best of blessings on this
> house, and all that shall hereafter inhabit. May none but
> honest and wise men ever rule under this roof.
> —President John Adams, in a letter to Abigail drafted
> after his first night in the White House

Can any American child grow up to be president? Probably not, however fond we might be of the idea. Perhaps a better question is: what well-adjusted tyke would *want* the job?[1] Not everyone finds the idea of being "the most powerful man in the world" intrinsically appealing, particularly when weighed against the enormous costs—physical and emotional—entailed in getting there and serving. Asked in 1998 whether he'd ever run for president, newly elected Minnesota governor Jesse Ventura demurred: "I've watched presidents and usually when they get elected, they look young and virile, and about four years later they look like they've aged 25 years. Life is too short."[2]

The Republic is probably no worse off for having missed out on the services of Jesse "The Body," but when an ex–Navy Seal like Ventura avers that he might not be tough enough for the job—when a former professional wrestler declines to enter the electoral circus—we might wonder what sort of person seeks it out.

It's not just the burdens of office that deter ordinary, level-headed people from seeking the presidency. It's what it takes to win the prize. The modern campaign trail is a waking life spent under the camera's merciless eye, a blur of glad-handing pancake breakfasts, hoarse-voiced platitudes, and long hours on the phone begging for cash. As the journalist Elizabeth Drew has observed, "Few human beings could emerge whole" from this "strange and brutal" competition.[3] Perhaps few human beings who were whole in the first place would feel compelled to enter such a contest.

If we're dissatisfied with the presidents we get—and we certainly seem to be—then instead of cursing our bad luck, it's worth examining why we get the presidents we do. Political leadership doesn't emerge in a vacuum, after all: the sorts of leaders any given regime generates depend on that regime's institutional design and the process it sets up for picking those who will rule.

F. A. Hayek addressed *The Road to Serfdom* to "the socialists of all parties," and in Chapter 10, "Why the Worst Get on Top," took them to task for their belief that the repellent features of socialist governments were a kind of historical accident. Hayek's adversaries recognized that people morally unsuited to rule had repeatedly seized power under socialism; yet, the democratic socialists of the West maintained, in effect, that "it is not the system which we need fear, but the danger that it might be run by bad men."[4]

What the socialists of all parties had overlooked, according to Hayek, was the close connection between the system and the type of leader it tended to produce. If bad men repeatedly rose to the top, it was because the nature of the regime itself had called them there, by setting up a self-selection process in which those attracted to absolute power and willing to wield it pitilessly would necessarily win out over their less ruthless compatriots.

Hayek's focus, of course, was on totalitarian governments; thankfully, in democratic, pluralist America, our problems are far less grave. Still, the insights contained in Chapter 10 of *The Road to Serfdom* have force even outside the context of the total state. Like Hayek's adversaries, today's "presidentialists of all parties" maintain that the problems of the presidency stem from bad leadership; the system itself is fundamentally sound.

The preceding chapters have, I hope, provided some reason to doubt that assessment. The modern conception of the president as the "man in charge" of finding solutions to all major problems in American life demands the impossible and, in the demanding, encourages concentration of power and erosion of civil liberties. The impossibility of the job, combined with Americans' enduring conviction that the "great" presidents are those who meet emergencies—real or manufactured—by expanding their powers and revolutionizing the American constitutional order—calls forth men and women who believe themselves fit for the task.

When the presidency demanded less, it attracted people with a different sort of temperament. In 1888's *The American Commonwealth*, Scotsman James Bryce attempted to explain "Why Great Men Are Not Chosen Presidents." One of the reasons Bryce offered was that the 19th-century presidency didn't require greatness:

> [European observers] forget that the president does not sit in Congress, that he ought not to address meetings, except on ornamental and (usually) nonpolitical occasions, that he cannot submit bills nor otherwise influence the action of the legislature. His main duties are to be prompt and firm in securing the due execution of the laws and maintaining the public peace.[5]

Today, the president's duties are immeasurably greater, and his powers correspondingly immense. The Framers constructed a system in which no one person or branch would be trusted with too much authority. The transformation of that system—the concentration of power that has come with increased presidential responsibility—means that being able to trust the man at the top is far more important than ever before. What sort of person does the transformed presidency call forth today? Are the candidates who hear the call worthy of such trust?

As this chapter will suggest, there's good reason to doubt that the system we have today selects for the virtues that would be necessary to wield the enormous powers of the modern presidency—if *anyone* is morally fit to be trusted with so much power. The modern campaign for the presidency has become a Darwinian contest rewarding bottomless ambition and moral flexibility—far more demanding than it used to be, and far more likely to deter well-adjusted, principled men and women from seeking the office. And the environment that the modern president enters into upon assuming office virtually ensures that even a conscientious, psychologically healthy person will become increasingly disconnected from reality. The demands of the job and the conditions of White House life warp personality, distort judgment, and encourage dysfunctional behavior.

The Framers hoped that the presidential selection system they designed would favor virtuous characters like Washington, who could wield power responsibly, and even renounce additional powers when proffered, if those powers were inconsistent with republican government. In this chapter, we'll look at how the process of selecting the president has changed over two centuries, in ways that frustrated the Framers' hopes.

After examining the way we choose the president, we'll turn to the ways in which the experience of being president has changed, and the effect those changes can be expected to have on the person occupying the office.

At this writing, as campaign 2008 gets under way, the roughly half of the electorate that identifies as Democratic appears especially energized by the impending election. At the rallies and on the blogs, a common theme that emerges is that George W. Bush's retirement and a Democratic restoration will end overweening executive power and restore wisdom and temperance to the presidency.

Hope springs eternal. But recent history suggests that trying to set things right by electing a better man or woman reflects hope's triumph over experience. Given the inordinate power and responsibility it grants to the president, the American system of government as currently constituted does not select for wisdom and temperance, nor does it encourage those qualities in office.

The Paradox of Choice

From the early 20th century on, Progressive Era reformers and their modern heirs have worked to increase citizen participation in the presidential selection process by expanding the use of primaries, disempowering party elites, and encouraging plebiscitary campaigns. In so doing, the Progressives hoped to energize American voters, inspiring them to rally behind popular, activist leaders.

The idea of democratizing the process of picking a democracy's chief executive officer has an intuitive appeal. Yet, as the University of Virginia's James W. Ceaser notes in his book *Presidential Selection: Theory and Development*, the Progressives' perspective departed radically from the Framers' central concern: the effect of the selection process on the presidency itself.[6] For the Constitution's architects, the important question was, what sort of man would tend to rise to the top?

"Characters Pre-eminent for Ability and Virtue"

The sort of man they wanted, of course, was Washington, the unanimous choice of the electors in 1789 and 1792. The Framers recognized that "enlightened statesmen would not always be at the helm,"[7] but they wanted a system that would improve the odds. A properly designed selection system would promote candidates with republican virtues; equally important, it would deter demagogues, discouraging the elevation of what the *Federalist* calls "those brilliant appearances of genius and patriotism, which, like transient meteors, sometimes mislead as well as dazzle."[8]

The Framers were confident they'd designed such a system. In *Federalist* no. 68, the sole essay devoted entirely to the method of choosing the president, Hamilton writes that the method of selecting the president was practically the only part of the proposed Constitution to escape criticism. That was for good reason, Hamilton argued: selection by the Electoral College allowed "the sense of the people" to operate on the choice of president, through knowledgeable intermediaries capable of cooling and refining public passions. Instead of crossing the country in search of support, rousing crowds and promising benefits, the president would be selected on the basis of reputation, by a body of "men most capable of analyzing the qualities adapted to the station," electors who would be "most likely to possess the information and discernment requisite to so complicated an investigation." In other systems, "talents for low intrigue, and the little arts of popularity," might win the day, but it would require "other talents, and a different kind of merit . . . to make [a person] a successful candidate for the distinguished office of President of the United States." "It will not be too strong to say," Hamilton concluded, "that there will be a constant probability of seeing the station filled by characters pre-eminent for ability and virtue."[9]

Things haven't quite worked out as planned. The modern presidency has become precisely what the Framers sought to avoid: an office for which popular appeals are the coin of the realm, the method by which the occupant seeks to mobilize the masses and reshape the constitutional order. The modern race for the presidency has been transformed accordingly, becoming a grueling plebiscitary marathon that rewards "talents for low intrigue and the little arts of popularity." And few among us feel moved to give thanks for having so many "characters pre-eminent for ability and virtue" among which to choose.

From Party Convention to Plebiscite

Many of the Framers' assumptions about how the selection process would work gave way within the first few election cycles under the new Constitution. The rise of factions meant that nomination and election of the president would no longer look like the neutral search for merit described in *Federalist* no. 68.[10] But the modern system—a plebiscitary campaign for a plebiscitary presidency—was a long time coming.

Nor had the Framers envisioned the system of nomination by national party conventions that had crystallized by 1832. Yet, that system still largely fulfilled their goals of constraining presidential ambition and deterring demagogic appeals. The leading candidates for president would not win the nomination on the basis of mass public campaigns; instead, they'd be vetted for suitability by party elites familiar with the candidates' reputations. And the republican norm against plebiscitary campaigning, which had remained surprisingly robust throughout the 19th century, meant that the race for the presidency was short, and not particularly onerous.

Political etiquette in the 19th century dictated that "the office of President of the United States should neither be sought nor declined," as James K. Polk put it upon accepting the 1844 Democratic nomination. Even those who violated that norm by campaigning on their own behalf, like 1872 Democratic candidate Horace Greeley, often felt compelled to apologize for breaking "the unwritten law of our country that a candidate for President may not make speeches."[11]

As the century progressed, the strictures against public appeals loosened somewhat. Yet, unless you were William Jennings Bryan, running for president wasn't particularly arduous. Republican candidates in the last two decades of the century generally ran "front porch" campaigns. In the 1888 campaign, Benjamin Harrison gave 94 speeches but never left his hometown of Indianapolis.[12] It wasn't easy to stoke popular fervor from your front porch, but at least it was comfortable.

If the presidents of the era were often uninspiring, then so much the better: the office wasn't designed to inspire. "Great men are not chosen presidents," Lord Bryce maintained, because such men are rare, because the American "method of choice does not bring them to the top," and because "they are not, in quiet times, absolutely needed."[13] They weren't needed—or much missed—in the "quiet times" that prevailed for the five decades from the end of the Civil War until American entry in World War I. If Bryce's contemporary, Lord Acton, was right that "great men are almost always bad men," then 19th-century Americans had reason to celebrate a system that elevated modest men to an office with modest powers.[14]

"The Cure for the Ills of Democracy Is More Democracy"

For the Progressive reformers of the early 20th century, however, presidential modesty was no virtue: they wanted a great office that would attract great men. Transforming the presidency demanded a new selection system that would allow Progressive presidents to carry out audacious reforms. Accordingly, the Progressives favored an open nominating process that would displace the corrupt party machines and empower the electorate. The "great army of the people" would be elevated and inspired by their ability to participate in the choice of candidates for national leader. The candidates chosen would run general election campaigns based on popular appeals, and the winner who emerged would then be able to claim a popular mandate for bold executive action.

For Woodrow Wilson, a pivotal figure in the development of the plebiscitary presidency, the president was to be the country's "one national voice": once he "takes the imagination of the country," "no other single force can withstand him."[15] What was needed, then, was a selection process that would allow the candidate to capture the country's imagination. In his 1913 State of the Union, the first in 112 years delivered in person before Congress, Wilson called for legislation providing "primary elections throughout the country at which the voters of the several parties may choose their nominees for the Presidency without the intervention of nominating conventions."[16] In 1916, Wilson became the first sitting president to travel the country stumping for his own reelection.

That year was roughly the high-water mark for Progressive Era electoral reforms. Though informal strictures against plebiscitary campaigning continued to erode, the Progressives' vision of a plebiscitary, primary-dominated selection system wouldn't be fully realized for nearly six decades.

In the so-called mixed system that had emerged by the 1950s, primaries were becoming increasingly important, but they weren't yet determinative. Sen. Estes Kefauver of Tennessee, who'd become a national figure by leading televised Senate hearings on organized crime, ran for the 1952 Democratic nomination while wearing his trademark coonskin cap, and won 12 of 15 primaries. Yet, since fewer than half the party delegates were selected through primaries, Adlai Stevenson managed to secure the nomination even though he hadn't actively campaigned. Senator Goldwater accomplished a similar feat in 1964, garnering the Republican nomination despite winning only one contested primary.[17]

Four years later, the furor surrounding the 1968 race set the stage for a transformation of the Democratic party's nomination process. Vice President Hubert Humphrey campaigned for the 1968 Democratic nomination on "the politics of joy." In the aftershock of Robert Kennedy's assassination, with anti-war activists and Mayor Daley's cops fighting it out in the streets of Chicago, the convention that gave Humphrey the nod wasn't a particularly joyful affair. Inside the convention hall, the warfare was less bloody, but tempers ran high. Eugene McCarthy supporters and other war opponents complained about the undemocratic delegate-selection procedures that had helped the party's old guard push Humphrey through. A late-night roll-call vote on the second day of the convention prepared the way for what would eventually become a major overhaul of the party's nominating rules. The resulting McGovern-Fraser Commission (chaired by South Dakota senator and 1972 presidential candidate George McGovern and Donald M. Fraser, a Minnesota congressman) proclaimed that "the cure for the ills of democracy is more democracy," and devised 18 rules on delegate selection designed to open up the process and weaken the control of party elites.[18]

One effect of the rule changes was to encourage the proliferation of presidential primaries. It turned out that adopting primaries was the easiest and surest way for a state party to insulate its delegates from challenge. The Republicans adopted similar reforms, albeit more slowly, and by 1976 both parties selected more than two-thirds of their delegates via primary votes.[19] For both parties, the presidential nominating system had completed its transformation from a convention-dominated system to a primary-dominated one.

What It Takes

If the result is more democratic, it's also far more demanding for the candidates, as political scientists Nelson Polsby and Aaron Wildavsky have described:

> The spreading out of preconvention party skirmishing, extending first to the primary phase and now to an ever lengthening pre-primary period, is, in part, a direct result of rules changes governing delegate selection to the national convention. . . . These rule changes have had the net effect of increasing the number of different people each candidate for the nomination must reach and, if possible, convince of his worthiness. The more people you have to reach, the more time and money it takes to do the job.[20]

And the smaller the increments in which the candidate is allowed to raise money, the more time and effort he or she will have to devote to it. The 1974 amendments to the Federal Elections Campaign Act, which limited individual contributions to $1,000 per candidate per election cycle, made it far more labor intensive to raise the necessary funds. As Bradley A. Smith, former head of the Federal Election Commission, has noted:

> A common complaint among the electorate is that campaigns have become too long. This is also, in part, a consequence of FECA. Because of the low fund raising limits and the corresponding time that must be spent raising funds, candidates must, as a

practical matter, declare their candidacies earlier with each election. . . . In 1968, before FECA, Senator Gene McCarthy was able to launch a challenge to President Lyndon Johnson, starting just a few months before the critical New Hampshire primary. He was able to do this because he was able to raise the necessary funds in a very short period of time, getting large, six figure contributions from Stewart Mott, Jack Dreyfuss, and a handful of others.[21]

Today, the ability to mount that sort of offensive is largely limited to rich eccentrics like H. Ross Perot. Thirty years of campaign finance reform have yet to "take money out of politics," but, together with the post-McGovern delegate-selection reforms, federal contribution limits have unintentionally made campaigning far more arduous.

Of course, the fact that campaigns have become more demanding is no reason to shed a tear for the suffering candidate; men and women who want to be president enlist voluntarily and they get what they deserve. Rather, the focus of our concern ought to be on the selection effects of a system that makes such enormous demands. Such a system necessarily deters those who aren't temperamentally suited to spending hours a day every day for two years on the phone asking for money. Worse still, the selection process encourages those who *are* so inclined—or those whose hunger for the presidency is so great that they're willing to do whatever it takes to get there.

Never Too Early

One of the things it takes today is a very early start. Surveying the data for the post-reform era, scholars Michael G. Hagen and William G. Mayer note that "a very large proportion of recent presidential contenders have announced their candidacies at least 400 days before the opening of their parties' national convention [and] at least a year and a half before the November election."[22] Running for president has never been easy, nor should it be. But it is only in the last three decades that it has become an all-consuming multiyear job. Warren Harding, elected to succeed Wilson in November 1920, began his 1920 campaign in earnest in June. John F. Kennedy officially entered the 1960 race in January of that year, and had found time in 1959 to make 77 percent of his Senate votes. That pattern was typical: mid-20th-century candidates generally announced their candidacies at the start of the election year or the winter before, and, of those running from the Senate or House, few found it hard to keep up their attendance before the election year.[23]

The modern race for the presidency demands a radically more intense commitment. Indiana senator Evan Bayh, who dropped out of the race in late 2006, had begun assembling his 2008 campaign team days after President Bush won reelection in 2004, and started campaigning hard early in 2005.[24] By February 2007, nearly two years before the next president's inauguration, all serious contenders in the Democratic field had made their official announcements and had begun campaigning nonstop.

The Candidate as Telemarketer

When not pressing the flesh, modern presidential aspirants need to be behind closed doors, pressing phone to ear. "You're talking about being locked in a hotel room for four to six hours a day making phone calls to a bunch who would rather spend money on things other than yourself," says one Republican political consultant of the demands on candidates.[25] "I feel like a trained dog," said Lamar Alexander after attending nearly 300 fundraising events the year before the 1996 race for the GOP nomination.[26]

The 2002 Bipartisan Campaign Reform Act, popularly known as McCain-Feingold, doubled the individual contribution limit, allowing people to give up to $2,000 per presidential candidate, per campaign (recently raised to $2,300).[27] Still, raising money isn't getting any easier. In March 2006, Federal Election Commission chairman Michael E. Toner predicted that there would be "a $100 million entry fee at the end of 2007 to be considered a serious candidate."[28] Latter-day Progressives often seize on such numbers to make the case that there's "too much money" in presidential politics. That's debatable: picking a president is fairly important. If, to convince primary voters of his or her worth, a candidate might need to spend roughly what Warner Brothers spent bringing *Catwoman* to theaters nationwide in 2004, who's to say that's excessive?

Instead, the excess we should worry about is the demands on the candidate's time when $100 million has to be raised in increments of $2,300 or less. Those demands will deter those whose desire for power is insufficiently robust to make the presidency seem an adequate reward for the nauseating labor required to win it.

Promises, Promises

As the 20th century advanced, the republican norm that the presidency should neither be sought nor declined went the way of knee breeches and powdered wigs. The normalization of the plebiscitary campaign means that during both the nominating and general election stages, credible candidates must make promises that no honest, intelligent, *credible* person could feel entirely comfortable making.

In the 1990s, Americans enjoyed a nervous laugh or two over the spectacle of Vladimir Zhirinovsky's rise to political prominence in newly noncommunist Russia. In his campaigns for the presidency, the quasi-fascist pol promised, among other things, free vodka, cheap underwear, and a husband for every lonely Russian woman. Electoral politics in America have not sunk quite so low—yet—but the modern presidential campaign abounds with promises only slightly less risible. Mike Huckabee swore that as president, he'd ensure that America achieves energy independence within eight years.[29] In his "Bold Education Agenda to Restore the Promise of America's Schools," John Edwards pledged to provide "An Excellent Teacher in Every Classroom," and to make "Every School an Outstanding School" (if *every* school can stand out from all the rest, then perhaps the miracle of Lake Wobegon is possible nationally as well, and all the children *can* be above average).[30]

Even a liar pays a certain kind of respect to the truth, writes Princeton philosopher Harry Frankfurt in his amusing little book *On Bullshit*:

> Someone who lies and someone who tells the truth are playing on opposite sides, so to speak, in the same game. Each responds to the facts as he understands them. . . . [But] the bullshitter . . . does not reject the authority of the truth, as the liar does, and oppose himself to it. He pays no attention to it at all. By virtue of this, bullshit is a greater enemy of the truth than lies are.[31]

"It is just this lack of connection to a concern with truth," Frankfurt writes, "this indifference to how things are—that I regard as the essence of bullshit."[32]

Edwards and Huckabee are intelligent men, intelligent enough, surely, to know that there isn't the slightest chance of public policy working the miracles they describe. Yet, anyone who feels uneasy about making promises he or she couldn't possibly deliver—anyone who prefers to have his or her statements correspond to objective reality—is preselected out of the race for the presidency. The contest the modern candidate enters into is characterized by a "lack of connection to a concern with the truth." Thus, the substance of the modern presidential campaign is—well, largely, the substance on which Frankfurt's book focuses.

And the promises made on the campaign trail have greater significance than those uttered during the average bull session. Candidates' vows to heal the sick, lift up the downtrodden, and democratize the world raise expectations for the office, and renew the perennial cycle of disappointment and centralization.

What Manner of Man?

Still, some defenders of the current nominating system argue that it selects for certain qualities that are essential to a successful presidency: stamina, ambition, and the ability to motivate and inspire large numbers of Americans.[33] And certainly there's something to that line of argument. But the post-1968 emphasis on Stakhanovite virtues has eclipsed other values, among them the Framers' emphasis on the importance of peer review.

"When the state presidential primaries became the mode rather than the exception after 1968," James L. Sundquist writes, "a basic safeguard in the presidential election process was lost." The "screening function" supplied, however imperfectly, by party leaders, could no longer operate in a process that privileged perseverance, name recognition, and fundraising ability.[34] Those are virtues of a sort, but ones that bear only a random relationship to the moral capacity to wield great power responsibly.

It would be a mistake to romanticize the old selection system, or to blame too many of our current difficulties on the new one. No doubt nomination-by-party-convention had abundant faults (though the fact that many analysts view Warren G. Harding's nomination as a showstopper argument against the "smoke-filled room" isn't very convincing if you appreciate Harding's many virtues as a president). Nor did selection by party convention prevent the elevation of men unfit for power; it gave us Woodrow Wilson, after all, who emerged victorious in 1912 after 46 ballots. The prereform "mixed system" gave us Kennedy, Johnson, and Nixon—three men whose character flaws led them to abuse their authority repeatedly. No selection regime can ever bar the gate permanently against corruption. The right question to ask is, compared with its predecessors, do we have reason to believe that the new system is doing *better* at selecting Americans who are fit to wield the powers of the modern presidency?

The demands of today's presidential race give the edge to those who, as Alan Ehrenhalt put it in his 1991 book *The United States of Ambition*, are driven by "a desire intense enough to keep their campaign going when any candidate of even modest intelligence is bound to realize just how mindless the whole enterprise can be."[35] Though that sort of drive will help a successful candidate hold up under the pressures of the modern presidency, it's unclear that it will make him or her a trustworthy leader. What sort of person wants the presidency *that* badly, after all?

"I will never depend on so slender a protection as the possibility of being represented by virtuous men," Patrick Henry proclaimed in 1788, arguing against the adoption of the new Constitution. Though the Framers disagreed with Henry's assessment of their handiwork, they shared his skepticism toward constitutional schemes that depended too heavily on the nobility of those wielding power. Even so, they thought it was important to craft institutional arrangements that would not, at the very least, disadvantage virtuous candidates.

Over the course of the 20th century, the presidency burst its constitutional bonds and accrued powers beyond the Framers' wildest imaginings. Given that the modern president has acquired the power to launch wars at will and reshape American law in accordance with wartime demands, the character of the person holding that office has become a matter of far greater consequence than it was at the Founding. And yet, while the presidency has grown, the method of selecting "the most powerful man in the world" has evolved in a way that makes the elevation of a latter-day Washington extremely unlikely. Probity and restraint don't seem to be the sort of virtues that regularly come

coupled with fundraising ability, popular appeal, and the sort of ambition that makes years of living out of a suitcase and constantly mouth-
ing inanities tolerable. It is, one supposes, *possible* that a character of
Cincinnatus-like integrity could emerge from the modern presidential
campaign, with all it demands—but if that happens, it's the sheerest of
accidents. And even a Cincinnatus would have his virtue sorely tested
by living for a few years in the atmosphere that surrounds the modern
president.

Kingly Isolation: The Modern White House Environment

As the race for the presidency has become increasingly democratic—
for good and ill—the life of the president has become increasingly regal, in ways that can't help but affect the judgment of the officeholder.[36]

For most of the 19th century, White House life was as "normal" as
one could possibly expect life to be for the chief magistrate of a great
republic. But today's president's surroundings are unimaginably different from those experienced by his predecessors. He lives behind a
paramilitary cordon, cut off from unscripted interaction with normal
Americans. He travels in a bubble of supplicants and sycophants jockeying for his attention. And he enjoys privileges that might make even
the most modest and unassuming of characters fancy himself a god.

In his 1970 book *The Twilight of the Presidency*, George Reedy warned
that the environment surrounding the chief executive was enough to
make even a well-grounded person delusional. Reedy arrived at that
conclusion through close observation, having served as Lyndon Johnson's press secretary from 1964 to 1965 and later as special assistant to
the president in 1968. It seems that Reedy did not entirely enjoy the experience. As a boss, Johnson was a "colossal son of a bitch," oscillating
unpredictably between sadistic abuse and kindness. Reedy has left us
a painfully honest—and, at times, bitterly funny—depiction of the sociology of power. Former Nixon aide John Dean, who knows something
about the darker side of the West Wing environment, calls *Twilight* "the
best book on the presidency."[37]

"The life of the White House," Reedy wrote, "is the life of a court.
It is a structure designed for one purpose and one purpose only—to
serve the material needs and the desires of a single man."[38] That man

is provided with the grandest perquisites imaginable, treated with extraordinary deference, and cut off almost entirely from communication with ordinary mortals. The president is simultaneously the center of attention and alone in the crowd:

> There is no position in the United States in which the isolation from equals is so complete as the presidency. To be the absolute superior in status to everyone else encountered throughout the day is an effective form of isolation. . . . In many respects, it is an even more effective form of isolation than physical confinement. The prisoner doing a spell in solitary *knows* that he is cut off from other human beings. The president, however, is surrounded by large, adoring groups that give him the illusion of human contact when all they really do is act as an echo chamber for his thoughts.[39]

Even before the modern presidency had fully formed, Calvin Coolidge noticed the distorting effect White House life could have on the president's judgment. "It is difficult," Coolidge wrote in his 1929 autobiography, "for men in high office to avoid the malady of self-delusion. They are surrounded by worshippers. . . . They live in an artificial atmosphere of adulation and exaltation, which sooner or later impairs their judgment. They are in grave danger of becoming arrogant or careless."[40] And if even a figure like Coolidge—a man who by temperament seemed immune to the trappings and privileges of the presidency—worried about the temptations that attach to the position, what then of today's "commander in chief"?

A Presidency on a Human Scale

To understand what the modern president confronts, it's worth looking at how staffing and security have changed as the office has grown.

When Coolidge served, White House life fell well short of what George Reedy would describe four decades later as "the life of a court." In the 1920s, as before, the public could walk uninvited onto the White House grounds without provoking a paramilitary response, and the president could, as Coolidge did, stand in the lobby to greet casual visitors touring the White House. Nor was the chief executive surrounded by the massive entourage that today accompanies him wherever he goes: when Coolidge took office, the White House office staff consisted of 38, mostly low-level employees.[41]

Skeleton Crew

Indeed, well into the 20th century, White House staffing was remarkably spartan, with the president receiving less clerical and administrative help than the CEO of a midsize company today. Congress didn't appropriate funds for White House staffers until 1857, when it provided for hiring a private secretary, a steward, and a messenger. Before that, presidents were expected to hire any help they needed using their salaries or other, private sources of income. The president usually got by with minimal manpower, often hiring relatives and paying their salaries out of his own pocket. Jefferson made do with one messenger and one secretary; Grant, with a staff of six. Years after the first telephone was installed in the White House, President Cleveland continued to answer it himself. Woodrow Wilson had only seven full-time aides, and often typed his own letters.[42]

The enormous growth of government's role and the large-scale delegation of legislative power to the executive during the Franklin Roosevelt administration meant that the president could no longer meet his ever-escalating responsibilities with a meager White House staff. In 1936, FDR established a Presidential Committee on Administrative Management to make recommendations on increasing White House and executive branch staffing so that the president could fulfill the public's burgeoning expectations for the office. "The president needs help" was the opening sentence of the report the committee issued the next year.[43] That help eventually came in the form of the establishment of the Executive Office of the President and a mushrooming presidential staff.

The Approachable Executive

The growth of the president's security detail followed a similar pattern, with the chief magistrate remaining surprisingly accessible well into the 20th century. Here again, the second Roosevelt's presidency was transformative. For most of FDR's first two terms, anybody could walk onto the White House grounds during daylight hours. But in 1939, with the visit of the king and queen of England on the eve of the Second World War, the White House gates were closed, and passes became mandatory for anyone entering the grounds.[44] With American entry into the war a year and a half later, those features became permanent.[45]

For the first century and a half of the presidency, however, even as threats to the chief executive increased, American political culture proved remarkably resistant to the idea of restricting public access to the president. Americans still believed that any chief executive who could hide behind a coterie of guards was one who had grown far too distant from the people he was supposed to serve.

In 1842, after a mob of drunken Whigs rioted outside the White House to protest President John Tyler's veto of a bill reviving the Bank of the United States, Tyler asked Congress to create a professional police force for the District of Columbia. The measure proved controversial, with Sen. John Crittenden of Kentucky warning that, under presidential control, the force "might be metamorphosed into a political guard for the Executive," which could eventually "overshadow the liberties of the people."[46] The bill that passed assigned several officers to the White House, but gave the mayor of Washington, not the president, the power to appoint them. Formally, the officers' job was to guard the White House grounds, not the president, and they'd be called "doormen." And if the president wanted personal protection when he traveled, he'd have to hire a bodyguard, as several presidents did. A Civil War–era children's primer summed up the 19th-century attitude toward the idea of a "palace guard":

> How are emperors and kings protected? By great troops of guards; so that it is difficult to approach them. How is the president guarded? He needs no guards at all; he may be visited by any persons like a private citizen.[47]

From 1865 to 1901, three presidents were assassinated: Lincoln, Garfield, and McKinley. Yet it wasn't until 1906, 5 years after the McKinley assassination and 117 years after the presidency was established, that Congress created a protective detail for the chief executive, with appropriations language allowing the Secret Service to perform that duty.[48] That came after a long and heated debate sounding the familiar anti-monarchical themes. To a proposal that Congress should establish a plainclothes army unit devoted to guarding the president, Sen. Stephen Mallory from Florida objected that "it is antagonistic to our traditions, to our habits of thought, and to our customs that the president should surround himself with a body of Janizarries or a sort of Praetorian guard and never go anywhere unless he is accompanied by men in uniform and men with sabers as is done by the monarchs in the continent of Europe."[49]

The military proposal never came to a vote; instead, in 1906, Congress authorized the Secret Service to carry out activities "for the protection of the person of the President of the United States."[50] Even that was only a temporary authorization in a rider to an appropriations bill. Though presidential security had increased greatly during FDR's presidency, permanent authorization for Secret Service protection wouldn't pass until 1951, after Puerto Rican nationalists tried to assassinate Harry Truman by shooting their way into the president's temporary residence at Blair House, across Pennsylvania Avenue from the White House.

"The Life of a Court"

As Fred Greenstein has noted, "Even a 1920s president would have difficulty making sense of the modern presidency."[51] By the time Harry Truman assumed office, the comparative normalcy the president enjoyed even two decades before had vanished. Early in his first term, Truman decided to head out on foot to visit the bank like a normal citizen, upsetting the Secret Service, which had grown used to Roosevelt's immobility. The agency kept a detail ready to accompany Truman on his unannounced departures, and even had the traffic lights en route to the bank rigged to turn red, stopping all traffic along the way.[52] That angered HST, and he ordered the practice stopped, but he eventually recognized that, given the enormous changes in the president's role, the president could no longer behave like a normal citizen.

Royal Entourage

No normal citizen, after all, could command the vast army of functionaries that the modern chief executive commands. The Executive Office of the President boasts over 1,500 staffers.[53] The budget for all this is tightly guarded, but one leading student of presidential staffing put it at nearly three-quarters of a billion dollars in 2001, and suggests that it is "almost certainly much more today."[54]

Everywhere he goes, today's president is shadowed by White House functionaries. NBC's *West Wing* often featured a "long take" where a single camera follows the president striding the White House corridors, absorbing information and issuing orders to a host of handlers and aides who busily circle and trail him. As a portrayal of the president's daily life, it's accurate enough. Yet, the overall impression is one of energy, motion, and purpose—the president in command of all that surrounds him and the government as a whole. And that may obscure a more fundamental aspect of the modern president's condition. During his tours at the White House, George Reedy observed that the enormous coterie of underlings answering to the president was as much obstruction as aid:

> From the president's standpoint, the greatest staff problem is that of maintaining his contact with the reality that lies outside the White House walls. . . . Since [presidential assistants] are the only people other than his family a president sees every day, they become to him the voice of the people. They are the closest he has to outside contacts, and it is inevitable that he comes to regard them as humanity itself.[55]

At the same time, an ever-larger chunk of the White House staff is tasked with convincing the press and the public of the president's superhero status: he is, by the testimony of every press release and every media appearance, hard at work solving America's problems, and even heading off problems Americans don't yet know they have. In 1973, Thomas Cronin marveled at the number of presidential staffers devoted to "busily selling and reselling the president." Such activity, he argued, "inevitably affects the presidency itself, by projecting or reinforcing images of the presidency that are almost imperial in their suggestions of omnipotence and omniscience."[56]

Palace Guard

The cordon of security around the president has expanded as radically as has the White House staff. The goal for the modern Secret Service, as explained by the agency's director during the Clinton administration, is to "provide a complete 24-hour-a-day, 365-day-a-year protective envelope" around the president. When the president travels, he's preceded by an advance team, and accompanied by Uniformed Division and Presidential Protective Division officers "who combine to form a moving protective perimeter surrounding the president at all times."[57] Even so, the agency also draws on local law enforcement to provide still more protection. In August 2004, when President Bush and Senator Kerry held simultaneous campaign rallies three blocks apart in Davenport, Iowa, police protection was so heavy that crooks managed to pull off three bank robberies unobstructed.[58]

Upon his return home, the president withdraws into a near-impregnable White House fortress where his palace guard tests his food and prevents anyone from approaching him unbidden.[59] The security perimeter around that fortress has expanded over the years due to increasing threats. After the 1995 Oklahoma City bombing, the executive branch closed off Pennsylvania Avenue to car traffic, and after September 11, the White House canceled daily public tours of the building. Limited public access to the White House resumed in 2003, but only for groups who make prior arrangements through their legislators and who have been prescreened by the Secret Service.

Some of the new restrictions are arguably excessive, but there's no doubt that increased security has been necessary. The standards of presidential accessibility that prevailed into the early 20th century would, if applied today, run a very large risk of getting presidents killed.[60] Increased protection comes with a price, however. Reflecting on his experiences as chief of staff and secretary of defense in the Ford administration, Donald Rumsfeld told an interviewer in 1992:

> One thing that is harmful and destructive to the way our system works is the system of security. . . . It has grown enormously since I went to Washington in the fifties. It happens incrementally. It may happen for good reason. . . . But the Secret Service and attendants have become so numerous and controlling that it is a put-off for the American people. A lot of people have stopped going to functions where the president and the vice president are because there is so much security. There is something about the total number of people in your entourage that defines your

importance. That is wrong. It is unhelpful to everyone. It inhibits communication.[61]

In one of Congress's first debates, arguing against the adoption of imperial titles for executive officers, James Madison stressed that "the more simple, the more republican we are in our manners, the more national dignity we will acquire." As Rumsfeld recognized in the 1970s, the modern presidency had drifted far from the dictates of republican modesty.

If Rumsfeld tried to correct that "harmful and destructive" tendency during his next stint in the White House, his efforts went unremarked. However, his comments highlighted an important problem. The regal atmosphere in which all modern presidents live may be a "put-off for the American people," but more importantly, it can hardly help but give the president an exaggerated sense of his own significance.

Fit for a King

Complaining about the restrictive security cordon that surrounds the president at all times, President Clinton once called the White House the "crown jewel of the federal prison system."[62] If so, with 132 rooms, 35 bathrooms, a swimming pool, a bowling alley, and a movie theater, it makes for a lovely jail.

The other perks that go with the office are magnificent as well. Chief among them is *Air Force One*. The Boeing 707 that served as Lyndon Johnson's presidential plane featured a "throne room" alcove in the presidential suite: "surrounded by a small desk that separated him from staff and guests, Johnson sat in a hydraulic 'king chair' that he could raise or lower to achieve the appropriate level of intimacy or intimidation."[63]

Today's *Air Force One* is a 231-foot Boeing 747 that has 4,000 square feet of space and is designed to withstand the electromagnetic pulse from a nuclear blast.[64] A 2000 General Accounting Office report estimated the cost of operating *Air Force One* at over $50,000 per hour of flight.[65] The plane and crew are in a constant state of readiness, prepared to take off at any time on the president's command. And wherever the plane happens to be in the United States, it goes to the front of the line for takeoff. Travelers at Los Angeles International Airport learned that to their chagrin in 1993, when they waited on the tarmac for 45 minutes while President Clinton had his hair cut by stylist-for-the-stars Cristophe aboard the presidential plane.

Similarly, if the president needs to get somewhere in a hurry, his attendants stand ready to clear the path. In August 2006, for example, when President Bush was scheduled to attend a fundraiser for then Republican senator George Allen, the Secret Service's attitude smacked of "make way, peasant!" The agency wanted to shut down several lanes on a Northern Virginia stretch of I-395 for six hours so Bush could get to the event with minimal inconvenience. That plan would have turned an already miserable Beltway commute into traffic hell, adding hours to the travel time of thousands of D.C. metro-area residents. Even so, it took Virginia transportation officials hours to talk the Secret Service down from the plan, and it seems that only the prospect of a "political nightmare" finally dissuaded them.[66]

Power Corrupts (Judgment)

In ancient Rome, when granted a triumph, a victorious general got to wear a purple toga and ride through the city in a golden chariot. But he had to share the ride with a slave whispering in his ear, "You are only a man." When a fellow is constantly surrounded by fawning assistants hanging on his every word—when his golden chariot is a modified 747—it might be hard for him to maintain the sense of perspective the Romans sought to instill in their military heroes.

We mortals—most of us, anyway—don't need a designated ego deflater to remind us of our unimportance. From the deli counter to the office, we're confronted daily with people who don't consider us anything special and don't particularly care what we think. The social environment in which the president operates is radically different, and it's easy to appreciate how that environment might distort his judgment.

"Acquired Situational Narcissism"?

Perhaps only the fabulously wealthy and the fabulously famous live in a milieu as unnatural as does the modern president. Like the president, rock stars, movie stars, famous athletes, and corporate "Masters of the

Universe" spend their lives immersed in adulation and surrounded by the trappings of wealth and power. And in 21st-century America, people who have it all should surely have their own syndrome. Thanks to Dr. Robert B. Millman, professor of psychiatry at Cornell Medical School, now they do: it's called acquired situational narcissism.

ASN is psychiatry's answer to the sorts of questions that occupy Americans, questions like, "What's Russell Crowe's problem, anyway?" The profitability of any number of magazines and entertainment news programs depends on celebrities displaying various pathologies, and that turns out to be a pretty sound business model.

But what explains the dependability of celebrity dysfunction? Standard psychology teaches that classical narcissism, with its symptoms of self-absorption, delusions of grandeur, and lack of empathy for others, originates in childhood. But as Dr. Millman sees it, "given the right situation, it [can] happen much later." It can happen, he says, when a person rises to fame, wealth, and power—and spends an extended period of time in an atmosphere of artificial deference:

> When a billionaire or a celebrity walks into a room, everyone looks at him. He's a prince. He has the power to change your life, and everyone is very conscious of that. So they're drawn to this person. What happens is he gets so used to everyone looking at him that he stops looking back at them.

Which is understandable, says the doctor: "why would they feel normal when every person in the world who deals with them treats them as if they're not?"[67]

Think what you will of our therapeutic culture, but whatever the scientific merit of the syndromes it ceaselessly generates, it's easy enough to imagine one's own character getting distorted by the conditions Dr. Millman describes. And there is evidence from experimental psychology that dominance warps judgment. In a series of experiments in 2006, scholars from Northwestern, New York University, and Stanford found that "power was associated with a reduced tendency to comprehend how others see the world, how others think about the world, and how others feel about the world."[68]

Whatever social power celebrities have over those who surround them—and it's considerable—the environment in which the president exists is even more unnatural. Rock stars and movie idols can order their functionaries around and buy their own planes, but they can't send the Seventh Fleet through the Taiwan Strait or bomb Iran. And the stakes are much smaller where Russell Crowe, Lindsay Lohan, or Tom Cruise are concerned. If fame and wealth go to a celebrity's head, he ends up jumping up and down on Oprah's couch, no harm done to the wider world. If the president loses his grip on things, there's rather more at stake.

Maintaining one's grip on reality may be difficult when one becomes the "commander in chief." The mere fact of ascending to office imbues the officeholder with an aura of magnificence and causes those around him—even lifelong friends—to treat him differently. President Carter tried, largely unsuccessfully, to have old friends, like communications director Gerald Rafshoon, call him "Jimmy" instead of "Mr. President." But Rafshoon acknowledges that, like almost everyone else in his position, "Once I got to the Oval Office, the atmosphere was such that I was intimidated."[69] Gerald Ford noted a similar phenomenon in his autobiography:

> Few people, with the possible exception of his wife, will ever tell a president that he is a fool. . . . There's a majesty to the office that inhibits even your closest friends from saying what is really on their minds. . . . You can tell them you want the blunt truth; you can leave instructions on every bulletin board, but the guarded response never varies.[70]

The growth of the White House staff may have made this problem worse. As the so-called presidential branch has grown, power has shifted from the president's cabinet to handpicked presidential assistants who do not need to be confirmed by the Senate. That in turn has reduced congressional influence on executive branch policymaking by concentrating power in the hands of unelected, unconfirmed staffers who are shielded from questioning by the doctrine of executive privilege. Increasingly, the president's closest advisers are people entirely beholden to him and who lack any sort of independent power base.[71] That enhances the danger that they'll serve as what Reedy described as "an echo chamber for [the president's] thoughts," even in matters of life and death.

"How could I have been so stupid?" John F. Kennedy asked himself after the Bay of Pigs fiasco. He wasn't the only one with bitter regrets. Arthur Schlesinger Jr., who had been at the table for the deliberations over whether to greenlight the attack on Cuba, reproached himself for "having kept so silent during those crucial discussions in the cabinet room." Schlesinger opposed the operation and had lodged his objections in a memo to the president. Yet, when the president's advisers lined up behind the plan, Schlesinger failed to do more than "raise a few timid questions."[72]

Reading Schlesinger's account years later, Yale psychologist Irving Janis was intrigued enough to shift his research focus from the study of individual, personal stress to the psychological dynamics of group deliberation. The result was his 1972 book *Victims of Groupthink: A Psychological Study of Foreign-Policy Decisions and Fiascoes.* Janis's concept of "groupthink" describes what happens in group deliberation "when the members' strivings for unanimity override their motivation to realistically appraise alternative courses of action."[73] As Janis noted, the problem of groupthink is only exacerbated when the most powerful man in the room—the president—tips his hand. Since everyone in the room wants what the president can provide—status and influence, among other things—there's enormous pressure for the rest of the group to ratify the Chief's preconceived notions, however unrealistic.

Since Janis wrote *Groupthink*, a great deal of work in experimental psychology has confirmed his basic insights: "One of the most robust findings in modern social science is that after deliberation, like-minded people tend to end up thinking a more extreme version of what they thought before deliberation began."[74]

Combating groupthink, ensuring effective deliberation, getting an assessment of available options and their desirability that's as accurate as possible—all require extraordinary self-awareness and subtlety on the part of a president. If he signals the direction in which he's leaning, the danger is that those surrounding him will believe he's already made up his mind, and that the right move is to fall in line. Again, Reedy described how it happens:

The first strong observations to attract the favor of the president become subconsciously the thoughts of everyone in the room. The focus of attention shifts from a testing of all concepts to a groping for means of overcoming the difficulties. A thesis that could not survive an undergraduate seminar in a liberal arts college becomes accepted doctrine, and the only question is not *whether* it should be done but *how* it should be done. A forceful public airing of the Bay of Pigs plan would have endangered the whole project, of course. It might also have prevented disaster.[75]

Smart presidents are conscious of that dynamic, as Eisenhower was when he took care to encourage open debate among his staffers during his 1954 deliberations about whether to commit ground troops to Vietnam:

> I know of only one way in which you can be sure you've done your best to make a wise decision. This is to get all of the people who have partial and definable responsibility in this particular field. Get them with their different viewpoints in front of you and listen to them debate.[76]

Indeed, the lessons the Kennedy administration learned about group decisionmaking after the Bay of Pigs—and the deliberative process JFK constructed during the Cuban Missile Crisis—may have helped save the world from nuclear war. In the meetings of the "ExCom" put together to plan the government's course of action during the 13 days of uncertainty, "protocol was suspended [and] the President was encouraged by some of his close associates to absent himself from some of the meetings when it was found that the process of mutual exploration of views was freer and more productive when he was not present."[77]

Getting good advice and ensuring that one does not poison the debate over policy can be a daunting task for any president. The strictures of the "White House prison"—physical and psychological—make it difficult for any president to get accurate information. Surrounded by sycophants, and conscious nonetheless that his policies are not working out as wonderfully as his advisers assured him they would, a president might, like Shakespeare's Henry V, feel the urge to walk among his public, and find out what they think of him. Yet unless, like Henry, the president goes in disguise, he may find it hard to make the connection he desires.

In early May 1970, tens of thousands of protesters had begun to descend on Washington, enraged by President Nixon's decision to send ground troops into Cambodia in late April and by the killings at Kent State several days later. Hundreds of army regulars were positioned within the Executive Office Building, and security officials lined up buses outside the White House grounds to form an extra barrier. At around 4:30 a.m. on May 9, a sleepless Nixon suddenly called for a car to take him to the Lincoln Memorial. A few minutes later, the Secret Service agents and staffers who had scrambled to keep up found Nixon standing on the memorial steps, ringed by a handful of shaggy protesters. Rambling on about his background growing up in a poor Quaker family, Nixon told the marchers, "I know probably most of you think I'm an S.O.B., but I want you to know that I understand just how you feel."[78]

The president returned to the White House at 7:30 a.m., after wandering through the Capitol with Manolo Sanchez, his Cuban valet, talking about religion to the cleaning ladies, and eating a breakfast of corned beef hash and eggs at a Connecticut Avenue restaurant. "The weirdest day yet," chief of staff H. R. Haldeman wrote in his diary, "I am concerned about his condition."[79]

The Lincoln Memorial incident is usually offered as a sign of Nixon's increasing disconnection from reality, and his deteriorating mental state brought on by the pressures of the Vietnam War. And it surely is that. But one could also see it as a halting, pitiful attempt to *reconnect* with reality. Absurd and fruitless though it was, Nixon's stab at protester outreach appears in retrospect as an awkward attempt to throw off his security cordon and engage the world around him. If Nixon somewhat overawed everyone he met—and if he spent far more time talking than listening—well, that too is understandable. The barriers that surround the president aren't limited to the merely physical—the "White House prison" is one he carries with him wherever he goes.

The "Decider" as Manager

It is, to say the least, difficult to imagine George W. Bush ditching his protective detail to talk to war protesters. Where other presidents have—with varying success—tried to fight the isolation inherent in the modern presidency, our 43rd president welcomed it. In his management of the Secret Service and his direction of the White House staff, President Bush operated, consciously or unconsciously, to ensure that he remained insulated from notice of dissent and disaffection.

"Free Speech Zones"

Some presidents have chafed against the security procedures the Secret Service insists upon. George W. Bush wasn't one of them. Perhaps more than any prior administration, the Bush team took elaborate steps to keep peaceful protesters far away from the president. Since Bush's inauguration in January 2001, in case after case, Secret Service agents or local authorities carrying out their requests have harassed nonviolent protesters at the president's public appearances. They've forced citizens carrying anti-Bush banners and placards to move out of the president's line of sight, to designated protest areas known as "free speech zones." Those "free speech zones" are often behind fences, or obstructions such as "Greyhound-sized buses" and far out of sight of the media covering the affair—in one case, the 2004 G-8 summit on Sea Island, Georgia, protesters were kept 10 miles away.[80] When protesters have failed to comply with the order to move, they have been arrested, and in some cases, prosecuted.[81]

"What the Secret Service does," according to Paul Wolf, an Allegheny County, Pennsylvania, police supervisor involved in planning a presidential visit to Pittsburgh in 2002, "is they come in and do a site survey, and say, here's a place where the people can be, and we'd like to have any protesters be put in a place that is able to be secured."[82] During the Pittsburgh visit, local authorities arrested retired steelworker Bill Neel, who was carrying an anti-Bush sign in an open public area, and charged him with disorderly conduct for refusing an order to move. As the arresting officer testified in the Neel case, the Secret Service had instructed local police to corral "people that were there making a statement pretty much against the president and his views."[83] Scores of other protesters have told similar stories.[84]

The "free speech zones" are, of course, patently unconstitutional.[85] The government interest in protecting the president does not come close to justifying the Secret Service's pattern and practice of harassing peaceful protesters. Though the agency is entitled to protect the president from potential threats, it cannot seriously be maintained that potential assassins like to draw attention to themselves by waving placards criticizing their target. Nor can the agency's other justification for free speech zones pass the straight-face test—which may be why the Secret Service's spokesman tried it out on the radio. On NPR in July 2003, agency spokesman Brian Marr suggested that free speech zones were designed to protect *protesters*, who might get so excited they'd "walk out into the motorcade route and be injured." The agency was determined, Marr said, to ensure that Bush's opponents have the right of free speech, but "we want to be sure that they are able to go home at the end of the evening and not be injured in any way."[86]

Reassuring as it might be to imagine a Secret Service so devoted to public safety that it wants to save protesters from themselves, a far more credible explanation is an agency culture that views dissent as tantamount to an assault on the executive branch. There has been little or no indication that any of the jailed protesters behaved in a threatening manner—unless one thinks that telling public officials what they don't want to hear is inherently threatening.

Unfortunately, that seems to be exactly how the Bush administration saw it. A lawsuit by two Americans arrested for wearing anti-Bush T-shirts to a presidential event led to the release of a "Presidential Advance Manual," the nonredacted portion of which confirms what had long been suspected about the administration's attitude toward dissenters at public events. Among other things, the manual orders Bush's attendants to designate "protest area[s] preferably not in view of the event site or motorcade route."[87] American law rejects the concept of lese majeste, the ancient crime of violating the sovereign's dignity; yet the president's protecters have gone beyond shielding his person—they appear to be actively engaged in shielding him from disagreement and slights.

Recall Senator Mallory's heated words from the 1906 debate over presidential protection: "Janissaries," "Praetorian guard," and so forth. That sort of 100-proof Jeffersonian rhetoric sounds anachronistic, even crankish, today. But when the president's protective detail makes clear that it could not care less about inconveniencing American citizens or trampling on their right to free speech, you might begin to wonder whether Mallory had a point. Under President Bush, the Secret Service came closer than ever before to justifying the fears of the early opponents of a presidential "palace guard." The president is in daily, direct contact with the agency, and is more than capable of ordering an end to its imperious behavior. If he hasn't, it may be because he thinks that this is the sort of treatment he's owed.

How Not to Fight Groupthink

The isolation inherent in the modern presidency can only be enhanced by turning the Secret Service loose to ensure that no murmurs of discontent ever reach the Chief's ears. What's even worse was that Bush's management style worked to suppress dissent and debate within the White House itself. If George W. Bush had deliberately set out to create an institutional culture designed to isolate the president from negative feedback, he could hardly have done a more thorough job.

All presidents prize loyalty among staffers, and well they should. Trying to control the great beast of the executive branch bureaucracy is a daunting task in its own right, but an impossible one without a staff fully dedicated to the president and his program. Yet, few presidents have prized loyalty as pathologically as our 43rd president.

From the beginning of his involvement in presidential politics, on his father's 1988 and 1992 campaigns, George W. Bush made loyalty a central and all-encompassing value. As George W. described his role in his father's campaigns: "I was a loyalty enforcer and a listening ear. . . . When someone wanted to talk to the candidate but couldn't, I was a good substitute. People felt if they said something to me, it would probably get to my dad. It did only if I believed it was important for him to know."[88]

A decade and a half later, that perspective would come to dominate the office culture of the George W. Bush administration. As a senior administration official put it in 2002, "The president finds out what he wants to know. But he does not necessarily find out what he might need to know."[89] Unfortunately, the current president does not appear particularly inquisitive. Former Bush speechwriter David Frum found George W. "often incurious and as a result ill-informed." In a 2003 interview, Fox's Brit Hume asked, "How do you get your news?" Bush replied, "I get briefed by Andy Card and Condi in the morning. . . . I glance at the headlines just to kind of [get] a flavor for what's moving. I rarely read the stories, and get briefed by people who are probably read[ing] the news themselves." He elaborated: "The best way to get the news is from objective sources. And the most objective sources I have are people on my staff who tell me what's happening in the world."[90]

Of course, it's unlikely that the president refrains from reading newspapers; his comment may instead have served to indicate his disdain for a press that he feels is biased against him. Even so, it's revealing that Bush identified his *employees*, people selected to begin with in large part because of their loyalty to him, as his "most objective sources" of information.

Worse still, Bush, by his own account, appears to interpret expressions of uncertainty and skepticism through the prism of loyalty—viewing doubt as a character flaw. "I don't need people around me who are not steady," Bush told Bob Woodward in a 2002 interview, "and if there's kind of a hand-wringing attitude going on when times are tough, I don't like it."[91] Inside and outside the administration, people have gotten the message. Asked if he ever openly disagreed with the president, Mark McKinnon, chief media adviser on Bush's two campaigns, said, "I prefer for others to go into the propeller first."[92]

In meetings with top advisers, the president apparently created an atmosphere in which skepticism was treated as a threat. As Bush told Woodward:

A president has got to be the calcium in the backbone. If I weaken, the whole team weakens. If I'm doubtful, I can assure you there will be a lot of doubt. . . . I mean, it's essential that we be confident and determined and united.[93]

Thus, as the situation in Iraq continued to deteriorate from 2003 onward, President Bush's posture in the White House Situation Room was as relentlessly optimistic as his public rhetoric: "We're on the right track here. We're doing the right thing for ourselves, for our own interest and for the world. And don't forget it. Come on, guys."[94]

If President Bush seemed to bristle when his assertions were challenged publicly—as he did in the 2004 debates with Senator Kerry—that may be because he's not used to being treated with anything but reverence. Robert Draper, a journalist granted unique access to Bush in 2006 and 2007 to write the president's biography, notes that in every cabinet meeting since White House Chief of Staff Josh Bolten took over for Andy Card in 2006, Bolten began by looking at Bush and saying, "Thank you for the privilege of serving today."[95] At no point, it seems, did Bush thank Bolten for his deference and then tell him to *cut it out.*

The Problem Is the Office, Not the Man

Here again, it's easy to understand why so many Americans think the problems of the presidency are really problems endemic to the *Bush* presidency. But George W. Bush is hardly the first president to become intoxicated by power and detached from reality. And whatever dysfunctional behavior Bush has exhibited pales in comparison to that of presidents past.

Fear and Loathing at 1600 Pennsylvania

Incensed by press criticism about the Vietnam War, Lyndon Johnson acted out in ways that caused some of his closest aides to question his sanity. In a private Oval Office meeting in 1967, asked by a reporter why America was in Vietnam, LBJ unzipped his fly, wagged the presidential member at his audience, and exclaimed "this is why!"[96] As the war bogged down, presidential aide Richard N. Goodwin witnessed episodes of "paranoid behavior" on Johnson's part, and believed the president had "taken a huge leap into unreason . . . almost frighteningly different from anything I had observed before." Both Goodwin and presidential assistant Bill Moyers consulted psychiatrists to ask about the president's behavior.[97]

Richard Nixon's aides also had many occasions to worry about the boss's sanity. As Watergate boiled to the surface, Secretary of Defense James Schlesinger began to fear a "Wag the Dog" incident and "directed all military commands not to accept any orders from the White House without his personal countersignature."[98] One of the episodes that prompted Schlesinger's concern was a story from the spring of 1974, reported to him by Office of Management and Budget official Joseph Laitin:

> I was on my way over to the West Wing of the White House to see Treasury Secretary George Shultz. I'd reached the basement, near the Situation Room. And just as I was about to ascend the stairway, a guy came running down the stairs two steps at a time. He had a frantic look on his face, wild-eyed, like a madman. And he bowled me over, so I kind of lost my balance. And before I could pick myself up, six athletic-looking young men leapt over me, pursuing him. I suddenly realized that they were Secret Service agents, that I'd been knocked over by the president of the United States.

Shocked, Laitin canceled his meeting and went back to his office to call the defense secretary. "I sat there stunned . . . and I thought, you know, 'That madman I have just seen has his finger on the red button.'"[99]

The Imperiling Presidency

As this book has emphasized, the presidency is a difficult, if not impossible, job. The man in charge is held accountable for events he cannot control, and he is repeatedly tempted to make up for his lack of control by exploiting or manufacturing crises and embracing militarism.

As difficult a job as the presidency is, its difficulty is only enhanced if the president behaves—as President Bush did—in ways that increase his isolation. If the president decides to favor "loyalty" above all else in those with whom he surrounds himself, if he refuses to brook dissent, and uses the Secret Service to keep protesters entirely outside his line of sight—it's virtually certain that he'll become untethered from reality. But even the most well-grounded of presidents, men who recognize the distorting effects power has on character and work to fight it, can succumb to its lures. President Bush was ill-equipped to deal with the environment of the modern presidency, but Bush's successors, Republicans and Democrats, will enter the same environment, with all the temptations it offers, all the pathologies it encourages. Some will handle that environment better than George W. Bush has; others will do even worse.

Over the course of the 20th century, Americans have transformed the presidency from a modest chief magistrate into a national father protector invested with the responsibility for fixing every major problem in American life. We've matched that responsibility with powers that are unlikely to meet those demands, but are virtually certain to threaten the American constitutional order.

How do we choose the person who will wield these powers? By accident more than by design, we've come to select the president via a competition that favors boundless ambition and power lust. The winner of that competition lives in a social environment that would corrupt a saint. And he walks the halls accompanied always by the military aide who carries the nuclear launch codes.

9

TOWARD NORMALCY

Garfield, Arthur, Harrison, and Hayes, time of my
father's time, blood of his blood, life of his life, . . . were
the lost Americans: their gravely vacant and bewhiskered
faces mixed, melted, swam together in the sea depths of
a past intangible, immeasurable, and unknowable as the
buried city of Persepolis. And they were lost. For who was
Garfield, martyred man, and who had seen him in the
streets of life? Who could believe that his footfalls ever
sounded on a lonely pavement? Who had heard the
casual and familiar tones of Chester Arthur? Where was
Harrison? Where was Hayes? Which had the whiskers,
which the burnsides: Which was which? Were they
not lost?

   —Thomas Wolfe, "The Four Lost Men" (1935)

After eight chapters covering the problems of the presidency, the
reader has every right to expect the payoff to come in the last in-
stallment, in which the author will provide a series of reforms
designed to solve the problems he's outlined. Natural as that expectation is, it's also unrealistic. As Theodore Lowi has put it: "Solutions are
for puzzles. Big government is not a puzzle. The plebiscitary presidency
is not a puzzle."[1] Rather, overweening government and the swollen

presidency that inevitably accompanies it are the product of incompatible public demands.

How did we get here, after all? What is it that transformed the presidency from an unassuming "chief magistrate" to the unholy and unnatural amalgam of genie, warlord, and shaman that it has become? How have we arrived at our current predicament, in which we regularly entrust our hopes and dreams—as well as the world's most powerful military—to whichever professional office-seeker dissembles most convincingly on the campaign trail? What have we done to deserve *this*?

Quite a lot, actually: We may not be happy with what presidential politics offers us, but we're far from blameless. We demand a government that will solve all our problems but will also have the decency to leave us alone. We want a president who knows his place, but we also long for a leader who can transform crisis into opportunity, helping us realize our collective potential in a grand national crusade.[2] We want what we cannot have, and as a result, we get what we do not like.

H. L. Mencken described democracy as "the theory that the common people know what they want and deserve to get it good and hard."[3] When it comes to the presidency, Mencken's aphorism needs qualification: American elites are at least as responsible as the ordinary citizen for what we're getting "good and hard." But Mencken was right to suggest that we're largely to blame for our own predicament. When our scholars lionize presidents who break free from constitutional restraints, when our columnists and talking heads repeatedly call upon the "commander in chief" to dream great dreams and seek the power to achieve them—when voters look to the president for salvation from all problems great and small—it's the sheerest hypocrisy for Americans to complain that the presidency has grown too big, too powerful, and too menacing.

If the presidency we have is, in large part, the creature of public demands, then it's naive to imagine that the office can be put in its proper constitutional place with a carefully designed package of legislative and judicial reforms. So long as Americans cling to the romance of the Heroic Presidency—so long as we demand what the office cannot provide—even the most well-crafted five-point plan for restoring the constitutional balance of power is likely to fail.

This chapter will nonetheless bow to convention and provide the obligatory reformers' wish list. At the same time, it will outline the difficulties and imperfections of each measure proposed. Legislative schemes for reining in rule by executive order, for cutting back on delegation of lawmaking authority and restraining executive war making are all worth trying, but they treat symptoms without addressing the underlying disease.

Accordingly, after exploring various reform proposals, we'll turn to the source of our affliction. Despite our rejection of what Nixon's chief of staff, H. R. Haldeman, described as "the implicit infallibility of presidents"—despite the more clear-eyed assessment of the office that Americans arrived at after Watergate—as a country, we still dream of Camelot. For all our skepticism, we still cling to the vision of the president as savior.

That vision is evident in popular entertainment, in academia, and among the pols and pundits who help frame Americans' conception of the president's proper role. And so long as we look to the presidency to provide protection and benefits beyond its capability, presidential politics will continue to follow the timeworn pattern: outsized expectations, dangerous centralization of power, and inevitable failure. The Cult of the Presidency persists, and its persistence means that there is no magic bullet—or bullet-pointed plan—for reform.

Looking out upon campaign 2008, with its depressing range of choices and familiar litany of false promises, hope seems audacious indeed. Yet, this book will not close with a counsel of despair. All is not lost.

In the nearly 220 years since the presidency's birth, the United States has grown from a weak frontier republic to a dynamic commercial empire of indescribable wealth. Yet, our 18th-century forebears would find some aspects of the modern American character entirely familiar. Our political culture retains its fundamental irreverence, its ornery resistance to being ruled. That resistance manifests itself in declining political trust, in a legal culture that's increasingly resistant to claims of unchecked power, and in the voters' growing preference for divided government. The 2008 presidential campaign certainly offers ample grounds for pessimism, but broader trends over the last four decades provide reason to hope that the Cult of the Presidency is a *dying* cult.

Bind Him Down from Mischief

Some of the problems identified earlier in this book defy any remotely plausible legislative solution. In Chapter 8, for instance, we looked at how our current system of selecting presidents calls forth men and women with an unhealthy desire for power and a disturbingly flexible relationship with the truth. But there's no chance of going back to the convention-dominated, smoke-filled-room method of picking our candidates, and perhaps we wouldn't want to even if we could. Similarly, it's hard to imagine how one might craft a statute that would solve the other major problem identified in that chapter: a White House environment that encourages presidential isolation and delusions of grandeur.[4] If we can't devise laws that would promote a better class of candidate or keep the winner from losing perspective, then it's all the more important to limit the powers of the office, so that anyone who attains it, whatever his or her predilections, is restrained from doing too much damage.

For other problems of the modern presidency—rule by executive order, excessive delegation, our drift toward presidential war making—we hardly lack for legislative proposals. In the 1970s, as America awakened to the problems of unchecked executive power, reformers in Congress tried to restrain the president with legislation like the War Powers Act, the Non-Detention Act, the Hughes-Ryan Amendment, and other measures that limited his discretion and commanded him to consult with Congress before acting. Those reforms largely failed to deimperialize the presidency, and their failure prompted scholars and legislators to think harder about how to return the chief magistrate to his proper constitutional role.

Though the president remains strongest in foreign affairs, he has, over the course of the 20th century, acquired significant powers over domestic policy as well. At times, he's seized those powers via executive order; at other times, he's received them as gifts from a Congress all too eager to delegate away its power over, and accountability for, the law. The post-Watergate era has seen any number of statutory schemes offered to address both problems.

In 1999, disturbed by President Clinton's late-term flurry of executive orders, Rep. Ron Paul (R-TX), the House's most reliable defender of constitutional government, introduced the Separation of Powers Restoration Act. That act would have required presidents to identify the specific constitutional or statutory provisions they're relying on to justify any given executive order; it would also have allowed legislators who believed a particular directive was illegal to challenge it in court.[5]

Others have suggested means by which Congress can bind itself, restraining its tendency toward overbroad delegations of authority. Few reforms could be more important: the collapse of the nondelegation doctrine after 1937 ensured that post–New Deal Congresses would rarely play the central role the Framers intended Congress to play. Once Congress became accustomed to ceding authority to the executive in domestic affairs, it was only natural that legislators would shrink from deciding the question of war or peace as well.

Post-Watergate Congresses never lost their taste for delegation, but they also tried to retain a check on executive lawmaking via the device of the legislative veto. Such provisions, inserted into statutes delegating power, allowed Congress to nullify executive branch regulations issued pursuant to the authority delegated.[6] In the 1983 case of *INS v. Chadha*, however, the Supreme Court struck down the legislative veto as an impermissible attempt to make law outside of the process that the Constitution contemplates.[7]

In a lecture given at the Georgetown University Law Center shortly after that decision, then judge, now justice, Stephen Breyer presented a plan for a "veto substitute" that would allow Congress to retain control of the law without violating the strictures of *Chadha*. Breyer suggested replacing the legislative veto with statutory language stating that "the agency's exercise of the authority to which the veto is attached is ineffective unless Congress enacts a confirmatory law within, say, sixty days." Such provisions, combined with changes to the House and Senate rules creating a special "fast track" for proposed regulations, would allow Congress to deny lawmaking power to the executive branch. Agencies could recommend particular courses of action, but their recommendations would not have the effect of law until they passed through the normal constitutional channels.[8]

After the GOP takeover of Congress in 1994, some enterprising Republican freshmen introduced a measure based on Breyer's idea. The Congressional Responsibility Act went further than Breyer did, applying his confirmatory law requirement to *all* executive branch regulations. The act's sponsors hoped to ensure "that Federal regulations will not take effect unless passed by a majority of the members of the Senate and House of Representatives."[9]

The Separation of Powers Restoration Act, the Breyer proposal, and the Congressional Responsibility Act are laudable attempts to prevent the president from exercising any authority beyond what the Constitution or Congress properly entrusts him with, but each has serious flaws. By giving aggrieved legislators the right to sue, the Separation of Powers Restoration Act aims to dragoon the courts into the fight over executive orders. But legislators cannot force judges to solve Congress's problems simply by passing a law. Federal courts rarely welcome the opportunity to sort out fights between the other two branches, and they've generally denied standing to legislators alleging an injury to Congress's institutional interests.[10] Likewise, forcing Congress to vote on significant federal rules is a noble idea, but the Breyer proposal and the Congressional Responsibility Act presuppose a Congress that's interested in taking responsibility for the law. That is not the Congress we have, or are likely to have, anytime soon.[11]

Statutes designed to return the war power to Congress suffer from similar problems, as the history of the War Powers Resolution makes clear. In the 35 years since the resolution's passage, presidents have put troops in harm's way repeatedly without letting the WPR cramp their style. The WPR's time limit is supposed to kick in when the president reports that he has sent American forces into hostilities or situations where hostilities are imminent. However, the statute is ambiguous enough to allow the president to "report" without starting the clock, and presidents have exploited that ambiguity. Of 111 reports submitted from 1975 to 2003, only one president deliberately triggered the time limit, and that was in a case where the fighting had ended before the report was made.[12]

Some prominent scholars have proposed amendments to the WPR that would give the resolution teeth. John Hart Ely's "Combat Authorization Act" would shorten the current 60-day "free pass" to 20 days and command the courts to hear suits by legislators seeking to start the clock. If the court determined that hostilities were imminent, and if Congress did not authorize the intervention, funds would automatically be cut off after the clock runs out.[13]

In the Bush years, WPR reform has taken on new urgency. Disturbed by the Iraq War disaster and President Bush's conviction that he has all the constitutional power he needs to start a war with Iran, Rep. Walter B. Jones Jr. (R-NC) recently drew up a bill that echoes Professor Ely's Combat Authorization Act.

Representative Jones has come a long way since 2003, when, in a fit of pique over France's refusal to back the Iraq War, he ordered the House cafeteria to rename french fries "Freedom Fries." Having soured on our Iraq adventure, the North Carolina Republican introduced the Constitutional War Powers Resolution in September 2007. The CWPR would allow the president to use force unilaterally only in cases involving an attack on the United States or U.S. forces, or to protect and evacuate U.S. citizens. As with Ely's Combat Authorization Act, the CWPR would give congressmen standing to "start the clock," and would cut off funding should Congress refuse to authorize military action.[14]

In 2005, foreign policy luminaries Leslie H. Gelb and Anne-Marie Slaughter proposed an even simpler solution to the problem of presidential war making: "A new law that would restore the Framers' intent by requiring a congressional declaration of war in advance of any commitment of troops that promises sustained combat." Under the Gelb-Slaughter proposal, the president could still, as the Framers contemplated, "repel sudden attacks," but any prolonged military engagement would require a declaration, otherwise "funding for troops in the field would be cut off automatically."[15]

Each of these proposals has the merit of demanding that Congress carry the burden the Constitution places upon it: responsibility for the decision to go to war. The Gelb-Slaughter plan shows particular promise. Though Congress hasn't declared war since 1942, reviving the formal declaration would make it harder for legislators to punt that decision to the president, as they did in Vietnam and Iraq. Hawks ought to see merit in making declarations mandatory, since a declaration commits those who voted for it to supporting the president and providing the resources he needs to prosecute the war successfully. Doves too should find much to applaud in the idea: forcing Congress to take a stand might concentrate the mind wonderfully and reduce the chances that we will find ourselves spending blood and treasure in conflicts that were not carefully examined at the outset.[16]

But again, each of these reforms presupposes a Congress eager to be held accountable for its decisions, a judiciary with a stomach for inter-branch struggles, and a voting public that rewards political actors who fight to put the presidency in its place. Representative Jones's Constitutional War Powers Resolution, which seeks to draw the judiciary into the struggle to constrain executive war making, ignores the Court's resistance to congressional standing, as well as the 30-year history of litigation under the War Powers Resolution, a history that shows how adept the federal judiciary is at constructing rationales that allow it to avoid picking sides in battles between Congress and the president.[17]

What's more, Representative Jones's proposal would require an extraordinary window of political opportunity to make it past a likely presidential veto. It took a moment of unusual presidential weakness to pass even the deeply flawed War Powers Resolution. Congress overturned Nixon's veto of the WPR at the height of the Watergate scandal, just weeks after the "Saturday Night Massacre."

Even if Representative Jones's Constitutional War Powers Resolution or Professor Ely's Combat Authorization Act could be passed today, and even if the courts, defying most past practice, grew bold enough to rule on whether hostilities were imminent, there would be still another difficulty; as Ely put it: "When we got down to cases and a court remanded the issue to Congress, would Congress actually be able to follow through and face the issue whether the war in question should be permitted to proceed? Admittedly, the matter is not entirely free from doubt."[18]

It's worth thinking about how best to tie Ulysses to the mast. But the problem with legislative schemes designed to force Congress to "do the right thing" is that Congress seems always to have one hand free. Even if any of these measures became law, Congress would remain free to avoid the pinch: ducking responsibility for new regulations and presidential wars. Statutory schemes designed to precommit legislators to particular procedures have a terrible track record. No mere statute can truly bind a future Congress. In areas ranging from agricultural policy to balanced budgets, Congress has rarely hesitated to undo past agreements in the pursuit of short-term political advantage.[19]

Hard as it is to design laws that can phase out farm subsidies or end deficit spending, reclaiming congressional authority over war is even harder. Congress has the power of the purse, but the commander in chief has control of the world's most powerful military. America spends more on "defense" than the next 12 countries combined and nearly half of what the rest of the world spends put together.[20] The troops the president commands are sprawled across the globe in 144 countries and over 700 military bases from South Korea to Qatar.[21] Thus the president has ample opportunity to act first and ask permission later—or, more likely, dare Congress to cut off funds for the troops he's sent into battle.

In some ways, that's nothing new; in 1846, James K. Polk showed that the president could usurp Congress's war powers by ordering troops into disputed territory and triggering a war. But the modern president has much more to work with than his 19th-century predecessors. The Constitution's allocation of war powers is, as Edward S. Corwin wrote, "an invitation to struggle for the privilege of directing American foreign policy."[22] By authorizing our imperial overstretch, Congress has given the president every advantage in that struggle. As then secretary of state Madeline Albright once remarked to a flabbergasted Colin Powell: "What's the point of having this superb military you're always talking about if we can't use it?"[23]

As we've seen, when the chief executive dons the uniform of the war president, he often seeks to increase his powers on the home front as well. The war on terror has provided a particularly striking example of that tendency: Bush administration officials argued that America is a battlefield, and the president needs as much discretion here as he does abroad. Efforts to check the powers advanced under that theory have run into the same obstacles of congressional cowardice and executive intransigence that have frustrated reform efforts since Watergate. The executive branch ought not to be able to listen in on Americans' international communications without a warrant—indeed, until Congress gutted it in 2007, we had a *law*, the Foreign Intelligence Surveillance Act, that criminalized such behavior. But when the president is determined to violate that law, and when Congress lacks the courage to address that violation, we have another problem that can't be solved with well-crafted legislation.

Efforts to address the other abuses identified in this book face similar difficulties. It would be wonderful if Congress strengthened the Posse Comitatus Act, eliminating the "drug war exceptions" passed in the 1980s.[24] Likewise, civil libertarians would have cause to rejoice if the federal judiciary took a stronger stand against aggressive use of the state secrets privilege and unilateral executive imprisonment of Americans suspected of terrorism. And they would have even more to cheer if Congress strengthened FISA and moved to restrain executive orders, promiscuous delegation, and presidential wars—despite the difficulties entailed in making those reforms stick.

An Enduring Cult?

All the above measures are worth pursuing, though in a sense they're superfluous. An America in which they were politically possible would have almost no need of them. An America that would demand such reforms would be a country that had changed its orientation toward the presidency—a country that thoroughly rejected the idea that it's the president's job to deliver us from evil and to invest our lives with meaning. We don't yet live in that country.

Today, Americans are far more suspicious of presidential power than they were in the 1950s and early 1960s. Yet, the fantasy of the redeemer president dies hard. That vision of the office can be found in almost every forum in which Americans interpret the presidency: in the movies, on television, in the perennial rankings of presidents, and on talk shows and op-ed pages. In each of those venues, the bipartisan romance with the Imperial Presidency smolders on.

The Pop Culture Presidency

The presidential movies and television programs of the past 15 years make plain America's bipolar attitude toward executive power. The Clinton era saw a burst of big-screen portrayals of the president, at least half of which reflected a post-Watergate sensibility, depicting the office-holder as worse than the ordinary run of humanity. In *Clear and Present Danger* (1994), for example, top CIA official Jack Ryan (Harrison Ford) battles with Colombian drug lords and his own crooked commander in chief, who has caused enormous bloodshed by ordering covert actions in defiance of Congress. "How dare you, sir?" Ryan demands of President Bennett in one memorable scene. In the 1997 thriller *Absolute Power*, the president's taste for rough sex leads to an elaborate cover-up after a resisting paramour gets shot by the Secret Service. And in *Mars Attacks!* (1996), *Murder at 1600* (1997), *Wag the Dog* (1997), *Primary Colors* (1998), and *Dick* (1999), the Hollywood president was a criminal, a fool, or—as often as not—both.

Yet, even amid the silver-screen cynicism, the yearning for Camelot persisted. Several of the more popular presidential movies of the 1990s enthusiastically embraced the Heroic Presidency. Rob Reiner's 1995 romantic comedy *The American President* featured Michael Douglas as President Andrew Shepherd, a Democrat and widower who falls in love with an environmental lobbyist (Annette Bening) and discovers his inner Bobby Kennedy. Toward the end of the movie, Shepherd breaks from his handlers' poll-tested script to tell America that by God, he'll fight for dramatic CO_2 reductions and a crime bill based on the premise that handguns are "a threat to national security." He closes the speech by vowing: "I'm gonna get the guns. . . . My name is Andrew Shepherd, and *I am the President*."

In the hit films *Independence Day* (1996) and *Air Force One* (1997), our superhero president fights all enemies foreign, domestic—and extraterrestrial. In *Independence Day*, Bill Pullman's President Thomas J. Whitmore, a Gulf War hero and former fighter pilot, takes to the skies to do battle against the aliens who threaten the American homeland. A year later, *Air Force One* made clear that Hollywood's Heroic President is always a Wilsonian. That film opens with a speech by President James Marshall (Harrison Ford), delivered on Russian soil, in which Marshall chastises his country and himself for being reluctant to use force when American interests are not at stake. On the flight home from Moscow, Russian fascists hijack the presidential plane. Ford's President Marshall deals with security threats even more directly than Pullman's President Whitmore, *personally* killing terrorists with his bare hands.

Ivan Reitman's 1993 comedy *Dave* didn't offer the cathartic violence of *Air Force One*, but it captured Americans' conflicting attitudes toward the office perhaps better than any other presidential movie of the era. In a twist on the familiar "evil twin" genre, *Dave* gave America *two* presidents, the corrupt William Harrison Mitchell and his noble doppelgänger Dave Kovic, both played by Kevin Kline.

"Dave" is an ordinary businessman who, taking advantage of his uncanny resemblance to Mitchell, also moonlights as a presidential impersonator. The real President Mitchell, much like Judson C. Hammond in 1933's *Gabriel over the White House*, is an amoral wretch who can't keep his hands off the help. Where Hammond fell into a coma after a car accident, Mitchell succumbs to a stroke while having sex with a presidential aide. With the real president incapacitated, his sinister chief of staff tries to seize power by covering up the coma and using Dave Kovic as a figurehead.[25] Kovic goes along with the scheme initially, but he soon proves impossible to control, deciding that as long as he holds the reins, he ought to use his powers to help Americans realize their dreams.

Kline's "Dave" is a Jimmy Stewart everyman who shows how easy fixing the country's problems can be when we have a president who is pure of heart. In one scene, Dave and his accountant buddy Murray sit down, roll up their sleeves, and, armed with only a pen, a legal pad, and their fundamental decency, draw up a new budget that saves money and cures homelessness.

By portraying the real president as a cad, *Dave* was at least willing to entertain the possibility that power corrupts. Aaron Sorkin's *The West Wing* found that notion unbearably pessimistic, and built one of the most popular political dramas in television history around the concept of an incorruptible president devoted to good works. In 1999, inspired by the research he did as the screenwriter for *The American President*, Sorkin sold NBC on the idea of a show designed to counter the prevailing cynicism about politics. Unabashed idealism proved to be a winning formula, as *West Wing* garnered high ratings and 26 Emmys over its seven-year run.

Yet, despite the snappy repartee and often-witty scripts, *West Wing* was a remarkably silly program. Has there ever been a group of *real* White House staffers as admirable and lovable as the *West Wing* ensemble, that selfless, high-minded, public-spirited, fundamentally decent pack of . . . political operators? Sorkin's White House existed in a Bizarro World where the Oval Office is apparently devoid of office politics. Fans of the show never saw the sort of infighting, backstabbing, and jockeying for position that appear in real-world accounts of White House life, like George Reedy's *Twilight of the Presidency* and John Dean's *Blind Ambition.*

It's nearly impossible to imagine any of the *West Wing* staffers behaving like a young John Dean, scheming to use the IRS against the administration's political enemies, or a young Bill Moyers, urging the FBI to spy on anti-war congressmen.[26] Could a Dick Morris or a David Addington ever walk the halls with saintly C.J. and noble Toby? In the fantasy world of *The West Wing*, that was unlikely: the arrogance of power was nowhere to be found. Sorkin had managed to design a show that—in 21st-century America—was markedly less cynical than Frank Capra's *Mr. Smith Goes to Washington.*

ABC's briefly popular *West Wing* knockoff *Commander-in-Chief* (2005) took the romance of the Imperial Presidency even further. In her first three days as president, Geena Davis's Mackenzie Allen proved as bellicose as any alpha male, sending the Seventh Fleet through the Taiwan Strait to intimidate China, and ordering U.S. troops into action twice, once to capture a drug-running, Noriega-like dictator from the country of "San Pascuale," and again to save a woman in Nigeria who's about to be executed under Sharia law for adultery. As U.S. Marines led the rescued prisoner to a waiting helicopter, the camera cut to President Allen delivering the line "I will always defend the Constitution"— a crashing non sequitur, given the context. Nonetheless, *National Review Online* gave Mac's decision an approving shout-out: "You go, girl."[27]

Presidential Pecking Order

Television executives and movie producers are paid to know their audience, so the fact that they repeatedly conjure up images of the Heroic Presidency says something about how Americans view the office. Oddly enough, though, American academics outdo the entertainment industry in their fondness for presidential adventurism. When ranking the presidents, scholars tend to downgrade any commander in chief who hasn't provided the audience sufficient explosions and drama.

In February 2007, as President Bush's troop surge began in Iraq, *U.S. News* ran a cover story on "America's Worst Presidents," asking "If there were a negative Mount Rushmore, which presidents would have their faces carved into it?" To find out, the magazine averaged the results of several recent scholarly polls to extract academia's consensus view on the 10 worst presidents in American history. Predictably, few activist presidents made the list. Instead, Warren G. Harding was number two, and William Henry Harrison, who died a month after his inauguration, number eight. Classifying Warren G. as the second-worst president in over two centuries was unfair, though hardly unexpected. But the fact that poor Harrison, who had even less time than inclination to attempt great works, garnered a spot on the scholars' wall of infamy was telling. Historians and political scientists seem to have little use for the presidential equivalent of the Hippocratic oath. In the presidential rankings game, "doing no harm" gets you nowhere; it might even cost you points.[28]

"The greatest presidents are those who exercise executive power most aggressively," John Yoo told a Federalist Society luncheon a few months later, insisting that historians would come to see George W. Bush's expansive view of presidential power as justified.[29] Most of the scholars who participate in presidential-ranking polls lean to the left, thus they're not particularly fond of the architect of the 9/11 presidency or the president he served. But it's hard to see what legitimate grounds they'd have for disagreeing with Yoo's assessment.

Indeed, more than five decades worth of scholarly surveys make it plain that American academics agree with John Yoo about the prerequisites for presidential magnificence. The scholarly arbiters of greatness reward those who centralize power—and some of them even admit it. In a 2003 article entitled "Reflections of a Presidency Rater," Barnard political scientist Richard M. Pious wrote that when he fills out presidential surveys, he rewards "the successful use of presidential prerogative power" and downgrades those who, like Harding, "left the presidential office weaker than when they entered."[30] That's a strange position to take, unless one believes that there has *never* been a time in American history when the presidency has been too strong.

According to Arthur Schlesinger Jr., President Kennedy, who had hired Schlesinger as an aide (perhaps to get a head start in the race for historians' favor) once observed that war "made it easier for a president to achieve greatness."[31] JFK wasn't the only president to make that assessment. Bill Clinton was obsessed with how historians might rank him. In 1996, he came up with his own list, dividing his predecessors into three brackets. He then approached Dick Morris, and the two spent hours mulling over what Clinton could do to end up in the top echelon.[32] "I envy Kennedy having an enemy," Clinton said at one point, imagining how much easier it must have been for the president to get his way by raising the specter of communist domination: "The question now is how to persuade people they could do things when they are not immediately threatened."[33]

The evidence bears out JFK's and Clinton's intuition. Leading or launching a war is one of the most reliable predictors of presidential greatness in scholarly surveys. Social psychologist Dean Keith Simonton used regression analysis to examine the factors that the rankers reward, demonstrating that, besides years in office, years at war are most strongly correlated with higher standing.[34] Another scholar who, like Simonton, ran the numbers on presidential greatness, concluded that "without the compelling urgency of war . . . a great individual will have considerable difficulty in gaining recognition as a great president."[35] In 2005, conservative law professor Eric Posner suggested that the academic consensus proved that "imperial presidents perform better than limited-power republican presidents." Posner looked at the 2000 presidential poll conducted by the *Wall Street Journal* and the Federalist Society (the first to control for the rankers' political affiliation) and categorized each of the presidents ranked in the poll as either "republican" or "imperial." The high status of the imperialists led Posner to conclude that there was a powerful argument for unleashing the Imperial Presidency: "Much of the structure of the presidency—especially in foreign affairs—is hampered by 18th-century restrictions that were motivated by fears of monarchy. By pushing against these restrictions, Bush . . . is further modernizing the office of the presidency and preparing it for the challenges ahead."[36]

In March 2005, the *WSJ* and the Federalist Society repeated their survey, again selecting an ideologically balanced panel of academics. This time, they broke down the results by rankers' party affiliations, revealing that five of right-wing academics' top 10 are warrior presidents. FDR, the court packer, the architect of the welfare state, the man who imprisoned over 110,000 innocent Japanese Americans, was, according to self-identified conservatives, the fifth best president in American history.[37]

In the perverse calculus that governs the presidential rankings, a man's worth is measured not by how much harm he avoided, not by how well he presided over domestic peace, but by how skillfully he exploited catastrophes to spur revolutionary change. Is it any wonder, then, that presidents, who walk the halls with the portraits of past greats, sometimes long for an enormous crisis in which to prove themselves? Should we be surprised if they're tempted to resort to militarism when the impossible tasks they've signed up for—"managing" the economy, keeping Americans safe from every sort of harm—up to and including spiritual "malaise"—prove difficult to fulfill? If presidents are too quick to invoke the war metaphor, if they find themselves drawn toward sweeping theories of executive power and an exalted, quasi-religious view of their station, then perhaps that's because the people who fill out their report cards reward such behavior.

American Caesaropapism

In his 1996 presidential ranking survey, Arthur Schlesinger Jr. insisted that a great president needed to "have a deep connection with the needs, anxieties, dreams of the people."[38] Of course, the ability to channel the collective spirit of the American *volk* isn't a skill that the chief magistrate needs to faithfully execute the laws or defend the country from foreign attacks. Schlesinger's theory of presidential greatness raises the question: are we picking a president—or a pope?

Yet, the idea expressed by the author of *The Imperial Presidency* is distressingly common. Far too many Americans credit or blame the president for the state of the "national soul," and look to him to bring unity to a fractious society, even if that unity can be achieved only in the crucible of war.

Foreign observers sometimes marvel at the aspirations Americans invest in whichever professional politician manages to claw his way up to the nation's highest office. In 1967, the British journalist Henry Fairlie compared the American orientation toward the presidency with "Caesaropapism": the union of secular and religious authority in the person of one national ruler, a leadership system usually associated with Constantine, the first Christian emperor of Rome. "The character of the presidency is such," Fairlie wrote, that the majority of the people can be persuaded to look to it for a kind of leadership which no politician, in my opinion, should be allowed, let alone invited, to give. "If people want a sense of purpose," [former British Prime Minister] Harold Macmillan once said to me, "they should get it from their archbishops."[39]

A few years later, fresh from his turn as a speechwriter for Democratic presidential candidate George McGovern, Catholic philosopher Michael Novak wrote an intriguing book called *Choosing Our King: Powerful Symbols in Presidential Politics*. In it, Novak echoed Fairlie's assessment, describing the presidency as "the nation's most central religious symbol."[40]

Choosing Our King is replete with vivid passages that bring home to the reader the peculiarity of images we normally take for granted—images that reveal an idolatrous orientation toward America's chief executive. Novak described campaign appearances in which "hands are stretched to [the president] over wire fences at airports, like hands extended toward medieval sovereigns or ancient prophets."[41] When Americans speak of "'saving the presidency,' of 'confidence' and 'faith' in the presidential office, of the 'sacredness' of that office, and of 'trust' in it," their language, Novak suggested, seemed "appropriate to religion, not to a secular state."[42]

Novak and Fairlie both found something ominous in Americans' tendency to invest the presidency with spiritual significance. Novak believed that tendency was endemic to man and thus unavoidable. Fairlie was more optimistic; he thought Americans could profit from the British example: "It was the true achievement of the Whigs to make the English monarchy dull and boring (and rather vulgar as well) and, in the process, to eliminate all concern with national and moral purpose from English politics—which does not mean from English society—for ever." "The presidency," Fairlie wrote during the twilight of the Johnson administration, "is very different."[43]

And so it remains today. Though Vietnam and Watergate tested Americans' trust in the office, turning many previously loyal suppliants into skeptics, we have not yet fully renounced our faith. Few Americans find anything inappropriate in the image of a president visiting a disaster area and promising to heal the afflicted, or constructing his stump speeches around the transparently false premise that the president controls the economy, or greeting the horror of September 11 with the promise to "rid the world of evil."

That's not quite right: many Americans *do* find something untoward in presidents' claims to be the Voice of the People, or in their periodic invocation of religious imagery. When Bill Clinton promised a "New Covenant" for middle-class taxpayers and when George W. Bush, in his 2003 State of the Union, adapted the hymn "There's Power in the Blood" to praise the "wonder-working power" of federally subsidized charity, some Americans took offense.[44] Yet, the level of offense taken, the degree to which particular groups resist the deification of the presidency, seems to depend on whether they identify with whichever faction currently holds the White House. All too often it seems that the virtues of a restrained presidency are best appreciated by those who've just been dislodged from power.

After *Choosing Our King,* Novak himself became an object lesson in the persistence of Situational Constitutionalism. During the 1970s, Novak drifted to the right and, toward the end of the decade, joined the conservative American Enterprise Institute. And as Republicans increasingly seemed to have a lock on the executive branch, Novak began to revise his views, becoming a reliable defender of presidential prerogative. In 1992, he rereleased *Choosing Our King,* this time under a tamer title that wouldn't perturb post-Reagan conservatives: *Choosing Presidents: Symbols of Political Leadership.*

In the introduction to the revised edition, Novak praised Reagan's skillful employment of "the symbolic power of the kingly office," and apologized for his previous misgivings about executive dominance: "Twenty years ago, many of us were perhaps too impressed by the presidential power exercised by Lyndon Johnson and Richard Nixon against our own wishes, especially with regard to Vietnam."[45] George W. Bush's second term found Novak taking a far more worshipful attitude toward the chief executive than he'd displayed in *Choosing Our King.* In an essay for *National Review,* Novak counted himself among those "who love and admire President Bush." As he saw it, Bush was "Our Bravest President," in large part because of his single-minded determination to democratize

Iraq, whatever the cost. Novak was sure that future generations would eventually revere Bush as "a president who changed the course of history, yes—and also one who did so against unprecedented opposition at home."[46]

High Priests of the Presidency

Novak and Fairlie believed that America had developed a "civil religion" in which the president was Pontiff in Chief. If the modern presidency has a priesthood, surely its ranks are thick with professional pundits, who use their column space and airtime to urge the president to think big and act boldly. Much of our pundit class seems convinced that the bourgeois tranquility America enjoys is hopelessly vacant and shallow. To save us all from Babbitry, we need a leader to set ablaze what Thomas Carlyle called our "common languid times," and bring us all together around the flames.

In 2000, David Brooks, the original National Greatness Conservative, published *Bobos in Paradise: The New Upper Class and How They Got There*, a charming foray into "comic sociology" that analyzes the emergent "Bourgeois Bohemian" class and its search for fresh arugula. In the book, Brooks worries that Americans aren't tough enough anymore, that opulence has made us soft and selfish. Globalization is glorious, Brooks tells us, but danger lurks amid our Belgian beers, slate shower stalls, and the knickknacks at Restoration Hardware: "American society is now rife with forces that encourage people to think about their own success, to cultivate their own gardens, to segment themselves off into their own cultural cliques."

What could we do to stop this epidemic of individualistic garden cultivating? As Brooks saw it, only "reform at home and activism abroad" could save us from the belief that "the pleasures of an oversized kitchen are more satisfying than the conflicts and challenges of patriotic service." We must, Brooks wrote, shoulder "the obligations that fall to the world's lead nation: promoting democracy and human rights everywhere and exercising American might in a way that reflects American ideals."[47]

Brooks wasn't the only pundit to lament the placidity of the post–Cold War era. In the years leading up to 9/11, many neoconservatives openly longed for war. In 1997, Fred Barnes of Fox News and the *Weekly*

Standard announced that he was "suffering from a bad case of ennui." Joy it was to be a Beltway journalist during the struggle against the Soviets, when tension filled the air and "the president might be called upon at a moment's notice to respond to a nuclear attack." "All this was great for journalism," Barnes wrote, remembering the thrill he used to get driving home past the Pentagon at night, looking at the packed parking lot, and imagining the war room "brimming with officers" busily developing battle plans: "Now when I drive by, the parking lot is practically empty."

In the boom times of the late 1990s, "nothing seem[ed] to matter very much," Barnes pouted, "normalcy turns out to be pretty slow-paced and dreary." He looked back wistfully to the Gulf War, "the last great moment in Washington":

> Every morning I turned to the *Washington Times* to find out which anti-war wussies it had put in its Desert Storm hall of shame. Every press conference, I watched. Desert Storm was all I thought about or talked about. My stories concentrated on President Bush's heroic role in the war.[48]

September 11 ended our long national nightmare of pundit boredom. As Ground Zero smoldered, many of America's opinion leaders hoped that the smoke heralded an opportunity to rally Americans to the cause of national greatness. Properly inspired, our "Bourgeois Bohemians" might become the "Greatest Generation" of the new century. In this new crusade, we'd each be called to different tasks: some would take point in Sadr City. Some would cheer them on in the *Weekly Standard*. But they also serve who only sit and write op-eds.

Two days after the World Trade Center's collapse, Chris Matthews, the host of MSNBC's *Hardball* and a former speechwriter for Jimmy Carter, praised George W. Bush's good fortune: "Lucky though he was, Bill Clinton never had his shot at greatness. He could lower the jobless rate, balance the budget, and console us after the Oklahoma City bombing. But he never got the opportunity George W. Bush was given: the historic chance to lead. Our American spirit, power and enterprise now stand ready for orders. Only the president can give them."[49]

By any normal standard, the sentiment that Barnes and Matthews express is *demented*. How else can we characterize the mindset of men who find peace boring and believe that carnage has its bright side, bringing with it a "historic chance to lead"? But that sentiment is all too common among America's opinion leaders. The "vital center" of the punditocracy ranges from the "National Greatness Conservatism" espoused by the *Weekly Standard* to the "National Greatness Liberalism" offered by its counterpart on the center left, the *New Republic*. Both camps seem to think American life is purposeless without a warrior president who can bring us together to fulfill our national destiny.

A Lover of Idols, A Worshipper of Kings

But perhaps we get the pundits we deserve as well. In darker moments, it's hard not to fear that the tendency to worship a leader—to look to him to give purpose to our lives—is equivalent to original sin—one of the flaws to which all flesh is heir.

Human affairs are chaotic, largely governed by chance, and not under the direction of any one person's will. The drama of the presidency rests on the notion that *one man* can vanquish our problems and impose order on the world. That drama may appeal to something deeply rooted in the human psyche. Political scientist Bruce Miroff suggests that the presidency provides the public with "a sense of personal power. Through skillful dramatic efforts, combined with projection on the part of the audience, a president can exhibit admirable and heroic qualities— such as decisiveness and courage—that most people cannot exhibit, or even feel, in their own lives."[50]

William Hazlitt, the early 19th-century English essayist and political radical, had a much less flattering take on our need to anoint and venerate a leader: "Man is a toad-eating animal," Hazlitt wrote in 1819, "naturally a worshipper of idols and a lover of kings."[51] In his essay "On the Spirit of Monarchy," Hazlitt noted that, as savages, we fashioned "Gods of wood and stone and brass," but now, thinking ourselves above superstition, "we make kings of common men, and are proud of our own handiwork." As Hazlitt saw it, behind that impulse lies a craven desire to dominate others, even if only vicariously: "Each individual would (were it in his power) be a king, a God; but as he cannot, the next best thing is to see this reflex image of his self-love, the darling passion of his breast, realized, embodied out of himself in the first object he can lay his hands on for the purpose."[52]

Sometimes it seems that we worship strange gods indeed. What *is* it that compels so many of us to invest ourselves so deeply in the fate of the office's current occupant? Considered dispassionately, very few, if any, of those who manage to get elected are remotely worthy of reverence. Why then do so many of the American intelligentsia place such high regard on the decidedly ordinary figures that occupy the Oval Office?

Hazlitt called the pundit class of his time the "intellectual pimps of power"[53]; one suspects that he wouldn't find much reason to dial back his assessment today. In the aftermath of the Lewinsky scandal, Nina Burleigh, former White House correspondent for *Time*, offered that she'd "be happy to give [Clinton oral sex] just to thank him for keeping abortion legal. I think American women should be lining up with their presidential kneepads on to show their gratitude for keeping theocracy off our backs."[54] Writing in 2005, John Hinderaker, Claremont Institute fellow, *National Review* contributor, and cofounder of the top-ranked conservative blog "Powerline," stopped short of Burleigh's salacious proposal, but gave George W. Bush a verbal stroking that was nearly as embarrassing: "It must be very strange to be President Bush. A man of extraordinary vision and brilliance approaching to genius, he can't get anyone to notice. He is like a great painter or musician who is ahead of his time, and who unveils one masterpiece after another to a reception that, when not bored, is hostile."[55]

It must be very strange to feel compelled to prostrate oneself before men like Bill Clinton, an Elmer Gantry risen far above his proper station, or George W. Bush, who as he approached 50, was notable mainly because he had a famous last name and had managed to quit drinking. Yet, from the cable talk shows to the voting booth, the propensity for leader-worship remains remarkably common, even when our leaders themselves are remarkably common. Hazlitt had an explanation for that phenomenon as well: If the man we designate a god appears distinctly ordinary, even mediocre, that in a way makes him *easier* to worship. "The less of real superiority or excellence there is in the person we fix upon as our proxy in this dramatic exhibition, the more easily can we change places with him, and fancy ourselves as good as he." "We see the symbols of Majesty," Hazlitt wrote, "we enjoy the pomp, we crouch before the power, we walk in the procession, and make part of the pageant, and we say in our secret hearts, there is nothing but accident that prevents us from being at the head of it."[56]

Stirrings of Heresy

At times—especially during presidential election years—Hazlitt's suspicion that we're hard-wired to worship kings seems depressingly accurate. But the American Revolution—the primal fact of our national identity—argues against that sort of despair. And promising developments in our political culture over the past 40 years suggest that we're not condemned to such a fate. The Spirit of '76 lives on—even if it manifests itself in thoroughly modern ways.

Civil libertarians and constitutionalists often talk about the post-9/11 presidency as if "It's Midnight in America." Given George W. Bush's insistence that the executive branch cannot be bound by law, and the considerable success his administration has had in pressing that claim, that pessimism is perfectly understandable. But a little reflection should serve to put the last seven years in perspective. In a way, it's astonishing that 9/11 didn't bring about a clampdown much worse than anything we've seen thus far.

In past wars, few Americans questioned the president's right to suppress dissent or abrogate constitutional protections. In World War I, the Wilson administration locked up anyone who dared question the war, and intimidated anyone who even thought about it. During World War II, home-front life tended to go easier for anyone not of Japanese descent. Even so, Americans were quite willing to endorse departures from settled constitutional norms.

In 1942, when FDR ordered secret military trials for the enemy saboteurs involved in the *Quirin* case, the public reaction was overwhelmingly supportive. Although one of the captured German agents was an American citizen, the *New York Times*, the *Washington Post*, and other publications applauded the president's decision. When the case reached the Supreme Court, even the *Nation* welcomed the Court's ruling that "unlawful combatants," including Americans, could be tried before a military tribunal.

Sixty years later, when George W. Bush announced that he intended to use military tribunals to prosecute *noncitizen* terrorist suspects, the same publications denounced his decision as a constitutional abomination. What explains the different reactions? Jack Goldsmith and Cass Sunstein suggest that the successive shocks of Vietnam, Watergate, and the Church Committee revelations spurred "a massively strengthened commitment to individual rights." "With respect to actions of the executive branch that might endanger civil liberties," Goldsmith and Sunstein write, "the nation is now far less trusting of government, and far more solicitous of the accused, than it was sixty years ago. This change counts as a genuine revolution not only in law but also in cultural attitudes."[57] That revolution has had enormous implications for the political fortunes of the Heroic Presidency.

Political scientists have often assumed that political trust is a dependent variable; from that perspective, if the trust indicator goes down, poor presidential leadership may be to blame. But Vanderbilt's Marc Hetherington has recently demonstrated that "trust's effect on feelings about the incumbent president . . . [are] even stronger than the reverse."[58] Resurgent distrust means that even a newly elected president with a clean record faces greater obstacles to his freedom of action than his predecessors did 40 years ago.

However fond tenured professors, Hollywood producers, and syndicated columnists may be of the Heroic Presidency, when ordinary Americans close the curtain behind them, they vote to check the hero's power. Hetherington notes that in the four presidential elections following the largest decline in political trust (1968, 1972, 1976, and 1992), the party that held the presidency lost it three times.[59] And of the 14 presidential elections between the end of World War II and September 11, 7 brought divided government.[60] Federalist Society founder Steven G. Calabresi, one of the pioneers of unitary executive theory, complains that after their initial election or reelection, presidents have to take "several steps back over the succeeding three years," because Americans favor the opposition party in off-year elections. "When a party wins the White House," Calabresi writes, "it gains on average only one governor's seat, while over the next three years the President's party loses on average four governorships, leaving it worse off than *before* it won the presidency."[61] It's almost as if the voters subconsciously regret their prior endorsement of presidential heroism, and decide to punish the figure that they've just rewarded.

It seems strange to try to check the president by voting against state officials who share his party affiliation, but to the extent that voters want greater oversight of the executive branch, electing a Congress dominated by the opposition party makes a great deal of sense. Political scientists William G. Howell and Jon C. Pevehouse have closely studied the data on divided government, and found that when the public rewards the opposition party during wartime, the result is more vigorous policing of the incumbent administration's conduct, including many more congressional oversight hearings.[62]

The Democratic Congress elected in November 2006 showed little inclination and even less skill when it came to restoring checks and balances and extricating the United States from the Iraq occupation. However, the very presence of an opposition-dominated legislature may help restrain the president from embarking on further foreign adventures. Howell and Pevehouse showed that "the White House's propensity to exercise military force steadily declines as members of the opposition party pick up seats in Congress."[63]

Pundits and pols wedded to the idea of the federal government as an all-purpose problem solver tend to interpret declining political trust as a political catastrophe. Whenever the trust indicator plunges, solemn op-eds lamenting the "trust crisis" are sure to follow. Given that many of the same commentators who agonize about declining trust also worry about unnecessary wars and the accompanying abuses of civil liberties, perhaps they ought to reflect on the fact that increased faith in government makes the very things they fear more likely. Hetherington notes that as political trust increases, so does support for military intervention.[64] Conversely, when trust declines, it diminishes support for adventurism abroad and also reduces the public's willingness to cede civil liberties for the illusory promise of greater security.[65]

Although American political elites seem to think that a trusting polity is a healthy polity, growing wariness about government power is better understood as a sign of cultural progress. For nearly three decades, the World Values Survey project, directed by University of Michigan political scientist Ronald Inglehart, has tracked the relationship between economic development and cultural change in dozens of countries worldwide. Inglehart's surveys have found that in all modern industrial societies, as per capita GDP increases, political distrust increases with it, and respect for hierarchical institutions declines.[66] Inglehart writes that "it seems clear that one of the most pervasive defining tendencies of the modernization era—the tendency to look to the state as the solution to all problems—has reached its limits."[67]

In the American context, it seems far too early to conclude that the tendency to look to the state—and the head of state—as the solution to all our problems "has reached its limits." But there are encouraging signs that suggest the era of the Heroic Presidency will not soon be repeated.

In the early 20th century, the growth of communications technology aided the growth of the plebiscitary presidency, giving Rossiter's Voice of the People a powerful microphone. Today, changing developments in that technology are starting to undermine the president's status as the central figure in American life.

In April 1971, when Richard Nixon gave a prime-time address on Vietnam, more than half the American viewing public watched. When George W. Bush wanted to explain his Iraq policy to the country in September 2003, he could do no better than 21 percent. In the heroic era, the president had a guaranteed audience, but today our national talk-show host suffers from declining Nielsens. The proliferation of cable television and VCRs during the 1980s gave Americans other options besides turning off the TV when a presidential address preempted network programming; TiVo, on-demand programming, and streaming Internet video continue to increase our choices about what to watch. "A whole generation has now grown up in the narrowcasting age," writes Martin Wattenberg, and to the extent that young Americans pay attention to the president, they seem to consider him a source of amusement.[68]

An enormous chunk of Generation Y, those born roughly after 1977, gets its political information from Comedy Central's *The Daily Show*, a comedy news program devoted to the idea that we're led by fools.[69] The sarcastic, impertinent spirit that characterized the private journals of William Maclay, the Jeffersonian senator who beat back John Adams's attempt to affix royal titles to executive officers, now has a mass audience, tuning in nightly to watch host Jon Stewart poke fun at people in power.

Stewart's merciless ridicule of President Bush has led some conservatives to complain that the show is politically biased. But the evidence doesn't support that complaint. In a 2006 study, the Center for Media and Public Affairs found that the only overarching prejudice *The Daily Show* displays is indiscriminate contempt for the political class. According to CMPA, 98 percent of *The Daily Show*'s coverage of Republicans was negative, compared with 96 percent of its commentary on Democrats.[70] The idea that anyone relying on the program as his or her main source of political news will end up woefully uninformed turns out to be false as well: *Daily Show* viewers tend to be more knowledgeable than most newspaper readers, even when factors such as education and political interest are taken into account.[71]

Some of the same earnest souls who lose sleep over the "trust crisis" also fret about declining "respect for the office" and the fact that more and more of the kids today get their information about public affairs from "fake news" programs. But if young Americans think that comedians provide the best possible source of political news, that probably says more about the quality of our leaders than it does about the fecklessness of youth.

In 2006, *Daily Show* alum Stephen Colbert was the featured comic at the White House Correspondents' Dinner, the annual gathering of D.C. journalists where the president is expected to show up and be a good sport by putting up with some gentle ribbing. Colbert wasn't gentle. In character as the moronic right-wing talk-show host he plays on the *Daily Show* spinoff *The Colbert Report*, Colbert compared the Bush administration with the *Hindenburg* disaster, sarcastically applauded our "success" in Iraq, and suggested that the president was an ignoramus who refused to seek accurate information because "reality has a well-known liberal bias." A former top administration aide who attended the dinner commented that the president was furious: he had "that look [like] he's ready to blow."[72]

Colbert's performance was open, in-your-face disrespect for the presidency, and many people didn't care for it. Many didn't like it 10 years earlier at the White House Correspondents' Dinner, when President Clinton had to sit uncomfortably while shock jock Don Imus cracked jokes about Clinton's marital infidelities (though, then as now, how offended one was largely depended on one's party affiliation).

Despite the vestiges of hero worship on display in the press and in popular entertainment, today we treat the presidency with less sentimentality and less respect than we have in years. American political culture in the 21st century is crass and ill-mannered; it holds no idols sacred, and for that reason it grates on those who prefer a more accommodating, respectful approach to political disagreement. But in its own way, our offensive, sometimes paranoid, and always confrontational orientation reflects an 18th-century American sensibility.

Mocking those who rule us might seem immature, but consider the alternative: From FDR through LBJ, for nearly four decades, Americans forgot their heritage of political distrust, and looked to the Oval Office with a childlike faith in the occupant's benevolence. The age of the Heroic Presidency left a legacy of ruinous wars, unrestrained executive surveillance, and repeated abuses of civil liberties. Perhaps a little disrespect is in order, and perhaps there are worse things, after all, than making the president a punching bag and punch line.

The Vision Thing

Accepting the Progressive Party's nomination for president in 1912, Teddy Roosevelt brought the delegates to their feet when he proclaimed: "We need leaders of inspired idealism, leaders to whom are granted great visions, who dream greatly and strive to make their dreams come true; who can kindle the people with the fire from their own burning souls." "The country ought not to take me unless it is in a heroic mood," TR warned.[73] The country got Wilson, but heroism aplenty nonetheless.

We too have suffered our share of executive branch heroism in the Bush years, under a liberator president who saw his role as lighting "a fire in the minds of men," as he put it in his second inaugural. As before, we've been stirred by the rhetoric, and, as before, we've come to be appalled by the results.

After the tragedy of World War I and the orgy of state repression it ushered in at home, Warren Harding came to office with a different prescription: "America's present need is not heroics but healing; not nostrums but normalcy; not revolution but restoration."[74] Pundits and historians rarely utter Harding's neologism "normalcy" without the verbal equivalent of a sneer. But what *is* it that's so contemptible about Harding's term and what it stands for: providing space for Americans to live their own lives, to build their own dreams? Normalcy isn't shallow; normalcy is noble. What more honorable goal could there be for government?

Judging by the presidents our professors and pundits glorify, though, keeping the peace and keeping faith with the Constitution aren't ambitious enough goals to make one a "great" president. Today's fights over the Bush legacy center on comparisons to Teddy Roosevelt and Harry Truman. Both the left and right hold up those authoritarian personalities as models for presidential greatness, differing only on whether the current president is worthy of the comparison. In 2006, former *New Republic* editor Peter Beinart, noting George W. Bush's fondness for invoking HST, accused the president of "tak[ing] Truman's name in vain."[75] Just who is Harry supposed to be in that metaphor?

There's an odd disconnect between the presidents that scholars and journalists worship and the ones that Americans actually *like* when they're in office. The public tends to be quite fond of presidents who preside over peace and prosperity. Neither Harding nor Coolidge ever measured up to historians' standards, but both were enormously more popular during their tenure than was the "heroic" HST. And if either Harding or his successor ever found themselves transfixed by "great visions" that set their souls afire, they had the good sense to keep quiet about it and rest until it passed. Perhaps there's a lesson here: where there is no vision, the people . . . do just fine, actually.

A healthier political culture would cease fighting over the legacies of Truman and TR, and recognize how much there is to admire in presidents who resist grand crusades, who content themselves with securing the peace and leaving well enough alone—in presidents who *preside*. Though we like our presidential clerks and timeservers well enough, we tend to forget about them after they've passed from the scene. But a country with a sounder orientation toward the presidency's potential would occasionally pause to acknowledge the merit of men like Cleveland, Taft, Harding, and Coolidge. A healthier political culture might even celebrate our forgotten presidents, our "lost men": those who could never have made the cut for Rushmore—those whose legacy is instead commemorated in highway rest stops and junior high schools across the land. Here's to the losers: bless them all.

Of course, a country that properly valued presidential restraint would also learn to restrain itself. It would no longer reflexively demand that the executive branch *do something* about any trick of fate notable enough to lead the nightly news. Suppressing that reflex is essential to restoring the limited presidency our Framers envisioned.

Demand and Supply

If presidents believe that the electorate will hold them accountable for providing protection that no free society can provide, they're likely to seek power that no free society ought to let them have. And if we recoil from the powers they claim, we need to recognize that our demands have encouraged them to seek those powers.

Jack Goldsmith's experience in the executive branch convinced him that every post-9/11 president from now on will be "acutely aware that he or she alone will be *wholly responsible* when thousands of Americans are killed in the next attack," and will act accordingly.[76] It is, of course, insane to hold the president "wholly responsible" for terrorist attacks on American soil; in an open society of 300 million people you can't put the homeland security equivalent of a child's bike helmet on every potential target. But it's not insane for presidents to think that the public will exact an enormous political price for their failure to stop such attacks. Who can doubt that a future Democratic president, publicly perceived as less willing to use force than his or her Republican opponents, will face tremendous pressure to take extreme, and possibly counterproductive, action if and when we're attacked again?

And we will be attacked again. If our experience since September 11 is any indication, then there will be a subway bombing, a mass shooting incident, or perhaps something worse every few years, somewhere in the West. The good news is that our chances of dying in a car wreck or ordinary foul play greatly outweigh our chances of dying in a terrorist incident, and there's no good reason that should change in the foreseeable future.[77]

When the Oklahoma City bombing happens, when Columbine or the Virginia Tech shooting happens, we mourn for the victims and then we go on about our lives. We recognize (or most of us do) that it's damned silly to transform American law in pursuit of perfect safety. We'd do well to adopt a similarly sensible perspective toward the terrorist threat—to accept that we'll suffer occasional losses, do what we can to combat terrorism, and renounce the notion that our Constitution itself is to blame for any losses we suffer.

One way to reduce our exposure to terrorism over the long term is to make fewer enemies abroad. Over the 20th century, an expansive view of America's historical mission led America to adopt a defense posture that often had little to do with defense, properly understood. Even if that posture was justified during the struggle against the Soviet Union, it surely deserved rethinking after 1989.

In going abroad in search of monsters to destroy, we've helped create new monsters in the process. Former deputy secretary of defense Paul Wolfowitz has admitted that the stationing of U.S. forces in Saudi Arabia was "Osama bin Laden's principal recruiting device."[78] The Pentagon's think tank, the Defense Science Board, and the best academic work on the motivations for terrorism confirm that American foreign policy has "elevated the authority of the Jihadi insurgents and tended to ratify their legitimacy among Muslims."[79] Interventionism has enhanced national security threats, which in turn have enhanced presidential power. The new enemies we've created may not represent an "existential threat" to America, but given our propensity for overreaction, we ought not to put ourselves at increased risk without good reason.

Our desire to spread the gift of American liberty worldwide is laudable, but the U.S. military is the wrong tool for that task. The principal responsibility of the American military establishment is to protect *American* national security. It is not, as the administration's 2002 *National Security Strategy* would have it, to make the *world* safer, let alone "better."[80] To say so is not to advocate "isolationism"—as if a globalized powerhouse like the United States could ever be "isolated" from the world community. Instead, it means rejecting the idea that global engagement means global policing. It means recognizing the difficulties of preserving a republic while operating a sprawling global empire. If Americans want to restore the constitutional separation of powers, then America needs to relinquish the idea of herself as a redeemer nation and what comes with that role: a redeemer president whose influence expands relentlessly into every sphere, foreign and domestic. America needs to become a normal country, not one that fancies herself chosen by God to pay any price, bear any burden to expand the American way of life by force of arms.

A normal country with a normal president: a government restrained, and a country set free. To some it will sound wonderful, but it's important to recognize the tradeoffs involved in achieving that vision. For one thing, a return to normalcy would condemn scores of bellicose pundits to lives of quiet desperation, forced to write columns about health care reform and tax policy—the unromantic, workaday business of a country at peace. It will not be easy for some of them, as each day they face the lonely drive home past a half-empty Pentagon parking lot. But nothing worth having in this world comes without sacrifice.

*　*　*

At this writing, three days after the Iowa caucuses, campaign 2008 has begun in earnest. Once again, we find ourselves drawn toward the horse race, and once again, despite our better judgment, we dare to hope that by electing a better man or woman, we can set the country and the world right. "Hope—hope in the face of difficulty. Hope in the face of uncertainty. The *audacity* of hope!" It's "God's greatest gift to us," Barack Obama intoned in his 2004 keynote address to the Democratic National Convention, this "belief in things not seen."

One doesn't wish to seem ungrateful, but our ability to believe in "things not seen" may not be the *greatest* gift bestowed upon us by the author of mankind. Believing in what you cannot see may lead to spiritual growth; but when it comes to politics, it makes you an easy mark. Sound political analysis rests on the lessons of experience: it's based on what we can observe, measure, and know. And if we know anything from the history of presidential politics, it's that the Audacity of Hope all too often gives rise to the Arrogance of Power.

If we're disappointed by the government we have, by the presidents we get, then perhaps we should tear our attention away from the current contest, and explore why we get the presidents we do. What do we want in a president? Can any president deliver it, without sacrificing other values we hold dear? If not, what *should* we want in a president?

Our major parties are convinced that what we want is a national parent; the result of that conviction is the long-running contest between the "Mommy Party" and the "Daddy Party."[81] Democrats haven't yet embraced the former designation, though some conservatives are proud to be members of the "Daddy Party."[82] It seems that they haven't thought through what that makes them—and us.

Though our politics retain a juvenile streak, we've grown up a lot since the Age of the Heroic Presidency. We've learned much since Vietnam and Watergate reminded us that, as H. R. Haldeman put it in 1971, "people do things the President wants to do even though it's wrong, and the President can be wrong."

We've come far, but we have farther still to go before we free ourselves of our atavistic tendency to see the chief magistrate as our national father or mother—responsible for our economic well-being, our physical safety, and even our sense of belonging. There's truth in the bitter adage that people—in the aggregate at least—get the government they deserve.

But we are capable of deserving so much better than the office has given us. Skepticism toward power is our constitutional birthright, and it teaches us that in politics, wherever there's a promise, there's an unspoken threat. We *know*, though we sometimes choose to forget, that when a presidential candidate promises to save the world and solve all our problems—it's not going to be free.

Perhaps, with wisdom born of experience, we can come once again to value a government that promises less, but delivers far more of what it promises. Perhaps we can learn to look elsewhere for heroes. But if we must look to the presidency for heroism, we ought to learn once again to appreciate a quieter sort of valor. True political heroism rarely pounds its chest or pounds the pulpit, preaching rainbows and uplift, and promising to redeem the world through military force. A truly heroic president is one who appreciates the virtues of restraint—who is bold enough to act when action is necessary, yet wise enough, humble enough to refuse powers he ought not have. That is the sort of presidency we need, now more than ever.

And we won't get that kind of presidency until we demand it.

AFTERWORD

Our Continuing Cult of the Presidency

March 2009

When *The Cult of the Presidency* came out in May 2008, many on the political right assumed it was yet another anti-Bush polemic. That was how a conservative magazine editor explained his decision not to commission a book review. He left the door open, though: "Talk to us after the election." Lately, a lot of people seem to think I wrote *Cult* with Barack Obama in mind, even though I finished it six months before he secured the nomination, at a time when I would have bet a nonessential appendage that Hillary Clinton would be our next president.

So it goes. In our increasingly tribal politics, we're expected to choose sides: Red Team or Blue, you're either "with us" or "against us." I don't know how *The Cult of the Presidency* will hold up over time, but there's one thing I'm pretty sure I did right with the book: I made it completely nonpartisan. The book is, I hope, relentlessly cynical about both sides of the political spectrum. After all, the imperial presidency is the classic bipartisan project: the left and the right have contributed equally to its growth.

Cynicism's out of vogue these days. In the 2008 campaign, both candidates identified distrust of government as a pernicious force in American life. John McCain had long warned of a specter haunting

America—a "pervasive public cynicism" toward government "as dangerous in its way as war and depression have been in the past"—and he continued to hammer that theme throughout his second bid for the presidency.[1]

Here, despite all their differences, was something on which McCain and Obama stood as one. In Obama's speech accepting the 2008 Democratic nomination, he decried "the cynicism we all have about government."[2] That sort of attitude wouldn't be tolerated in the Age of Hope, Michelle Obama made clear at a rally on UCLA's campus; Barack Obama would "demand that you shed your cynicism . . . and that you engage."[3]

In his inaugural address, President Obama emphasized inclusiveness, "Our patchwork heritage is a strength." "Christians and Muslims, Jews and Hindus, and nonbelievers," Americans "of every language and culture, drawn from every end of this Earth," would join together to renew the country's greatness. But there was one group, at least, whose membership in the American family was suspect: the "cynics" weren't quite welcome. "There are some," Obama intoned, "who question the scale of our ambitions, who suggest that our system cannot tolerate too many big plans. Their memories are short, for they have forgotten what this country has already done, what free men and women can achieve when imagination is joined to common purpose. . . . What the cynics fail to understand is that the ground has shifted beneath them."[4]

But after eight years of George W. Bush, how could any sober citizen resist casting a skeptical eye on grand presidential plans to remake the country and the world? Reacting to Obama's inaugural address, my colleague Will Wilkinson wrote:

Can you recall the scale of our recent ambitions? The United States would invade Iraq, refashion it as a democracy and forever transform the Middle East. Remember when President Bush committed the United States to "the ultimate goal of ending tyranny in our world"? That is ambitious scale.

Not only have some of us forgotten "what this country has already done . . . when imagination is joined to a common purpose," it's as if some of us are trying to erase the memory of our complicity in the last eight years—to forget that in the face of a crisis we did transcend our stale differences and cut the president a blank check that paid for disaster. How can we not question the scale of our leaders' ambitions? How short would our memories have to be?[5]

In these early days of the Obama administration, however, it looks as though our memories are short indeed. Intoxicated by the aura of Hope surrounding our new president, once again, many Americans look to the office to unite us behind a common cause, deliver us from evil, and help us realize our dreams. And once again, I suspect, we'll have cause to regret our infatuation with the false promise of presidential power.

We still look to the presidency to solve problems it was never designed to solve—problems that no single man or woman could solve—problems that may well be beyond the capacity of *any* political institution, however constituted, to solve. As Theodore Lowi has suggested, the "Pogo Principle" is the key factor behind our metastasizing executive branch: "We have met the enemy, and he is us." The irrational expectations we invest in the office drive the growth of presidential power. When you ask a man to perform miracles, don't be surprised when he seeks powers to match that responsibility. And, having demanded the impossible, don't be surprised when you're disappointed with the results.

A lot has happened since *The Cult of the Presidency* was first published. But through the long campaign and the dawning of the Obama era, nothing has emerged to undermine the book's basic themes. We continue to reward candidates who dream big and promise miracles. Congress remains as eager as ever to abandon its constitutional responsibilities—handing the president vast powers to fight the war on terror and, increasingly, to reshape the economy as well. In the midst of crisis, all eyes still turn to the chief executive, demanding presidential rescue plans for anything that ails the body politic. The president continues to use the language of war and emergency to stoke public demands for bold executive action. And as ever before, crisis is the health of the presidency.

Barack Obama is a fascinating and frustrating figure, whose views on the president's role are riddled with tensions. On the campaign trail, Obama simultaneously promised to roll back executive power and to greatly expand the bounties that the president can provide. And, whether by accident or design, he's become the focal point of an enormous and unsettling cult of personality.

How will those tensions play out in the years to come? Will Obama make good on his promise to end presidential excesses in the fight against terrorism, restoring the rule of law and, as he put it in his inaugural address, reconciling "our safety and our ideals"? Will he prove the cynics wrong and radically reshape the American political landscape? Or will the scale of his ambitions prove too vast?

Predicting the future is always a risky enterprise, but the smart money says that Obama's will be a failed presidency. That does not mean, however, that he will leave the office weaker than he found it. When Obama's tenure comes to a close, four or eight years from now, he'll probably end up one of the least popular presidents in the modern era—and also one of the most powerful.

The Cult of the Presidency in Campaign 2008

There was a revealing moment in the first presidential debate in September 2008, when moderator Jim Lehrer asked the candidates, "Are you willing to acknowledge, both of you, that this financial crisis is going to affect the way you *rule the country* as president of the United States?"[6] Neither McCain nor Obama objected to Lehrer's phrasing. Both, it seemed, were perfectly comfortable with the idea that it's the president's job to "rule the country."

A disturbing sentiment in a country born through rejection of monarchy. But you could see how the candidates might get the idea that "ruling the country" was the president's job. By the time both major parties had settled on their nominees for the 2008 race, it had become clear that whoever won would, as Yale Law professor Jack Balkin observed, "inherit more constitutional and legal power than any president in U.S. history."[7] Both campaigns struggled to prove that their man was worthy of such power, making exorbitant promises and describing their respective candidates as God-touched beings come to deliver Americans from all that plagued them.

In the revival-tent atmosphere of Obama's campaign, the preferred hosanna of hope was "Yes we *can!*" We *can*, the Democratic candidate promised, not only create "a new kind of politics" but "transform this country," "change the world," "end the age of oil in our time,"[8] deliver "a complete transformation of the economy,"[9] and even "create a Kingdom right here on earth."[10] With the presidency, it seems, all things are possible.

One of McCain's more effective campaign ads skewered Obama's messianic posturing. Mockingly titled "The One," the ad mixed clips of Obama speeches with a video of Charlton Heston as Moses parting the waters. "And the world shall receive [Obama's] blessings," the narrator intoned.[11]

But the 2008 campaign made it clear that *both* parties viewed the presidency in quasi-religious terms. For Republicans as much as Democrats, the office was a fount of miracles and a wellspring of national redemption. In his keynote address at the Republican National Convention in St. Paul, Minnesota, former New York City mayor Rudy Giuliani declared that we could "trust [John McCain] to deal with anything that nature throws our way, anything that terrorists do to us. . . . We will be safe in his hands, and our children will be safe in his hands."[12] (He's got the whole world in his hands.)

McCain began his acceptance speech with a note of humility—a sharp contrast to the biographical video that introduced the speech. The video described McCain's near-death experience in 1967, when a missile accidentally went off on the deck of the USS *Forrestal* and caused a catastrophic fire. "One hundred and thirty-four men lost their lives," the narrator tells us, but "John McCain's life was somehow spared. Perhaps *he had more to do*."[13] Apparently, McCain too had been chosen by God.

The Last Days of George W. Bush

But God, it seemed, was determined to be difficult. The weeks after the Republican National Convention saw an intensification of the ongoing financial meltdown with the collapse of Lehman Brothers, the federal takeover of Fannie Mae and Freddie Mac, and the bailout of mega-insurer American International Group. McCain's poll numbers, which had enjoyed a brief, post-convention bounce, fell rapidly. After his gimmicky late-September decision to suspend his campaign and push for a bank bailout, McCain's campaign never recovered.

George W. Bush's lame-duck period repeated the pattern that had prevailed throughout his two terms: the announcement of an unprecedented crisis, demands for new presidential powers to meet that crisis, and—after some perfunctory grumbling—Congress's capitulation to those demands.

In his seminal book *Presidential Power and the Modern Presidents*, Richard Neustadt argued that the presidency is an inherently weak office, and to grow its powers, the president needs to build up political capital and spend it wisely. But oddly enough, although our massively unpopular president's political capital had evaporated early in his second term, George W. Bush continued to secure broad new grants of authority from Congress. Nobody liked the president, nobody trusted him—but everybody looked to him to solve all of America's problems.

Treasury Secretary Henry Paulson's original three-page proposal for a bank bailout demanded unchecked power over some $700 billion in taxpayer assets, "Decisions by the Secretary pursuant to the authority of this Act are non-reviewable and committed to agency discretion, and may not be reviewed by any court of law or any administrative agency."[14] That provision didn't make it into the final bill, the Emergency Economic Stabilization Act of 2008, which passed on October 3, allowing the executive branch to set up the Troubled Assets Relief Program (TARP) to purchase toxic mortgage-backed securities. Nonetheless, by the end of 2008, Paulson looked a lot like the modern equivalent of a Roman dictator for economic affairs, using a broad delegation of authority from Congress to decide which financial institutions would live and which would die.

In December 2008, American automakers General Motors and Chrysler tottered on the brink of bankruptcy, while Congress debated legislation to provide some $15 billion to keep two of the "Big Three" alive. On December 11, the auto bailout bill failed to pass a key procedural vote in the Senate. But a week later, Bush announced that, despite the bill's failure, he had decided to lend the car companies $17.4 billion. White House spokesman Tony Fratto explained:

Congress lost its opportunity to be a partner because they couldn't get their job done. . . . This is not the way we wanted to deal with this issue. We wanted to deal with it in partnership. What

Congress said is . . . "We can't get it done, so it's up to the White House to get it done."[15]

As the Bush administration saw it, then, by not giving the president the power to bail out the automakers, Congress "lost its opportunity to be a partner," and the president had every right to order the bailout anyway.

Some commentators cited that decision as yet another example of Bush administration lawlessness.[16] The president claimed that he had the power to act under TARP, the operative clause of which gave the secretary of the treasury the power to buy "troubled assets" from "financial institutions." The Bush administration had interpreted that authority broadly, abandoning the original plan almost immediately and using TARP to buy shares in banks—some of which, such as Wells Fargo, weren't "troubled." But using the legislation to bail out car companies seemed a bridge too far. How could a statute empowering the executive branch to buy mortgage-backed securities from banks be used to lend money to automakers, which surely couldn't qualify as "financial institutions"? Having repeatedly insisted that he could not be bound by validly enacted statutes in matters related to national security, it seemed that President Bush had decided he couldn't be bound by clear statutory language when it came to addressing the nation's economic woes.

The truth was even more disturbing. A closer look at the TARP statute reveals that Congress wrote legislative language so irresponsibly broad that the administration actually had a colorable argument that it could reshape the bailout as it saw fit.[17]

Various members of Congress angrily protested that the president had gone from buying toxic assets to recapitalizing banks to bailing out carmakers—shifting priorities almost daily, regardless of what Congress believed it had authorized. But after ceding vast authority to the president, legislators' outrage was more than a day late and $700 billion short. Once again, on a core issue of governance, Congress had abdicated its legislative responsibilities, leaving the hard choices to the president. The buck stops *there*.

Two weeks after Bush bailed out GM and Chrysler, *Newsweek's* cover story focused on presidential power. The lead article, by Stuart Taylor Jr.

and Evan Thomas, rang the changes on an all-too-familiar theme: the dangers of an enervated executive branch. "By trying to strengthen the presidency," Taylor and Thomas argued, Bush and Cheney "weakened it." They quoted former Office of Legal Counsel head Jack Goldsmith, who maintained that we should be "less worried about an out-of-control presidency than an enfeebled one."[18]

At a time when the Treasury secretary was busily reshaping the commanding heights of finance with precious little input from Congress, it was hard to understand how anyone could think that the executive branch had lost power during the previous eight years. But Taylor and Thomas were on to something when they argued that Obama might be pressured into maintaining certain aspects of the Bush approach to the war on terror.

The conventional narrative about the Bush power grab blames Dick Cheney, David Addington, John Yoo, and the other administration figures whose ideological commitment to unchecked executive power long predated September 11. The conventional narrative isn't wrong; it's just incomplete. It ignores the role of public demands for presidential action, which can force presidents to seek or accept new powers they'd never previously craved.

In his swan-song press conference on January 12, 2008, a worn-out George W. Bush grew momentarily animated when asked about the damage to America's "moral standing" that resulted from Guantanamo Bay and "enhanced interrogation" techniques. Bush shot back:

> All these debates will matter naught if there's another attack on the homeland. The question won't be, you know, "Were you critical of this plan or not?" The question's going to be, "Why didn't you do something?"
>
> Do you remember what it was like right after September the 11th around here? . . . people were saying, "How come they didn't see it? How come they didn't connect the dots?"
>
> Do you remember what the environment was like in Washington—I do—when people were hauled in front of Congress and members of Congress were asking questions about, "How come you didn't know this, that, or the other?"[19]

"Why didn't you do something?" Much of the Bush administration's relentless drive to expand its powers can be explained as an attempt to avoid ever having to answer that question again.

That question, "Why didn't you do something?" also explains much of the Bush team's push for enhanced presidential powers in the aftermath of the Katrina debacle and in the midst of the 2008 financial crisis. Key administration figures had long argued that the president needed more authority in the foreign affairs arena, but none of them had spent the 1990s writing position papers about the need for unchecked executive power to fight hurricanes or bail out banks. No matter: They found themselves forced to seek that authority anyway. They won't be the last of the president's men to face that dilemma.

Obama on Presidential Power: A Bundle of Contradictions

On the campaign trail, Barack Obama signaled that, if elected, he'd take a very different approach to executive power. He'd forcefully criticized Bush's claim to be sole constitutional "decider" on all matters involving national security. And in Obama's answers to reporter Charlie Savage's December 2007 executive power questionnaire, he made it clear that he *didn't* think Article II of the Constitution gave the president unchecked power. "The President," Senator Obama wrote, "does not have power under the Constitution to unilaterally authorize a military attack in a situation that does not involve stopping an actual or imminent threat to the nation." Neither, in Obama's view, did he have the power to ignore statutes governing surveillance and treatment of enemy combatants.[20]

As he came closer to winning the office, however, he reversed himself on national security wiretapping. When Senator Obama acquiesced to the FISA Amendments Act in summer 2008, he broke an explicit campaign promise to filibuster any legislation that would grant immunity to FISA-flouting telecom companies. And by voting for the bill, Obama helped legalize large swaths of a dragnet surveillance program he'd long claimed to oppose.

Perhaps some were comforted by Obama's "firm pledge" that "as president, I will carefully monitor the program."[21] But our constitutional structure envisions stronger checks than the supposed benevolence of our leaders. Civil libertarians had good reason to fear that, once elected, Obama would, like other presidents, "grow in office."

And yet, in the early days of his administration, Obama seemed determined to confound the cynics. In his first full day as president, Obama halted all military commission trials.[22] At a swearing-in ceremony for senior executive branch officials, he told the attendees, "For a long time now, there's been too much secrecy in this city." He issued a directive to "the Heads of Executive Departments and Agencies" on interpreting the Freedom of Information Act, "All agencies should adopt a presumption in favor of disclosure, in order to renew their commitment to the principles embodied in FOIA, and to usher in a new era of open Government. The presumption of disclosure should be applied to all decisions involving FOIA."[23]

Call it the "soft bigotry of low expectations," if you will, but it was genuinely heartening when, the next day, the new president ordered the executive branch to *obey the law*. Obama issued an executive order making it clear that the executive branch had to comply with federal statutes governing torture.[24]

Equally important were Obama's appointments to the Office of Legal Counsel, the institution that provides legal advice to the president as to the limits of his Article II powers. The people Obama picked to set legal policy for the executive branch made for a stark contrast with the Bush administration. John Ashcroft, who, as attorney general, turned out to be what passed for a civil libertarian in the Bush White House, had a nickname for Bush OLC official John Yoo: "Dr. Yes."[25] Obama's appointments to OLC suggested that he valued attorneys who were willing to say "no" to the president. Dawn Johnsen, Obama's pick for OLC head, had a long record of condemning Bush administration abuses and advocating a restrained approach to executive power. Noting the Johnsen appointment, a *Wall Street Journal* editorialist lamented, "Mr. Obama has nominated as his main executive branch lawyer someone who believes in diminishing the powers of the executive branch." Johnsen, the *Journal* complained, "seems to think her job isn't to defend the Presidency."[26] The horror, the horror! What's next? Judges who refuse to legislate from the bench? Members of Congress who respect enumerated powers? *Where will it all end?*[27]

Civil libertarian euphoria faded rather quickly, however. A few weeks after the initial flurry of executive orders, in a case alleging that the Bush administration had broken the law by facilitating the torture of terrorist suspects, the Obama legal team took the same position the Bush administration had. They argued that the State Secrets Privilege didn't merely prevent the disclosure of sensitive pieces of evidence. It allowed the federal government to suppress the entire lawsuit and to send the litigants home. Shortly thereafter, Obama's lawyers took the same position in a case that challenged Bush's warrantless wiretapping program, making the administration complicit in covering up illegal activity by its predecessor.[28] In early March 2009, the president issued his first signing statement, objecting to several provisions in a $410 billion omnibus spending bill. Reserving the right to ignore or evade one such provision—which would restrict his ability to place U.S. troops under foreign command—Obama invoked his authority under the Commander-in-Chief clause.

As of this writing, the evidence is mixed, and it's far too early to tell whether Obama intends to meaningfully relimit executive power in the war on terror. If he does, he deserves enormous credit. Presidential self-restraint is a rare thing, and we ought to applaud it if and when it happens. The perennial presidential ranking polls show that far too many scholars overvalue strong presidents—where "strong" is defined as aggressively expanding the powers of the office. What the presidential rankers too often miss is that it takes a strong president to *resist* maximizing his power.

Laudable as it is, though, presidential self-restraint is far from a robust or lasting solution to the imperial presidency. Executive orders can be overturned, and personnel can be changed—by future presidents, or by this president, should political conditions change.

The threat of terrorism is no longer as vivid in the public mind as it was a few years ago, but all that could change quite rapidly. If a bomb goes off in a subway or a terrorist carries out a shooting spree at a shopping mall, it will be very difficult for any president—particularly one with political opponents eager to paint him as "soft on terror"—to resist pushing his authority beyond constitutional limits.

Lasting restraint needs to come from external sources: the courts, the Congress, and the general public. The Supreme Court has lately shown greater willingness to check presidential power in foreign affairs. However, there's little evidence that the public has moderated its demands for bold presidential action to solve all manner of problems. And Congress remains as pliable as ever.

Jack Goldsmith and others have argued that George W. Bush's greatest mistake was acting unilaterally instead of going to Congress for further grants of power. It's unlikely that Barack Obama will make the same mistake. Should Obama feel the need to expand his powers, instead of secretly ordering his administration to violate the laws, he'll probably go to Congress. And if the last eight years tell us anything, Obama will get most of what he wants. Having secured congressional authorization, he'll be on firmer legal ground and less likely to get rebuked by the courts. But the result will be the same: enormous concentration of power in one man's hands for precious little gain in terms of national security.

Moreover, Obama has always been a bundle of contradictions when it comes to the role of the presidency and the use of executive power. Although his team has backed away from the war metaphor when it comes to international affairs and homeland security, the Obama administration seems all too willing to employ the language of war and crisis to increase federal power over economic affairs. "We are at war," Joe Biden told congressional leaders at an economic summit on January 5, 2009.[29] "The time for talk is over," Obama insisted in February as he demanded passage of his $800 billion "stimulus package," 2009's equivalent of the Patriot Act: a preexisting wish list of Democratic priorities forced through amid cries of "emergency." Any delay could "turn a crisis into a catastrophe," the president warned.[30] And as Chief of Staff Rahm Emanuel helpfully explained, "You never want a serious crisis to go to waste."[31]

Obama has suggested that he *doesn't* think the president has the power to do whatever he wants in the name of national security. Yet he seems quite comfortable with vast grants of power that allow him to remake the economy by executive fiat. On the day that Bush decided to bail out GM and Chrysler, Obama issued a press release supporting Bush's decision: "Today's actions are a necessary step to help avoid a collapse in our auto industry that would have devastating consequences for our economy and our workers."[32] And Obama took a page from

Bush's playbook when he announced his housing bailout plan in mid-February. The bulk of the plan, which has enormous repercussions for the U.S. economy, will be enacted without any action by Congress.[33]

How these contradictions will play out in the years to come remains to be seen. But in the end, it is highly unlikely that Barack Obama will leave the presidency weaker than he found it.

Great Expectations

It was never terribly plausible to suppose that a man running as the re-incarnation of John F. Kennedy would reduce the presidency's power and prominence in American life. Obama has done more than any candidate in living memory to raise expectations for the office—expectations that were absurdly high to begin with.

Obama's inaugural address began somberly, emphasizing that "we are in the midst of crisis." But even in the midst of crisis, our possibilities were virtually limitless. United behind our president, we could "wield technology's wonders" to improve health care, "harness the sun and the winds and the soil to fuel our cars and run our factories," and "transform our schools and colleges and universities to meet the demands of a new age. All this we can do. All this we will do."

If the early polls were any indication, Obama had little to fear from the cynics, who seemed pretty thin on the ground. He entered office with a 79 percent favorability rating, the highest in more than 30 years.[34] Eight in 10 Americans expected Obama to improve conditions for minorities and the poor. Seven in 10 believed he'd improve education and the environment, and 60 percent expected him to usher in a robust economy and keep Americans safe from terrorism.[35] In fact, the only modern president to rival Obama's popularity on the eve of his inauguration was Jimmy Carter—something that should have given our new president pause.

As the Carter experience suggests, in presidential politics, great expectations often lead to crashing disappointments. The Obama era began amid an infectious atmosphere of hope. But there's no reason to believe that Obama will escape what scholar Barbara Hinckley dubbed "the decay curve"—the steady decline in popularity that all modern presidents have experienced as the public recognizes that they're unable to deliver the miracles they've promised.[36] Obama, after all, has inherited a budgetary and financial disaster; he faces significant constraints, and he is likely to see some of his more ambitious plans run aground on fiscal reality.

Even when it comes to racial healing, where high hopes seem justified, Americans might do better to moderate their expectations. Seven in 10 Americans expect race relations to improve under Obama, according to a post-election Gallup poll.[37] It's not hard to understand why. The election of an African-American president shows genuine progress toward resolving the "American dilemma," and whatever one's politics, it's an event that's cause for celebration.

But even here, the modern presidency is likely to disappoint. Obama's tenure may lead to politics that are more racially charged and, thus, even more rancorous than we're accustomed to. That's so for reasons that have more to do with the nature of the modern presidency than with Obama himself. Americans expect the president to right the wrongs that plague us—and we blame him when he fails. Because we invest impossible expectations in the presidency, the presidency has become an impossible job. And once the honeymoon period inevitably fades, the modern president becomes a lightning rod for discontent, often catching blame for phenomena beyond the control of any one person, however powerful. In the Obama presidency, America's unhealthy obsession with race may collide with our equally unhealthy obsession with the modern presidency—and the results might make us long for the relative placidity of the Bush years.

Over and over again, we begin by looking to the president as the solution to all our problems, and we end up believing he's the *source* of all our problems. If history is any guide, when Obama fails to fully heal our financial troubles, stop the oceans' rise, and rescue us from spiritual malaise, his hope-addled rhetoric will seem all the more grating, and the public will increasingly come to see him as the source of all American woes. As his popularity dwindles, many of Obama's supporters will view attacks on him through the prism of race, forgetting or ignoring the fact that nearly every president eventually morphs from superhero to scapegoat in the public mind. Race will take on undue relevance because the presidency is far more powerful and far more important than it ought to be.

Perhaps, then, we ought to rethink what we ask of the presidency. Our Constitution's Framers thought the president had an important job, but they never looked to him to heal all the nation's wounds and save the national soul. Far from serving as a national guardian angel, the president was to be a limited constitutional officer whose main job was to execute the laws. Until we return to the Framers' modest, businesslike view of the presidency, we cannot expect any president to be "a uniter, not a divider" in American life.

Our outsized demands have left us with a presidency that is a constitutional monstrosity: at once menacing and ineffectual. After our century-long drift away from the Framers' vision, can we possibly return to a humbler set of expectations for the office and a less powerful chief executive? Perhaps we can. Unfortunately, it's part of the American character that we periodically get drunk on the romance of the presidency. But, happily, it's also part of the American character that we eventually sober up and feel disgusted with ourselves. And then we take the long walk of shame back to the well-lit dorm room of political sanity.

Barack Obama is bound to disappoint. How could he not? What is the "Audacity of Hope," after all, but the eternal—and eternally false—notion that the presidency is the vehicle of American redemption?

So vast are the promises that Obama has made—so fervent the hopes he has inspired—that his failure may serve to heighten the contradictions inherent in modern Americans' view of the presidency. And when disappointment comes, it could be the beginning of political maturity for us to recognize that the fault lies not in our leaders, but in ourselves.

First Edition

It probably wasn't the brightest idea for me, as a first-time author, to tackle a subject so immense that no one could ever read everything intelligent that's been written about it. "A man's got to know his limitations," as Dirty Harry Callahan once put it. I don't know if I'd try this sort of thing again. It wrecked my social life and made my back hurt. On the other hand, writing this book was also far more rewarding than I could have imagined, so who knows?

My friend and colleague John Samples, a first-time author himself in 2006, told me I could do it and seemed to think it was important that I try. So I'll steal a couple of appropriate lines from the acknowledgments to John's book: "Libertarians are often said to be overly individualistic and against social cooperation. Nothing could be less true."

That's been my experience as well. I had the help of many friends and colleagues who were unfailingly generous with their time and their wisdom. Much of the credit—and none of the blame—for what you've read or skimmed goes to them.

The following people read and commented on some or all of the manuscript: Jude Blanchette, David Boaz, George Carey (TME), Ted Galen Carpenter, Vincent Getz, John Healy, Jeffrey Rogers Hummel, Tom Jenney, Bob Levy, Justin Logan, Tim Lynch, Mark Moller, Jim Powell, Chris Preble, John Samples, and Peter Van Doren. They provided invaluable help, ranging from slimming down flabby prose and unearthing grammatical errors and typos, to identifying weak arguments and suggesting better ones. Others, including Brooke Oberwetter, Vin Getz, and, of course, my mom and dad, provided moral support on the days when writing a book felt like digging my way out of prison with a spoon.

A succession of Cato's dedicated interns assisted on the research, among them Lauren Drew, Seth Feldman, Ashley Frohwein, Sonya Jones, Andrew Perraut, Kevin Ross, Anastasia Uglova, and Jason Vines. On production, I'd like to thank Pat Bullock, Claudia Ringel, and the unflappable David Lampo, who put up with more than his fair share of blown deadlines and first-time author anxieties. Art director Jon Meyers deserves special thanks for creating a terrific cover that looks like it leapt full-blown from my fevered brain (that's a compliment, Jon). Our book marketing team, Bob Garber, Camille Cooke, Scott Manning, and Diane Zoerb, has already done a tremendous job working to get the book in front of the right reviewers and me in front of the right audiences. So many people helped out along the way that I'm sure I've lost track of a few, so I apologize to anyone I've forgotten.

This book would not have been possible were it not for Ed Crane, whom the *Washington Post* once described as the only D.C. think tank founder who says he "doesn't like politicians and people who like politics." Behind that uncooperative comment lies a political theory that represents the best of the American tradition, a theory that accords politics only a limited role in our lives, and that only grudgingly. There's no other institution in Washington where I'd feel quite so at home, and no other think tank that would have given me the time and the space to pursue this project. Thus I owe Ed, David Boaz, and the Cato Institute's supporters an enormous debt of gratitude.

Finally, I'd like to dedicate this book to two people: my mother, who loves me far more than I deserve, and whose support has been the foundation for anything worthwhile I've ever achieved. And to my father, who, in his curmudgeonly way, taught me long before I'd ever read Jefferson that men are not born with saddles on their backs, nor others born booted and spurred to ride them.

2024 Edition

The Cult of the Presidency has had a longer shelf life than most public policy books, in part because it deals with one of the most intractable and menacing problems in American politics. We're forced to take interest in the presidency because the presidency is interested in us. As an author, I'm happy that the book has stayed relevant; as an American, I hold out hope for reforms that make the office *less* interesting—and less dangerous—by re-limiting its powers.

The Cult of the Presidency has been a Cato product from start to finish, so thanks first and foremost go to the Cato Institute and its CEO and president, Peter Goettler, who's ensured that the Institute remains the rare place in Washington, D.C., where you can call them like you see them, without fear or favor.

Updating a book is a lot easier than writing one, but this revised edition still took extra work from key members of Cato's dedicated staff. Special thanks go to Eleanor O'Connor, managing director of Cato books, who came up with the idea for a revised edition of *Cult* and, with the right mix of patience and perseverance, kept at me to make sure it happened.

Tom Ryan provided crucial research support and did yeoman's work hunting down cites, while Anna Keyes and Alex Kolonchin helped updated the index and proof the text. Justin Logan, Ryan Bourne, John Samples, Jonathan Fortier, and Ivan Osorio gave me valuable comments and edits on the new preface. As before, much of the credit and none of the blame for how it turned out goes to them.

I'm especially grateful to my wife, Caitlyn, who cheerfully took on the extra burden when this project bled into odd hours and weekends. Finally, I'd like to dedicate this edition to our three daughters, Maddie, Liddy, and Lucie, in the hopes that they'll come of age in a world where the president matters less.

Preface

1. Andy Kessler, "The Presidency, I'm against It," *Wall Street Journal*, April 7, 2024.

2. *Federalist* 68, in George Carey and James McClellan, eds., *The Federalist* (Indianapolis: Liberty Fund, 2001), p. 354.

3. Gene Healy, *The Cult of the Presidency: America's Dangerous Devotion to Executive Power* (Washington: Cato Institute, 2008), p. 235, 233–65.

4. The phrase is P. J. O'Rourke's; see Nick Gass, "P.J. O'Rourke Hate-Endorses Hillary Clinton on NPR Quiz Show," *Politico*, May 9, 2016.

5. Andrew Romano, "Poll: 'Dread' Tops List of Americans' Feelings about 2024 Election," *Yahoo News*, September 21, 2023.

6. "Biden's Age Is a Significant Concern for Voters," AP-NORC Center for Public Affairs Research, August 28, 2023.

7. Cormac McCarthy, *Suttree* (New York: Vintage Books, 1979), p. 372.

8. Theodore J. Lowi, *The Personal President: Power Invested, Promise Unfulfilled* (Ithaca, NY: Cornell University Press, 1985), p. 11.

9. Eli J. Finkel et al., "Political Sectarianism in America," *Science* 370, no. 6516 (October 2020): 533.

10. *Federalist* 69, in George Carey and James McClellan, eds., *The Federalist* (Indianapolis: Liberty Fund, 2001), p. 361.

11. Gene Healy, *The Cult of the Presidency: America's Dangerous Devotion to Executive Power* (Washington: Cato Institute, 2008), p. 3.

12. Matt McDonald, "'The Seal Is Now Broken': Trump's Post-Arraignment Speech at Bedminster," *The Spectator*, June 13, 2023.

13. "Donald Trump Hosts First 2024 Presidential Campaign Rally in Waco, Texas Transcript," Rev, March 27, 2024.

14. "Donald Trump Hosts First 2024 Presidential Campaign Rally in Waco, Texas Transcript," Rev, March 27, 2024 (emphasis added).

15. "Remarks by President Biden on the Continued Battle for the Soul of the Nation," speech, White House, September 1, 2022.

16. "Trump: View Each Day as TV Episode," *Axios*, December 10, 2017.

17. See David Brooks, "Joe Biden and the Struggle for America's Soul," *New York Times*, April 27, 2023.

18. Jack Shafer, "How Baby Donald Slew the Imperial Presidency," *Politico*, March 10, 2017.

19. Jeffrey M. Jones, "Trust in Federal Government Branches Continues to Falter," *Gallup*, October 11, 2022.

20. Micah Zenko, "Obama's Final Drone Strike Data," *Politics, Power, and Preventive Action* (blog), Center for Preventive Action, Council on Foreign Relations, January 20, 2017.

21. Mark Landler, "For Obama, an Unexpected Legacy of Two Full Terms at War," *New York Times*, May 14, 2016.

22. Louis Fisher, "The Law: Military Operations in Libya: No War? No Hostilities?," *Presidential Studies Quarterly* 42, no. 1 (March 2012).

23. Curtis A. Bradley and Jack Goldsmith, "Obama's AUMF Legacy," *American Journal of International Law* 110 (2016).

24. Greg Miller, "Legal Memo Backing Drone Strike That Killed American Anwar Al-Awlaki Is Released," *Washington Post*, June 23, 2014. See also Ryan Patrick Alford, "The Rule of Law at the Crossroads: Consequences of Targeted Killing of Citizens," *Utah Law Review* 2011, no. 4 (2011): 1203. Two weeks later, when another strike eliminated al-Awlaki's teenage son, press secretary Robert Gibbs cracked that he should've had a "more responsible father." Conor Friedersdorf, "How Team Obama Justifies the Killing of a 16-Year-Old American," *The Atlantic*, October 24, 2012.

25. See Charlie Savage, *Power Wars: Inside Obama's Post-9/11 Presidency* (New York: Little, Brown and Company, 2015), 161–64.

26. Gene Healy, *The Cult of the Presidency: America's Dangerous Devotion to Executive Power* (Washington: Cato Institute, 2008), p. 218.

27. Todd Zywicki, "The Auto Bailout and the Rule of Law," *National Affairs* (Spring 2011).

28. Gene Healy, *False Idol: Barack Obama and the Continuing Cult of the Presidency* (Washington: Cato Institute, 2012), pp. 36–65.

29. Andrew Romano, "President Obama's Executive Power Grab," *Newsweek*, October 22, 2012.

30. Gene Healy, "Trump the Decider," *Cato at Liberty* (blog), Cato Institute, January 8, 2020.

31. Jacob Pramuk, "Congress Fails Again to Stop Trump from Using Military Money for His Border Wall," CNBC, October 17, 2019.

32. Donald J. Trump (@realDonaldTrump), "I am giving consideration to a QUARANTINE of developing 'hot spots,'" X post, March 28, 2020, 13:31 p.m.; Gene Healy, "Posse Comitatus and Interstate Travel Bans," *Cato at Liberty* (blog), Cato Institute, April 1, 2020.

33. Jennifer Jacobs, Justin Sink, and Saleha Mohsin, "Trump Declares He Has 'Total' Authority to Reopen after Virus," *Bloomberg*, April 13, 2020; and Donald Trump (@realDonaldTrump), "With Universal Mail-In Voting (not Absentee Voting, which is good), 2020 will be the most INACCURATE & FRAUDULENT Election in history. It will be a great embarrassment to the USA. Delay the Election until people can properly, securely and safely vote???," X post, July 30, 2020, 8:46 a.m.

34. "Executive Order on Protecting the Federal Workforce and Requiring Mask-Wearing," Presidential Actions, White House, January 20, 2021; Jeff Stein et al., "Biden Administration Moves to Block Evictions in Most of US Following Liberal Backlash," *Washington Post*, August 3, 2021; and Jon O. Shimabukuro,

"Supreme Court Stays OSHA Vaccination and Testing Standard," Congressional Research Service, January 21, 2022.

35. David Zweig, "How Twitter Rigged the COVID Debate," *Free Press*, December 26, 2022.

36. *Missouri v. Biden*, 5th Cir. R. 23-30445 (2023), p. 62.

37. Adam Liptak, "What Is the HEROES Act?," *New York Times*, June 30, 2023.

38. Joe Biden (@JoeBiden), "The Supreme Court tried to block me from relieving student debt," X post, May 29, 2024, 8:04 p.m.

39. Shanto Iyengar and Masha Krupenkin, "The Strengthening of Partisan Affect," *Advances in Political Psychology* 39, no. 1 (February 2018): 201–218.

40. "Partisanship and Political Animosity in 2016," Pew Research Center, June 22, 2016.

41. Eli J. Finkel et al., "Political Sectarianism in America," *Science* 370, no. 6516 (October 2020): 533.

42. "As Partisan Hostility Grows, Signs of Frustration with the Two-Party System," Pew Research Center, August 9, 2022.

43. Nathan P. Kalmoe and Lilliana Mason, "Lethal Mass Partisanship: Prevalence, Correlates & Electoral Contingencies" (paper prepared for the National Capital Area Political Science Association American Politics Meeting, Washington, DC, January 2019), pp. 18, 22.

44. Eli J. Finkel et al., "Political Sectarianism in America," *Science* 370, no. 6516 (October 2020): 533.

45. John O. McGinnis and Michael B. Rappaport, "Presidential Polarization," *Ohio State Law Journal* 83, no. 1 (2022): 7.

46. John O. McGinnis and Michael B. Rappaport, "Presidential Polarization," *Ohio State Law Journal* 83, no.1 (2022): 5.

47. "President Calls for Constitutional Amendment Protecting Marriage," White House, February 24, 2004.

48. Luisa Blanchfield, "Abortion and Family Planning-Related Provisions in US Foreign Assistance Law and Policy," Congressional Research Service, updated July 15, 2022, pp. 10–11.

49. "Executive Order on Advancing Racial Equity and Support for Underserved Communities Through the Federal Government," White House, January 20, 2021.

50. John B. Judis and Ruy Teixeira, "New York's Race-Based Preferential Covid Treatments," *Wall Street Journal*, January 7, 2022.

51. "Executive Order on Guaranteeing an Educational Environment Free from Discrimination on the Basis of Sex, Including Sexual Orientation or Gender Identity," White House, March 8, 2021.

52. Zach Montague and Erica L. Green, "Biden Administration Released Revised Title IX Rules," *New York Times*, April 19, 2024.

53. Rachel N. Morrison, "HHS's Proposed Nondiscrimination Regulations Impose Transgender Mandate in Health Care," *FedSoc Blog* (blog), Federalist Society, September 8, 2022.

54. "Remarks by President Biden and First Lady Jill Biden at Pride Celebration," speech, White House, June 10, 2023.

55. Gene Healy, "Biden's New Federal Czar for the Middle-School Library," *Cato at Liberty* (blog), Cato Institute, August 8, 2023.

56. "President Trump's Plan to Protect Children from Left-Wing Gender Insanity," Agenda47, Donald J. Trump for President 2024, February 1, 2023.

57. Andrew Restuccia and Aaron Zitner, "Trump's Second-Term Plans: Anti-'Woke' University, 'Freedom Cities,'" *Wall Street Journal,* December 2, 2023.

58. "Texas Woman Indicted for Transporting Minor for Female Genital Mutilation," press release, Department of Justice, January 13, 2021.

59. *Federalist 70,* in George Carey and James McClellan, eds., *The Federalist* (Indianapolis: Liberty Fund, 2001), p. 362.

60. Coral Davenport, "How Abrupt U-turns Are Defining US Environmental Regulations," *New York Times,* April 26, 2024.

61. Lisa Friedman, "Five Major Climate Policies Trump Would Probably Reverse if Elected," *New York Times,* April 26, 2024.

62. Lisa Friedman, "Five Major Climate Policies Trump Would Probably Reverse if Elected," *New York Times,* April 26, 2024.

63. Thomas B. Edsall, "'Gut-Level Hatred' Is Consuming Our Political Life," *New York Times,* July 19, 2023.

64. John O. McGinnis and Michael B. Rappaport, "Presidential Polarization," *Ohio State Law Journal Vol.* 83, no. 1 (2022): 8.

65. Publius Decius Mus, "The Flight 93 Election," *Claremont Review of Books,* September 5, 2016.

66. "Few Adults Like the Idea of Unilateral Action by Presidents," AP-NORC Center, University of Chicago, April 5, 2024.

67. Nicholas Riccardi and Linley Sanders, "Americans Think a President's Powers Should Be Checked, AP-NORC Finds—Unless Their Side Wins," Associated Press, April 5, 2024.

68. Gene Healy, *The Cult of the Presidency: America's Dangerous Devotion to Executive Power* (Washington: Cato Institute, 2008), p. 3.

Introduction

1. "Meet the Press transcript for Jan. 28, 2007," available at http://www.msnbc .msn.com/id/16785556/ (emphasis added).

2. John McCain, "Theodore Roosevelt," in *Presidential Leadership: Rating the Best and the Worst in the White House,* ed. James Taranto and Leonard Leo (New York: Free Press, 2004, 2005) pp. 126, 128.

3. Ed Crane, "Is Hillary Clinton a Neocon?" *Financial Times,* July 11, 2007.

4. "President Bush Visits Greensburg, Kansas to Survey Tornado Damage, Offer Condolences," May 9, 2007.

5. Bill Broadway, "War Cry from the Pulpit," *Washington Post,* September 22, 2001 (emphasis added).

6. Clinton quoted in Anna Quindlen, "Public and Private: America's Sleeping Sickness," *New York Times,* October 17, 1993; Bush: President's State of the Union Address, January 29, 2002.

7. 1959 national poll cited in Roberta S. Sigel, "Image of the American Presidency—Part II of an Exploration into Popular Views of Presidential Power," *Midwest Journal of Political Science* 10 (February 1966): 128.

8. "Americans Distrust Government, but Want It to Do More," *NPR Online,* July 28, 2000; "Attitudes toward Government," *NPR-Kaiser-Kennedy School Poll.*

9. Richard J. Ellis and Aaron B. Wildavsky, *Dilemmas of Presidential Leadership: From Washington through Lincoln* (New Brunswick, NJ: Transaction Publishers, 1989), p. 14.

10. Arthur M. Schlesinger Jr., "Rating the Presidents: Washington to Clinton," *Political Science Quarterly* 112 (Summer 1997): 189.

11. James Lindgren, "The Federalist Society and the *Wall Street Journal* Present: Rating the Presidents of the United States, 1789–2000: A Survey of Scholars in History, Political Science, and Law," November 16, 2000; "Our study, conducted in October 2000, found remarkably similar results to the last Schlesinger study. The correlation between the ranks in the two studies is a staggeringly high .94," p. 5.

12. Clinton Rossiter, *The American Presidency* (Baltimore: Johns Hopkins University Press, 1956, 1987), pp. 2–3.

13. All quotes from Rossiter, *The American Presidency*, chapter 1, "The Powers of the Presidency."

14. Theodore Roosevelt, "A Confession of Faith," delivered August 6, 1912, to Progressive Party Convention in Chicago, Illinois.

15. Quoted in James Chace, *1912: Wilson, Roosevelt, Taft and Debs—The Election That Changed the Country* (New York: Simon & Schuster, 2004), p. 221.

16. President Bill Clinton, first inaugural address, January 20, 1993.

17. See, for example, Elvin T. Lim, "Five Trends in Presidential Rhetoric: An Analysis of Rhetoric from George Washington to Bill Clinton," *Presidential Studies Quarterly* 32 (June 2002): 328–66.

18. Steroids, State of the Union address, January 20, 2004; gangs, State of the Union address, February 2, 2005; "petroleum-based economy" and "freedom's advance," State of the Union address, January 31, 2006.

19. Theodore J. Lowi, *The Personal President: Power Invested, Promise Unfulfilled* (Ithaca, NY: Cornell University Press, 1985), p. 20.

20. See Daniel W. Drezner, "Mind the Gap," *The National Interest*, no. 87 (January–February 2007).

21. *Federalist* no. 8, in George W. Carey and James McClellan, eds., *The Federalist* (Indianapolis, IN: Liberty Fund, 2001), p. 34.

22. Chris Hedges, *War Is a Force That Gives Us Meaning* (New York: Anchor Books, 2002).

23. J. Richard Piper, "Situational Constitutionalism and Presidential Power: The Rise and Fall of the Liberal Model of Presidential Government," *Presidential Studies Quarterly* 24 (Summer 1994): 577–96.

24. "President Interviewed by Joe Klein, *New Yorker*," October 10, 2000.

Chapter 1

1. James McClellan and M. E. Bradford, eds., *Elliot's Debates, Vol. III: Debates in the Federal Convention of 1787* (Richmond: James River Press, 1989), pp. 45–46.

2. See, for example, Pinckney, June 1; Randolph, June 1; McClellan and Bradford, *Elliot's Debates*, pp. 45–46.

3. Richard M. Pious, *The American Presidency* (New York: Basic Books, 1979), pp. 21–22.

4. *The Journal of William Maclay, United States Senator from Pennsylvania, 1789-1791* (New York: Albert & Charles Boni, 1927), p. 23.

5. Sidney M. Milkis and Michael Nelson, *The American Presidency: Origins and Development, 1776-1998*, 3rd ed. (Washington: CQ Press, 1999), p. 70.

6. David McCullough, *John Adams* (New York: Touchstone, 2001), p. 407.

7. James H. Hutson, "John Adams' Title Campaign," *New England Quarterly* 41 (March 1968): 32-33.

8. *Maclay*, pp. 1, 24, and 36.

9. *Maclay*, p. 12.

10. *Maclay*, p. 21.

11. One of the first reviewers of the unexpurgated Maclay (a bowdlerized version had been released in the 1880s) condemns the senator for his "narrow and illiberal spirit" and tendency toward "splenetic indulgences." W. P. Trent, "Review: *Journal of William Maclay, United States Senator from Pennsylvania, 1789-1791*, by Edgar S. Maclay," *Political Science Quarterly* 6 (June 1891): 366.

12. *Maclay*, p. 3.

13. *Maclay*, p. 29.

14. *Maclay*, p. 27.

15. *Maclay*, p. 34.

16. *Maclay*, p. 27.

17. Stanley Elkins and Eric McKitrick, *The Age of Federalism: The Early American Republic, 1788-1800* (New York: Oxford University Press, 1993), p. 48. Though, as Gordon Wood has noted, at one time Washington had favored "His High Mightiness, the President of the United States and Protector of Their Liberties," Gordon S. Wood, "The Man Who Would Not Be King," *New Republic*, December 20, 2004, pp. 33-37.

18. Glenn A. Phelps, *George Washington and American Constitutionalism* (Lawrence: University Press of Kansas, 1994), p. 141.

19. *Federalist* no. 69, in *The Federalist*, ed. George W. Carey and James McClellan (Indianapolis, IN: Liberty Fund, 2001), p. 361.

20. Jeffrey K. Tulis, "The Two Constitutional Presidencies," in *The Presidency and the Political System*, 5th ed., ed. Michael Nelson (Washington: CQ Press, 1998), p. 93.

21. Peter Augustine Lawler, "*The Federalist*'s Hostility to Leadership and the Crisis of the Contemporary Presidency," *Presidential Studies Quarterly* 17 (Fall 1987): 718.

22. Theodore J. Lowi, *The Personal President: Power Invested, Promise Unfulfilled* (Ithaca, NY: Cornell University Press, 1985), p. 40.

23. Steven G. Calabresi and Kevin H. Rhodes, "The Structural Constitution: Unitary Executive, Plural Judiciary," *Harvard Law Review* 105 (April 1992): 1165-66.

24. See, for example, Charles Thatch's discussion of the so-called removal debate of 1789, which concerned the structure of the executive departments, and whether the president alone could decide to dismiss subordinate officers. Thatch argues that "the power of removal was derived from the general executive power of administrative control. The latter power has not been an extra-constitutional growth. It was the conscious creation of the men who made the Constitution." Charles C. Thatch Jr., *The Creation of the Presidency: 1775-1789, A Study in Constitutional History* (Baltimore: Johns Hopkins University Press, 1923, 1969), pp. 158-59.

25. See, for example, Charlie Savage, "Hail to the Chief: Dick Cheney's Mission to Expand—or 'Restore'—the Powers of the Presidency," *Boston Globe*, November 26, 2006.

26. See, for example, Willmoore Kendall, "The Two Majorities," *Midwest Journal of Political Science* 4 (November 1960): 317–45 and the discussion on pages 124–27 of this book.

27. Jeffrey Rosen, "The Power of One," *New Republic*, July 24, 2006.

28. Paul M. Barrett, "A Young Lawyer Helps Chart Shift in Foreign Policy," *Wall Street Journal*, September 12, 2005.

29. See, for example, John C. Yoo, "The Continuation of Politics by Other Means: The Original Understanding of War Powers," *California Law Review* 84 (March 1996): 167–305.

30. Peter Slevin, "Scholar Stands by Post-9/11 Writings on Torture, Domestic Eavesdropping," *Washington Post*, December 26, 2005.

31. John Yoo, *The Powers of War and Peace: The Constitution and Foreign Affairs After 9/11* (Chicago: University of Chicago Press, 2005), p. x.

32. John Yoo and Robert J. Delahunty, "Book Review: Thinking about Presidents," *Cornell Law Review* 90 (May 2005): 1176.

33. Yoo, *Powers of War and Peace*, pp. 112–13.

34. McClellan and Bradford, *Elliot's Debates*, pp. 46–47.

35. Plutarch, "Poplicola," in *The Lives of the Noble Grecians and Romans*, ed. Arthur Hugh Clough (New York: Random House, 1992), pp. 129–46.

36. *Federalist* no. 69, p. 355.

37. It's worth noting in this context that Jefferson's oft-repeated story about Hamilton telling him that Julius Caesar was "the greatest man that ever lived" may have been a politically motivated distortion. Hamilton condemned Caesar repeatedly in public and private. See Thomas P. Govan, "Alexander Hamilton and Julius Caesar: A Note on the Use of Historical Evidence," *William and Mary Quarterly* 32 (July 1975): 475–80; and Richard Brookhiser, *Alexander Hamilton, American* (New York: Touchstone, 1999), pp. 191–92.

38. McClellan and Bradford, *Elliot's Debates*, p. 136.

39. See Louis Fisher, *Presidential War Power* (Lawrence: University Press of Kansas, 1995), pp. 18, 20–21. In his debates with Madison over Washington's 1793 Neutrality Proclamation, Hamilton argued that, in the absence of guidance from Congress, the executive had the power to reaffirm the existing state of peace, leaving it to *Congress* to change peace into war. That's what passed for a rabidly pro-executive view in the early republic. But Hamilton was quite clear about which branch retains control over the war power: "It is the province and duty of the executive to preserve to the nation the blessings of peace. The legislature alone can interrupt them by placing the nation in a state of war," he writes in the first Pacificus letter. In 1798, at the start of the Quasi-War with France over harassment of American shipping, Hamilton wrote that any naval actions beyond the merely defensive "must fall under the idea of *reprisals* & require the sanction of that Department which is to declare or make war." See also, Richard Loss, "Alexander Hamilton and the Modern Presidency: Continuity or Discontinuity," *Presidential Studies Quarterly* 12 (Winter 1982): 6–25.

40. McClellan and Bradford, *Elliot's Debates*, p. 621.

41. Bernard Bailyn, *The Ideological Origins of the American Revolution* (Cambridge, MA: Belknap Press, 1967, 1992), pp. 59–60.

42. Benjamin F. Wright, "The Federalist on the Nature of Political Man," *Ethics* 59 (January 1949): 4. NB: the precise quote, from a letter written 100 years after the Philadelphia Convention, is "Power tends to corrupt and absolute power corrupts absolutely." J. Rufus Fears, ed., *Essays in Religion, Politics, and Morality: Selected Writings of Lord Acton*, Vol. 3 (Indianapolis, IN: Liberty Classics, 1988), p. 519. See also James P. Scanlan, "The Federalist and Human Nature," *Review of Politics* 21 (October 1959).

43. Bailyn, *Ideological Origins*, p. 379.

44. *Federalist* no. 47, p. 249.

45. Quoted in Michael J. Rosano, "Liberty, Nobility, Philanthropy, and Power in Alexander Hamilton's Conception of Human Nature," *American Journal of Political Science* 47 (January 2003): 68.

46. *Federalist* no. 51, p. 268.

47. *Federalist* no. 48, p. 257.

48. Jess Bravin, "Judge Alito's View of the Presidency: Expansive Powers," *Wall Street Journal*, January 5, 2006.

49. David P. Currie, *The Constitution in Congress: The Federalist Period, 1789–1801* (Chicago: University of Chicago Press, 1997), p. 177: "The difference in phrasing . . . may well have been accidental." On the other hand, Charles Thatch believes that New York's Gouverneur Morris, who favored a powerful executive, made the change "with full realization of its possibilities." That he managed to slip the change past the convention "admitted an interpretation of executive power which would give to the President a field of action much wider than that outlined by the enumerated powers." Thatch, *Creation of the Presidency*, p. 139.

50. Curtis A. Bradley and Martin S. Flaherty, "Executive Power Essentialism and Foreign Affairs," *University of Michigan Law Review* 102, no. 4 (February 2004): 591: "There is not a single reference to the Vesting Clause Thesis in all of the records of the Federal Convention."

51. Jack N. Rakove, "Taking the Prerogative out of the Presidency: An Originalist Perspective," *Presidential Studies Quarterly* 37, no. 1 (March 2007): 98. To be sure, Anti-Federalists suggested the president might come to resemble a king; Rakove's point is that unitarians have not identified any who pointed to the vesting clause as the source of the danger.

52. *Federalist* no. 45, p. 241.

53. *Federalist* no. 84, p. 445. Bradley and Flaherty provide a powerful case against the vesting clause thesis in "Executive Power Essentialism and Foreign Affairs," from which a number of the points are drawn.

54. See generally Gene Healy and Timothy Lynch, "Power Surge: The Constitutional Record of George W. Bush," Cato Institute White Paper, May 1, 2006.

55. See, for example, Lawrence Lessig and Cass Sunstein, "The President and the Administration," *Columbia Law Review* 94, no. 1 (January 1994): 47–48.

56. As Cass Sunstein notes:

> The claim for the unitary executive is not a general claim about the President's power to act on his own or to contradict the will of Congress. You can believe in a strongly unitary executive branch while also believing that the President cannot make war, or torture people, or engage in foreign surveillance without congressional authorization.

Cass Sunstein, "What the 'Unitary Executive' Debate Is and Is Not About," University of Chicago Law School Faculty Blog, August 6, 2007.

Indeed, not all unitarians believe that the president's possession of "The executive Power" means that Congress is powerless to restrain him in wartime. For example, Michael Ramsey, one of John Yoo's most powerful critics, believes that the vesting clause gives the president significant power in foreign affairs, but Ramsey denies that those powers allow the president to start wars or ignore statutes banning torture. Michael D. Ramsey, "Torturing Executive Power," *Georgetown Law Journal* 93, no. 4 (April 2005).

57. Henry P. Monaghan, "The Protective Power of the Presidency," *Columbia Law Review* 93, no. 1 (January 1993): 11.

58. "William Blackstone, Commentaries 1:254," *The Founders' Constitution* (online); Vol. 4, Art. 2, Sec. 2, Cl. 1, Doc. 2. For Yoo on Blackstone, see, for example, *Powers of War and Peace*, pp. 41–42.

59. *Federalist* no. 4, p. 13.

60. James Madison, "Helvidius No. IV," in *The Letters of Pacificus and Helvidius (1845) with the Letters of Americanus* (New York: Scholars' Facsimiles & Reprints, 1976), pp. 89–90.

61. McClellan and Bradford, *Elliot's Debates*, pp. 45–46.

62. Quoted in Norman A. Graebner, "The President as Commander in Chief: A Study in Power," *Journal of Military History* (January 1993): 112, "in remarks recorded by Rufus King of Massachusetts."

63. McClellan and Bradford, *Elliot's Debates*, pp. 451–52.

64. Other important war-making powers include the power "to raise and support armies, but no Appropriation of Money to that Use shall be for a longer Term than two years" and the power "to provide for calling forth the Militia to execute the Laws of the Union, suppress Insurrections and repel invasions."

65. *Federalist* no. 69, p. 357.

66. John Yoo, "A President Can Pull the Trigger," *Los Angeles Times*, December 20, 2005.

67. John Yoo, *Powers of War and Peace*, p. 145.

68. *Federalist* no. 25, p. 124.

69. John C. Yoo, "Continuation of Politics," pp. 206–7 and Yoo, *Powers of War and Peace*, pp. 33–34.

70. Michael D. Ramsey, "Text and History in the War Powers Debate: A Reply to Professor Yoo," *University of Chicago Law Review* 69 (Autumn 2002): 1685.

71. Quoted in Ramsey, "Textualism and War Powers," *University of Chicago Law Review* 69, no. 4 (Autumn 2002): 1545. That proposition is further supported by Emmerich de Vattel, "the international law writer best known to the Framers," who explained that "when one nation takes up arms against another, she from that moment declares herself an enemy to all the individuals of the latter, and authorizes them to treat her as such." See also Michael D. Ramsey, *The Constitution's Text in Foreign Affairs* (Cambridge, MA: Harvard University Press, 2007).

72. "President Bush Announces Major Combat Operations in Iraq Have Ended," White House press release, May 1, 2003.

73. Ramsey, "Textualism and War Powers." Ramsey also points out that a formal proclamation was not necessary in the 18th century to invoke the laws of

war, one of the two main purposes Yoo ascribes to the congressional power to declare war.

74. See, for example, *Federalist* no. 41: "Security against foreign danger is one of the primitive objects of civil society. It is an avowed and essential object of the American Union. The powers requisite for attaining it must be effectually confided to the federal councils. Is the power of declaring war necessary? No man will answer this question in the negative."

75. As Ramsey notes, "In my own review of the ratification debates I have found no passage in which anyone asserted broad presidential war powers, and Professor Yoo has not pointed to any such passage." Ramsey, "Text and History in the War Powers Debate," p. 1712.

76. "James Wilson, Pennsylvania Ratifying Convention," *The Founders' Constitution* (online), Vol. 1, Chap. 7, Doc. 17.

77. "Pierce Butler, South Carolina Legislature," *The Founders' Constitution* (online), Vol. 3, Art. 1, Sec. 8, Cl. 11, Doc. 5. Butler's assurance should perhaps carry special weight, given that at the Philadelphia Convention it was Butler himself who argued for giving the president the power "to make war."

78. Louis Fisher, *Presidential War Power*, p. 18.

79. David P. Currie, "Rumors of Wars: Presidential and Congressional War Powers, 1809–1829," *University of Chicago Law Review* 67, no. 1 (Winter 2000): 40; David P. Currie, *The Constitution in Congress: The Jeffersonians, 1801–1829* (Chicago: University of Chicago Press, 2001), p. 195 ("Neither Madison nor his supporters in Congress even remotely suggested that the President had inherent authority to initiate hostilities without congressional approval"). Abraham D. Sofaer, whose 1976 book *War, Foreign Affairs and Constitutional Power* remains the most comprehensive study of the constitutional history of American foreign policy, came to the same conclusion as Professor Currie: "At no point during the first forty years of activity under the Constitution, did a President or any other important participant claim that Presidents could exercise force independently of congressional control." Abraham D. Sofaer, "War and Responsibility: A Symposium on Congress, the President, and the Authority to Initiate Hostilities," *University of Miami Law Review* 50, no. 1 (October 1995): 50–51. Sofaer places more weight on early presidents' conduct than does Currie, noting that they repeatedly took independent action that could be expected to lead to military conflict. But the fact that early presidents felt compelled to publicly observe the forms of deference even while pushing the limits of their authority casts serious doubt on John Yoo's claim that, in the original understanding, the president had the "right to start wars."

80. Jeffrey K. Tulis, "The Two Constitutional Presidencies," p. 112.

81. *Federalist* no. 1, p. 3; *Federalist* no. 85, p. 457. The observation is Tulis's, p. 95.

82. Robert Schmuhl, "Over to You, President Bush; The Consequences of Shaping the World's Most Powerful Office," *Chicago Tribune*, January 18, 2001.

83. Robert A. Dahl, "Myth of the Presidential Mandate," *Political Science Quarterly* 105, no. 3 (Autumn 1990): 369.

84. Jeffrey K. Tulis, *The Rhetorical Presidency* (Princeton, NJ: Princeton University Press, 1987), p. 6.

85. Lynn Hudson Parsons, *John Quincy Adams* (Lanham, MD: Rowman & Littlefield, 1999), p. 185.

86. Tulis, *The Rhetorical Presidency*, p. 66.

87. Jason W. A. Bertsch, "Chatterbox," *Public Interest* (Summer 1996). Some scholars argue that Tulis draws the contrast between what he calls "the Old Way" and "the New Way" too sharply. Terri Bimes and Quinn Mulroy find that "a strong vibrant tradition of populist leadership existed among nineteenth century Democratic presidents." "The Rise and Decline of Presidential Populism," *Studies in American Political Development* 18, no. 2 (Fall 2004): 137. Michael J. Korzi recognizes that "the nineteenth-century president was constrained in being a popular leader, and, to be sure, he rarely made direct, popular appeals." But Korzi argues that there is also "significant evidence that [19th-century presidential] candidates actually were expected to present their political opinions and pledges to the people, which, as we have seen, would have been anathema to the founders." Michael J. Korzi, "The Seat of Popular Leadership: Parties, Elections, and the Nineteenth-Century Presidency," *Presidential Studies Quarterly* 29, no. 2 (June 1999): 351, 356.

88. "The message was generally known as 'the President's Annual Message to Congress' until well into the 20th century. Although some historians suggest that the phrase 'State of the Union' emerged only after World War II, President Franklin Roosevelt's 1934 message is identified in his papers as his "Annual Message to Congress on the State of the Union." Thomas H. Neale, "The President's State of the Union Message: Frequently Asked Questions," *CRS Report for Congress*, Order Code RS20021, updated March 7, 2006.

89. George Washington, First Annual Address, January 8, 1790. See discussion in David P. Currie, *Constitution in Congress: Federalist Period*, pp. 29–30.

90. George Washington, "Communication of Sentiments to Benjamin Hawkins," in *The Writings of George Washington 1790–1794*, Vol. 12, ed. Worthington Chauncey Ford (New York and London: G.P. Putnam' Sons, 1891), p. 73.

91. Quoted in Phelps, *George Washington and American Constitutionalism*, p. 141.

92. Thomas Jefferson, First Annual Message, December 8, 1801.

93. Tulis, *The Rhetorical Presidency*, p. 56.

94. In their deference to Congress, early presidents went well beyond anything required by the Constitution's text. Far from hermetically sealing off legislative functions within the legislative branch, that document gives an important role to the president in the lawmaking process. In addition to the veto power, the Constitution stipulates that the president "shall from time to time give to the Congress information of the state of the union, and recommend to their consideration such measures as he shall judge necessary and expedient." The language of that clause ("shall," not "may"), and its inclusion amid a list of duties of the president, suggest that the chief executive is not just entitled to, but constitutionally required to, make policy recommendations to Congress. Vasan Kesavan and J. Gregory Sidak, "The Legislator-in-Chief," *William and Mary Law Review* 44, no. 1 (October 2002): 7–13.

95. Aaron Wildavsky, "'Greatness' Revisited: Evaluating the Performance of American Presidents in Terms of Cultural Dilemmas," in *The Beleaguered Presidency* (New Brunswick, NJ: Transaction, 1991), p. 11.

96. *Federalist* no. 51, p. 269.

97. Quoted in James Burnham, *Congress and the American Tradition* (Chicago: Henry Regnery Company, 1959), p. 92.

98. *Federalist* no. 14, p. 67.

99. Leonard W. Levy, *Jefferson and Civil Liberties: The Darker Side* (Chicago: Ivan R. Dee, Inc., 1989), p. 119. Madison, Jefferson's secretary of state and successor, played a key role in pushing the coercive and disastrous embargo policy. Garry Wills explains that Madison and Jefferson supported that policy because they thought it would keep the United States out of war, and the pair "had an ideological block about war of any kind." Garry Wills, *James Madison* (New York: Times Books, 2002), p. 62.

100. James T. Patterson, "The Rise of Presidential Power before World War II," *Law and Contemporary Problems* 40, no. 2 (Spring 1976): 39.

101. Quoted in Marcus Cunliffe, *The Presidency*, 3rd ed. (Boston: Houghton Mifflin Co., 1987), p. 132.

102. See David K. Nichols, *The Myth of the Modern Presidency* (University Park: Pennsylvania State University Press, 1994).

103. For a discussion of the Louisiana Purchase and Jefferson's desire for a constitutional amendment that would ratify his actions, see David N. Mayer, *The Constitutional Thought of Thomas Jefferson* (Charlottesville: University of Virginia Press, 1994, 1997), pp. 244–51.

104. Quoted in Patterson, "Rise of Presidential Power," p. 43.

105. *Federalist* no. 73, p. 381. See also Frank Easterbrook, "Presidential Review," *Case Western Reserve Law Review* 40 (1990): 907–8.

106. Nichols, *Myth of the Modern Presidency*, p. 27.

107. As Madison had put it during the removal debate, "The power of removal was an executive power, and as such belonged to the president, by the express words of the constitution: 'the executive power shall be vested in a President of the United States of America.'" See Thatch, *Creation of the Presidency*, p. 151.

108. Tulis, *The Rhetorical Presidency*, p. 73.

109. Quoted in Fisher, *Presidential War Power*, p. 30.

110. Fisher, *Presidential War Power*, p. 34.

111. Lincoln, to William H. Herndon, February 15, 1848, in *Lincoln: Selected Speeches and Writings*, ed. Don E. Fehrenbacher (New York: Vintage Books, 1989), pp. 67–68.

112. Jeffrey Rogers Hummel, *Emancipating Slaves, Enslaving Free Men: A History of the American Civil War* (Chicago: Open Court Press, 1996), p. 256. In March 1863, Congress ratified Lincoln's suspension of habeas corpus.

113. *The Prize Cases*, 67 U.S. 635, 668 (1862). The administration itself admitted as much at oral argument, when district attorney Richard Henry Dana Jr., arguing the case for the president, affirmed that the questions before the Court had nothing to do with "the right to initiate a war, as a voluntary act of sovereignty. That is vested only in Congress." David Gray Adler, "The Law: The Clinton Theory of the War Power," *Presidential Studies Quarterly* 30, no. 1 (March 2000).

114. Quoted in Fisher, *Presidential War Power*, p. 88. See also Raoul Berger, *Executive Privilege: A Constitutional Myth* (Cambridge, MA: Harvard University Press, 1974), pp. 75–77. That is not, of course, to suggest that none of these incidents were significant. The Quasi-War with France (1798–1800) and Jefferson's actions against the Barbary powers were important conflicts carried out without declarations of war. In the second chapter of his book *Presidential War Power*, "Precedents from 1789 to 1900," constitutional scholar Louis Fisher argues that

Congress authorized the use of force in both incidents, and he examines other, smaller 19th-century interventions that better fit Corwin's description.

115. James Madison, *Letters and Other Writings*, Vol. 4, pp. 491–92.

116. Walter A. McDougall, *Promised Land, Crusader State* (Boston: Houghton Mifflin Co., 1997), p. 48.

117. Thomas Jefferson, First Inaugural Address, March 4, 1801.

118. Eric A. Nordlinger, *Isolationism Reconfigured: American Foreign Policy for a New Century* (Princeton, NJ: Princeton University Press, 1995), p. 186.

119. Nordlinger, *Isolationism Reconfigured*, p. 242.

120. Stanton's removal violated the Tenure of Office Act, a measure of dubious constitutionality that Congress had passed to protect him.

121. U.S. Senate, *Proceedings in the Trial of Andrew Johnson* (Washington: 1869).

122. Tulis, *The Rhetorical Presidency*, p. 93.

123. Quoted in James T. Patterson, "Rise of Presidential Power," p. 48.

124. Samuel Kernell and Gary C. Jacobson, "Congress and the Presidency as News in the Nineteenth Century," *Journal of Politics* 49, no. 4 (November 1987): 1016–35.

125. Tulis, *The Rhetorical Presidency*, pp. 15–17.

126. See figures cited in Jonathan Monten, "The Roots of the Bush Doctrine: Power, Nationalism, and Democracy Promotion in U.S. Strategy," *International Security* 29, no. 4 (Spring 2005).

127. Thomas Carlyle, "The Leader as Hero," in *Political Leadership: A Source Book*, ed. Barbara Kellerman (Pittsburgh: University of Pittsburgh Press, 1986), p. 7.

128. *The Papers of Woodrow Wilson*, Vol. 1, ed. Arthur S. Link (Princeton, NJ: Princeton University Press, 1966), p. 125.

129. Garry Wills, "The Presbyterian Nietzsche," *New York Review of Books*, January 16, 1992.

130. Woodrow Wilson, *Congressional Government*, p. 27.

131. Woodrow Wilson, *Congressional Government*, p. 185.

132. Howard K. Beale, *Theodore Roosevelt and the Rise of America to World Power*, p. 50, 1967 ed.

133. Woodrow Wilson, *Congressional Government*, pp. 22–23.

Chapter 2

1. Woodrow Wilson, *Constitutional Government in the United States* (New York: Columbia University Press, 1908, 1917), p. 46.

2. Richard Hofstadter, ed., *The Progressive Movement: 1900–1915* (Englewood Cliffs, NJ: Prentice-Hall, 1963), pp. 1–2.

3. Robert E. Gallman, "Economic Growth and Structural Change in the Long Nineteenth Century," in *The Cambridge Economic History of the United States, Vol. II: The Long Nineteenth Century*, ed. Stanley L. Engerman and Robert E. Gallman (Cambridge: Cambridge University Press, 2000), p. 23.

4. Quoted in Sean Dennis Cashman, *America in the Gilded Age* (New York: New York University Press, 1993), p. 354.

5. Richard Hofstadter, "Introduction: The Meaning of the Progressive Movement," in *The Progressive Movement: 1900–1915*, ed. Richard Hofstadter (Englewood Cliffs, NJ: Prentice-Hall, 1963), pp. 4–5.

6. M. J. C. Vile, *Constitutionalism and the Separation of Powers*, 2nd ed. (Indianapolis: Liberty Fund, 1998), p. 292.

7. Richard A. Epstein, Roger Pilon, Geoffrey R. Stone, John Yoo; Moderator: William H. Pryor Jr., Debate: "Federalism and Separation of Powers: Executive Power in Wartime," *Engage* 8, no. 2 (May 2007), p. 58.

8. Quoted in Raymond Tatelovich and Thomas S. Engeman, *The Presidency and Political Science: Two Hundred Years of Constitutional Debate* (Baltimore: Johns Hopkins University Press, 2002), p. 77.

9. Tatelovich and Engeman, *The Presidency and Political Science*, p. 85.

10. Samuel Kernell and Gary C. Jacobson, "Congress and the Presidency as News in the Nineteenth Century," *Journal of Politics* 49 (November 1987): 1031–32.

11. Wilson, *Constitutional Government*, p. 56. See also Christopher Wolfe, "Woodrow Wilson: Interpreting the Constitution," *Review of Politics* 41 (January 1979).

12. Wilson, *Constitutional Government*, p. 56.

13. Wilson, *Constitutional Government*, p. 70.

14. Gary L. Gregg II, "Whiggism and Presidentialism: American Ambivalence toward Executive Power," in *The Presidency Then and Now*, ed. Philip G. Henderson (Lanham, MD: Rowman & Littlefield, 2000), p. 84.

15. Herbert Croly, *The Promise of American Life* (New York: Macmillan Co., 1909), p. 400. Even Jefferson, who had a more sanguine view of human nature than most of his contemporaries, summed up his constitutional vision in decidedly un-Progressive terms: "In questions of power, then, let no more be heard of confidence in man, but bind him down from mischief by the chains of the Constitution." Jefferson, "The Kentucky Resolutions," in *The Portable Thomas Jefferson*, ed. Merrill D. Peterson (New York: Penguin Books, 1977), p. 288.

16. Herbert Croly, *Progressive Democracy* (New York: Macmillan Co., 1915), pp. 370–71. It should be noted that not all Progressives shared Croly's enthusiasm for central direction of the economy. The "New Freedom" Progressives, whose leader was, for a time, Woodrow Wilson, shared many of the reformers' goals, but thought they were better achieved through harnessing competitive forces. Thus, for example, "New Freedom" Progressives thought vigorous enforcement of antitrust laws—breaking up the trusts to restore competition—was preferable to the increased regulation of corporate behavior favored by TR's "New Nationalist" Progressives. In office, however, Wilson drifted toward New Nationalism: "In the wake of the excitement aroused by the Progressive Party, Wilson, whose New Freedom campaign was far more sympathetic to the decentralized state of courts and parties than TR's, felt compelled, as president, to govern as a New Nationalist Progressive." See Sidney M. Milkis, "Why the Election of 1912 Changed America," *Claremont Review of Books*, February 15, 2003. Howard Gillman writes that under Wilson, the New Freedom agenda "was discarded in favor of a conception of governmental responsibilities that included rationalizing an [erratic] market through independent agencies and bureaus guided by the standards of scientific management." Howard Gillman, "The Constitution Besieged: TR, Taft, and Wilson on the Virtue and Efficacy of a Faction-Free Republic," *Presidential Studies Quarterly* 19 (1989): 195–96.

17. Croly, *Promise of American Life*, p. 312.

18. William James, "The Moral Equivalent of War," in *Memories and Studies* (New York: Longmans, Green & Co., 1935), p. 291. See also Linda Schott, "Jane Ad-

dams and William James on Alternatives to War," *Journal of the History of Ideas* 54 (April 1993): 241–54.

19. Edward Mandell House, *Philip Dru: Administrator* (Whitefish, MT: Kessinger Publishing's Rare Reprints, 1912, 2004), pp. 92–93.

20. William E. Leuchtenburg, "The New Deal and the Analogue of War," in *Change and Continuity in Twentieth-Century America*, ed. John Braeman, Robert H. Bremner, and Everett Walters (Columbus: Ohio State University Press, 1964), p. 502.

21. Wilfred M. McClay, "Croly's Progressive America," *Public Interest*, Fall 1999.

22. Croly, *Promise of American Life*, p. 173.

23. Milkis, "Why Election of 1912 Changed America."

24. TR was a fan of proto-Nazi Madison Grant, whose 1916 book *The Passing of the Great Race*—"a capital book," in Roosevelt's estimation—called for the "elimination of those who are weak or unfit" and "worthless race types." Michael Chapman, "TR: No Friend of the Constitution," *Cato Policy Report* 24 (November/December 2002). See also Gary Gerstle, "Theodore Roosevelt and the Divided Character of American Nationalism," *Journal of American History* 86 (December 1999): 1281 ("Roosevelt's nationalism expressed itself as a combative and unapologetic racial ideology that thrived on aggression and the vanquishing of savage and barbaric peoples").

25. The first observation ("celebrity president") is Lewis L. Gould, "Theodore Roosevelt, Woodrow Wilson, and the Emergence of the Modern Presidency: An Introductory Essay," *Presidential Studies Quarterly* 19 (Winter 1989): 43, and the second ("initials"), Sidney M. Milkis and Michael Nelson, *The American Presidency: 1776–1998* (Washington: CQ Press, 1999), p. 194.

26. Quoted in Richard J. Ellis, "The Joy of Power: Changing Conceptions of the Presidential Office," *Presidential Studies Quarterly* 33 (June 2003): 282.

27. Theodore Roosevelt, *Theodore Roosevelt: An Autobiography* (New York: Macmillan Co., 1913), p. 383. There's some debate about whether TR actually used the term "bully pulpit." Sidney M. Milkis and Michael Nelson write that "there is no direct evidence that Theodore Roosevelt ever spoke or wrote this term." Milkis and Nelson, *American Presidency*, n. 17, p. 218. But Donald J. Davidson quotes TR as saying, "I suppose my critics will call that preaching, but I have got such a bully pulpit." Donald J. Davidson, ed., *The Wisdom of Theodore Roosevelt* (New York: Citadel Press, 2003), p. 11.

28. Jeffrey K. Tulis sees TR as representing a "middle way" between the reserved presidency of the 19th century and the fully developed "rhetorical presidency" of the 20th. Jeffrey K. Tulis, *The Rhetorical Presidency* (Princeton, NJ: Princeton University Press, 1987), p 95.

29. James Bennet, "True to Form, Clinton Shifts Energies Back to U.S. Focus," *New York Times*, July 5, 1998.

30. "Executive Orders," American Presidency Project, June 1, 2024.

31. Sidney M. Milkis, "Theodore Roosevelt and the Birth of the Modern Presidency," *Miller Center Report*, Fall/Winter 2003. Another unilaterally expanded a federal entitlement by providing a disability pension to all Civil War veterans over age 62. William J. Olson and Alan Woll, "Executive Orders and National Emergencies: How Presidents Have Come to 'Run the Country' by Usurping Executive Power," Cato Institute Policy Analysis no. 358, October 28, 1999, p. 15.

32. Bill Kauffman, "T.R. vs. the Dictionary," *The American Enterprise*, January 1, 2001.

33. In his autobiography, Roosevelt noted the weakness of his constitutional authority here: "There was no duty whatever laid upon me by the Constitution in this matter, and I had in theory no power to act directly unless the Governor of Pennsylvania or the legislature, if it were in session, should notify me that Pennsylvania could not keep order." Roosevelt, *Autobiography*, p. 505.

34. Lewis L. Gould, *The Presidency of Theodore Roosevelt* (Lawrence: University Press of Kansas, 1991), p. 69.

35. Edmund Morris, *Theodore Rex* (New York: Random House, 2001), p. 165. Constitutional or not, the gambit worked: the strike settled when the owners agreed to arbitration.

36. Louis Fisher, *Presidential War Power* (Lawrence: University Press of Kansas, 1995), p. 49.

37. Panama and the Great White Fleet aside, Roosevelt's record was not as bellicose as one might have expected given his romantic view of war. He won the Nobel Peace Prize for negotiating an end to the Russo-Japanese War in 1905. He pulled U.S. troops out of Cuba and supported U.S. withdrawal from the Philippines. See John B. Judis, *The Folly of Empire: What George W. Bush Could Learn from Theodore Roosevelt and Woodrow Wilson* (New York: Scribner, 2004); Tom Parker, "The Realistic Roosevelt," *National Interest* (Fall 2004).

38. William Michael Treanor, "Fame, the Founding, and the Power to Declare War," *Cornell Law Review* 82 (May 1997): 764.

39. James Chace, *1912: Wilson, Roosevelt, Taft & Debs—The Election That Changed the Country* (New York: Simon & Schuster, 2004), p. 161.

40. Quoted in Chace, p. 111.

41. "Taft Tells His Campaign Views; Interview with a New York Times Correspondent on the Issues to Be Met," *New York Times*, August 13, 1912.

42. Roosevelt, *Autobiography*, p. 389.

43. William Howard Taft, *Our Chief Magistrate and His Powers* (New York: Columbia University Press, 1925), p. 144. See generally Michael J. Korzi, "Our Chief Magistrate and His Powers: A Reconsideration of William Howard Taft's 'Whig' Theory of Presidential Leadership," *Presidential Studies Quarterly* 33 (June 2003). Taft had a less restrictive view of the president's freedom to act in foreign affairs, as evidenced by his unilateral actions in Nicaragua. See Fisher, *Presidential War Power*, pp. 52–54. Domestically, he was an exponent of "narrow" unitarianism. See *Myers v. U.S.*, 272 U.S. 52 (1926).

44. Quoted in Forrest McDonald, *The American Presidency: An Intellectual History* (Lawrence: University Press of Kansas, 1994), pp. 359–60.

45. Quoted in Francis D. Wormuth and Edwin B. Firmage, *To Chain the Dog of War: The War Power of Congress in History and Law* (Champaign: University of Illinois Press, 1986, 1989), p. 289.

46. Quoted in Chace, *Wilson, Roosevelt, Taft & Debs*, p. 268.

47. Arthur M. Schlesinger Jr., "Annual Messages of the Presidents: Major Themes of American History," in *The State of the Union Messages of the Presidents 1790–1966*, Vol. 1, ed. Fred L. Israel (New York: Chelsea House, 1966), p. xvii.

48. Quoted in Henry A. Turner, "Woodrow Wilson: Exponent of Executive Leadership," *Western Political Quarterly* 4 (March 1951): 99, 105.

49. Of course, not all Progressives were militarists and imperialists. Prominent anti-war Progressives included Robert LaFollette, Jane Addams, and William Borah. But they were a minority. See William E. Leuchtenburg, "Progressivism and Imperialism: The Progressive Movement and American Foreign Policy, 1898–1916," *Mississippi Valley Historical Review* 39 (December 1952); Charles Hirschfeld, "Nationalist Progressivism and World War I," *Mid-America: An Historical Review* 45 (July 1963); Richard Hofstadter, *The Age of Reform* (New York: Vintage Books, 1955), pp. 272–82.

50. Quoted in Arthur A. Ekirch Jr., "The Reform Mentality, War, Peace, and the National State: From the Progressives to Vietnam," *Journal of Libertarian Studies* 3 (1979): 63.

51. Richard Weiss, "The Patrician as Patriot," *Reviews in American History* 13 (September 1985): 405.

52. John Patrick Diggins, "The New Republic and Its Times," *New Republic*, December 10, 1984, pp. 23, 25.

53. Quoted in Hirschfeld, "Nationalist Progressivism," p. 142.

54. Quoted in Ekirch, "The Reform Mentality," p. 64.

55. Ekirch, "The Reform Mentality," p. 64.

56. John Dos Passos, *Nineteen Nineteen* (New York: Signet Classic, 1932, 1979), pp. 120–21.

57. A. F. Beringause, "The Double Martyrdom of Randolph Bourne," *Journal of the History of Ideas* 18 (October 1957): 597.

58. Randolph Bourne, "The State," in *The Radical Will: Selected Writings 1911–1918*, ed. Olaf Hansen (New York: Urizen Books, 1977), pp. 356–57.

59. Quoted in Kendrick A. Clements, "Woodrow Wilson and World War I," *Presidential Studies Quarterly* 34 (March 2004): 78.

60. Quoted in Walter A. McDougall, *Promised Land, Crusader State: The American Encounter with the World Since 1776* (New York: Houghton Mifflin Co., 1997), p. 136.

61. In the 1914 occupation of Veracruz, Wilson requested congressional authorization, while maintaining he did not need it, then ordered U.S. Marines ashore before the Senate had voted. In 1915 he ordered American troops to Haiti without authorization. See Fisher, *Presidential War Power*, pp. 50–52.

62. Fisher, *Presidential War Power*, p. 57.

63. Quoted in Olaf Hansen, ed., "Introduction," *The Radical Will*, p. 55.

64. *See* Robert Higgs, *Crisis and Leviathan* (New York: Oxford University Press, 1987), pp. 123–58; Bruce D. Porter, *War and the Rise of the State: The Military Foundations of Modern Politics* (New York: Free Press, 1994), pp. 269–72.

65. Quoted in Beringause, "Double Martyrdom," p. 602.

66. Geoffrey R. Stone, *Perilous Times: Free Speech in Wartime from the Sedition Act of 1798 to the War on Terrorism* (New York: W.W. Norton & Co., 2004), p. 156.

67. G. J. A. O'Toole, *Honorable Treachery: A History of U.S. Intelligence, Espionage, and Covert Action from the American Revolution to the C.I.A.* (New York: Atlantic Monthly Press, 1991), p. 278.

68. Joan M. Jensen, *Army Surveillance in America, 1775–1980* (New Haven, CT: Yale University Press, 1991), pp. 176–77.

69. Geoffrey R. Stone, *Perilous Times*, pp. 151–52, 186.

70. Michael Linfield, *Freedom under Fire: U.S. Civil Liberties in Times of War* (Boston: South End Press, 1990), p. 45.

71. Stone, *Perilous Times*, pp. 172–73. Even so, Wilson thought Congress had given him insufficient power to maintain order at home. He pushed unsuccessfully for a measure that would have given censorship powers directly to the president, and he wanted the suppression of dissent to continue in peacetime, pocket-vetoing a bill to repeal the Espionage and Sedition Acts in 1920. Garry Wills, "The Presbyterian Nietzsche," *New York Review of Books*, January 16, 1992.

72. Quoted in Porter, *War and the Rise of the State*, p. 276.

73. Robert Higgs, *Crisis and Leviathan*, pp. 123–58; Porter, *War and the Rise of the State*, p. 160.

74. Christopher S. Yoo, Steven G. Calabresi, and Laurence D. Nee, "The Unitary Executive during the Third Half-Century, 1889–1945," *Notre Dame Law Review* 80 (November 2004).

75. See Fisher, *Presidential War Power*, pp. 70–72.

76. Quoted in Walter A. McDougall, *Promised Land*, p. 142.

77. Thomas Fleming, *The Illusion of Victory: America in World War I* (New York: Basic Books, 2003), p. 460.

78. Warren G. Harding, First Annual Message, December 6, 1921.

79. Richard Vedder and Lowell Gallaway, "Rating Presidential Performance," in *Reassessing the Presidency: The Rise of the Executive State and the Decline of Freedom*, ed. John V. Denson (Auburn, AL: Mises Institute, 2001), p. 19.

80. Robert Sobel, *Coolidge: An American Enigma* (Washington: Regnery, 1998), p. 291.

81. Quoted in Paul Johnson, *Modern Times: The World from the Twenties to the Nineties*, rev. ed. (New York: Harper Perennial, 1992), p. 216.

82. Stone, *Perilous Times*, p. 230. Alas, Attorney General Stone also appointed J. Edgar Hoover to head the FBI. But it took 12 years and an administration more accommodating than Coolidge's to set Hoover free to spy at will. Stone, p. 249.

83. Quoted in Morton H. Halperin, Jerry J. Berman, Robert L. Borosage, and Christine M. Marwick, *The Lawless State: The Crimes of the U.S. Intelligence Agencies* (New York: Penguin Books, 1976), p. 95.

84. Quoted in Sobel, *Coolidge*, p. 237.

85. Quoted in Sobel, *Coolidge*, p. 244.

86. David Greenberg, "Help! Call the White House!" Slate.com, Tuesday, September 5, 2006; Sobel, *Coolidge*, pp. 315–17.

87. Schlesinger, "Annual Messages of the Presidents," p. xvi.

88. For Coolidge's innovations, including, surprisingly, a historic number of press conferences, see Elmer E. Cornwell Jr., "Coolidge and Presidential Leadership," *Public Opinion Quarterly* 21 (Summer 1957), who notes nonetheless that Coolidge's radio addresses "were admirably calculated to convey a general impression of the man and his ideas without in the least offending by their partisanship" (p. 269).

89. H. L. Mencken, "Coolidge," in *The Vintage Mencken*, ed. Alistair Cooke (New York: Vintage Books, 1955), p. 223.

90. Aaron L. Friedberg, *In the Shadow of the Garrison State: America's Anti-Statism and Its Cold War Grand Strategy* (Princeton, NJ: Princeton University Press, 2000), pp. 19–20.

91. Higgs, *Crisis and Leviathan*, pp. 123–58; Porter, *War and the Rise of the State*, p. 161.

92. Franklin D. Roosevelt, First Inaugural Address, March 4, 1933.

93. William E. Leuchtenburg, "The New Deal," pp. 92–93, 109.

94. Higgs, *Crisis and Leviathan*, p. 180.

95. Quoted in David Schoenbrod, *Power without Responsibility: How Congress Abuses the People through Delegation* (New Haven, CT: Yale University Press, 1993), p. 38.

96. Quoted in Leuchtenburg, "The New Deal," p. 120.

97. John A. Garraty, "The New Deal, National Socialism, and the Great Depression," *American Historical Review* 78 (October 1973): 925.

98. James, "Moral Equivalent of War," p. 290.

99. Porter, *War and the Rise of the State*, p. 278.

100. Leuchtenburg, "The New Deal," p. 115.

101. Michael S. Sherry, *In the Shadow of War: The United States since the 1930s* (New Haven, CT: Yale University Press, 1995), p. 21.

102. See Fisher, *Presidential War Power*, pp. 63–67; for a qualified defense of FDR, see Arthur Schlesinger Jr., *The Imperial Presidency* (Boston: Houghton Mifflin Co., 1973), pp. 105–14.

103. Halperin et al., *The Lawless State*, pp. 95–96.

104. Stone, *Perilous Times*, p. 249.

105. Halperin et al., *The Lawless State*, p. 96.

106. Stone, *Perilous Times*, pp. 249–50.

107. Halperin, et al., *The Lawless State*, p. 96.

108. Barton J. Bernstein, "The Road to Watergate and Beyond: The Growth and Abuse of Executive Authority since 1940," *Law and Contemporary Problems* 40 (Spring 1976): 63.

109. Edward S. Corwin, *Total War and the Constitution* (New York: Albert A. Knopf, 1947), p. 179.

110. See *Helvering v. Davis*, 301 U.S. 619 (1937) (upholding the Social Security Act of 1935 under the general welfare clause: "Congress may spend money in aid of the 'general welfare.' . . . The discretion belongs to Congress. . . . Needs that were narrow or parochial a century ago may be interwoven in our day with the well-being of the nation"); *N.L.R.B. v. Jones & Laughlin Steel Corp.*, 301 U.S. 1 (1937) (upholding regulation of manufacturing and labor relations under the commerce clause); *Wickard v. Filburn*, 317 U.S. 111 (1942) (Congress can regulate noncommercial activity that taken in the aggregate with other, similar activities substantially affects interstate commerce).

111. Along with the growth in presidential power came growth in quasi-independent administrative agencies, insulated from presidential control by law or practice. See Cass R. Sunstein, "Constitutionalism after the New Deal," *Harvard Law Review* 101 (December 1987): 444: "There was some tension in the New Deal vision of the executive branch. The increase in presidential power was based on a belief in a direct relationship between the will of the people and the will of the President; hence the presidency, rather than the states or the common law courts, was regarded as the primary regulator. In contrast the faith in bureaucratic administration was based on the ability of regulators to discern the public interest and to promote, though indirectly and through their very insulation, democratic goals."

112. The Supreme Court's 1935 decision striking down the industrial code provisions of the NIRA on nondelegation grounds helped inspire FDR's attempt to subvert the judiciary's independence by enlarging the Court. In *Schechter Poultry Corp. v. United States*, 295 U.S. 495 (1935), the Court, led by Chief Justice Hughes, held that "Congress is not permitted to abdicate or to transfer to others the essential legislative functions with which it is thus vested." But after Roosevelt's effort to pack the Court, the judiciary never again struck down a New Deal statute for impermissible delegation.

113. *Yakus v. U.S.*, 321 U.S. 414 (1944).

114. Theodore J. Lowi, *The Personal President: Power Invested, Promise Unfulfilled* (Ithaca, NY: Cornell University Press, 1985), pp. 45–48, quote on p. 46 (emphasis in original).

115. Lowi, *The Personal President*, p. 51.

116. Lowi, *The Personal President*, p. 52.

117. The original 100 Days began with Bonaparte's return to Paris on March 20, 1815, and ended with Louis XVIII's restoration on June 28. William Safire, "Language: Breaking the Hours Barrier," *International Herald Tribune*, January 28, 2007.

118. Franklin D. Roosevelt, State of the Union Message to Congress, January 11, 1944.

119. Leila A. Sussmann, "FDR and the White House Mail," *Public Opinion Quarterly* 20 (Spring 1956): 10.

120. James T. Patterson, "The Rise of Presidential Power before World War II," *Law and Contemporary Problems* 40 (Spring 1976): 54.

121. Willam E. Leuchtenburg, "The Twentieth-Century Presidency," *Miller Center Report* (Spring 2000); Fred I. Greenstein, "Change and Continuity in the Modern Presidency," in *The New American Political System*, ed. Anthony King (Washington: American Enterprise Institute, 1978).

Chapter 3

1. Michael Nelson, "Evaluating the Presidency," in *The Presidency and the Political System*, 5th ed. (Washington: CQ Press, 1998), p. 5.

2. John F. Kennedy, "The Presidency in 1960," National Press Club, Washington, D.C., January 14, 1960.

3. American National Election Studies, "Trust the Federal Government (4-point Scale)," *ANES Guide to Public Opinion and Electoral Behavior*.

4. Roberta S. Sigel, "Image of the American Presidency—Part II of an Exploration into Popular Views of Presidential Power," *Midwest Journal of Political Science* 10 (February 1966): 128.

5. Thomas Cronin, "Superman: Our Textbook President," *Washington Monthly* (October 1970): 50. Chapter 2 of Cronin's 1975 book *The State of the Presidency*, "The Cult of the Presidency: A Halo for the Chief," expands on his 1970 essay and touches on other themes I explore in this book. Cronin, *The State of the Presidency* (Boston: Little, Brown and Co., 1975), pp. 23–51.

6. Fred I. Greenstein, "The Benevolent Leader: Children's Images of Political Authority," *American Political Science Review* 54 (December 1960).

7. Fred I. Greenstein, "More on Children's Images of the President," *Public Opinion Quarterly* 25 (Winter 1961): 648–54.

8. Roberta S. Sigel, "An Exploration into Some Aspects of Political Socialization," *American Political Science Review* 62 (March 1968).

9. Neustadt and Schlesinger quoted in Nelson, *The Presidency and the Political System*, pp. 4–5.

10. James MacGregor Burns, *The Deadlock of Democracy: Four-Party Politics in America* (Englewood Cliffs, NJ: Prentice-Hall, 1963), p. 337.

11. Peter Augustine Lawler, "The *Federalist's* Hostility to Leadership and the Crisis of the Contemporary Presidency," *Presidential Studies Quarterly* 17 (Fall 1987): 721, fn. 9; James MacGregor Burns, *The Power to Lead* (New York: Simon & Schuster, 1984), p. 17.

12. Burns, *The Power to Lead*, p. 330.

13. David McCullough, *Truman* (New York: Simon & Schuster, 1992), p. 591.

14. Quoted in James T. Patterson, "The Rise of Presidential Power before World War II," *Law and Contemporary Problems* 40 (Spring 1976): 52.

15. Sidney M. Milkis and Michael Nelson, *The American Presidency: Origins and Development, 1776–1998*, 3rd ed. (Washington: CQ Press, 1999), pp. 288–89.

16. Milkis and Nelson, *The American Presidency*, p. 293.

17. Lyn Ragsdale and John J. Theis III, "The Institutionalization of the American Presidency, 1924–92," *American Journal of Political Science* 41 (October 1997): 1296.

18. William P. Quigley, "The Right to Work and Earn a Living Wage: A Proposed Constitutional Amendment," *New York City Law Review* 2 (Summer 1998).

19. Ulysses S. Grant, Sixth Annual Message, December 7, 1874.

20. Article I, Section 8, Cl. 15, Art. IV, Sec. 4.

21. Rossiter, *The American Presidency* (Baltimore: John Hopkins University Press, 1956, 1987), p. 21.

22. 18 *Cong. Rec.* 1875 (1887). For an argument that such refusals were a rarity, and that constitutional constraints played little role in early debates over federal relief policy, see Michele L. Landis, "Let Me Next Time Be 'Tried by Fire': Disaster Relief and the Origins of the American Welfare State 1789–1874," *Northwestern University Law Review* 92 (Spring 1998).

23. See Henry B. Hogue and Keith Bea, "Federal Emergency Management and Homeland Security Organization: Historical Developments and Legislative Options," *CRS Report for Congress RL33369*, April 19, 2006.

24. Willard M. Oliver, *The Law and Order Presidency* (Upper Saddle River, NJ: Prentice-Hall, 2003), pp. 72–74.

25. Lyndon B. Johnson, "Statement by the President upon Signing the Omnibus Crime Control and Safe Streets Act of 1968," June 19, 1968.

26. William Henry Seward, ed., *Life and Public Services of John Quincy Adams* (New York: C. M. Saxton, Barker & Co., 1860), p. 132.

27. John F. Kennedy, Inaugural Address, January 20, 1961.

28. Rossiter, *The American Presidency*, p. 27.

29. Quoted in Rossiter, *The American Presidency*, p. 18.

30. The phrase "rhetorical common law" is from Jeffrey K. Tulis, *The Rhetorical Presidency* (Princeton, NJ: Princeton University Press, 1987), p. 61.

31. Elvin T. Lim, "Five Trends in Presidential Rhetoric: An Analysis of Rhetoric from George Washington to Bill Clinton," *Presidential Studies Quarterly* 32 (June 2002): 343.

32. David F. Ericson, "Presidential Inaugural Addresses and American Political Culture," *Presidential Studies Quarterly* (Fall 1997): 739. Ericson notes that some of the prevalence of this theme in early addresses can be attributed to the fact that the integrity of the Union was less secure before the Civil War.

33. Lim, "Five Trends in Presidential Rhetoric," p. 339.

34. George Washington, First Inaugural Address, April 30, 1789; Franklin D. Roosevelt, First Inaugural Address, March 4, 1933.

35. Lim, "Five Trends in Presidential Rhetoric," pp. 335, 337.

36. Rossiter, *The American Presidency*, p. 11.

37. Quoted in Louis Fisher, "The Korean War: On What Legal Basis Did Truman Act?" *American Journal of International Law* 89 (January 1995): 33–34.

38. Under the charter, commitment of troops would be undertaken by means of "special agreements" between participating nations and the Security Council, and those agreements would be issued pursuant to member nations' "respective constitutional processes." Moreover, the UN Participation Act makes those agreements "subject to the approval of the Congress by appropriate Act or joint resolution." See John Hart Ely, *War and Responsibility: Constitutional Lessons of Vietnam and Its Aftermath* (Princeton, NJ: Princeton University Press, 1993), p. 11, n. 60; Louis Fisher, *Presidential War Powers* (Lawrence: University Press of Kansas, 1995), p. 80.

39. Quoted in Ronald Radosh, *Prophets on the Right: Profiles of Conservative Critics of American Globalism* (New York: Free Life Editions, 1975), p. 174.

40. Arthur Schlesinger Jr., *The Imperial Presidency* (Boston: Houghton Mifflin Co., 1973), p. 139.

41. Norman A. Graebner, "The President as Commander in Chief: A Study in Power," *Journal of Military History* 57 (January 1993): 124.

42. Quoted in Francis D. Wormuth and Edwin B. Firmage, *To Chain the Dog of War: The War Power of Congress in History and Law* (Chicago: University of Illinois Press, 1989), p. 291.

43. P.L. 88-408 (August 10, 1964).

44. John Hart Ely, "The American War in Indochina, Part I: The (Troubled) Constitutionality of the War They Told Us About," *Stanford Law Review* 42 (April 1990): 886, 888.

45. Quoted in John Prados, "Essay: 40th Anniversary of the Gulf of Tonkin Incident," George Washington University National Security Archive, August 4, 2004.

46. "Gulf of Tonkin, USS *Maddox* Reports for 2 and 4 August 1964," *Selected Naval Documents: Vietnam*; also, it seems that the *Maddox* shot first. Tim Weiner, *Legacy of Ashes: The History of the CIA* (New York: Doubleday, 2007), p. 241.

47. Robert J. Hanyok, "Skunks, Bogies, Silent Hounds, and the Flying Fish: The Gulf of Tonkin Mystery, 2–4 August 1964," *Cryptologic Quarterly* (approved for Release by NSA on November 3, 2005).

48. James P. Pfiffner, "The Contemporary Presidency: Presidential Lies," *Presidential Studies Quarterly* 29 (December 1999).

49. Jack Beatty, "The One-Term Tradition," *Atlantic Monthly*, September 2003.

50. Quoted in Jonathan Monten, "The Roots of the Bush Doctrine: Power, Nationalism, and Democracy Promotion in U.S. Strategy," *International Security* 29 (Spring 2005).

51. Quoted in Sen. J. William Fulbright, *The Arrogance of Power* (New York: Vintage Books, 1966), p. 53.

52. Lyndon B. Johnson, "Remarks at the University of Michigan," May 22, 1964.

53. Quoted in Walter A. McDougall, *Promised Land, Crusader State* (Boston: Houghton Mifflin Co., 1997), p. 189. Though perhaps one could call it a "New Deal War" as well, given Johnson's pledge to seek funding for a TVA-style project on the Mekong River. Lyndon B. Johnson, Address at Johns Hopkins University: Peace without Conquest, April 7, 1965.

54. George C. Herring, *America's Longest War*, 2nd ed. (New York: Alfred A. Knopf, 1986), p. 158.

55. Charles Hirschman, Samual Preston, and Vu Manh Loi, "Vietnamese Casualties during the American War: A New Estimate," *Population and Development Review* 21 (December 1995): 790.

56. Tim Weiner, *Legacy of Ashes*, p. 109.

57. Quotations taken from the Operation Northwoods memo, which can be found in George Washington University's National Security Archive.

58. Quotations taken from the Operation Northwoods memo, p. 8.

59. Quotations taken from the Operation Northwoods memo, pp. 8–9.

60. William D. Hartung, "Shadow Warriors," *Washington Post Book World*, May 27, 2001, p. To9. For further information on Operation Northwoods, see David Ruppe, "Friendly Fire Book: U.S. Military Drafted Plans to Terrorize U.S. Cities to Provoke War with Cuba," ABCNews.com, November 7, 2001; Michael Young, "Spy Watch: Behind Closed Doors at the National Security Agency," *Reason*, March 1, 2002.

61. Richard A. Epstein, Roger Pilon, Geoffrey R. Stone, John Yoo; Moderator: William H. Pryor Jr., Debate: "Federalism and Separation of Powers: Executive Power in Wartime," *Engage* 8, no. 2 (May 2007).

62. Quoted in Graham T. Allison, *Essence of Decision: Explaining the Cuban Missile Crisis* (Boston: Little, Brown and Co., 1971), pp. 195–96.

63. Richard Rhodes, *Dark Sun: The Making of the Hydrogen Bomb* (New York: Simon & Schuster, 1995), pp. 565–66.

64. James Carroll, "Seeds of Salvation," *The Boston Globe*, June 26, 2006.

65. Rhodes, *Dark Sun*, p. 573.

66. Rhodes, *Dark Sun*, p. 575.

67. Rhodes, *Dark Sun*, p. 576.

68. Clinton Rossiter, *Constitutional Dictatorship* (New Brunswick, NJ: Transaction Publishers, 1948, 2002), p. 314.

69. Quoted in W. James Antle III, "Conservative Crack-Up: Will Libertarians Leave the Cold War Coalition?" *The American Conservative*, November 17, 2003.

70. See Aaron L. Friedberg, *In the Shadow of the Garrison State: America's Anti-Statism and Its Cold War Grand Strategy* (Princeton, NJ: Princeton University Press, 2000).

71. Though Truman vetoed the bill on civil liberties grounds, he did not appear overly concerned with the internment provisions. His main objection was to

the provisions of the act that required registration of so-called communist front organizations, provisions that "would open a Pandora's box of opportunities for official condemnation of organizations and individuals for perfectly honest opinions which happen to be stated also by communists." His objections to the internal detention provisions were tepid at best, noting that the bill might cause legal confusion because Congress hadn't suspended habeas corpus. Harry S. Truman, "Veto of the Internal Security Bill," September 22, 1950.

72. Cornelius P. Cotter and J. Malcolm Smith, "An American Paradox: The Emergency Detention Act of 1950," *Journal of Politics* 19 (February 1957): 20. See also Morton H. Halperin, Jerry J. Berman, Robert L. Borosage, and Christine M. Marwick, *The Lawless State: The Crimes of the U.S. Intelligence Agencies* (New York: Penguin Books, 1976), p. 111.

73. Michael Linfield, *Freedom under Fire: U.S. Civil Liberties in Times of War* (Boston: South End Press, 1990), p. 80.

74. McCullough, *Truman*, pp. 501, 506.

75. Executive Order 10340, "Directing the Secretary of Commerce to Take Possession of and Operate the Plants and Facilities of Certain Steel Companies," April 8, 1952.

76. Quoted in David Gray Adler, "The Steel Seizure Case and Inherent Presidential Power," *Constitutional Commentary* 19 (Spring 2002): 161.

77. *Youngstown Co. v. Sawyer*, 343 U.S. 579, 587 (1952).

78. *Youngstown*, 343 U.S. at 650.

79. William J. Olson and Alan Woll, "Executive Orders and National Emergencies: How Presidents Have Come to 'Run the Country' by Usurping Legislative Power," Cato Institute Policy Analysis no. 358, October 28, 1999, pp. 12–13.

80. Ragsdale and Theis, "Institutionalization of the American Presidency," pp. 1288–90.

81. Executive Order 9981, July 26, 1948.

82. *Federalist* no. 47, pp. 250–51.

83. Arvin S. Quist, "Security Classification of Information, Vol. 1: Introduction, History, and Adverse Impacts," September 20, 2002.

84. Quist, Chapter 3, "Classification under Executive Orders."

85. Melissa Healy, "Science of Power and Weakness: In the Name of the Cold War, Researchers Took the Disadvantaged and Made Them Subjects of Risky Radiation Tests," *Los Angeles Times*, January 8, 1994.

86. *Federalist* no. 62, p. 321.

87. William G. Howell and Kenneth R. Mayer, "The Last One Hundred Days," *Presidential Studies Quarterly* 35 (September 2005): 551.

88. "E. Political Use of Intelligence Information," Select Committee to Study Governmental Operations with Respect to Intelligence Activities, United States Senate, *Intelligence Activities and the Rights of Americans: Book II, Final Report*, April 26, 1976.

89. Barton J. Bernstein, "The Road to Watergate and Beyond: The Growth and Abuse of Executive Authority since 1940," *Law and Contemporary Problems* 40 (Spring 1976): 71.

90. John F. Kennedy, Press Conference, April 11, 1962.

91. Victor Lasky, *It Didn't Start with Watergate* (New York: Dial Press, 1977) p. 69.

92. Lasky, *It Didn't Start with Watergate*, p. 72.

93. Robert Novak, "Removing J. Edgar's Name," CNN.com, December 1, 2005; Laurence H. Silberman, "Hoover's Institution," *Wall Street Journal*, July 20, 2005.

94. Lasky, *It Didn't Start with Watergate*, pp. 171–72.

95. Lee Edwards, *Goldwater: The Man Who Made a Revolution* (Washington: Regnery, 1997), p. 310.

96. Quoted in John Herbers, "The 37th President; In Three Decades, Nixon Tasted Crisis and Defeat, Victory, Ruin and Revival," *New York Times*, April 24, 1994.

97. Paul Johnson, *A History of the American People* (New York: Harper Collins, 1998), p. 904 (emphasis added).

Chapter 4

1. See generally Peter E. Quint, "The Separation of Powers under Nixon: Reflections on Constitutional Liberties and the Rule of Law," *Duke Law Journal* 1981 (February 1981).

2. *American Federation of Government Employees v. Phillips*, 358 F. Supp. 60, 77 (D.C. 1973).

3. Philip Jenkins, *Decade of Nightmares* (New York: Oxford University Press, 2006), p. 49.

4. Christopher H. Pyle, "CONUS Intelligence: The Army Watches Civilian Politics," *Washington Monthly*, January 1970.

5. Morton H. Halperin, Jerry J. Berman, Robert L. Borosage, and Christine M. Marwick, *The Lawless State: The Crimes of the U.S. Intelligence Agencies* (New York: Penguin Books, 1976), p. 155.

6. Select Committee to Study Governmental Operations with Respect to Intelligence Activities, "Improper Surveillance of Civilians by the Military," (Church Committee) *Book III: Supplementary Detailed Staff Reports on Intelligence Activities and the Rights of Americans*, 1976.

7. Halperin et al., *The Lawless State*, p. 165.

8. Church Committee, "COINTELPRO: The FBI's Covert Action Programs against American Citizens," *Book III*, 1976.

9. James Kirkpatrick Davis, *Spying on America: The FBI's Domestic Counterintelligence Program* (New York: Praeger, 1992), p. 172. One of the Hoodwink memos is available at http://www.thesmokinggun.com/archive/hoodwink1.html.

10. Halperin et al., *The Lawless State*, p. 127.

11. Allan M. Jalon, "A Break-In to End All Break-Ins; In 1971, Stolen FBI Files Exposed the Government's Domestic Spying Program," *Los Angeles Times*, March 8, 2006.

12. Though at first Nixon saw possible political benefits in the publication of material damaging to JFK's reputation. Richard Reeves, *President Nixon: Alone in the White House* (New York: Touchstone, 2002) p. 331.

13. Morton H. Halperin, "Bush Is No Nixon—He's Worse," *Los Angeles Times*, July 16, 2006.

14. Halperin et al., *The Lawless State*, pp. 191–92.

15. David Frum, *How We Got Here: The 70's, the Decade That Brought You Modern Life—For Better or Worse* (New York: Basic Books, 2000), p. 48.

16. William Shawcross, *Sideshow: Kissinger, Nixon, and the Destruction of Cambodia* (London: Fontana Paperbacks, 1980); Christopher Hitchens, "The Case against Henry Kissinger—Former Secretary of State," *Harpers Magazine*, February 2001.

17. John Hart Ely, *War and Responsibility: Constitutional Lessons of Vietnam and Its Aftermath* (Princeton, NJ: Princeton University Press: 1993), p. 98.

18. Richard M. Nixon, remarks at the Veterans of Foreign Wars National Convention, New Orleans, Louisiana, August 20, 1973.

19. *New York Times Co. v. United States*, 403 U.S. 713 (1971).

20. *New York Times Co. v. United States*, at 718, J. Black concurring.

21. "Oval Office Meeting with Bob Haldeman, 3:09 PM," Nixon Presidential Materials Project, National Security Archive, George Washington University, June 14, 1971.

22. *United States v. United States District Court*, 407 U.S. 297 (1972).

23. Quint, "Separation of Powers," pp. 19–20.

24. *Keith*, 407 U.S. at 317.

25. *United States v. Nixon*, 418 U.S. 683 (1974).

26. Quoted in Andrew Rudalevige, *The New Imperial Presidency: Renewing Presidential Power after Watergate* (Ann Arbor: University of Michigan Press, 2005), p. 105.

27. Quint, "Separation of Powers," p. 30.

28. Quoted in Paul Haskell Zernicke, "Presidents on the Textbook Presidency," *Social Science Journal* 30 (October 1, 1993).

29. Tim Weiner, "Hoover Planned Mass Jailing in 1950," *New York Times*, December 23, 2007.

30. 18 U.S.C. §4001(a). See Louis Fisher, "Detention of U.S. Citizens," *CRS Report for Congress*, RS22130, April 28, 2005.

31. Harold C. Relyea, "National Emergency Powers," *CRS Report for Congress 98-505 GOV*, updated September 15, 2005, pp. 3–4.

32. P.L. 93-148, Sec. 2(a).

33. The president can extend the 60-day deadline by 30 days if he certifies that there is an "unavoidable military necessity respecting the safety of United States Armed Forces," Sec. 5(b)(3).

34. P.L. 93-189. See Andrew Rudalevige, *The New Imperial Presidency: Renewing Presidential Power after Watergate* (Ann Arbor: University of Michigan Press, 2005), chap. 4 and 5, for a discussion of Watergate reforms and their unraveling.

35. "Veto Battle 30 Years Ago Set Freedom of Information Norms," *National Security Archive Electronic Briefing Book No. 142*, posted November 23, 2004. Other reforms helped bolster the new policy of openness. Keeping secret files on Americans would be harder after the passage of the Privacy Act of 1974, which gave U.S. citizens presumptive access to information about them held by the executive branch and limited the transfer of such information between agencies. P.L. 93-579.

36. P.L. 95-511.

37. For instance, the independent counsel provisions of 1978's Ethics in Government Act aimed at a real problem: the difficulties inherent in expecting the executive branch to investigate itself. But the mechanism it set up to address that problem was constitutionally dubious and would result in a number of expen-

sive, distracting prosecutions that the public would have been better off without. See Linda Greenhouse, "Blank Check; Ethics in Government: The Price of Good Intentions," *New York Times*, February 1, 1998. Another "clean government" initiative, the 1974 amendments to the Federal Election Campaign Act, placed tight limits on campaign contributions and put federal regulators in the business of regulating and rationing political speech. See generally John Samples, *The Fallacy of Campaign Finance Reform* (Chicago: University of Chicago Press, 2006).

38. David Frum, *How We Got Here*, p. 32.

39. Not an acronym. Apparently, the CIA just thought "CHAOS" had a nice ring to it. Agents conducted "black-bag jobs" (burglaries for the purpose of gathering information), opened mail, and kept files on thousands of Americans. See Halperin et al., *The Lawless State*, pp. 148–54.

40. Church Committee, "CIA Intelligence Collection about Americans; CHAOS and the Office of Security," *Book III*; Rudalevige, *The New Imperial Presidency*, p. 66.

41. See generally Frederick A. O. Schwarz Jr. and Aziz Huq, "Revelations of the Church Committee," in *Unchecked and Unbalanced: Presidential Power in a Time of Terror* (New York: New Press, 2007), pp. 19–47.

42. Church Committee, "Conclusions and Recommendations," *Book II: Intelligence Activities and the Rights of Americans*.

43. American National Election Studies, "Trust the Federal Government (4–point Scale)," *The ANES Guide to Public Opinion and Political Behavior*.

44. F. Christopher Arterton, "Watergate and Children's Attitudes toward Political Authority Revisited," *Political Science Quarterly* 90 (Autumn 1975).

45. Alan Schroeder, *Celebrity-in-Chief: How Show Business Took over the White House* (Boulder, CO: Westview Press, 2004), p. 285.

46. John Matvitko, "Television Satire and the Presidency: The Case of Saturday Night Live," in *Hollywood's White House: The American Presidency in Film and History*, ed. Peter C. Rollins and John E. O'Connor (Lexington: University Press of Kentucky, 2004), 336–37; and "SNL Transcripts: Ron Nessen: 4/17/76," SNL Transcripts Tonight, transcript.

47. S. Robert Lichter, Linda S. Lichter, and Daniel Amundson, "Government Goes Down the Tube: Images of Government in TV Entertainment, 1955–1998," *Harvard International Journal of Press/Politics* 5 (March 2000): 98.

48. Thomas Patterson, *Out of Order* (New York: Vintage Books, 1994), p. 19.

49. Richard Reeves, *President Kennedy: Profile of Power* (New York: Touchstone, 1993), p. 110.

50. Steven E. Clayman, Marc N. Elliot, John Heritage, and Laurie L. McDonald, "Historical Trends in Questioning Presidents, 1953–2000," *Presidential Studies Quarterly* 36 (December 2006): 580. Though some might suspect that growing Republican dominance of the executive branch and partisan bias by reporters explain much of the enhanced assertiveness, the authors find the "liberal media bias" explanation unpersuasive: "Although it is true that the more volatile dimensions [of reportorial aggressiveness] steadily rose during mostly Republican administrations (Nixon through first-term Reagan), the subsequent period of decline also occurred under Republicans (second-term Reagan through Bush), and the more recent increase occurred when a Democrat (Clinton) occupied the

White House. The volatile dimensions thus do not correlate with the president's party affiliation."

51. Peter Wallsten, "All This President's Men; Watergate's Links to the Bush White House," *Toronto Star*, June 11, 2005.

52. Richard B. Cheney, "The Significance of Campaign '84," *Presidential Studies Quarterly* 14 (Summer 1984): 334.

53. Conservatives had also pushed unsuccessfully for the Bricker Amendment, which would have restricted the use of executive agreements with other countries and limited the president and the Senate's ability to weaken the U.S. Constitution through use of the treaty power. See Nelson Richards, "The Bricker Amendment and Congress's Failure to Check the Inflation of the Executive's Foreign Affairs Powers, 1951–1954," *California Law Review* 94 (January 2006).

54. Russell Kirk, "Ten Conservative Principles (1993)," Russell Kirk Center for Cultural Renewal.

55. Willmoore Kendall, "The Two Majorities," *Midwest Journal of Political Science* (November 1960): 344.

56. Russell Kirk and James McClellan, *The Political Principles of Robert A. Taft* (New York: Fleet Press, 1967), p. 163.

57. James Burnham, *Congress and the American Tradition* (Chicago: Henry Regnery Co., 1959), p. 352. Burnham recognized that "by the intent of the Founding Fathers and the letter and tradition of the Constitution, the bulk of the sovereign war power was assigned to Congress." But he doubted that congressional control of the war power could be maintained, given the demands of modern war. See pp. 191–92.

58. Quoted in Marcus Cunliffe, *The Presidency* (Boston: Houghton Mifflin Co., 1987), p. 120.

59. Ronald Reagan, "Address on Behalf of Senator Barry Goldwater," October 27, 1964.

60. In 1960's *The Conscience of a Conservative*, Goldwater described the actions he thought the United States ought to take in the event of another Eastern European uprising along the lines of the 1956 Hungarian Revolution:

> In such a situation, we ought to present the Kremlin with an ultimatum forbidding Soviet intervention, and be prepared, if the ultimatum is rejected, to move a highly mobile task force equipped with appropriate nuclear weapons to the scene of the revolt. Our objective would be to confront the Soviet Union with superior force in the immediate vicinity of the uprising and to compel a Soviet withdrawal. An actual clash between American and Soviet armies would be unlikely; the mere threat of American action, coupled with the Kremlin's knowledge that the fighting would occur amid a hostile population and could easily spread to other areas, would probably result in Soviet acceptance of the ultimatum.

Of course, such a policy would put the United States on the brink of nuclear war without any decision by Congress. As Goldwater admitted a paragraph later, "Any policy that successfully frustrates the Communist aim of world domination runs the risk that the Kremlin will choose to lose in a kamikaze-finish." Barry Goldwater, *The Conscience of a Conservative* (New York: McFadden Capitol Hill Books, 1960), pp. 124–26.

61. J. Richard Piper, "Presidential-Congressional Power Prescriptions in Conservative Political Thought since 1933," *Presidential Studies Quarterly* 21 (Winter 1991): 40–41.

62. Piper, "Presidential-Congressional Power," p. 40.

63. Willmoore Kendall and George W. Carey, *Liberalism versus Conservatism: The Continuing Debate in American Government* (Princeton, NJ: D. Van Nostrand Company, Inc., 1966), pp. 224–25.

64. Rick Perlstein, "'I Didn't Like Nixon *until* Watergate': The Conservative Movement Now," *Huffington Post*, December 5, 2005.

65. Jeffrey Hart, "The Presidency: Shifting Conservative Perspectives?" *National Review*, November 22, 1974. In recent years, Hart has had occasion to rethink the virtues of a powerful presidency. He wrote in 2006 that

> because Bush is an ideologue remote from fact, he has failed comprehensively and surely is the worst president in American history—indeed, in the damage he has caused to the nation, without a rival in the race for the bottom. Because Bush is generally called a conservative, he will have poisoned the term for decades to come.

Jeffrey Hart, "What Is Left? What Is Right?" *The American Conservative*, August 28, 2006.

66. Piper, "Presidential-Congressional Power Prescriptions," p. 44 and Table 2, p. 45.

67. J. Richard Piper, "Situational Constitutionalism and Presidential Power: The Rise and Fall of the Liberal Model of Presidential Government," *Presidential Studies Quarterly* 24 (Summer 1994).

68. Irving Kristol, "The Inexorable Rise of the Executive," *Wall Street Journal*, September 20, 1974.

69. Tom Morganthau with Margaret Garrand Warner and Pat Wingert, "Four More Years? An Unlikely Movement Pushes to Repeal the Constitution's 22nd Amendment," *Newsweek*, September 8, 1986.

70. Newt Gingrich, "Foreword," in *The Imperial Congress: Crisis in the Separation of Powers*, ed. Gordon S. Jones and John A. Marini (New York: Pharos Books, 1988), p. ix. Other conservative books taking similar positions include L. Gordon Crovitz and Jeremy A. Rabkin, eds., *The Fettered Presidency: Legal Constraints on the Executive Branch* (Washington: American Enterprise Institute, 1989); and Terry Eastland, *Energy in the Executive: The Case for the Strong Presidency* (Toronto: Maxwell MacMillan International, 1992).

71. Ryan J. Barilleaux, *The Post-Modern Presidency: The Office After Ronald Reagan* (New York: Praeger, 1988), p. 55.

72. P.L. 98-473; see Louis Fisher, *Constitutional Conflicts between Congress and the President*, 4th ed. rev. (Lawrence: University Press of Kansas, 1997), pp. 219–20.

73. See Richard F. Grimmett, "The War Powers Resolution after Thirty Years," *CRS Report for Congress RL 32267*, March 11, 2004.

74. Planning for the invasion had begun before the truck bombing, so it's not clear what effect the events in Lebanon had on the decision to authorize the invasion. Denise M. Bostdorff, *The Presidency and the Rhetoric of Foreign Crisis* (Columbia: University of South Carolina Press, 1994). p. 182.

75. Charlie Savage, *Takeover: The Return of the Imperial Presidency* (New York: Little, Brown and Co., 2007), p. 61.

76. Scott Peterson, "In War, Some Facts Less Factual," *Christian Science Monitor*, September 6, 2002.

77. James David Barber, "Empire of the Son; How George Bush Rewrote the Book on the Imperial Presidency," *Washington Monthly*, October 1991.

78. Quoted in Fisher, *Presidential War Power* (Lawrence: University Press of Kansas, 1995), p. 151.

79. See generally Gene Healy, "Arrogance of Power Reborn: The Imperial Presidency and Foreign Policy in the Clinton Years," Cato Institute Policy Analysis no. 389, December 13, 2000.

80. Chris Black, "Gov. Clinton of Arkansas Joins the Presidential Race," *Boston Globe*, October 4, 1991; Martha Sherrill, "Hillary Clinton's Inner Politics: As the First Lady Grows Comfortable in Her Roles, She Is Looking Beyond Policy to a Moral Agenda," *Washington Post*, May 6, 1993.

81. William G. Howell, *Power without Persuasion: The Politics of Direct Presidential Action* (Princeton, NJ: Princeton University Press, 2003), pp. 5–6.

82. Sen. J. William Fulbright, *The Arrogance of Power* (New York: Vintage Books, 1966), p. 248.

83. Quoted in *Congressional Record*, August 5, 1994, 140, S10,663.

84. Jim Landers, " Expanded Role for Troops Detailed," *Dallas Morning News*, June 8, 1995; Kathryn Q. Seelye, "House Defeats Bid to Repeal 'War Powers,'" *New York Times*, June 8, 1995.

85. See Major Geoffrey S. Corn, "Clinton, Kosovo, and the Final Destruction of the War Powers Resolution," *William and Mary Law Review* 42 (April 2001).

86. Quoted in Charles Lane, "TRB: Something to Declare," *New Republic*, May 17, 1999.

87. See David Gray Adler, "*The Law:* The Clinton Theory of the War Power," *Presidential Studies Quarterly* 30 (March 2002).

88. Quoted in Jake Tapper, "Declaring War on Undeclared War," *Salon*, May 6, 1999.

89. Michael J. Fitts, "Symposium: The Legalization of the Presidency: A Twenty-Five Year Watergate Retrospective," *St. Louis Law Journal* 43 (Summer 1999): 733.

90. James Risen and David Johnston, "Experts Find No Arms Chemicals at Bombed Sudan Plant," *New York Times*, February 9, 1999.

91. "Remarks by President Clinton on Iraq," United Press International, December 16, 1998.

92. David Broder, "Hard Faces of Partisanship," *Washington Post*, December 19, 1998.

93. William Safire, "On Impeachment Eve," *New York Times*, December 17, 1998.

94. Ambrose Bierce, *The Devil's Dictionary* (New York: Dover Publications, 1993), p. 21.

95. Gregory D. Hess and Athanasios Orphanides, "War Politics: An Economic, Rational-Voter Framework," *American Economic Review* 85 (September 1995): 842.

96. James Madison, "Helvidius No. IV," in *The Letters of Pacificus and Helvidius (1845) with the Letters of Americanus* (New York: Scholars' Facsimiles & Reprints, 1976), pp. 89–90.

97. Trust rebounded somewhat after 1994. By 2000, the National Election Studies numbers for "Most of the Time/Just about Always" had reached 44 percent, but

remained still well below the 60-plus figures that prevailed before 1970. See "Trust the Federal Government," *ANES Guide to Public Opinion and Electoral Behavior.*

98. Susan J. Pharr, Robert D. Putnam, and Russell J. Dalton, "A Quarter-Century of Declining Confidence," *Journal of Democracy* 11 (April 2000): 9.

99. "Tapes Show Nixon Ordering Theft of Files," *New York Times*, November 22, 1996; Christopher Matthews, "Nixon Personally Ordered Break-In: He's on Tape Demanding Theft at Brookings Think Tank," *San Francisco Examiner*, November 21, 1996.

100. Bernard Bailyn, *The Ideological Origins of the American Revolution* (Cambridge, MA: Belknap Press, 1967, 1992), p. 368.

101. P.L. 100-707.

102. Gary L. Wamsley and Aaron D. Schroeder, "Escalating in a Quagmire: The Changing Dynamics of the Emergency Management Policy Subsystem," *Public Administration Review* 56 (May/June 1996): 236.

103. James Bovard, " Disaster Racketeering for Political Profit," *Washington Times*, October 2, 1996.

104. Andrew Reeves, "Political Disaster? Presidential Disaster Declarations and Electoral Politics," January 2004; Thomas A. Garrett and Russell S. Sobel, "The Political Economy of FEMA Disaster Payments," *Economic Inquiry* 41 (July 2003): 496–509.

105. Task Force on Federalization of Criminal Law, American Bar Association, Criminal Justice Section, "The Federalization of Criminal Law" (1998). See generally Gene Healy, ed., *Go Directly to Jail: The Criminalization of Almost Everything* (Washington: Cato Institute, 2004).

106. John S. Baker Jr., "Measuring the Explosive Growth of Federal Crime Legislation," *Federalist Society Review* 5, no. 2 (October 2004).

107. Elvin T. Lim, "Five Trends in Presidential Rhetoric: An Analysis of Rhetoric from George Washington to Bill Clinton," *Presidential Studies Quarterly* 32 (June 2002): 339.

108. George H. W. Bush, State of the Union address, January 28, 1992; William Jefferson Clinton, State of the Union address, February 4, 1997.

109. Pew Research Center for the People and the Press, "How Americans View Government: Deconstructing Distrust," Washington, March 10, 1998, p. 1.

110. Pew, "How Americans View Government," p. 46.

111. Pew, "How Americans View Government," p. 39.

112. Pew, "How Americans View Government," p. 38.

113. "The 1992 Campaign; Transcript of 2d TV Debate between Bush, Clinton and Perot," *New York Times*, October 16, 1992 (emphasis added).

114. Joe Klein, "The Nervous '90s," *Newsweek*, May 1, 1995: "'I would have told that guy to get a hold of himself, get a life,' says William Bennett, author of the *Book of Virtues.* "

115. "The 1992 Campaign."

116. "Nixon and Kissinger: Triumph and Trial," *Time*, January 1, 1973.

117. Sandra Sobieraj, "Gore: Militias and 'Extreme Individualism,'" Associated Press, June 12, 1997. Interestingly, both Nixon's and Gore's comments can be read as mild critiques of the Denton Walthall mentality. In the interview, Nixon continued, "If on the other hand you make [the average American] completely dependent and pamper him and cater to him too much, you are going to make him soft, spoiled

and eventually a very weak individual." In Gore's speech, the "grandparents" line is preceded by "the federal government should never be the baby sitter, the parents." But even as they invoked notions of individual responsibility, neither Nixon nor Gore found anything inappropriate about comparing Americans with children.

118. Clinton Rossiter, *The American Presidency* (Baltimore: Johns Hopkins University Press, 1956, 1987), p. 23.

119. Rossiter, *The American Presidency,* p. 28.

120. "Contemporary presidential approval ratings generally peak 10% to 15% below those achieved at the beginning of the survey era." Marc J. Hetherington, "The Political Relevance of Political Trust," *American Political Science Review* (December 1998): 791.

Chapter 5

1. Kenneth T. Walsh, "A New World Disorder: Untested No More, the New President Faces a Historic Challenge," *U.S. News and World Report,* September 14, 2001.

2. Bill Sammon, "Suddenly, a Time to Lead: 'Difficult Moment for America' Transforms the President," *Washington Times,* October 7, 2002.

3. Sammon, "A Time to Lead."

4. Jerry Schwartz, "Planes Crash into World Trade Center, Creating Horrifying Scene; No Word on Casualties," Associated Press, September 11, 2001.

5. William Langley, "Revealed: What Really Went on during Bush's 'Missing Hours,'" *Telegraph,* December 16, 2001.

6. Statement by the President in His Address to the Nation, September 11, 2001.

7. Bill Broadway, "War Cry from the Pulpit," *Washington Post,* September 22, 2001 (emphasis added).

8. Barton Gellman and Mike Allen, "The Week That Redefined the Bush Presidency; President Sets Nation on New Course," *Washington Post,* September 23, 2001.

9. George W. Bush, Address to a Joint Session of Congress and the American People, September 20, 2001.

10. Presidential speech, *ABC News* Special Report, September 20, 2001.

11. "Washington Post Poll: War on Terrorism," *Washington Post,* September 28, 2001.

12. Leonie Huddy, Nadia Khatib, and Theresa Capelos, "The Polls—Trends: Reactions to the Terrorist Attacks of September 11, 2001," *Public Opinion Quarterly* 66 (Fall 2002): 431.

13. Gary C. Jacobson, "The Bush Presidency and the American Electorate," *Presidential Studies Quarterly* 33 (December 2003).

14. Gary L. Gregg II, "Crisis Leadership: The Symbolic Transformation of the Bush Presidency," *Perspectives on Political Science* 32 (Summer 2003): 143.

15. Roger Rosenblatt, "The Age of Irony Comes to an End," *Time,* September 24, 2001.

16. Dick Polman, "A President Pardoned," *Philadelphia Inquirer Magazine,* January 6, 2002.

17. J. Hoberman, "That's Our Bush!" *OC Weekly,* September 5, 2003.

18. Peggy Noonan, "God Is Back," *Wall Street Journal,* September 28, 2001.

19. Peggy Noonan, "The Phony War," *Wall Street Journal*, November 9, 2001.

20. Peggy Noonan, "Why Did They Do It?" *Wall Street Journal*, April 24, 2000.

21. Fred Barnes, "Man with a Mission," *Weekly Standard*, October 8, 2001.

22. Todd S. Purdum, "What, Us Worry?" *New York Times*, March 19, 1995.

23. Thomas H. Sander and Robert D. Putnam, "Walking the Civic Talk after Sept. 11," *Christian Science Monitor*, February 19, 2002.

24. Robert Putnam, "Bowling Together: The United State of America," *American Prospect*, February 11, 2002.

25. Peter Beinart, "A Fighting Faith," *New Republic*, December 13, 2004.

26. Beinart, "A Fighting Faith"; Lawrence F. Kaplan, "American Idle: Four Years after September 11, We're Still Bowling Alone," *New Republic*, September 12, 2005.

27. See, for example, Robert E. Litan, "September 11, 2001: The Case for Universal Service," *Brookings Review*, September 22, 2002; E. J. Dionne, Kayla Meltzer Drogosz, and Robert E. Litan, eds., *United We Serve: National Service and the Future of Citizenship* (Washington: Brookings Institution Press, 2003).

28. Chris Hedges, *War Is a Force That Gives Us Meaning* (New York: Anchor Books, 2002).

29. See, for example, David Brooks, "TR's Greatness," *Weekly Standard*, November 19, 2001.

30. David Brooks, "A Return to National Greatness: A Manifesto for a Lost Creed," *Weekly Standard*, March 3, 1997.

31. William Kristol and David Brooks, "What Ails Conservatism," *Wall Street Journal*, September 15, 1997.

32. Virginia Postrel, "The Croly Ghost: Exorcising the Specter Haunting American Politics," *Reason*, December 1997.

33. Brooks, "A Return to National Greatness."

34. William Kristol and Robert Kagan, "Toward a Neo-Reaganite Foreign Policy," *Foreign Affairs*, July/August 1996.

35. Jonathan Clarke, "The Guns of 17th Street," *National Interest*, Spring 2001.

36. David Brooks, "Normal, U.S.A.: Amidst the Terror, We're Turning Back to the Attitudes Which Made America Great," *Weekly Standard*, October 5, 2001.

37. Damian Whitworth, "Utah Goes on to War Footing for Winter Games," *Times* (London), February 8, 2002.

38. *Youngstown Sheet & Tube Co. v. Sawyer*, 343 U.S. 579, 644 (1952), J. Jackson concurring.

39. Kim Barker and Tom McCann, "Sense of Necessity Tempers the Fear," *Chicago Tribune*, October 8, 2001.

40. Michael Grunwald, "Terrorists Hijack 4 Airliners, Destroy World Trade Center, Hit Pentagon; Hundreds Dead," *Washington Post*, September 12, 2001.

41. Mike Glover, "Gore Sets Solemn Tone in Low-Key Swing through Iowa," Associated Press, September 29, 2001.

42. Kent Ward, "Catchy Slogans, Logos and the Upside-Down 'WIN' Button," *Bangor (ME) Daily News* August 5, 2006.

43. Judy Keen and Laurence McQuillan, "President Prepares for Strong Response," *USA Today*, September 13, 2001.

44. Colin S. Gray, *Maintaining Effective Deterrence* (Carlisle, PA: Strategic Studies Institute, U.S. Army War College, 2003), p. 5.

45. George W. Bush, State of the Union address, January 29, 2002.

46. Quoted in Tom Jackman, "U.S. a Battlefield, Solicitor General Tells Judges," *Washington Post*, July 20, 2005.

47. George W. Bush, *The National Security Strategy of the United States of America* (Washington: White House, September 17, 2002), p. 5.

48. "Elmo Testifies at Congressional Hearing to Ask for Federal Money to Help Provide Music Education in Elementary Schools," CBS News Transcripts, *CBS Morning News*, April 24, 2002.

49. Amy Fagen, "Elmo Goes to Bat for Education: Sesame Street Puppet Plugs Music Programs in School," *Washington Times*, April 24, 2002; "Mr. Elmo Goes to Washington," CNN.com, April 24, 2002.

50. Arthur Schlesinger Jr., *The Imperial Presidency* (Boston: Houghton Mifflin Co., 1973), p. ix.

51. *Chevron v. Natural Resources Defense Council*, 467 U.S. 837 (1984).

52. See Gary Lawson, "The Rise and Rise of the Administrative State," *Harvard Law Review* 107 (April 1994); David Schoenbrod, *Power without Responsibility: How Congress Abuses the People through Delegation* (New Haven, CT: Yale University Press, 1993).

53. David Schoenbrod and Jerry Taylor, "The Delegation of Legislative Powers," *Cato Handbook for the 108th Congress* (Washington: Cato Institute, 2002), p. 80.

54. Elizabeth McCaughey, "No Exit," *New Republic*, February 7, 1994.

55. Adam Nagourney, "'McCain-Feingold School' Finds Many Bewildered," *New York Times*, February 19, 2003.

56. Thomas S. Vontz and Sarah E. Drake, "Teaching about the U.S. Congress," *ERIC Digest*, Educational Resources Information Center, March 2001.

57. Abraham Lincoln, First Annual Message, December 3, 1861.

58. In the 108th Congress, for example, any representative who cared to read the 1,507-page fiscal year 2003 Omnibus Appropriations Bill had 12 hours to do so. Members would have had to read the FY 04 defense authorization bill at a rate of three pages a minute during the five hours it was available before the floor vote to discharge their responsibilities. House Rules Committee Minority Office, "Broken Promises: The Death of Deliberative Democracy," March 8, 2005, p. 39.

59. In November 2003, under pressure from the Bush administration, the Republican leadership gave members just over 24 hours to review the 850-page Medicare prescription drug bill, the largest expansion of a federal entitlement program since the Great Society. House Rules Committee, "Broken Promises," p. 42. It later emerged that in the effort to force the bill through, the Bush administration had suppressed cost estimates showing that over the first 10 years, the bill would cost $139 billion more than had been advertised—an estimate that itself turned out to be understated. Amy Goldstein, "Foster: White House Had Role in Withholding Medicare Data," *Washington Post*, March 19, 2004.

60. Jake Tapper, "Squabbling Returns," Salon.com, October 3, 2001.

61. Jesse Walker, "Panic Attacks: Drawing the Thin Line between Caution and Hysteria after September 11," *Reason*, March 1, 2002. Of course, even if they'd had the bill, and the time and inclination to read it, members still might not have understood what they were voting for or against. The Patriot Act was 346 pages of dense legalese.

62. Nancy Kassop, "The War Power and Its Limits," *Presidential Studies Quarterly* 33 (September 1, 2003).

63. P.L. 107-40, Sec. 2(a) (emphasis added).

64. Sec. 7(b)(2) of the military order provides, "The individual shall not be privileged to seek any remedy or maintain any proceeding, directly or indirectly, or to have any such remedy or proceeding sought on the individual's behalf, in (i) any court of the United States, or any State thereof." That order has been superseded by the Military Commissions Act (P.L. 109-366) passed on October 17, 2006.

65. By holding that the president had exceeded his constitutional and statutory authority in the November 2001 military order, the Supreme Court's 2006 *Hamdan* decision forced Congress to act, at which point Congress, in the Military Commissions Act of 2006, codified most of what the president had ordered unilaterally five years before.

66. Mike Allen and Juliet Eilperin, "Bush Aides Say Iraq War Needs No Hill Vote; Some See Such Support as Politically Helpful," *Washington Post*, August 26, 2002.

67. Memorandum from John Yoo, Deputy Assistant Attorney General, Office of Legal Counsel, to Timothy Flanigan, Deputy Counsel to the President, "The President's Constitutional Authority to Conduct Military Operations against Terrorists and Nations Supporting Them," September 25, 2001.

68. David Rogers, "Pentagon Funded Mideast Plans in Secret prior to Iraq-War Vote," *Wall Street Journal*, April 22, 2004.

69. The amount is disputed. The administration admits that Central Command requested over $700 million, but asserts that only $178.4 million was committed. Bob Woodward, in his book *Plan of Attack*, writes that the administration drew some $700 million from prior appropriations, including funds to fight the war in Afghanistan. See also Cass R. Sunstein, "The Secret $700 Million," Salon.com, April 22, 2004.

70. Allen and Eilperin, "Iraq War Needs No Hill Vote."

71. David Firestone with David E. Sanger, "Traces of Terror: Washington; Congress Now Promises to Hold Weeks of Hearings about Iraq," *New York Times*, September 6, 2002.

72. How could a joint resolution passed in 1991 to authorize Gulf War I be read to authorize Gulf War II in 2002? A good question, the answer to which was not at all apparent from reading the resolution. The key clause of the Gulf War resolution incorporates a dozen United Nations Security Council resolutions and authorizes using the U.S. armed forces to implement them. None of the enumerated Security Council resolutions even mentions weapons of mass destruction or Hussein's involvement with international terrorism. Instead, they all condemn the dictator's swallowing Kuwait and focus on various means to get him to disgorge it. P.L. 102-1. By authorizing a war to expel Hussein from Kuwait, did Congress in 1991 somehow delegate warmaking authority in perpetuity to the president— authorizing any future war that might be contemplated in the region?

73. "Dugout Briefing with Senate Minority Leader Trent Lott (R-MS)," Federal News Service, July 31, 2002.

74. Among them, Defense Secretary Donald Rumsfeld's assertions that there was "bulletproof" evidence of a Saddam–al Qaeda link and Vice President Cheney's

claim that "we do know, with absolute certainty, that [Saddam Hussein] is using his procurement system to acquire the equipment he needs in order to enrich uranium to build a nuclear weapon." That too was a misrepresentation, unless one entirely discounted strong doubts about that claim by the State Department's intelligence service and the Department of Energy's nuclear experts. Despite being directly informed by Central Intelligence Agency Director George Tenet in September 2002 about those doubts and the fact that they were shared by some CIA analysts, President Bush repeated the claim in an October 7 speech in Cincinnati. For an overview of false and misleading administration claims in the Iraq War, see Chaim Kaufmann, "Threat Inflation and the Failure of the Marketplace of Ideas: The Selling of the Iraq War," *International Security* 29 (Summer 2004); James Pfiffner, "Did President Bush Mislead the Country in His Arguments for War with Iraq?" *Presidential Studies Quarterly* 34 (March 2004): 26. Murray Waas, "Prewar Intelligence: Insulating Bush,"*National Journal*, March 30, 2006.

75. "President Bush Outlines Iraqi Threat," Cincinnati, OH, October 7, 2002. In the National Intelligence Estimate, the director of Air Force intelligence maintained that the Iraqi unmanned aerial vehicles were unsuited to carry weapons of mass destruction and were most likely for reconnaissance missions. Joseph Cirincione, Jessica Tuchman Mathews, and George Perkovich, with Alexis Orton, "WMD in Iraq: Evidence and Implications," Carnegie Endowment for International Peace, Washington, January 2004, p. 42.

76. Greg Bruno and Sharon Otterman, "INTELLIGENCE: National Intelligence Estimates," *Backgrounder*, Council on Foreign Relations, July 15, 2004, last updated May 14, 2008.

77. Adam Entous, "Kerry Didn't Read Iraq Report before Vote—Aides," *Reuters*, July 14, 2004.

78. Patrick Healy and Marc Santora, "Aide Says Edwards Misspoke on Reading Classified Iraq Report," *New York Times*, June 1, 2007.

79. Dana Priest, "Congressional Oversight of Intelligence Criticized," *Washington Post*, March 27, 2004. The October 2002 NIE was under 100 pages, and, judging by the portions declassified in July 2003, well within the reading comprehension abilities of your average senator or representative. It is available at the Federation of American Scientists Intelligence Resource Program.

80. They could have read the dissenting views on Iraqi WMDs offered by the State Department's Bureau of Intelligence and Research, which said the government "lack[ed] persuasive evidence that Baghdad has launched a coherent effort to reconstitute its nuclear weapons program." Dana Milbank and Mike Allen, "Iraq Flap Shakes Rice's Image," *Washington Post*, July 27, 2003. They would have learned that both the State Department and nuclear experts from the Department of Energy believed that Iraq had purchased aluminum tubes not for use in centrifuges, but "most likely for the production of artillery shells." Murray Waas, "Prewar Intelligence."

81. By late September 2002, the administration had backed off a bit from the rationale that the Gulf War I resolution authorized Gulf War II. But the Bush team still, unsurprisingly, pushed for a broader grant of authority than it needed. The original resolution offered by the administration included the phrase "to use all means that he determines to be appropriate" to "restore international peace and security in the region," a formulation that could be construed—especially by an

administration as dedicated as this one to stretching its authority to the utmost—to authorize action against other malefactors like Syria and Iran. Todd S. Purdum and Elisabeth Bumiller, "Threats and Responses: White House; Bush Seeks Power to Use 'All Means' to Oust Hussein," *New York Times*, September 20, 2002.

82. P.L. 107-243, Sec. 3(a).

83. Anne Q. Hoy, "Clinton, Schumer Weigh Iraq Proposals," *Newsday*, October 6, 2002.

84. Ken Fireman and Anne Q. Hoy, "CIA's View of Iraq; Documents Say Unprovoked Attack by Hussein Unlikely," *Newsday*, October 9, 2002.

85. Elisabeth Bumiller and Carl Hulse, "Threats and Responses: The Overview; Bush Will Use Congress Vote to Press U.N.," *New York Times*, October 12, 2002.

86. David Firestone, "Threats and Responses: The Debate; 2 Critics of Bush Iraq Policy Say They'll Back Resolution," *New York Times*, October 10, 2002.

87. Maggie Haberman, "Hillary Does Iraq Flip," *New York Post*, January 23, 2007.

88. Gaillard Hunt, ed., *The Writings of James Madison*, Vol. 6 (New York: G. P. Putnam's Sons, 1906), p. 148 (emphasis in original).

89. Arthur Schlesinger, Jr., *The Imperial Presidency*, pp. 28–29.

90. S. 3111; S. 3118; H.R. 4015.

91. Editorial: "Spinning on Iraq," *Washington Post*, September 26, 2002.

92. Steven Thomma, "Bush's Push for War Changes Political Landscape of Elections," Knight Ridder Washington Bureau, September 27, 2002.

93. In November 2002, Kerry pushed ahead with a bill he cosponsored to relieve major telecom companies like Verizon and AT&T from paying more than $16 billion for spectrum licenses purchased at government auction. Around the same time, Kerry moved to increase funding for the Small Business Administration's key loan program, a program that had been cut because of the unusually high default rate on the loans. Cromwell Schubarth, "Bizlines; SBA Program Knows Its Limitations," *Boston Herald*, November 14, 2002. Later, as the battle for Baghdad raged in April 2003, Senator Kerry's website boasted that he had helped secure a $3.75 million loan for the Massachusetts Museum of Contemporary Art. "Kerry, Kennedy, and Olver Announce $3.75 Million for Mass MoCA," press release, April 8, 2003.

94. See generally David R. Mayhew, *Congress: The Electoral Connection* (New Haven, CT: Yale University Press, 1974).

95. Charles Babington and Dan Balz, "Democrats Press Bush Harder on Iraq," *Washington Post*, June 22, 2005.

96. John Hart Ely, *War and Responsibility* (Princeton, NJ: Princeton University Press, 1993), p. 52.

97. "The Big Picture: 2004 Cycle, Reelection Rates over the Years," OpenSecrets.

98. Remarks by Senator Miller to the Republican National Convention, September 1, 2004 (emphasis added).

99. Michael Nelson, "George W. Bush and Congress: The Electoral Connection," *Perspectives on Political Science* 32 (June 22, 2003).

Chapter 6

1. Transcript, *Meet the Press with Tim Russert*, February 8, 2004.

2. Office of Homeland Security, *National Strategy for Homeland Security*, July 2002, p. 48.

3. Mary H. Cooper, "The New Defense Priorities," *Congressional Quarterly Weekly*, September 13, 2002.

4. Robert Block and Gary Fields, "Is the Military Creeping into Domestic Spying and Enforcement?" *Wall Street Journal*, March 9, 2004.

5. Kevin Baker, "We're in the Army Now: The GOP's Plan to Militarize Our Culture," *Harper's Magazine*, October 2003.

6. For martial themes in American presidential campaigns, see Christine Scriabine, "American Attitudes towards a Martial Presidency: Some Insights from Material Culture," *Military Affairs* 47 (December 1983).

7. Lawrence F. Kaplan, "Apocalypse Kerry," *TNR Online*, July 30, 2004.

8. Andrew J. Bacevich, *The New American Militarism: How Americans Are Seduced by War* (New York: Oxford University Press, 2005), pp. 30–31.

9. Arthur Ekirch, *The Civilian and the Military: A History of the American Antimilitarist Tradition* (Colorado Springs: Ralph Myles, 1972), pp. 22, 43.

10. Bernard Bailyn, *The Ideological Origins of the American Revolution* (Cambridge, MA: Belknap Press, 1967, 1992), pp. 61–62, quoting John Trenchard.

11. Andrew J. Bacevich, *The New American Militarism: How Americans Are Seduced by War* (New York: Oxford University Press, 2005), pp. 32–33 (emphasis in original).

12. James Madison, "Political Observations," *Letters and Other Writings of James Madison* (Philadelphia: J. B. Lippincott, 1865), pp. 491–92.

13. James McClellan and M. E. Bradford, eds., *Elliot's Debates, Vol. III: Debates in the Federal Convention of 1787* (Richmond, VA: James River Press, 1989), p. 208.

14. Chitra Ragavan, "Cheney's Guy: He's Barely Known outside Washington's Corridors of Power, but David Addington Is the Most Powerful Man You've Never Heard of. Here's Why," *U.S. News & World Report*, May 21, 2006.

15. See "A Guide to the Memos on Torture," *New York Times*.

16. 18 U.S.C. § 2340A; 18 U.S.C. § 2441. See "U.N. Convention against Torture (CAT): Overview and Application to Interrogation Techniques," *CRS Report for Congress*, RL32438, February 10, 2005; and "The War Crimes Act: Current Issues," *CRS Report for Congress*, RL33662, September 25, 2006, on the War Crimes Act of 1996, which criminalizes violations of Common Article 3 of the Geneva Conventions.

17. The legal reasoning employed in the August 2002 memo resurfaces in a March 2003 Pentagon memo prepared for Secretary of Defense Donald Rumsfeld, which holds that "any effort by Congress to regulate the interrogation of unlawful combatants would violate the Constitution's sole vesting of the Commander-in-Chief authority in the President." "Working Group Report on Detainee Interrogations in the Global War on Terrorism: Assessment of Legal, Historical, Policy, and Operational Considerations," April 4, 2003.

18. William Blackstone, *Commentaries* 1:254 (on king's "sole power").

19. Other powers bearing on Congress's ability to proscribe torture include the power to "make Rules concerning Captures on Land and Water," and the power to "make all Laws which shall be necessary and proper for carrying into Execution . . . all other Powers vested by this Constitution in the Government of the United States." See Michael D. Ramsey, "Torturing Executive Power," *Georgetown Law Journal* 93 (April 2005): 1240.

20. *Federalist* no. 69. The "Take Baghdad from the north" example was borrowed and adapted from Michael D. Ramsey, "Torturing Executive Power."

21. Nat Hentoff, "Don't Ask, Don't Tell," *Village Voice*, February 7, 2006 (emphasis added).

22. "Transcript: Exclusive Bush Interview, President Bush Sits Down with Bob Schieffer," *CBS News*, January 27, 2006.

23. See Elizabeth B. Bazan, "Assassination Ban and E.O. 12333: A Brief Summary," *CRS Report for Congress*, RS21037, January 4, 2002.

24. "The executive branch shall construe Title X in Division A of the Act, relating to detainees, in a manner consistent with the constitutional authority of the President to supervise the unitary executive branch and as Commander in Chief and consistent with the constitutional limitations on the judicial power, which will assist in achieving the shared objective of the Congress and the President . . . of protecting the American people from further terrorist attacks." President's statement on signing H.R. 2863, the "Department of Defense, Emergency Supplemental Appropriations to Address Hurricanes in the Gulf of Mexico, and Pandemic Influenza Act, 2006," December 30, 2005. See also Charlie Savage, "Bush Could Bypass New Torture Ban," *Boston Globe*, January 4, 2006. Using the presidential signing statement to signal his interpretation of new laws—and to indicate the provisions he believes to be nonbinding—had become one of the president's favorite legal tactics. Other presidents had used signing statements for similar purposes in the past, but none with the frequency or aggressiveness that George W. Bush displayed. See Charlie Savage, "Bush Challenges Hundreds of Laws," *Boston Globe*, April 30, 2006; Phillip J. Cooper, "George W. Bush, Edgar Allan Poe, and the Use and Abuse of Presidential Signing Statements," *Presidential Studies Quarterly* 35 (September 2005).

25. Dana Milbank, "Bob Barr, Bane of the Right?" *Washington Post*, February 11, 2006.

26. See, for example, Andrew C. McCarthy, "Comforting the Enemy," *National Review Online*, December 19, 2003. Commenting on the Second Circuit's 2003 ruling that the president lacked inherent constitutional authority to confine Padilla permanently without due process, McCarthy wrote, "If you were under the impression that the 9/11 atrocities marked the long-overdue end of a suicidal government philosophy that terrorists and bombs should be fought with indictments and trials instead of missiles in the air and boots on the ground, guess again."

27. *Hamdi v. Rumsfeld*, 542 U.S. 507, 554–55, (2004), Scalia, J. dissenting.

28. Eugene Fidell, "Martial Law, 2001-Style," unpublished manuscript on file with author.

29. "Declaration of Michael H. Mobbs," from *Rumsfeld v. Padilla*, 542 U.S. 426 (2004).

30. In Padilla's federal court trial in 2006, the government produced an al Qaeda training camp application bearing Padilla's fingerprints. "Enemy Combated; José Padilla," *The Economist*, August 25, 2007.

31. *Jose Padilla v. Commander C.T. Hanft*, 389 F. Supp. 2d 678, 690 (D.S.C. 2005).

32. "Oral Arguments in the Case of Donald H. Rumsfeld versus Jose Padilla," *Federal News Service*, April 28, 2004 (emphasis added).

33. *Ex Parte Milligan*, 71 U.S. 2 (1866) at 120.

34. Quoted in John Herbers, "The 37th President; In Three Decades, Nixon Tasted Crisis and Defeat, Victory, Ruin and Revival," *New York Times*, April 24, 1994. Your author is among the offenders; see Gene Healy and Timothy Lynch, "Power Surge: The Constitutional Record of George W. Bush," Cato Institute White Paper, May 1, 2006, p. 8.

35. Louis Fisher, "Detention of U.S. Citizens," *CRS Report for Congress*, RS22130, April 28, 2005, p. 2.

36. *Jose Padilla v. Commander C.T. Hanft* at 690.

37. "Improper Surveillance of Private Citizens by the Military," in *Final Report of the Select Committee to Study Governmental Operations with Respect to Intelligence Activities, United States Senate, Book III: Supplementary Detailed Staff Reports on Intelligence Activities and the Rights of Americans*, pp. 789, 804. Plainclothes military intelligence operatives fanned out across the United States, infiltrating protest groups and monitoring anti-war activists. Among other activities, army agents joined a yippie commune in Washington, D.C.; posed as students to monitor a "Black Studies" class at New York University; and infiltrated a Colorado Springs coalition of church youth groups protesting the Vietnam War.

38. Shane Harris, "National Security: Signals and Noise," *National Journal*, June 17, 2006. Poindexter's convictions were later reversed on appeal.

39. One wonders what sort of "veterinary" data DARPA envisioned using. The Electronic Privacy Information Center has compiled a history of key developments in the TIA program, accessible at http://www.epic.org/privacy/profiling/tia/.

40. Nathan Hodge, "DARPA Official Stumps for 'Total Information Awareness'" *Defense Week*, November 18, 2002.

41. See P.L. 108-7, Sec. 111(a), "Limitation on Use of Funds for Research and Development on Total Information Awareness Program."

42. Shane Harris, "TIA Lives On," *National Journal*, February 26, 2006.

43. James Risen and Eric Lichtblau, "Bush Lets U.S. Spy on Callers without Courts,"*New York Times*, December 16, 2005.

44. Press briefing with Attorney General Alberto Gonzales and General Michael Hayden, principal deputy director for national intelligence (December 19, 2005).

45. "National Security Agency Surveillance Affecting Americans," in *Final Report of the Select Committee to Study Governmental Operations with Respect to Intelligence Activities, United States Senate, Book III: Supplementary Detailed Staff Reports on Intelligence Activities and the Rights of Americans*, p. 749.

46. "National Security Agency Surveillance Affecting Americans," p. 765.

47. See Robert A. Levy, "Wartime Executive Power and the NSA's Surveillance Authority," testimony submitted to the United States Senate, Committee on the Judiciary, February 28, 2006.

48. U.S. Department of Justice, "Legal Authorities Supporting the Activities of the National Security Agency Described by the President," January 19, 2006.

49. House Judiciary Committee hearing, 109th Congress, Subject: Department of Justice Oversight, April 6, 2006, transcript, U.S. Government Publishing Office.

50. "Memorandum of Points and Authorities in Support of the United States' Assertion of the Military and State Secrets Privilege," *Center for Constitutional Rights v. George W. Bush*, Case No. 06-CV-313 (S.D.N.Y.).

51. William G. Weaver and Robert M. Pallitto, "State Secrets and Executive Power," *Political Science Quarterly* 120 (2005): 97, quoting Blackstone.

52. *U.S. v. Reynolds*, 345 U.S. 1, 10 (1953).

53. *Black v. U.S.*, 62 F.3d 1115, 1119 n. 5 (8th Cir. 1995).

54. *Reynolds*, 345 U.S. at 10.

55. *Reynolds*, 345 U.S. at 8.

56. William G. Weaver and Robert M. Pallitto, "State Secrets and Executive Power," *Political Science Quarterly* 120 (2005): 101.

57. OpenTheGovernment.org, "Secrecy Report Card 2007," p. 13.

58. *Hepting v. AT&T*, 439 F. Supp. 2d 974, 993 (N.D. Cal. 2006).

59. L. Stuart Ditzen, "Unearthed Military Secret Brings New Life to Old Case," *Philadelphia Inquirer*, March 5, 2003; Tim Lynch, "In '48 Crash, U.S. Hid behind National Security," *Washington Post*, June 22, 2003.

60. The phrase "posse comitatus," Latin for "the power or force of the county," refers to the sheriff's common-law power to call upon the male population of a county for assistance in enforcing the laws, and the act is designed to prevent use of the armed forces for that purpose. The PCA had its immediate origins in Reconstruction-era concerns about the use of federal troops to influence elections in the formerly rebellious Southern states. Supporters of domestic militarization have tried to use the act's origins to discredit it. But as historian Joan M. Jensen explains, dismissing the Posse Comitatus Act as a "Reconstruction law" is historically inaccurate:

> Democrats were still concerned about a Republican president using the army in the South, but with troops already withdrawn from the South, it is unlikely that Southern Democrats would have been able to get support for the bill had Northern members of Congress not responded to the rhetoric expressing opposition to a standing army. By . . . raising the specter of the army being used against laboring men, and examining the difference between suppressing domestic violence and the execution of the law, proponents were able to convince many members that the act merely declared a truth about the limits of the military in American society.

Joan M. Jensen, *Army Surveillance in America, 1775–1980* (New Haven, CT: Yale University Press, 1991), p. 36. Indeed, the supporters of the act saw themselves as affirming principles that were already embodied in the Constitution. According to Rep. Richard Townsend of Illinois, "it was the real design of those who framed our Constitution that the Federal Army should never be used for any purpose but to repel invasion and to suppress insurrection when it became too formidable for the State to suppress it." 6 *Cong. Rec.* 287, 45th Cong., 1st sess., pt. 1 (November 8, 1877).

61. As amended, the act reads, "Whoever, except in cases and under circumstances expressly authorized by the Constitution or Act of Congress, willfully uses any part of the Army or Air Force as a posse comitatus or otherwise to execute the laws shall be fined under this title or imprisoned not more than two years, or both." 18 U.S.C.§ 1385.

62. Kim Lane Scheppele, "Does the Posse Comitatus Act Still Exist?" *Balkinization* blog, Balkin.com.

Of course, the act's proscription against using the military to "execute the laws" does not bar the use of military forces to ward off a military-style attack. Few, if any, suggested that post-9/11 air force patrols aimed at shooting down hijacked planes violated the Posse Comitatus Act. It is important, however, to recognize the limits of the military purpose exception, lest it be warped into an exception that swallows the Posse Comitatus Act rule. It is true that the ultimate purpose of any post-9/11 military involvement in domestic law enforcement would be to deter and neutralize al Qaeda operatives at war with the United States. But that does not allow the U.S. military to take over all aspects of local law enforcement simply because by so doing soldiers might catch some terrorists. To slide down that slope is essentially to say that the act does not apply during wartime so long as saboteurs may be afoot—which appears to be John Yoo's position.

63. Jefferson Morris, "Official: NORTHCOM Will Plan for Worst-Case Scenarios," *Aerospace Daily*, September 27, 2002.

64. April Fulton, "Transportation Secretary Seeks Military Security on Airplanes," *Government Executive*, September 13, 2001.

65. Oliver Poole, "Thanksgiving Gestures Focus on Servicemen," *Daily Telegraph* (London), November 24, 2001, p. 15.

66. Bradley Graham, "War Plans Drafted to Counter Terror Attacks in U.S.," *Washington Post*, August 8, 2005.

67. For army enforcement of the fugitive slave laws, see James M. McPherson, *Battle Cry of Freedom* (New York: Oxford University Press, 1988), p. 83; for suppression of unions, see Jerry M. Cooper, "Federal Military Intervention in Domestic Disorders," in *The United States Military under the Constitution of the United States, 1789–1989*, ed. Richard H. Kohn (New York: New York University Press, 1991), p. 123. McPherson recounts an 1851 incident involving Thomas Sims, a 17-year-old escaped slave working in Boston as a waiter. The U.S. army provided sufficient firepower to thwart any abolitionist vigilantes that might try to free him. Three hundred armed federal deputies and soldiers led Sims and his captor from the courthouse to the navy yard, where 250 more army regulars waited to put them on a ship heading south. Cooper provides details on the army's involvement in suppressing the 1899 miners' strike in Coeur d'Alene, Idaho. Army regulars under the command of Brig. Gen. Henry C. Merriam engaged in house-to-house searches and assisted in more than a thousand arrests, violating the rights of countless citizens. U.S. troops arrested every adult male in the area and locked them up without charges for weeks. The occupation lasted for two years and destroyed the union, as was intended. See also Jensen, *Army Surveillance in America*, p. 139.

68. *United States v. McArthur*, 419 F. Supp. 186, 193–94 (D.N.D. 1975).

69. Quoted in Douglas Holt, "DA Questions Military Account of Border Slaying Drug Unit Spokeswoman Calls Remarks Surprising," *Dallas Morning News*, June 4, 1997.

70. *Oversight Investigation of the Death of Esequiel Hernandez, Jr.: A Report of Chairman Lamar Smith to the Subcommittee on Immigration and Claims of the Committee on the Judiciary, House of Representatives*, 150th Congress (Washington: Government Printing Office, November 1998).

71. As the DOJ criminal civil rights investigation into the Hernandez incident put it, "The minimal, perhaps ambiguous, training given to the Marines on this mission should be compared to the clear training provided in basic infantry tactics." The *Marine Battle Skills Training Handbook*, Book 2, describes how a marine must react to enemy small-arms fire. It directs, among other things,

"[m]aneuver to a better vantage point to deliver more effective fire upon the enemy." Included as Appendix E to Smith, *Oversight Investigation*, p. 97.

72. U.S. General Accounting Office, "Homeland Defense: DOD Needs to Assess the Structure of U.S. Forces for Domestic Military Missions," Report to the Chairman, Subcommittee on National Security, Emerging Threats, and International Relations, Committee on Government Reform, House of Representatives, July 2003.

73. That is, it has been fairly restrained when it comes to the seizure of citizens and the active employment of the military on U.S. soil. Surveillance programs conducted under the president's theory of inherent authority are much easier to shield from scrutiny, and, as noted, administration officials have been very guarded in their testimony when asked about the existence of NSA programs beyond that revealed by the *New York Times* in late 2005.

74. To clarify, Jose Padilla is neither the only citizen nor the only person captured on American soil to be imprisoned at the will of the executive. The administration also invoked the "enemy combatant" theory in the cases of Yaser Esam Hamdi (an American citizen captured abroad) and Ali Saleh Kahlah al-Marri (a resident alien seized on American soil), but Padilla is thus far the only American seized in America to be subject to detention without charges or trial.

75. The six pled guilty and are now in federal prison.

76. Michael Isikoff, "The Other Big Brother; The Pentagon Has Its Own Domestic Spying Program. Even Its Leaders Say the Outfit May Have Gone Too Far," *Newsweek*, January 30, 2006. Lisa Myers, Douglas Pasternak, Rich Gardella, and the NBC Investigative Unit, "Is the Pentagon Spying on Americans?" NBC News, December 14, 2005.

77. Robert Block and Jay Solomon, "Neighborhood Watch: Pentagon Steps Up Intelligence Efforts inside U.S. Borders," *Wall Street Journal*, April 27, 2006.

78. William M. Arkin, "Mission Creep Hits Home; American Armed Forces Are Assuming Major New Domestic Policing and Surveillance Roles," *Los Angeles Times*, November 23, 2003.

79. Pamela Hess, "Pentagon Agrees to Help DC Sniper Hunt," *Washington Times*, October 16, 2002. See also Elaine M. Grossman, "Former JAG: Military Aid in D.C. Sniper Pursuit May Have Broken Law," *Inside the Pentagon*, November 14, 2002.

80. Adam Clymer, "Big Brother Joins the Hunt for the Sniper," *New York Times*, October 20, 2002.

81. Rowan Scarborough, "Military Training of Civilian Police Steadily Expands; Congress Has Paved Way with Legislation," *Washington Times*, September 9, 1999.

82. David B. Kopel and Paul H. Blackman, *No More Wacos* (Amherst, NY: Prometheus, 1997), p. 86. U.S. Army special forces soldiers also helped the Bureau of Alcohol, Tobacco and Firearms rehearse its aggressive initial raid on the Davidians' home. Lee Hancock, "ATF Official Defends Raid Planning," *Dallas Morning News*, March 27, 1993.

83. Lawyers for the Branch Davidians, seeking to determine what role Delta Force operatives played at Waco, were told that they could only submit written questions and receive anonymous answers from military personnel involved in the incident. While three Delta operatives were eventually deposed, the Department of Defense refused to declassify 5,000 pages of documents the Davidians' lawyers claimed were instrumental to resolving whether military personnel acted

illegally during the standoff. Lee Hancock, "Government Seeks Delay on Waco Files; White House Weighs Withholding Documents," *Dallas Morning News*, November 2, 1999. In the Hernandez case, the Pentagon and other federal agencies repeatedly stonewalled in response to state authorities conducting a homicide investigation, according to Rep. Lamar Smith (R-TX), who conducted a congressional oversight investigation into the circumstances surrounding Hernandez's slaying. *Oversight Investigation*.

84. Charlie Savage, "Mitt Romney Q&A," *Boston Globe*, December 20, 2007.

85. For the origins of the phrase, see George P. Fletcher, "The Cliché That 'the Constitution Is Not a Suicide Pact,'" Findlaw.com, January 7, 2003.

86. Jack Goldsmith, *The Terror Presidency: Law and Judgment inside the Bush Administration* (New York: W.W. Norton & Company, 2007), p. 71.

87. Goldsmith, *The Terror Presidency*, p. 82.

88. John Mueller, *Overblown: How Politicians and the Terrorism Industry Inflate National Security Threats and Why We Believe Them* (New York: Free Press, 2006), p. 13.

89. Mueller, *Overblown*, pp. 14–23.

90. "Terrorism Statistics: Terrorist Acts, 1968–2006, Deaths to Incidences Ratio (Most Recent) by Country," Nationmaster.com, using statistics compiled from the Memorial Institute for the Prevention of Terrorism Database.

91. "Bush Campaign to Base Ad on Kerry Terror Quote," CNN.com, October 11, 2004.

92. One involved an FBI informant's "fake terrorist plot" to assassinate a Pakistani diplomat. Three others (the Lackawanna Six case, the Virginia "paintball jihadis," and a case involving a father lying to the FBI about whether his son had attended a terrorist training camp) apparently didn't involve any specific plots at all. James Jay Carafano, "U.S. Thwarts 19 Terrorist Attacks against America since 9/11," Heritage Foundation Backgrounder no. 2085, November 13, 2007.

93. "6 Arrested in Fort Dix Plot," *Associated Press*, May 8, 2007.

94. Micah Morrison, "The Mena Coverup," *Wall Street Journal*, October 18, 1994; Dorothy Rabinowitz, "Juanita Broaddrick Meets the Press," *Wall Street Journal*, February 19, 1999.

95. Ion Mihai Pacepa, "Propaganda Redux," *Wall Street Journal*, August 7, 2007.

96. Harvey C. Mansfield, "The Case for the Strong Executive," *Wall Street Journal*, May 2, 2007.

97. Charlie Savage, "Candidates on Executive Power: A Full Spectrum," *Boston Globe*, December 22, 2007.

98. Goldsmith, *The Terror Presidency*, pp. 189–90.

99. Todd S. Purdum, "Clinton Seeks New Welfare Bill, Saying G.O.P. Plan Is Too Harsh," *New York Times*, April 19, 1995.

100. "The Clinton Years," transcript, *Frontline*.

101. Norman C. Bay, "Executive Power and the War on Terror," *Denver University Law Review* 83 (2005): 353.

102. Testimony of David B. Kopel, "Hearings on Wiretapping and Other Terrorism Proposals," Committee on the Judiciary, United States Senate, May 24, 1995. According to Kopel, the anti-terrorism bill backed by Clinton defined "almost every violent and property crime, no matter how trivial, as 'terrorism,'" and au-

thorized "'the Army, Navy, and Air Force' to render assistance against 'terrorism' whenever requested by the attorney general."

103. "Congress Reached Compromise on Anti-Terrorism Bill," CNN.com, April 16, 1996: "The Republicans also dropped the additional wire-tap authority the Clinton administration wanted."

104. Quoted in Carol K. Winkler, *In the Name of Terrorism: Presidents on Political Violence in the Post–World War II Era* (Albany: State University of New York Press, 1996), p. 145.

105. Christopher S. Kelley, letter to the editor, *New Republic*, September 11, 2006.

106. Jeffrey Rosen, "Power of One," *New Republic*, July 8, 2006. Dellinger stopped short of arguing that the president could launch ground wars without congressional approval. Instead, he maintained, among other things, that the Haiti operation was not a "war" in the constitutional sense because it was to be undertaken at the invitation of the island's legitimate government (i.e., President Aristide). In their response to Dellinger's memo, a group of law professors noted dryly, "presumably, at the outset of World War II, General de Gaulle could not have nullified the Constitution's requirement of congressional approval by 'inviting' the United States to invade occupied France."

107. Randolph D. Moss, "Authorization for Continuing Hostilities in Kosovo," December 19, 2000.

108. Michael Crowley, "Hillary's War," *New Republic*, April 2, 2007.

109. Jack M. Balkin and Sanford V. Levinson, "The Processes of Constitutional Change: From Partisan Entrenchment to the National Surveillance State," *Fordham Law Review* 75, no. 2 (2006): 101, 141–42.

110. Richard E. Neustadt, *Presidential Power and the Modern Presidency: The Politics of Leadership from Roosevelt to Reagan* (New York: Free Press, 1991).

Chapter 7

1. Quoted in Glenn Greenwald, *A Tragic Legacy: How a Good vs. Evil Mentality Destroyed the Bush Presidency* (New York: Crown, 2007), p. 75.

2. Chuck Leddy, "'Denial' Lays Blame at White House Door," *Boston Globe*, October 3, 2006.

3. G. Calvin Mackenzie and Judith M. Labiner, "Opportunity Lost: The Rise and Fall of Trust and Confidence in Government after September 11," Center for Public Service, Brookings Institution, Washington, May 30, 2002.

4. In 2004, 37 percent trusted government, only a point above 2000's score of 36. American National Election Studies, "Trust in Government Index," *ANES Guide to Public Opinion and Electoral Behavior.* The NES index is an average of the "trust the government in Washington" question and three others: "Would you say the government is pretty much run by a few big interests looking out for themselves or that it is run for the benefit of all the people?"; "Do you think that people in the government waste a lot of money we pay in taxes, waste some of it, or don't waste very much of it?"; "Do you think that quite a few of the people running the government are (1958–1972: a little) crooked, not very many are, or do you think hardly any of them are crooked (1958–1972: at all)?"

5. Gallup presidential approval polls, available at http://www.pollingreport .com/BushJob1.htm.

6. Peter Baker, "Disfavor for Bush Hits Rare Heights," *Washington Post*, July 25, 2007.

7. George W. Bush, commencement address at the United States Military Academy at West Point, May 27, 2006.

8. *Economist*, November 11, 2006.

9. Albert R. Hunt, "The Incredible Shrinking President," *Wall Street Journal*, September 8, 2001.

10. Arthur Schlesinger Jr., "So Much for the Imperial Presidency," *New York Times*, August 3, 1998.

11. *Hamdi v. Rumsfeld*, 542 U.S. 507, 536 (2004).

12. *Padilla v. C.T. Hanft*, 432 F.3d 582 (4th Cir. 2005).

13. Fourth Circuit Court of Appeals Order, No. 05–6396, December 21, 2005.

14. Warren Richey, "Was Jose Padilla Tortured by US Military?" *Christian Science Monitor*, February 16, 2007; Padilla's motion containing the torture allegation is available at http://www.discourse.net/archives/docs/Padilla_Outrageous _Government_Conduct.pdf.

15. "Oral Arguments in the Case of Donald H. Rumsfeld versus Jose Padilla," *Federal News Service*, April 28, 2004.

16. *Hamdan v. Rumsfeld*, 126 S. Ct. 2749 (2005).

17. *Hamdan*, 126 S.Ct. at 2774, n. 23. Justice Kennedy's concurrence invoked *Youngstown* as well, 126 S. Ct. at 2800.

18. See, for example, Jack Balkin, "Hamdan and the NSA Dispute," *Balkinization* blog, Balkin.com. June 30, 2006.

19. Dan Eggen, "Court Will Oversee Wiretap Program," *Washington Post*, January 18, 2007.

20. Colleen J. Shogan, "The Contemporary Presidency: The Sixth Year Curse," *Presidential Studies Quarterly* 36 (March 2006): 90. Of course, not every second-term president suffers from each aspect of the curse, as President Clinton demonstrated in the 1998 elections, when his party picked up five House seats and avoided losses in the Senate.

21. "Contemporary presidential approval ratings generally peak 10% to 15% below those achieved at the beginning of the survey era." Marc J. Hetherington, "The Political Relevance of Political Trust," *American Political Science Review* (December 1998): 791. Michael A. Fitts, "The Paradox of Power in the Modern State: Why a Unitary, Centralized Presidency May Not Exhibit Effective or Legitimate Leadership," *University of Pennsylvania Law Review* 144 (January 1996): 836.

22. See, for example, Richard W. Waterman, Hank C. Jenkins-Smith, and Carol L. Silva, "The Expectations Gap Thesis: Public Attitudes toward an Incumbent President," *Journal of Politics* 61 (November 1999); George C. Edwards III, *The Public Presidency: In Pursuit of Popular Support* (New York: St. Martin's Press, 1983).

23. Bruce Miroff, "Monopolizing the Public Space: The President as a Problem for Democratic Politics," in *Rethinking the Presidency*, ed. Thomas E. Cronin (Boston: Little, Brown and Co., 1982), p. 220.

24. Michael A. Fitts suggests that the public's overestimation of the president's responsibility for the fate of the nation reflects the "availability heuristic" studied by social psychologists. The public has a "heuristic bias toward overestimating the causal significance of readily accessible factors" widely discussed in the media. Fitts, "Paradox of Power," p. 886.

25. Thomas E. Cronin, "Superman: Our Textbook President," *Washington Monthly*, October 1970, p. 53.

26. Michael A. Fletcher, "President Again Takes on Role of 'Consoler in Chief,'" *Washington Post*, April 18, 2007.

27. Michael Abramowitz, "Bush Urges Stepped-Up Campaign against Childhood Obesity," *Washington Post*, February 2, 2007.

28. Marc J. Hetherington, "The Effect of Political Trust on the Presidential Vote, 1968–96," *American Political Science Review* 93 (June 1999): 312.

29. Matthew Eshbaugh-Soha and Jeffrey S. Peake, "Presidents and the Economic Agenda," *Political Research Quarterly* 58 (March 2005): 128.

30. "'West Wing' Debate Throws Out the Rules," Associated Press, November 6, 2005.

31. Christopher H. Achen and Larry M. Bartels, "Musical Chairs: Pocketbook Voting and the Limits of Democratic Accountability," Princeton University, unpublished paper, 2004, p. 36. The patient's assessment of the experience is also greatly affected by the most intense moment therein—the sharpest pain, for instance, not simply the level of sensation at the end of the experience. Keith James Holyoak and Robert G. Morrison, *The Cambridge Handbook of Thinking and Reasoning* (New York: Cambridge University Press, 2005), p. 284.

32. Achen and Bartels, "Musical Chairs," p. 36. Interestingly, though, Achen and Bartels find evidence for the existence of the "political business cycle," the idea that politicians stimulate the economy during election years to gain reelection. According to Achen and Bartels, income growth in election years is an average of 1.5 percent higher than in other years, which suggests political manipulation of the economy. Even so, that doesn't change the assessment that the president's power to generate desired economic results is limited and dwarfed by larger trends.

33. Jodi Wilgoren, "The 2004 Campaign: The Massachusetts Senator: Kerry Outlines His Jobs Program in Swing through Midwest," *New York Times*, April 29, 2004.

34. "Rebuilding the Middle Class: Hillary Clinton's Economic Blueprint for the 21st Century," October 8, 2007.

35. See, for example, Thomas A. Garrett and Russell S. Sobel, "The Political Economy of FEMA Disaster Payments," Working Paper 2002-012B, Federal Reserve Bank of St. Louis (finding that "States politically important to the president have a higher rate of disaster declaration by the president, and nearly half of all disaster relief is motivated politically rather than by need").

36. "Disasters and Other Declarations," FEMA.gov.

37. David Weigel, "Skirting Political Disaster: Mother Nature's Wrath Brings Out Best and Worst in Candidates," *Campaigns and Elections*, December/January 2005.

38. Dana Milbank, "A 'Unified Command Structure' in Search of a Leader," *Washington Post*, March 21, 2006 (emphasis added).

39. William L. Waugh Jr., "Terrorism and the 'All-Hazards' Model," revised version of paper presented on the IDS Emergency Management On-Line Conference, June 28–July 16, 2004, p. 1:

> The media, political leaders, influential residents, or influential participants in the planning process or the larger community may encourage attention to hazards of very low probability or even of no

discernible possibility. Media attention can make hazards and disasters seem much worse or more frequent than they really are. That is the so-called "CNN effect." Personal and family traumas may create champions for lesser risks. The point is that these less probable or even improbable hazards may be included in the planning. That's politics and the planning process is, after all, political as well as technical. It is also human nature. If the community is lucky, the planners give greatest attention to the biggest risks. All-hazards planning, then, is based upon the most likely disasters and the most "popular."

40. *I, Claudius*, Episode no. 2, first broadcast September 20, 1976, by the BBC, directed by Herbert Wise and written by Jack Pulman.

41. Gregory D. Hess and Athanasios Orphanides, "War Politics: An Economic, Rational-Voter Framework," *American Economic Review* 85 (September 1995).

42. Patrick James and John R. Oneal, "The Influence of Domestic and International Politics on the President's Use of Force," *Journal of Conflict Resolution* 35 (1991): 307–32; Charles W. Ostrom Jr. and Brian L. Job, "The President and the Political Use of Force," *American Political Science Review* 80 (1986): 541–66.

43. See, for example, William D. Baker, "The Dog That Won't Wag: Presidential Uses of Force and the Diversionary Theory of War," *Strategic Insights* 3 (May 2004) (finding that presidential uses of force are more likely when presidential approval and consumer confidence are higher than average, and that the proximity of elections does not correlate with militarized disputes).

44. William G. Howell and Jon C. Pevehouse, *While Dangers Gather: Congressional Checks on Presidential War Powers* (Princeton, NJ: Princeton University Press, 2007), p. 107.

45. Robin F. Marra, Charles Ostrom Jr., and Dennis M. Simon, "Foreign Policy and Presidential Popularity: Creating Windows of Opportunity in the Perpetual Election," *Journal of Conflict Resolution* 34 (1990): 618–19. See also Patrick James and Jean-Sebastian Rioux, "International Crises and Linkage Politics: The Experiences of the United States, 1953–1994," *Political Research Quarterly* 51 (1998): 781–812; Bradley Lian and John R. Oneal, "Presidents, the Use of Military Force, and Public Opinion," *Journal of Conflict Resolution* 37 (1993): 277–300; James and Oneal, "The Influence of Domestic and International Politics."

46. William D. Baker, "The Dog That Won't Wag," p. 40.

47. Sheldon Solomon, Jeff Greenberg, and Tom Pyszczynski, "Fatal Attraction: A New Study Suggests a Relationship between Fear of Death and Political Preferences," *APS Observer* 17 (October 2004).

48. Mark J. Landau, Sheldon Solomon, et al., "Deliver Us from Evil: The Effects of Mortality Salience and Reminders of 9/11 on Support for President George W. Bush," *Personality and Social Psychology Bulletin* 30 (September 2004); John B. Judis, "Death Grip: How Political Psychology Explains Bush's Ghastly Success," *New Republic*, August 27, 2007; Cass Sunstein, "Mortality Salience and Politics," University of Chicago Law School Faculty Blog, October 1, 2006.

49. Robb Willer, "The Effects of Government-Issued Terror Warnings on Presidential Approval Ratings," *Current Research in Social Psychology* 10 (September 2004).

50. Eric Schmitt and Thom Shanker, "Washington Recasts Terror War as 'Struggle,'" *International Herald Tribune*, July 27, 2005.

51. Richard W. Stevenson, "President Makes It Clear: Phrase Is 'War on Terror,'" *New York Times*, August 4, 2005.

52. Dan Eggen and Shailaigh Murray, "FBI Raid on Lawmaker's Office Is Questioned," *Washington Post*, May 23, 2006.

53. General Michael V. Hayden, "What American Intelligence and Especially the NSA Have Been Doing to Defend the Nation," address to the National Press Club, Washington, January 23, 2006.

54. Leslie Cauley, "NSA Has Massive Database of Americans' Phone Calls," *USA Today*, May 10, 2006.

55. P.L. 109-366; Sec. 948(b)(g), "No alien unlawful enemy combatant subject to trial by military commission under this chapter may invoke the Geneva Conventions as a source of rights"; Sec. 7(a), "No court, justice, or judge shall have jurisdiction to hear or consider an application for a writ of habeas corpus filed by or on behalf of an alien detained by the United States who has been determined by the United States to have been properly detained as an enemy combatant or is awaiting such determination." However, in *Al-Marri v. Wright*, 487 F.3d 160 (4th Cir. 2007), a case involving a legal resident of the United States picked up on American soil and subjected to military detention, the Fourth Circuit Court of Appeals recently held that "the MCA was not intended to, and does not, apply to aliens like al-Marri, who have legally entered, and are seized while legally residing in, the United States."

56. Sec. 948a(1); see Robert A. Levy, "Does the Military Commission Act Apply to U.S. Citizens?" *Cato at Liberty* (blog), February 6, 2007.

57. P.L. 110-55.

58. *Hamdi v. Rumsfeld*, 542 U.S. at 575 (2004) (Scalia, J., dissenting). Jack Goldsmith agrees that *Hamdi* did not significantly constrain the president. He wrote that *Hamdi* and another June 2004 Supreme Court decision, *Rasul v. Bush*, 542 U.S. 466 (2004) (holding that the judiciary could rule on the legality of the detentions at Guantanamo Bay), "were really little more than slaps on the wrist." Jack Goldsmith, *The Terror Presidency: Law and Judgment inside the Bush Administration* (New York: W. W. Norton & Co., 2007), p. 135. See also Harvey Silverglate, "Civil Liberties and Enemy Combatants: Why the Supreme Court's Widely Praised Rulings Are Bad for America," *Reason*, January 2005.

59. Of course, without legal discovery, it's impossible to verify all of el-Masri's claims, but German Chancellor Angela Merkel has confirmed that Secretary Rice "admitted this man had been erroneously taken." David G. Savage, "'State Secrets' Case May Get Airing," *Los Angeles Times*, October 8, 2007.

60. *El-Masri v. United States, cert denied*, 2007 U.S. LEXIS 11351 (2007).

61. ACLU Petition for Writ of Certiorari, p. 30.

62. Following Robert A. Dahl and Gerald N. Rosenberg, political scientists and legal scholars have made a related argument about the Court's capacity to carry out constitutional revolutions without the cooperation of the coordinate branches. These analysts cast doubt on the notion that the judiciary can, by itself, force large-scale social change on a resisting public. See, for example, Robert A. Dahl, "Decision Making in a Democracy: The Supreme Court as National Policy Maker," *Journal of Public Law* 6 (1957): 279–95; Gerald N. Rosenberg, *The Hollow Hope: Can Courts Bring about Social Change?* (Chicago: University of Chicago Press, 1991).

63. Jack M. Balkin and Sanford V. Levinson, "The Processes of Constitutional Change: From Partisan Entrenchment to the National Surveillance State," *Fordham Law Review* 75 (2006): 101, 112.

64. Balkin and Levinson, "The Processes of Constitutional Change," p. 102.

65. Balkin and Levinson believe that "the most important part of the Bush Administration's constitutional agenda" is "the enhancement of presidential power." Balkin and Levinson, "The Processes of Constitutional Change," 128.

66. Alexander Bolton, "Soothing the Seething Right Wing," *The Hill*, October 4, 2005.

67. Jeffrey Rosen, "Samuel Alito, Executive Assistant," *New Republic*, January 30, 2006.

68. See, for example, Jeffrey Rosen, "Power of One," *New Republic*, July 24, 2006: "Bush's extremism may have ultimately weakened executive power in the same way Clinton did when the Supreme Court rejected his sweeping assertions of executive privilege in the Monica Lewinsky investigation. By taking implausibly aggressive positions before the Supreme Court, both presidents precipitated a judicial backlash that left their own authority diminished. And that may be the ultimate irony that both sides failed to anticipate."

69. Goldsmith, *The Terror Presidency*, p. 181. For a comprehensive account of Cheney and Addington's long allegiance to expansive theories of executive power, see generally Charlie Savage, *Takeover: The Return of the Imperial Presidency* (New York: Little, Brown and Co., 2007).

70. "President Discusses Hurricane Relief in Address to the Nation," September 15, 2005.

71. Robert Burns, "Military May Play Bigger Relief Role," *Newsday*, September 17, 2005.

72. Bill Nichols and Richard Benedetto, "Govs to Bush: Relief Our Job," *USA Today*, October 2, 2005.

73. Patrik Jonsson, "A Native Son Takes Charge in Gulf Coast," *Christian Science Monitor*, September 9, 2005.

74. Brian Thevenot and Gordon Russell, "Rumors of Deaths Greatly Exaggerated," *New Orleans Times-Picayune*, September 23, 2005.

75. Jim Dwyer and Christopher Drew, "Fear Exceeded Crime's Reality in New Orleans," *New York Times*, September 29, 2005. ABT Associates, Inc., "Estimating Loss of Life from Hurricane-Related Flooding in the Greater New Orleans Area," final report, prepared for Paul Scodari, U.S. Army Corps of Engineers, Institute for Water Resources, May 19, 2006.

76. Louisiana Department of Health and Hospitals, "Hurricane Katrina: Reports of Missing and Deceased," August 2, 2006.

77. Louisiana Department of Health and Hospitals, "Updated Number of Deceased Victims Recovered Following Hurricane Katrina," news release, February 23, 2006; "Vital Statistics of All Bodies at St. Gabriel Morgue," February 23, 2006.

78. Susan B. Glasser and Michael Grunwald, "The Steady Buildup to a City's Chaos; Confusion Reigned at Every Level of Government," *Washington Post*, September 11, 2005; Ellen Knickmeyer, "Troops Head Home to Another Crisis," *Washington Post*, September 2, 2005; Times Staff Writer, "Q&A: Hurricane Katrina," *St. Petersburg Times*, September 3, 2005.

79. John Riley, "Brown's Out in New Orleans," *Newsday*, September 10, 2005.

80. Pam Zubek, "Bush Arrives to Monitor Operations," *Colorado Springs Gazette*, September 24, 2005.

81. Charles Aldinger, "Bush Wants Right to Use Military if Bird Flu Hits," Reuters, October 4, 2005.

82. Michael Isikoff and Mark Hosenball, "Domestic Defense," *Newsweek*, October 5, 2005.

83. U.S Department of Health and Human Services, *Pandemic Influenza Plan*, November 2005, p. 333.

84. Clinton Rossiter, *The American Presidency* (Baltimore: Johns Hopkins University Press, 1956, 1987), pp. 2–3.

85. Clinton Rossiter, "The Presidents and the Presidency," *American Heritage*, April 1956.

86. Joel Roberts, "Poll: Katrina Response Inadequate," CBSnews.com, September 8, 2005.

87. "Bush Approval Rating at 40 Percent," CNN.com, September 19, 2005.

88. Russell S. Sobel and Peter T. Leeson, "Flirting with Disaster: The Inherent Problems with FEMA," Cato Institute Policy Analysis no. 572, July 19, 2006, p. 5.

89. James Kitfield, "Poor Communications Slowed Military's Hurricane Response," *National Journal*, September 19, 2005.

90. Kitfield, "Poor Communications."

91. "Former FEMA Director Michael Brown Testifies before Congress; Rescue from Rita," *CNN Live Event/Special*, aired September 27, 2005.

92. Susan Roesgen, "New Orleans Evacuation Plan Has Holes," CNN.com, May 11, 2006.

93. Colby Cosh, "Katrina-ism 6.0: The Triumph of Government?" September 10, 2005.

94. P.L. 109-364, Sec. 1076.

95. Jennifer K. Elsea and R. Chuck Mason, "The Use of Federal Troops for Disaster Assistance: Legal Issues," Congressional Research Service, November 5, 2012, p. 2: "Language was subsequently added to the FY2008 Defense Authorization bill repealing the expanded authority (P.L. 110-181, 122 Stat. 325 (January 28, 2008)); returning the Insurrection Act to what had been in effect prior to the FY2007 Defense Authorization bill and returning the authority to utilize the National Guard, during domestic emergencies, to the state governors."

96. Frank Newport, "Americans' Confidence in Congress at All-Time Low," Gallup News Service, June 21, 2007.

97. "American Coup d'Etat: Military Thinkers Discuss the Unthinkable," *Harper's*, April 2006.

98. P.L. No. 97-86.

99. National Security Decision Directive 221, Narcotics and National Security, April 8, 1986.

100. President Reagan, "Address to the Nation on the Campaign against Drug Abuse," September 14, 1986.

101. Actually, the administration had to go to great lengths to stage the drug buy in Lafayette Park. Michael Isikoff, "Drug Buy Set Up for Bush Speech, DEA Lured Seller to Lafayette Park," *Washington Post*, September 22, 1989.

102. George Bush, "Address to the Nation on the National Drug Control Strategy," September 5, 1989.

103. Radley Balko, "Overkill: The Rise of Paramilitary Police Raids in America," Cato Institute White Paper, July 17, 2006.

104. Homeland Security Council, *National Strategy for Homeland Security*, October 2007, p. 3.

105. Goldsmith, *The Terror Presidency*, p. 79 (emphasis added).

106. The phrase was coined by security consultant Bruce Schneier in *Beyond Fear: Thinking Sensibly about Security in an Uncertain World* (New York: Springer, 2003), p. 39.

107. Ron Suskind, "Faith, Certainty and the Presidency of George W. Bush," *New York Times Magazine*, October 17, 2004.

108. Thomas Cronin, "Superman: Our Textbook President," p. 50.

109. See, for example, James Bowman, "The Elite Force: War and Masculinity and the Pundits and Thinkers Who Don't Get It," *National Review Online*, August 14, 2003.

Chapter 8

1. In fact, 8 out of 10 *don't* want to be president, according to a 2004 ABC News poll. Dalia Sussman, "No Thanks; Poll: Most Teens Don't Want to Be President," ABCNews.com, January 22, 2004.

2. "Ventura: Not Eyeing WH 2000. Yet," *Hotline*, November 4, 1998.

3. Philip H. Melanson, *The Secret Service: The Hidden History of an Enigmatic Agency* (New York: Carroll & Graf, 2002, 2005), p. 286.

4. F. A. Hayek, *The Road to Serfdom* (Chicago: University of Chicago Press, 1944), p. 135.

5. James Bryce, "Why Great Men Are Not Chosen Presidents," in *Classics of the American Presidency*, ed. Harry A. Bailey Jr. (Oak Park, IL: Moore Publishing Co., 1980), p. 375.

6. See generally James W. Ceaser, *Presidential Selection: Theory and Development* (Princeton, NJ: Princeton University Press, 1979); see also James Ceaser, "Presidential Selection," in *The Presidency in the Constitutional Order*, ed. Joseph Bessette and Jeffrey Tulis (Baton Rouge: Louisiana State University Press, 1981), p. 238.

7. *Federalist* no. 10, in *The Federalist*, ed. George W. Carey and James McClellan (Indianapolis, IN: Liberty Fund, 2001), p. 45.

8. *Federalist* no. 64, p. 333.

9. *Federalist* no. 68, p. 352.

10. The Framers did not distinguish sharply between nomination and election, perhaps supposing that "the Electoral College would be the vehicle for presidential nominations, forwarding a field of worthy candidates to the House of Representatives, which would make the final selection." Rhodes Cook, *The Presidential Nominating Process: A Place for Us?* (Lanham, MD: Rowman & Littlefield, 2004), p. 12.

11. Richard J. Ellis and Mark Dedrick, "The Rise of the Rhetorical Candidate," in *The Presidency Then and Now*, ed. Philip G. Henderson (Lanham, MD: Rowman & Littlefield, 2000), p. 190.

12. Ellis and Mark Dedrick, "The Rise of the Rhetorical Candidate," p. 192.

13. Bryce, "Why Great Men Are Not Chosen Presidents," p. 377.

14. J. Rufus Fears, ed., *Essays in Religion, Politics, and Morality: Selected Writings of Lord Acton*, Vol. 3 (Indianapolis, IN: Liberty Classics, 1988), p. 519.

15. Woodrow Wilson, *Constitutional Government in the United States* (New York: Columbia University Press, 1908, 1917), p. 68.

16. Woodrow Wilson, First Annual Message, December 2, 1913.

17. Cook, *Presidential Nominating Process*, p. 38.

18. The Democratic National Committee approved the rules in early 1971, and they would become mandatory for all state parties by the 1972 nomination race. See generally Michael Nelson, ed., *Congressional Quarterly's Guide to the Presidency*, 2nd ed. (Washington: Congressional Quarterly, Inc., 1996), pp. 210–16.

19. Michael G. Hagen and William G. Mayer, "The Modern Politics of Presidential Selection: How Changing the Rules Really Did Change the Game," in *In Pursuit of the White House 2000: How We Choose Our Presidential Nominees*, ed. William G. Mayer (New York: Chatham House, 2000), p. 11.

20. Nelson W. Polsby and Aaron Wildavsky, *Presidential Elections: Contemporary Strategies of American Electoral Politics* (London: Collier Macmillan, 1988), p. 88.

21. Bradley A. Smith, "Campaign Finance Reform: Soft Money and the Presidential Campaign System," testimony before United States Senate, Committee on Rules and Administration, May 14, 1997. See also Richard W. Waterman, Robert Wright, and Gilbert St. Clair, *The Image-Is-Everything Presidency: Dilemmas in American Leadership* (Boulder, CO: Westview Press, 1999), p. 90.

22. Hagen and Mayer, "Modern Politics of Presidential Selection," p. 25.

23. Hagen and Mayer, "Modern Politics of Presidential Selection," pp. 21, 30–31.

24. Dan Balz, "Clinton, Obama Clearing the Field," *Washington Post*, December 24, 2006.

25. Brooks Jackson, "Financing the 1996 Campaign: The Law of the Jungle," in *Toward the Millennium: The Elections of 1996*, ed. Larry J. Sabato (Boston: Allyn and Bacon, 1997), p. 230.

26. Michael Duffy, "The Money Chase," *Time*, March 13, 1995.

27. Federal Election Commission, "FEC Announces Updated Contribution Limits," press release, January 23, 2007.

28. Thomas B. Edsall and Chris Cillizza, "Money's Going to Talk in 2008," *Washington Post*, March 11, 2006.

29. David Brooks, "From the Back of the Pack," *New York Times*, October 19, 2007.

30. "Edwards Announces Bold Education Agenda to Restore the Promise of America's Schools," press release, John Edwards for President, September 21, 2007.

31. Harry G. Frankfurt, *On Bullshit* (Princeton, NJ: Princeton University Press, 2005), pp. 60–61.

32. Frankfurt, *On Bullshit*, p. 34.

33. See, for example, Robert E. DiClerico, "In Defense of the Presidential Nominating Process," in *Choosing Our Choices: Debating the Presidential Nominating Process*, ed. Robert E. DiClerico and James W. Davis (Lanham, MD: Rowman & Littlefield, 2000).

34. James L. Sundquist, "The Crisis of Competence in Our National Government," *Political Science Quarterly* 95 (Summer 1980): 193.

35. Alan Ehrenhalt, *The United States of Ambition* (New York: Times Books, 1991), p. 255. As for the argument that the demands of the modern campaign promote the "fire in the belly" needed for a candidate to become a successful president, Ehrenhalt writes that "stamina and intensity are useful qualities in a president, as they are in countless other roles in life, but anybody who thinks about the problem can easily imagine someone who hates campaigning and has never thirsted for public office but would make a superb president" (p. 266).

36. In an intriguing book, part of the post-Watergate backlash against president worship in political science, Bruce Buchanan examined the ways in which the presidential environment might distort personality. Some of this account draws on his insights. See Bruce Buchanan, *The Presidential Experience: What the Office Does to the Man* (Englewood Cliffs, NJ: Prentice-Hall, 1978).

37. John Dean, "The Best Book on the Presidency: Comments on a Classic That Is Particularly Trenchant in Times of War," Findlaw.com, March 14, 2003.

38. George Reedy, *Twilight of the Presidency* (New York: Mentor Press, 1970, 1987), p. 26.

39. Reedy, *Twilight of the Presidency,* pp. 150–51.

40. Robert Sobel, *Coolidge: An American Enigma* (Washington: Regnery, 1998), p. 371.

41. Lyn Ragsdale, *Vital Statistics on the Presidency: Washington to Clinton* (Washington: CQ Press, 1996), p. 257. John Hart, *The Presidential Branch: From Washington to Clinton,* 2nd ed. (Chatham, NJ: Chatham House Publishers, 1995), p. 23.

42. John P. Burke, *The Institutional Presidency* (Baltimore: Johns Hopkins University Press, 2000), p. 6.

43. Hart, *The Presidential Branch,* p. 3.

44. Ronald Kessler, *Inside the White House* (New York: Simon & Schuster, 1995), p. 69.

45. U.S. Treasury Department, *Public Report of the White House Security Review,* May 1995.

46. Melanson, *Secret Service,* pp. 132–33.

47. Melanson, *Secret Service,* p. 130 (emphasis in original).

48. Frederick M. Kaiser, "Origins of Secret Service Protection of the President: Personal, Interagency, and Institutional Conflict," *Presidential Studies Quarterly* 18 (Winter 1988): 102. The Secret Service had begun to take on this duty in the second Cleveland administration and agents were present at the McKinley assassination (to no avail), but even that violated a clear statutory prohibition on spending agency funds on purposes other than those, like anti-counterfeiting operations, enumerated in the relevant appropriations bills.

49. The House Judiciary Committee echoed that complaint, fearing that the secretary of war would send the agents "among the people to act under secret orders. When such laws begin to operate in the Republic, the liberties of the people will take wings and fly away." Melanson, *Secret Service,* pp. 30–33.

50. Melanson, *Secret Service,* pp. 31–32.

51. Fred I. Greenstein, "Change and Continuity in the Modern Presidency," in *Classics of the American Presidency,* p. 411.

52. Melanson, *Secret Service,* p. 292.

53. Lyn Ragsdale, *Vital Statistics*, p. 261.

54. Bradley H. Patterson, "The White House Budget—What It Isn't, What It Is: And a Five-Year Comparison," *White House Studies*, Winter 2005.

55. Reedy, *Twilight of the Presidency*, p. 84.

56. Thomas E. Cronin, "The Swelling of the Presidency," in *Classics of the American Presidency*, p. 157.

57. "Secret Service Director's Declaration," Washingtonpost.com, May 20, 1998.

58. "Three Bank Robberies for Iowa Town during Bush, Kerry Visits," CNN .com, August 6, 2004.

59. Tim Weiner, "In the Bubble, No Food Is Left Untouched," *The New York Times*, December 3, 2006.

60. That's not just because of the terrorist threat. It's also because the larger-than life presidency seems to act as a sort of "lone-nut" magnet for increasing numbers of the mentally disturbed. Samuel Byck, the unemployed former tire salesman portrayed by Sean Penn in *The Assassination of Richard Nixon* tried to hijack a plane so that he could crash it into the White House. Gerald Ford, though hardly larger than life himself, suffered two assassination attempts in the space of two weeks, first from former Manson girl Lynette "Squeaky" Fromme, then from left-wing activist Sara Jane Moore. There were four "lone-nut" attacks on the White House in 1994 alone. Melanson, *Secret Service*, pp. 96–106.

61. Kessler, *Inside the White House*, p. 74.

62. Evan Thomas, "Bush in the Bubble," *Newsweek*, December 19, 2005.

63. Michael John Burton, "*The Contemporary Presidency:* The 'Flying White House': A Travel Establishment within the Presidential Branch," *Presidential Studies Quarterly* 36 (June 2006): 303.

64. Kenneth T. Walsh, *Air Force One: A History of Presidents and Their Planes* (New York: Hyperion, 2003), p. 32. It's two planes, actually. "Air Force One" is merely the call sign for the president's plane, and the federal government owns two nearly identical 747s that regularly serve as *Air Force One*.

65. Burton, "The 'Flying White House,'" p. 305.

66. Michael D. Shear, "HOV Traffic Waits for No Man, Even the President," *Washington Post*, August 25, 2006.

67. Stephen Sherrill, "The Year in Ideas: A to Z: Acquired Situational Narcissism," *New York Times*, December 9, 2001; James Langton, "When Fame Is the Illness," *Evening Standard* (London), January 10, 2002.

68. Adam D. Galinsky, Joe C. Magee, M. Ena Enisi, and Deborah H. Gruenfeld, "Power and Perspectives Not Taken," *Psychological Science* 17 (2006): 2. Among the experiments conducted by the researchers was one in which subjects were primed by asking them to write down a memory in which they held power over other people, and then they were asked to write the letter "E" on their forehead. "Participants primed with high power compared to low power were more likely to draw an 'E' on their forehead in a self-oriented direction, indicating less of an inclination to spontaneously adopt another's visual perspective." See also Shankar Vedantam, "What the Bard and Lear Can Tell a Leader about Yes Men," *Washington Post*, March 18, 2007.

69. Libby Copeland and Mark Leibovich, "First Buddy: Andy Card Hopes His White House Resignation Is the Beginning of a Beautiful Friendship," *Washington Post*, March 29, 2006.

70. Ford's autobiography quoted in Kessler, *Inside the White House*, p. 81.

71. In 1973, Thomas Cronin noted that the "Presidential Establishment . . . has become a powerful inner sanctum of government, isolated from traditional, constitutional checks and balances," Cronin, "The Swelling of the Presidency," p. 153.

72. Irving L. Janis, *Victims of Groupthink: A Psychological Study of Foreign Policy Decisions and Fiascos* (Boston: Houghton Mifflin Co., 1972), p. 40.

73. Janis, *Victims of Groupthink*, p. 9.

74. Cass R. Sunstein, "Minimalism at War," *University of Chicago Supreme Court Review* 47 (2004): 69.

75. Reedy, *Twilight of the Presidency*, p. 34.

76. Thomas Preston, *The President and His Inner Circle: Leadership Style and the Advisory Process in Foreign Affairs* (New York: Columbia University Press, 2000), p. 83.

77. Alexander L. George, "The Case for Multiple Advocacy in Making Foreign Policy," *American Political Science Review* 66 (September 1972): 764.

78. Richard Reeves, *President Nixon: Alone in the White House* (New York: Simon & Schuster, 2001), p. 220.

79. Reeves, *President Nixon*, p. 222.

80. Emanuel Margolis, "Penning the First Amendment against Free Speech Rights," *Connecticut Law Tribune*, August 23, 2004.

81. That's what happened to Brett Bursey during a presidential visit to Columbia, South Carolina, October 24, 2002. Bursey stood at the side of a public road near the Columbia Metropolitan Airport, awaiting the president's arrival for a political rally at an airport hangar. Hundreds of Bush supporters, some bearing pro-administration signs, were in the area awaiting admission to the hangar. Bursey carried a sign reading "No War for Oil," which attracted the attention of a Secret Service agent. The agent ordered Bursey to move to a "demonstration area" three-quarters of a mile away. When he refused, airport police arrested him at the agent's request on a state trespass charge, which was later dropped, since Bursey was on public property. Over four months after Bursey's initial arrest, U.S. Attorney Strom Thurmond Jr. charged Bursey with violation of a federal statute prohibiting "willfully and knowingly" entering any "restricted area of a building or grounds where the President or other person protected by the Secret Service is or will be temporarily visiting," a charge for which he was convicted on January 6, 2004. See *United States v. Bursey*, No. 044832 (4th Cir. 2005) 2005 U.S. App. LEXIS 15152.

82. Dave Lindorff, "Keeping Dissent Invisible: How the Secret Service and the White House Keep Protesters Safely Out of Bush's Sight—and off TV," Salon.com, October 16, 2003.

83. *Pennsylvania v. Neel* transcript. Magistrate Judge Shirley R. Trkula dismissed the charge of disorderly conduct on October 31, 2002, stating "this is America, and that's why our forefathers came here, for freedom of speech."

84. In St. Charles, Missouri, on November 4, 2002, police arrested activist Bill Ramsey when he tried to unfurl an anti-Bush sign and refused to leave a crowd of Bush supporters while Bush was visiting a local airport. The officers "said they'd been ordered to [arrest him] by the Secret Service." Again in January 2003, St. Louis police arrested information technology worker Andrew Wimmer on a public street for refusing to move his "Instead of war, invest in people" sign to a free speech zone three blocks away from the presidential motorcade route. A woman with a

sign reading "Mr. President, we love you" was allowed to remain. According to Wimmer, the police told him "the Secret Service wanted protesters in the protest area." Dave Lindorff, "Keeping Dissent Invisible." And then there is Colorado resident Stephen Howards, who was walking his 11-year-old son to piano class when he came across Vice President Dick Cheney at a public event at an outdoor mall and told him "your policies in Iraq are reprehensible." A few minutes later, as Howards walked back across the mall accompanied by his younger son, 8-year-old Jonah, a Secret Service agent approached him, accused him of assault, cuffed him, put him in a black SUV, and took him to jail. J. K. Perry, "Man Sues Over Cheney Confrontation," *Vail Daily News*, October 3, 2006.

85. When citizens are expressing themselves in a public forum, the federal government cannot discriminate among them based on the views they express, forcing some out of the president's sight while leaving his supporters unmolested. The government cannot, as one federal judge has put it, "license one side to fight freestyle, while forbidding the other to fight at all." *Mahoney v. Babbitt*, 105 F.3d 1452 (D.C. Cir. 1997). See also *U.S. v. Grace*, 461 U.S. 171 (1983).

86. Melanson, *Secret Service*, p. 359. James Bovard, "'Free-Speech Zone': The Administration Quarantines Dissent," *American Conservative*, December 15, 2003.

87. Office of Presidential Advance, "Presidential Advance Manual," October 2002, p. 34.

88. Christopher Cooper, "White House Information Flow Is Tested," *Wall Street Journal*, May 27, 2005. For its coverage of the 2000 campaign, the *New York Times* used Freedom of Information Act requests to secure the father-and-son correspondence between George H. W. Bush and his sons in 1988. Unlike brother Jeb, George W. Bush showed little interest in matters of policy. Statements like "Don Ensenat is a very good man and good friend of all Bushes" made up the substance of the future 43's messages to the soon-to-be 41. Nicholas D. Kristof, "The 2000 Campaign: The 1988 Campaign; For Bush, Thrill Was in Father's Chase," *New York Times*, August 29, 2000.

89. Dan Balz and Bob Woodward, "Bush Awaits History's Judgment," *Washington Post*, February 3, 2002.

90. "An Exclusive Interview with President Bush," Fox Special Report with Brit Hume, September 23, 2003.

91. Bob Woodward, *State of Denial* (New York: Simon & Schuster, 2006), p. 326.

92. Elisabeth Bumiller, "The White House without a Filter," *New York Times*, June 4, 2006. A foreign diplomat who, understandably, preferred to remain anonymous told *Newsweek* in 2005 that Secretary of State Rice told him not to give the president bad news: "Don't upset him." Evan Thomas and Richard Wolffe, "Bush in the Bubble," *Newsweek*, December 19, 2005.

93. Woodward, *State of Denial*, p. 326. A similar dynamic prevailed during the president's cabinet meetings, which were carefully scripted: as former Treasury secretary Paul O'Neill told reporter Ron Suskind, before most meetings, senior White House officials would provide cabinet secretaries with instructions detailing what they were expected to speak about and for how long, "kill[ing] off the whole purpose of bringing people together," to O'Neill's mind. Ron Suskind, *The Price of Loyalty: George W. Bush, the White House, and the Education of Paul O'Neill* (New York: Simon & Schuster, 2004), p. 147.

94. Woodward, *State of Denial*, p. 371.

95. Max Hastings, "Never a Doubt, Never a Waver," *Sunday Times*, September 30, 2007.

96. Robert Dallek, *Flawed Giant: Lyndon Johnson and His Times, 1961–1975* (New York: Oxford University Press, 1998), p. 491.

97. Stanley A. Renshon, *The Psychological Assessment of Presidential Candidates* (New York: New York University Press, 1996), p. 102. Some of Johnson's aides disagreed with this characterization, notably Jack Valenti. See Renshon, *Psychological Assessment*, p. 109.

98. Renshon, *The Psychological Assessment*, p. 101.

99. Anthony Summers, *The Arrogance of Power: The Secret World of Richard Nixon* (New York: Viking Press, 2000), p. 478.

Chapter 9

1. Theodore J. Lowi, *The Personal President* (Ithaca, NY: Cornell University Press, 1986), p. 210.

2. Among the "paradoxes of the American presidency" identified by Thomas Cronin and Michael A. Genovese in their 2004 book of that name are Americans' tendency to "demand powerful, popular presidential leadership that solves the nation's problems," coupled with our inherent suspicion "of strong centralized leadership." "We admire power, but fear it. We love to unload responsibilities on our leaders, yet we intensely dislike being bossed around." Thomas E. Cronin and Michael A. Genovese, *The Paradoxes of the American Presidency*, 2nd ed. (New York: Oxford University Press, 2004), p. 4.

3. Quoted in Terry Teachout, *The Skeptic: A Life of H. L. Mencken* (New York: Harper Collins, 2002), p. 216.

4. Some analysts have proposed measures designed to address each problem, though most such proposals seem likely to be unachievable, ineffective, or both. See, for example, Richard Rose, "Learning to Govern or Learning to Campaign," in *Presidential Selection*, ed. Alexander Heard and Michael Nelson (Durham, NC: Duke University Press, 1987), pp. 71–73 (proposing a national primary system that might lead to shorter campaigns and selection of nominees by party delegates); and Bruce Buchanan, *The Presidential Experience: What the Office Does to the Man* (Englewood Cliffs, NJ: Prentice-Hall, 1978), pp. 174–76 (proposing reviving the congressional censure motion and instituting an American variation on the "Question Time" procedure used in the UK).

5. H.R. 2655, 106th Congress.

6. See Andrew Rudalevige, *The New Imperial Presidency: Renewing Presidential Power after Watergate* (Ann Arbor: University of Michigan Press, 2005), p. 115: "While they varied in form and stringency, legislative vetoes enabled all or part of Congress to review the executive branch's use of a given power statutorily delegated to it before the executive decision took final effect. . . . Often the action could be vetoed—sometimes merely by a committee, sometimes by one chamber, sometimes by both." Rudalevige cites a study showing that 423 such provisions were passed in the 1970s.

7. *INS v. Chadha*, 462 U.S. 919 (1983). Specifically, the Court struck down a one-house veto provision in the Immigration and Nationality Act that allowed

either House to veto the attorney general's decision, pursuant to authority Congress had delegated, to allow a legally deportable alien to remain in the United States. According to the Court, the veto provision at issue violated the Constitution's requirements of bicameralism and presentment embodied in the lawmaking procedure outlined in Art. I, Sec. 7.

8. Stephen Breyer, "The Thomas F. Ryan Lecture: The Legislative Veto After *Chadha*," *Georgetown Law Journal* 72 (February 1984): 785–99.

9. H.R. 2727, 104th Congress.

10. See *Raines v. Byrd*, 521 U.S. 811 (1997); see also Ryan McManus, "Note: Sitting in Congress and Standing in Court: How Presidential Signing Statements Opened the Door to Legislator Lawsuits," *Boston College Law Review* 48 (May 2007): 739–80.

11. It's often argued that abandoning delegation would be impossible because Congress simply would not have the time to make the laws we live under. There's some force to that objection, though it ignores the fact that, as David Schoenbrod and Jerry Taylor write,

> delegation forces Congress to spend a large chunk of its time constructing the legislative architecture—sometimes over a thousand pages of it—detailing exactly how various agencies are to decide important matters of policy. Once that architecture is in place, members of Congress find that a large part of their job entails navigating through those bureaucratic mazes for special interests jockeying to influence the final nature of the law. Writing such instructions and performing agency oversight to ensure that they are carried out would be unnecessary if Congress made the rules in the first place.

David Schoenbrod and Jerry Taylor, "The Delegation of Legislative Powers," *Cato Handbook for Policy* (Washington: Cato Institute, 2005), p. 157. But an end to delegation—whether piecemeal (as with the Breyer proposal) or wholesale (as per the Congressional Responsibility Act)—would force Congress to prioritize. That might mean a return to prescriptive laws, a new respect for federalism, and a renewed appreciation of the Framers' view that the chief danger to republican government lies in legislative overzealousness, not legislative inaction. A Congress that wanted to reclaim control of the law would have to do less, do it constitutionally, and be held accountable for the results. For most legislators, that's hardly an attractive proposition.

12. That occurred in the 1975 *Mayaguez* affair. See Richard F. Grimmett, "The War Powers Resolution after Thirty Years," *CRS Report for Congress*, RL 32267, March 11, 2004.

13. John Hart Ely, *War and Responsibility: Constitutional Lessons of Vietnam and Its Aftermath* (Princeton, NJ: Princeton University Press, 1993), p. 138. See also Constitution Project, "Deciding to Use Force Abroad: War Powers in a System of Checks and Balances," 2005.

14. "Constitutional War Powers Amendments of 2007," H.J. Res. 53.

15. Leslie H. Gelb and Anne Marie Slaughter, "Declare War: It's Time to Stop Slipping into Armed Conflict," *Atlantic Monthly*, November 2005.

16. For a discussion of the benefits of requiring a formal declaration, see J. Gregory Sidak, "To Declare War," *Duke Law Journal* 27 (1991): 27–121. Some analysts have argued that congressionalists ought to be "careful of what they wish for" when they advocate reviving the formal declaration, since a formally declared

war activates a number of federal statutes that enhance presidential power at home. See, for example, Roger Pilon, *Cardozo Public Law, Policy & Ethics Journal* 2 (December 2003): 57. Many of the same analysts also seem convinced that the president has all those enhanced powers and more whether or not war is formally declared, so it's difficult to understand the nature of their objection. For instance, in *The Powers of War and Peace*, John Yoo argues that even though the president, under Yoo's theory, can take the country into war whenever he chooses, the congressional power to *declare* war remains a significant power because, "a declaration of war places the nation in a state of total war, which triggers enhanced powers on the part of the federal government." Among the powers Yoo mentions is "conducting warrantless surveillance." John Yoo, *The Powers of War and Peace* (Chicago: University of Chicago Press, 2005), p. 151. To bolster that point, he cites the provision of the Foreign Intelligence Surveillance Act that temporarily suspends the warrant requirement following a declaration of war. But it's hard to believe that Yoo offered that argument in good faith. He wrote those words knowing what the rest of the country learned only months later: that the president, following Yoo's own legal advice, was even then secretly ignoring FISA's warrant requirement despite the fact that Congress had not declared war. And since leaving the Bush administration, Yoo has ardently defended the propositions that the president has unrestricted surveillance and detention powers in wartime, declaration or no. In any event, even if offered in good faith, the argument that declared wars give the president too much power isn't a strong one. If existing law gives the president too much power in formally declared wars, the proper solution isn't to forever renounce formal declarations of war. Instead, we should either amend existing law or exercise more caution about entering "wars of choice."

17. See Richard F. Grimmett, "The War Powers Resolution."

18. Ely, *War and Responsibility*, p. 130.

19. David Orden and Robert Paarlberg, "The Withering of Farm Policy Reform," Cato Institute, April 16, 2002; Louis Fisher, *Constitutional Conflicts between Congress and the President*, 4th ed. (Lawrence: University Press of Kansas, 2007), pp. 207–11.

20. Richard K. Betts, "A Disciplined Defense," *Foreign Affairs* (November/December 2007); Gordon Adams and John Diamond, "Don't Grow the Army," *Washington Post*, December 29, 2006.

21. Edward F. Bruner, "U.S. Military Dispositions: Fact Sheet," *CRS Report for Congress*, RS20649, January 30, 2007; Department of Defense, *Base Structure Report (A Summary of DoD's Real Property Inventory)*, 2006, p. 22.

22. Quoted in Arthur Schlesinger Jr., *The Imperial Presidency* (Boston: Houghton Mifflin Co., 1973), p. 7.

23. Andrew J. Bacevich, *American Empire: The Realities and Consequences of U.S. Diplomacy* (Cambridge, MA: Harvard University Press, 2002), p. 48.

24. Charles Bloeser suggests an additional PCA reform: "Because military personnel are often underpaid and expected to follow orders," Congress should "provide by statute that a victim of a PCA violation may recover compensatory—or if malice was present, punitive—damages from the branch responsible for the violation." Charles Bloeser, "Revising the Posse Comitatus Act after 9/11," *Federal Lawyer*, May 2003, pp. 24–31.

25. *Dave's* screenwriter, Gary Ross, said in 1993 that "if this movie serves as a reminder that politics ought to be, like Dave, uncynical, then I'm really happy.

That's the point. It should be uncynical." Bernard Weinraub, "For the Writer of 'Dave,' Cynicism and Politics Don't Mix on Screen," *New York Times*, May 11, 1993.

26. Morton H. Halperin, "Bush Is No Nixon—He's Worse," *Los Angeles Times*, July 16, 2006; Robert Dallek, *Flawed Giant: Lyndon Johnson and His Times, 1961–1975* (New York: Oxford University Press, 1998), p. 353. Myron A. Levine notes that "nowhere does *The West Wing* focus on the potential for groupthink and the dangers of presidential isolation in a White House of yes-men (and yes-women)," Myron A. Levine, " *The West Wing* (NBC) and The West Wing (D.C.): Myth and Reality in Television's Portrayal of the White House," in *The West Wing: The American Presidency as Television Drama*, ed. Peter C. Rollins and John E. O'Connor (Syracuse, NY: Syracuse University Press, 2003), p. 58.

27. Louis Wittig, "It's Commander-in-Chief G. I. Jane," *National Review Online*, September 27, 2005.

28. Jay Tolson, "The 10 Worst Presidents," *U.S. News and World Report*, February 26, 2007.

29. Dan Froomkin, "Bush Gets Outraged," Washingtonpost.com, September 20, 2007.

30. Richard M. Pious, "Reflections of a Presidency Rater," *White House Studies* 3 (Winter 2003). That Pious made such a statement was surprising, because some of his work reflects a critical approach to expansive claims of presidential authority. See, for example, Richard M. Pious, *The American Presidency* (New York: Basic Books, 1979).

31. Arthur Schlesinger Jr., "Rating the Presidents: Washington to Clinton," *Political Science Quarterly* 112 (Summer 1997): 180.

32. Michael Nelson, "Where Have You Gone, Franklin Roosevelt?" *The American Prospect*, November 6, 2000.

33. Richard Reeves, "Why Clinton Wishes He Were JFK," *Washington Monthly*, September 1995.

34. Dean Keith Simonton, "Presidential Greatness: The Historical Consensus and Its Psychological Significance," *Political Psychology* 7 (1986): 273. See also Jack E. Holmes and Robert E. Elder Jr., "Our Best and Worst Presidents: Some Possible Reasons for Perceived Performance," *Presidential Studies Quarterly* 19 (Summer 1989): 543 ("Significantly more war years are found in the case of the top third than the bottom third of presidents").

35. David C. Nice, "The Influence of War and Party System Aging on the Ranking of Presidents," *Western Political Quarterly* 37 (September 1984): 454.

36. Eric A. Posner, "All Hail . . . King George?" Foreignpolicy.com, March 2005.

37. James Taranto and Leonard Leo, eds., *Presidential Leadership: Rating the Best and Worst in the White House* (New York: Wall Street Journal Books, 2004), pp. 268–72.

38. Arthur Schlesinger Jr., "Rating the Presidents," p. 186.

39. Henry Fairlie, "Thoughts on the Presidency," *Public Interest* (Fall 1967): 44.

40. Michael Novak, *Choosing Our King: Powerful Symbols in Presidential Politics* (New York: Macmillan Publishing Co., 1972), p. xiv.

41. Novak, *Choosing Our King*, p. 5.

42. Novak, *Choosing Our King*, p. xv.

43. Fairlie, "Thoughts on the Presidency," p. 45.

44. George W. Bush, State of the Union address, January 28, 2003.

45. Michael Novak, *Choosing Presidents: Symbols of Political Leadership* (New Brunswick, NJ: Transaction Publishers, 1992), pp. xix, xxii.

46. Michael Novak, "Our Bravest President: This Guy Is Good," *National Review Online*, May 23, 2006.

47. David Brooks, *Bobos in Paradise: The New Upper Class and How They Got There* (New York: Simon & Schuster), 2000, p. 272.

48. Fred Barnes, "Past Tension," *Weekly Standard*, February 24, 1997.

49. Chris Matthews, "Bush's War," *San Francisco Chronicle*, September 13, 2001.

50. Bruce Miroff, "Monopolizing the Public Space: The President as a Problem for Democratic Politics," in *Rethinking the Presidency*, ed. Thomas E. Cronin (Boston: Little, Brown and Co., 1982), p. 224.

51. William Hazlitt, "Man Is a Toad-Eating Animal," in *Selected Writings*, ed. Ronald Blythe (Baltimore: Penguin Books, 1970), pp. 378–79.

52. William Hazlitt, "On the Spirit of Monarchy," in *On the Pleasure of Hating* (New York: Penguin Books, 2005), p. 48.

53. Hazlitt, *Selected Writings*, p. 379.

54. "And the Winner Is . . ." editorial, *Manchester Union-Leader*, December 31, 1998.

55. John Hinderaker, "A Stroke of Genius?" Powerline, July 28, 2005.

56. Hazlitt, *On the Pleasure of Hating*, p. 49. Ironically, as if illustrating his own warnings about man's tendency toward hero-worship, Hazlitt penned a hagiographic *Life of Napoleon Buonaparte* that took "a sentimental view of Caesarism." Herschel Baker, *William Hazlitt* (Cambridge, MA: Belknap Press, 1962), p. 330.

57. Jack Goldsmith and Cass R. Sunstein, "Military Tribunals and Legal Culture: What a Difference Sixty Years Makes," *Constitutional Commentary* 19 (Spring 2002): 282, 289.

58. Marc J. Hetherington, "The Political Relevance of Political Trust," *American Political Science Review* 92 (December 1998): 791.

59. Marc J. Hetherington, "The Effect of Political Trust on the Presidential Vote, 1968–96," *American Political Science Review* 93 (June 1999): 312. Hetherington's article was written before the post-9/11 spike and decline; George W. Bush's reelection would make it three out of five.

60. See Michael E. Bailey, "The Heroic Presidency in the Era of Divided Government," *Perspectives on Political Science* 31 (Winter 2002): 41.

61. Steven G. Calabresi, "The President: Lightning Rod or King?" *Yale Law Journal* 115 (September 2006): 2612.

62. William G. Howell and Jon C. Pevehouse, "When Congress Stops Wars: Partisan Politics and Presidential Power," *Foreign Affairs* (September/October 2007).

63. Howell and Pevehouse, "When Congress Stops Wars," p. 99. See also Howell and Pevehouse, *While Dangers Gather: Congressional Checks on Presidential War Powers* (Princeton, NJ: Princeton University Press, 2007); and William A. Niskanen, "Give Divided Government a Chance," *Washington Monthly*, October 2006.

64. Marc J. Hetherington, *Why Trust Matters: Declining Political Trust and the Demise of American Liberalism* (Princeton, NJ: Princeton University Press, 2005), p. 143.

65. "At every level of concern about another terrorist attack, increased trust in the government is associated with a greater exchange of civil liberties for security." Darren W. Davis and Brian D. Silver, "Civil Liberties vs. Security: Public Opinion in the Context of the Terrorist Attacks on America," *American Journal of Political Science* 48 (January 2004): 39.

66. In the main, this happens without any corresponding decrease in interpersonal trust: "it is specifically a withdrawal of confidence from authoritarian institutions." Though the United States saw a downturn in interpersonal trust during the period of rising distrust of the government, that downturn was atypical in the countries studied; in fact, "interpersonal trust *rose* in 13 of the 19 countries in which change was observed." Ronald Inglehart, *Modernization and Postmodernization* (Princeton, NJ: Princeton University Press, 1997), p. 305.

67. Inglehart, *Modernization and Postmodernization,* p. 306.

68. Martin P. Wattenberg, "The Changing Presidential Media Environment," *Presidential Studies Quarterly* 34 (September 2004). See also Matthew A. Baum and Samuel Kernell, "Has Cable Ended the Golden Age of Presidential Television?" *American Political Science Review* 93 (March 1999): 99–114.

69. Almost half of all television viewers between 18 and 24 watch the show at least occasionally. Jody Baumgartner and Jonathan S. Morris, "*The Daily Show* Effect," *American Politics Research* 34 (May 2006): 344.

70. "Daily Show: Night-Time Nabobs of Negativity?" Center for Media and Public Affairs, December 20, 2006.

71. "Daily Show Viewers Knowledgeable about Presidential Campaigns," National Annenberg Election Survey, September 21, 2004.

72. Dan Froomkin, "The Colbert Blackout," Washingtonpost.com, May 2, 2006.

73. Quoted in Robert Sobel, *Coolidge: An American Enigma* (Washington: Regnery, 1998), p. 328.

74. Quoted in William C. Spragens, *Popular Images of American Presidents* (New York: Greenwood Press, 1988), p. 281.

75. Peter Beinart, "Hijacking Harry Truman," *Washington Post*, June 1, 2006.

76. Jack Goldsmith, *The Terror Presidency* (New York: W.W. Norton & Co., 2007), p. 190 (emphasis added).

77. Even in 2001, the year of terrorism's ghastliest success, 12 times as many Americans died of the flu. Benjamin H. Friedman, "The Hidden Cost of Homeland Defense," The Audit of Conventional Wisdom, MIT Security Studies Program, November 2005, p. 1.

78. Quoted in John Hendren, "An Architect of War Draws Blueprint for Peace," *Los Angeles Times*, April 13, 2003.

79. *Report of the Defense Science Board Task Force on Strategic Communication*, September 2004, p. 40. ("American direct intervention in the Muslim World has paradoxically elevated the stature of and support for radical Islamists, while diminishing support for the United States to single-digits in some Arab societies. . . . Muslims do not 'hate our freedom,' but rather, they hate our policies."); Robert A. Pape, *Dying to Win: The Strategic Logic of Suicide Terrorism* (New York: Random House, 2005).

80. *The National Security Strategy of the United States of America*, September 2002, p. 5.

81. Patrick Healy, "A Mom Running to Lead the Mommy Party," *New York Times*, May 14, 2007.

82. See, for example, Jay Nordlinger, "Political Virility: Real Men Vote Republican," OpinionJournal.com, September 17, 2003.

Afterword

1. John McCain, "Address by Senator John McCain to the Johns Hopkins University Class of 1999," speech, Johns Hopkins University, Baltimore, MD, May 27, 1999.

2. Barack Obama, "Barack Obama's Acceptance Speech," speech, Democratic National Convention, Denver, CO, August 28, 2008.

3. Michelle Obama, "Michelle Obama Speaks at UCLA Rally," speech, University of California, Los Angeles, February 2, 2009.

4. Barack Obama, "President Barack Obama's Inaugural Address," speech, U.S. Capitol, January 20, 2009.

5. Will Wilkinson, "We Need Cynics," *The Week*, January 29, 2009.

6. "First Presidential Debate," *New York Times*, September 26, 2008.

7. Jack Balkin, "Obama and the Imperial Presidency," *The Guardian*, November 12, 2008.

8. Jake Tapper and Sunlen Miller, "Obama Promises to 'End the Age of Oil in Our Time,'" ABCNews.com, August 5.

9. Barack Obama, "Remarks from Senator Obama: Energy Town Hall," speech, Youngstown, OH, August 5, 2008.

10. Peter Hanby, "Obama: GOP Doesn't Own Faith Issue," *CNN.com*, October 8, 2007.

11. John McCain, "The One," political advertisement, YouTube, August 1, 2008.

12. "Rudolph W. Giuliani's Speech at the Republican National Convention," New York Times, September 3, 2008.

13. "John McCain Introduction at the 2008 Republican National Convention," C-SPAN, September 4, 2008.

14. "Text of Draft Proposal for Bailout Plan," *New York Times*, September 20, 2008.

15. David Cho and Zachary A. Goldfarb, "UAW Vows to Fight Wage Concessions," *Washington Post*, December 24, 2008.

16. Jacob Sullum, "Illegal Lending Practices," *Reason Online*, December 17, 2008.

17. Under the law, a "troubled asset" is "any . . . financial instrument" the secretary of the treasury "determines the purchase of which is necessary to promote financial market stability," and "financial institution" is defined as " *any institution*, including, *but not limited to*, any bank, savings association, credit union, security broker or dealer, or insurance company, established and regulated under the laws of the United States or any State, territory, or possession of the United States" (emphasis added). *Emergency Economic Stabilization Act of 2008*, Public Law 110-343, *U.S. Statutes at Large* 110 (2008).

18. Stuart Taylor Jr. and Evan Thomas, "Obama's Cheney Dilemma," *Newsweek*, January 10, 2009.

19. "Press Conference by the President," White House, transcript, January 12, 2009.

20. Charlie Savage, "Barack Obama's Q&A," *Boston Globe*, December 20, 2007.

21. Gail Russell Chaddock, "Congress Wrestles over Spying Bill," *The Christian Science Monitor*, June 23, 2008.

22. One judge refused his request. *See* Demetri Sevastopulo, "Setback to Guantánamo Closure Hopes," *Financial Times*, January 29, 2009.

23. "President Obama Delivers Remarks at Swearing-In Ceremony," January 21, 2008.

24. Barack Obama, "Ensuring Lawful Interrogations," Executive Order 13491, *Federal Register* 74, no. 16 (January 22, 2009): 4894. He also ordered the closure of the prison at Guantánamo Bay within a year, and he stipulated that Common Article 3 of the Geneva Conventions would apply to any interrogations conducted there in the interim. Barack Obama, "Review and Disposition of Individuals Detained at the Guantánamo Bay Naval Base and Closure of Detention Facilities," Executive Order 13492, *Federal Register* 74, no. 16 (January 22, 2009): 4897.

25. Jason Ryan and Z. Byron Wolf, "DOJ Probes Legality of Waterboarding," ABCNews.com, February 22, 2008.

26. "President Gulliver's Lawyer," *Wall Street Journal*, January 10, 2009.

27. And the *Wall Street Journal's* editorialist was right. As Johnsen has written, "When providing legal advice to guide contemplated executive branch action, OLC should provide an accurate and honest appraisal of applicable law, even if that advice will constrain the administration's pursuit of desired policies. The advocacy model of lawyering, in which lawyers craft merely plausible legal arguments to support their clients' desired actions, inadequately promotes the President's constitutional obligation to ensure the legality of executive action." Dawn E. Johnsen, "Faithfully Executing the Laws: Internal Legal Constraints on Executive Power," Indiana University School of Law, Bloomington Legal Studies Research Paper Series no. 84, July 2007.

28. Carol J. Williams, "Wiretapping Case May Have Its Day in Court," *Los Angeles Times*, February 28, 2009.

29. Jonathan Martin, "Biden on Economy: We Are at War," *Politico*, January 5, 2009.

30. Sheryl Gay Stolberg and Helene Cooper, "Obama Makes Case as Bill Clears Hurdle," *New York Times*, February 9, 2009.

31. Gerald F. Seib, "In Crisis, Opportunity for Obama," *Wall Street Journal*, November 21, 2008.

32. "Auto Industry Assistance Package Statement from the President Elect," Change.gov, The Office of the President-Elect, December 19, 2009.

33. Sheryl Gay Stolberg and Edmund L. Andrews, "$275 Billion Plan Seeks to Address Housing Crisis," *New York Times*, February 18, 2009.

34. Michael D. Shear and Jon Cohen, "Nation's Hopes High for Obama," *Washington Post*, January 17, 2009.

35. Jill Lawrence, "Hopes Are High for Obama, Poll Shows," *USA Today*, November 12, 2008.

36. Tom Jacobs, "Congratulations, Obama: Here's Your Decay Curve," *Miller-McCune*, January 20, 2009.

37. Sarah Kershaw, "Talk about Race? Relax, It's OK," *New York Times*, January 14, 2009.

GENE HEALY is senior vice president for policy at the Cato Institute. His research interests include executive power and the role of the presidency as well as federalism and overcriminalization.

He is the author of, among other works, *Indispensable Remedy: The Broad Scope of the Constitution's Impeachment Power* (2018) and *False Idol: Barack Obama and the Continuing Cult of the Presidency* (2012). Healy has appeared on *PBS NewsHour* and NPR's *Talk of the Nation,* and his work has been published in the *Los Angeles Times,* the *New York Times,* the *Chicago Tribune,* the *Legal Times,* and elsewhere.

Healy holds a BA from Georgetown University and a JD from the University of Chicago Law School. He lives in Leesburg, Virginia, with his wife, Caitlyn, and their three ungovernable daughters.

Founded in 1977, the Cato Institute is a public policy research foundation dedicated to broadening the parameters of policy debate to allow consideration of more options that are consistent with the traditional American principles of limited government, individual liberty, and peace. To that end, the Institute strives to achieve greater involvement of the intelligent, concerned lay public in questions of policy and the proper role of government.

The Institute is named for *Cato's Letters*, libertarian pamphlets that were widely read in the American Colonies in the early 18th century and that played a major role in laying the philosophical foundation for the American Revolution.

Despite the achievement of the nation's Founders, today virtually no aspect of life is free from government encroachment. A pervasive intolerance for individual rights is shown by government's arbitrary intrusions into private economic transactions and its disregard for civil liberties.

To counter that trend, the Cato Institute undertakes an extensive publications program that addresses the complete spectrum of policy issues. Books, monographs, and shorter studies are commissioned to examine the federal budget, Social Security, regulation, military spending, international trade, and myriad other issues.

In order to maintain its independence, the Cato Institute accepts no government funding. Contributions are received from foundations, corporations, and individuals, and other revenue is generated from the sale of publications. The Institute is a nonprofit, tax-exempt, educational foundation under Section 501(c)3 of the Internal Revenue Code.

CATO INSTITUTE
1000 Massachusetts Ave. NW
Washington, D.C. 20001
www.cato.org